Television, Japan, and Globalization

Michigan Monograph Series in Japanese Studies
Number 67

Center for Japanese Studies
The University of Michigan

Television, Japan, and Globalization

Edited by Mitsuhiro Yoshimoto,
Eva Tsai, and JungBong Choi

Center for Japanese Studies
The University of Michigan
Ann Arbor, 2010

Published by the Center for Japanese Studies,
The University of Michigan
1007 E. Huron St.
Ann Arbor, MI 48104-1690

Library of Congress Cataloging in Publication Data

Television, Japan, and globalization / edited by Mitsuhiro Yoshimoto, Eva Tsai,
and JungBong Choi.
    p. cm. — (Michigan monograph series in Japanese studies ; no. 67)
    Includes bibliographical references and index.
    ISBN 978-1-929280-58-2 (cloth : alk. paper) — ISBN 978-1-929280-59-9
(pbk. : alk. paper)
    1. Television broadcasting—Japan.   2. Television programs—Japan.
    3. Television and globalization—Japan.   I. Yoshimoto, Mitsuhiro,
1961–   II. Tsai, Eva, 1975–   III. Choi, JungBong, 1969–   IV. Title.   V. Series.

PN1992.3.J3T37 2010
302.23'450952--dc22

                                                            2009048563

This book was set in Palatino Macron.

Printed in the United States of America

Contents

Preface

Television, Japan, and Globalization tries to do two things. First, the book is edited with the explicit intent of introducing Japanese television as a significant scholarly topic. Whereas extensive scholarship on Japanese television already exists in Japan, not enough attention has been paid by scholars in the United States to this dominant cultural force and its socio-economic impact on contemporary Japanese everyday life. For various reasons, Japanese television has fallen through the cracks in the disciplinary politics of the U.S. academia. Although it is simply presumptuous to even suggest a single book could create a new space for examining Japanese television in a new and critical way, it is my hope that *Television, Japan, and Globalization* makes a small contribution to the further development of an emerging field.

The second objective of the book is to problematize the "Japaneseness" of Japanese television. This may sound contradictory to what I said in the previous paragraph, but what makes Japanese television a worthy scholarly topic now is precisely its non-Japaneseness. Dissemination of Japanese television programs goes beyond the boundaries of the Japanese nation-state. Even what looks like a domestic dimension of Japanese television often turns out to be inexplicable until it is reexamined in relation to globalization and the regional dynamics of economic competition and cultural markets. *Television, Japan, and Globalization* attempts to drive a wedge in "Japanese television" by closely analyzing the political economy of the global media industry, the formal features and contents of popular television genres, and the reception and consumption of Japanese programs outside Japan, among other issues.

The production of this book has been a long and strenuous process, which would not have come to an end without a close working relationship among the three editors. My co-editors Eva Tsai and JungBong Choi opened up my eyes to the importance of transdisciplinary dialogues and collaboration when we met numerous times to discuss ideas for the book at coffee shops in Iowa City. I thank them for their unfailing kindness and camaraderie. I would also like to thank Markus Nornes, Bruce Willoughby, and all the contributors to the volume for their hard work, encouragement, and, above all, patience.

Mitsuhiro Yoshimoto
February 2010

Why Japanese Television Now?

Mitsuhiro Yoshimoto

Not long time ago, the sign "Japan" was synonymous with hyperconsumerism, high-tech spectacles, and a post-Fordist system of flexible accumulation, that is, postmodernism. In the midst of its phenomenal economic success and prosperity, Japan was simultaneously celebrated and criticized as a quintessential postmodern nation. When the economic bubble burst in the early 1990s, however, the debates on postmodernism were quickly forgotten as things of the past. Although it is by no means a mere reflection of Japan's troubled identity in the age of recession and globalization, Japan after the fall of postmodernism emerged as a contested site of difference and disagreement. The alleged homogeneity of Japanese society was attacked on all fronts; the dominant history was rewritten through a critique of representation and by listening to the repressed voices of the past; the old literary canon, which had reigned supreme during the cold war period, began to fall apart as critics convincingly revealed its ideological biases and political unconscious. Yet it is not so clear whether we should see in this paradigmatic discursive shift an unmistakable sign of progress because scholarly attention to differences, otherness, and margins does not always lead to genuine problematization of Japan's fixed identity. As long as Japan remains the absolute horizon of interpretive coherence, heterogeneity can easily be domesticated by a centralizing logic of the nation-state and at best regurgitated as a variant of multiculturalism.

The reason why postmodern discourse and its short-lived popularity are brought up here is not to rescue postmodernism from its theoretical

1

fatigue. In fact, there is no need to "[run] the risk of breathing new life into postmodernist orthodoxy at a moment when it is showing all the signs of senile decay."[1] But it is still important to point out that the premature disappearance of the discourse on postmodernism and Japan has to do with the institutional politics of disciplines as much as postmodernism's own limitations. If postmodern debates have had no lasting impact on the scholarship on Japan, it is partly because of the potential threat they posed to the institutional structure in which Japan became an object of knowledge. For instance, blurring boundaries of serious art and mass entertainment, which would require a thorough reexamination of the idea of culture, have been absorbed into the existing structure of area studies and the division of disciplinary labor. Although it is commonly assumed that area studies has been going through a process of transformation since the collapse of the cold war system in the 1990s, we should seriously entertain the possibility that in fact nothing has fundamentally changed in area studies and that most of what appears to be a new development is for the most part a cosmetic adjustment or repetition of a debunked old paradigm.

A gradual shift of attention from traditional arts to popular culture in Japanese studies is a reflection of the globalization of capital and consumer culture. At the same time, it has also ushered in something similar to a pre-cold-war orientalist gaze through which Japanese popular culture is transformed into curiosities and exotic items on display in a shop window or at a net auction web site. This return of the repressed is closely linked to the virtual fetishization of material objects and images that have become a ubiquitous presence in the everyday life of global consumer space. As the reorientalizing tendency of Japanese studies becomes more conspicuous, it is imperative to foreground and tackle the problematic of media and representation as a central focus of critical intervention. Instead of examining any particular commodity or image as a privileged yet isolated specimen of contemporary Japanese popular culture, we need to put it back in the transnational networks of production, distribution, and consumption in which Japan does not occupy any uniquely privileged position. Global commodities originally coming out of Japan demand new scholarly approaches that not only will make full use of theoretical advances in allied disciplines including media studies, film studies, and cultural studies, but also will reveal the shortcomings of these disciplines and the limitations of area studies.

Studied by film specialists for many years, Japanese film is now rapidly reemerging as a key object marking a "visual turn" in Japanese studies. Equally important for this scholarly reorientation is Japanese animation, or anime, which raises a number of important questions concerning culture and global capital, visual literacy, and new media among others. Surprisingly, compared to film and anime, Japanese television has not received much scholarly attention so far. The development of new media and other information technologies may account for the dearth of critical materials on Japanese television, which seems to be already obsolete as a medium of mass communication and entertainment. Another reason may be Japanese television's alleged insularity, that is, television has been so thoroughly integrated into the fabric of Japanese everyday life that it would lose its intelligibility if it were removed from the symbiotic space of televisual images and specifically national viewers. But these assumptions do not accurately represent the state of Japanese television. For example, despite a radically transfigured media landscape, television in Japan occupies center stage in the government-initiated policy of digitalization of media, culture, and the economy. Instead of rendered obsolete by information technology, television is regarded as a strategic medium of technological convergence that is necessary if Japan is to recapture a leading position in the ever more fierce global economic competition. The so-called Japaneseness of Japanese television is also not as self-evident as it may seem at first. Technological inventions and appropriations connect old and new audiences to the content, form, and ideological infrastructures of Japanese television, joining new meaning-making experiences with a cultural object that was once safely imagined within the Japanese national boundary. Recorded media such as VCDs, DVDs, cable and satellite TV, and increasingly the Internet, have given rise to televisual flows that are not primarily regulated along the lines of national boundaries. In such transnational space of televisual flows, the original intentions of producers are often less important than the effects of circulation and consumption, which problematize the nationality of media images and the positionality of actual viewers.

Televisually, constructed boundaries of the Japanese national space are neither as self-evident nor as impenetrable as it may seem at first glance because, regardless of the viewers' awareness, Japanese television is firmly embedded in the global media network. As Lisa Parks and Shanti Kumar argue, global television "is part of the very social fabric that gives shape to us as individual subjects and imagined communities," that is, "no matter where we live in the world we are implicated within it."[2] Yet there is no global television as such but a number of different televisual landscapes where the instance of the global emerges only through complex negotiations between the local and the regional, the national and the transnational, the private and the public, the domestic and the foreign, and so forth. Constituting such a televisual landscape, Japanese television exceeds the limits of the Japanese nation.

Despite the undeniable significance of global television as a new horizon of analysis and interpretation, the status of globalization as a critical concept remains ambiguous. The idea of globalization often ends up reaffirming the status quo of global capitalism in the name of critical analysis. Many analyses of cultural globalization suspiciously resemble celebratory discourses of globalization apologists. Globalization is commonly discussed as a new state of the world that makes obsolete an old paradigm of scholarship centered around nation-states as a fundamental unit of identity. For example, a conspicuous casualty of globalization discourse in film studies is the idea of national cinema, which is increasingly regarded as an obstacle to the discipline's regeneration and further growth. The "national," however, creeps back into the argument on global cinema in the form of distinct national and cultural identities, which have supposedly survived as indispensable ingredients of a localization process. It is said that form is certainly global yet content is derived from specifically local identities and cultural traditions. In such an argument, the globalization of cinema is understood as a simultaneous process of stylistic standardization à la Hollywood and thematic diversification due to cultural differences. Reminding us of the Japanese slogan *wakon yosai* (Japanese spirit combined with Western learning), the dichotomy of global style and local cultural identity is an exact reversal of the older paradigm of film studies. In poststructuralist film theory, which once dominated film scholarship, content is pushed to the periphery of discussion as mere themes and cultural variations. The real political battleground is film style and formal conventions, which are believed to construct ideologically determined subject positions for spectators. Although the abstract determinism of poststructuralist theory has lost much of its persuasiveness, the question of ideology of form is becoming far more important in the face of instrumentalism and the culturalism of globalization discourse in film and media studies.

The identitarian assumptions of cultural globalization discourse does not in the end tell us anything particularly new or significant about what is actually happening in the contemporary world of global capital. National identity is not the only major issue at stake in the globalization of media production, distribution, and consumption. Nor is the successful participation in global markets as a producer of blockbuster films and television dramas always a good thing unless, of course, the success is measured only by financial gain. What makes the discourse on cinema and media globalization problematic is its use of the notion of culture, which, on the one hand, functions as a code word for the national and, on the other, conceals the production of unevenness. Discussions on global cinemascape and televisualscape must go beyond the idea of culture, the pervasive use of which is a symptom of global capital rather than a theoretical intervention in the imperial dynamic of capitalism.

Japanese television does not simply mean television in Japan or television produced and/or consumed by Japanese. A study of Japanese television is a simultaneous process of defining what it is and questioning any new definition that appears as a result of such an attempt. Lacking anything naturally obvious, Japanese television will emerge as an object of critical analysis when it is clearly situated in the intersections of competing and often contradictory discourses on media, national identity, and globalization currently popular in various academic fields. What is at stake is not just the meanings of *Japanese* and *television* but also a larger context of capitalism and globalization outside of which the former two terms become empty signifiers. At the same time, these two terms acquire concrete meanings only when the specificity of television as a medium and the history of Japan as a modern nation-state are critically scrutinized. Japanese television can potentially give rise to new critical approaches that will not be recycled by the paradigms of area studies and cultural globalization. And it is mostly as an object of such possibility that Japanese television deserves our serious critical attention.

NOTES

1. Alex Callinicos, "Toni Negri in Perspective," in Gopal Balakrishnan, ed., *Debating Empire* (London: Verso, 2003), 139.

2. Lisa Parks and Shanti Kumar, "Introduction," in Lisa Parks and Shanti Kumar, eds., *Planet TV: A Global Television Reader* (New York: New York University Press, 2003), 3.

Banishment of Murdoch's Sky in Japan: A Tale of David and Goliath?

JungBong Choi

On 29 August 2003, Rupert Murdoch's News Corporation, Inc., made a startling announcement. The company decided to relinquish its entire stake in SkyPerfecTV, the leading communications satellite (CS) television platform in Japan, to which Murdoch himself had given life. Pulling out of the worlds' second-largest media market was a disgrace for the transnational media titan, which has wielded during the last two decades enormous sway over the global media market. At the same time, however, it is a stimulating case that problematizes the accepted view of media globalization as an unstoppable juggernaut steered by transnational media conglomerates. In addition, the case compels scholars in global media to reexamine the fabled demise of cultural sovereignty of the local/national in an era of planetary media integration.

In the wake of Murdoch's departure from SkyPerfecTV, this essay explores the institutional and cultural milieu that forced his withdrawal from the most lucrative and fastest-growing niche in Japan's media business. The focal point of this essay is the intersection where the trajectories of Murdoch's Sky television in Japan encountered a set of deregulatory measures implemented by the country. I submit that Japan's deregulatory measures in digital CS exhibit characteristics akin to ventriloquism and a hypochondriac mentality. Although they were initiated to lure foreign capital into its burgeoning digital CS television market, Japan's deregulatory policies have enacted subtle forms of control guided by the ethos of renationalization. At the same time, Japan's media industry and policy agents have counteracted the incursion of transnational media corporations, siphoning off their capital, business leadership, and technological knowhow, as exemplified by Murdoch's case.

On a more theoretical front, this essay counters the supposed chimerical omnipotence of global media titans, on the one hand, and critiques the valorization of the local/national media as underdogs capable of trouncing their oversized foes on the other. Scholarship in the study of media globalization tends to fall into polarity: those focusing on the relentless expansion of multinational media Goliaths,[1] and those focusing on the clever jockeying of local/national media guerrillas.[2] Nevertheless, the two polarized camps commonly subscribe to a transparent antithesis between local/national media and transnational media. Preoccupied with the adversarial *collision* of the local/national and global media, both groups remain inattentive to voluntary and compulsory *collusions* between the two allegedly conflicting forces.

This essay contravenes the categorical clarity between multinational media corporations as domineering predators and local/national media as beleaguered preys. Their resemblance in orientation and praxis, it seems to me, outstrips their dissimilarity in size and geocultural habitation. Also, tactics and strategies the local/national media employ are analogous with and equally problematic as those harnessed by the transnational titans. I will suggest in what follows that the sudden withdrawal of News Corporation from the frontier of Japanese media is an event that blows the whistle on the alarming rise of local, petit media tyrants, who, like ethnologists, duplicate and proliferate the domineering practices of transnational media behemoths. Methodologically, I circumnavigate a range of interlaced instances—economic, legal, cultural, historical, ideological, and so on—orbiting the rise and fall of Murdoch's Sky television in Japan. I chose to do so because the incident under consideration here involves components external to what classical political-economic or institutional approaches would encompass. It is hoped that this approach will galvanize discussions that may refine our grasp on the multifarious trajectories of media globalization in a vexing time of deregulation and reregulation.

CONTROLLED GLASNOST

Roughly speaking, broadcasting via digital communications satellite is an enterprise that bundles many channels together and wholesales the package. Of all the present forms of broadcast television (terrestrial, cable, and satellite), digital CS is most critical to the establishment of a multichannel environment in Japan. Currently, there are more than 300 CS channels (249 for television and 52 for datacasting) run by approximately 125 broadcasters (content providers and distributors combined) nationwide.[3] But the super-abundance of Japan's CS was made possible largely by transnational media corporations. Being a central conduit through which transnational media conglomerates entered Japan's media market, digital CS has been a major battlefield between Japan-based media companies and foreign capital.

Broadcasting by CS in Japan began in 1992 with the conventional analog system. Four years later digital CS broadcasting got off the ground when PerfecTV opened business by taking over Japan's first analog CS service, Skyport. PerfecTV was then run by the Japan Digital Broadcasting Service, a company funded by twenty-eight Japanese trading and financial corporations, including Itochu, Nissho Iwai, Sumitomo, and Mitsui. Contrary to expectations, PerfecTV drew meager attention from scholars, policymakers, and even broadcasting entrepreneurs. It was at this time that officials in the Ministry of Posts and Telecommunications (MPT) were timidly dwelling on gains and losses in introducing a full-scale digital plan.[4] Because of the indecisiveness of policymakers, the potential subscribers stood back uninterested and few Japanese broadcasting corporations dared to embark on digital CS.

Amid this vacuum, a host of corporations that had not previously entered the media industry traversed the threshold of the hitherto well-sheltered enclave. Toyota Motor Corporation, for instance, bid for a niche in the segment of CS digital broadcasting with the intent to offer programs related to automobile navigation and other transportation-specific services. Another notable contender was Sony, which had long been geared up to provide a variety of next generation digital services ranging from movies and television programs to interactive data transmission and Internet-based commerce. The Japanese government, in the meantime, responded to the entrepreneurial enthusiasm with propitious legislative packages. A set of bylaws adopted by the Diet lowered the admissions bar for the broadcasting industry by relieving aspirants of the burden of committing enormous sums of money to satellite equipment. In the same spirit, a new licensing policy introduced in June 2001 substituted a simplified registration system for an inspection-based approval process.

Japanese businessmen were not the only ones enthused by the legal arrangement. Foreign media conglomerates, which had long sought to penetrate Japan's media fortress, were also elated since the revision of the Broadcast Law in 2001 further relaxed regulations on foreign media capital from the initial benchmark of 1989. The effect of this second legal reorganization loomed most tangibly in digital CS broadcasting. However, opening the door to digital CS did not mean an unrestrained liberalization of Japan's domestic television market. Rather, it has been a tightly controlled glasnost with two main purposes: complying with the hegemonic doctrines of international free trade, on one hand; and capitalizing on massive financial and program inputs from transnational media firms on the other.

Needless to say, attempts to make headway into Japan's broadcasting arena by multinational media corporations preceded the recent wave of deregulation on foreign media capital. Since the early 1980s, the liberalization of Japan's telecommunications and broadcasting markets has been a perennial issue compelled by delegates from the United States and European Union in major conventions of the G8, Asia-Pacific Economic Cooperation (APEC), the World Trade Organization, and other trade-relevant groups. One of the most contentious issues during the 1990s was the high interconnection rate that Japan's National Telegraph and Telephone Company charged international telecommunications carriers who wished to enter the Japanese market.[5]

But the opening of Japan's media industry was by no means a reluctant and imposed move. Apart from the external pressure, a wide consensus was being forged among Japanese officials, especially those in the Ministry of International Trades and Industries (MITI). Well cognizant of Japan's lag in digital broadcasting vis-à-vis its American and Western European counterparts, the MITI elites put forth plans to entice multinational media companies to bankroll burgeoning media technologies such as satellite broadcasting, cable broadcasting, and other digital telecommunications. The confluence of domestic impetus and foreign pressure expedited the induction of foreign capital in Japan's media industry, a tendency that became increasingly pronounced in the domain of CS broadcasting around the mid-1990s.

Participation by foreign media capital occurred first in the telecommunications sector. Microsoft and Telecommunications International (now Liberty Media) were the first to set foot in Japan in January 1995. They partially funded the venture of two multiple system operators (MSOs) named Jupiter Telecom (better known as J-COM) and TITUS.[6] A few months later, the MPT approved the operation of overseas satellite programs received in Japan by subjecting them to the directives of Japan's Broadcast Law. The number of foreign satellite broadcasters operating in Japan grew at a breathtaking pace. By June 1997, roughly two years after the initial authorization, eleven overseas broadcasters with twenty-two satellite channels had entered the market. The rising number of foreign broadcasters at this time caused little angst among Japan's policymakers and media entrepreneurs since most of the foreign firms were headquartered outside Japan and did not muddle the ownership structure of the Japanese media industry. The advent of Murdoch's JSkyB,[7] however, triggered a sequence of shockwaves.

PERRY'S BLACK SHIPS AND MURDOCH'S SKY CHANNEL

Before News Corporation's arrival, there was another foreign company that hovered around Japan's CS broadcasting: DirecTV, which had inaugurated a CS platform in October 1997. While PerfecTV was fully subsidized by Japan-based corporations, DirecTV was a mélange in its financial and management composition. Major sponsors of DirecTV were Hughes Electric (owned by General Electric), representing American capital (35 percent), and Matsushita and Mitsubishi, representing Japanese capital (65 percent). The two early settlers of Japan's digital CS broadcasting frontier were soon joined by Murdoch's JSkyB in 1998.

Shortly after the successful launch of BSkyB in Britain, Rupert Murdoch held a press conference in Tokyo on 12 June 1996 and unveiled his plan to embark on a satellite Sky television platform in Japan, namely, JSkyB. In order to kick-start his proposed mammoth CS platform, which would have over one hundred channels, Murdoch needed a domestic partner that could furnish JSkyB with ample content favored by Japanese viewers. It was TV Asahi that came into Murdoch's line of sight. In an attempt to milk TV Asahi of its rich media software, Murdoch acquired 21.4 percent of Asahi National Broadcasting stock, an event that badly wounded the nation's pride in its advanced broadcasting system and immaculate record of self-governance. Since the introduction of television broadcasting in 1953, Japan had remained "unsoiled" by foreign media capital and had preserved an astounding level of self-sufficiency across the fields of production, distribution, management, and ownership.[8]

Hence, some Japanese newspapers went so far as to compare Murdoch's landing to the arrival of Black Ships (*kurofune*) led by Commodore Matthew Perry in 1853. As is widely known, the arrival of Black Ships in Kanagawa Prefecture near Tokyo marks one of the most critical moments in the modern history of Japan. It heralded the onset of turbulent modernization, bringing to an end the nation's insularity, which had lasted for several centuries. The incident is remembered with profound ambivalence both as a marker of feeble nationhood that caused the opening of the country to alien forces and as the watershed from which the rearward-looking legacies of the feudal regime were relinquished. Murdoch's entrance into Japan reinvoked the jumbled emotions of apprehension and anticipation that the Japanese people had experienced two centuries before. Newspaper headlines such as "Sudden Arrival of Black Ships" in the *Sankei Shinbun* and "Breaking the Isolationism of Japanese Broadcasters" in the *Asahi Shinbun* aptly illustrate these mixed feelings.[9] Yet the prevalent tenor in the analogy of the Black Ships was skewed toward self-traumatization and victimization. As Iwabuchi Koichi notes, "The threat posed by Murdoch to Japan" was perceived as "the possibility of control of the Japanese media industry by foreign capital."[10]

The discourse of self-victimization before the "incursion" of foreign capital is a narrative neither unprecedented nor unique to Japan's broadcasting industry. Japanese business elites and policy bureaucrats have routinely rekindled it during the 1990s to the degree that alarm bells over the arrival of foreign capital can now be deemed a hollow ritual. Similarly, state officials in America, too, would vocalize the hyperbolized threat posed by alien enterprises. It was only two decades earlier that the specter of "Japan, Inc.," loomed menacingly over the United States. Overwhelmed by Japan's then advanced telecommunications and television technologies, U.S. business leaders and politicians rushed to ring the jingoistic bell, dubbing Japan an "economic fox" and "trade predator."[11] As a result of the witch hunt, according to a Harris Survey, the American people saw Japan as a greater threat than the Soviet Union and its nuclear arsenal.[12] On both sides of the Pacific, the level of jeopardy presented by foreign media capital has been consistently overstated during the economic cold war between Japan and the United States.

Although the shrill siren that greeted Murdoch's entry into Japan was something of a customary bellyache, it nevertheless augured the tough challenge that Murdoch had to face in making headway in Japan's digital CS business. Well aware of the potential cultural resistance lurking on his route to Japan, Murdoch shrewdly formed a strategic partnership with the Softbank Corporation, a major computer software company based in Japan that commands a stellar public reputation. Murdoch's alliance with Softbank had two main purposes. First, it was intended to circumvent the restriction on foreign investment in Japan's media industry as stipulated in the Japanese Radio Law. The law limits the percentage of foreign capital in a Japan-based broadcasting company to 20 percent or lower while leaving a huge loophole for indirect possession through a joint venture, as in Murdoch's case. The other rationale behind the joint acquisition was to use Softbank as a buffer lest the acquisition of Asahi's stock inflame the nationalist sentiments of the Japanese people and media industry.[13]

Although Sky entrance engendered major public unease, Japan's broadcasting industry was not as vulnerable or fragile as it was made out to be. Time and again, it outperformed, stymied, or drained off the assets of the savvy media mogul who was well versed in mergers and acquisitions. For example, Murdoch's plan to leverage a vast range of media archives owned by TV Asahi was far from trouble free. The *Asahi Shinbun*, a major stakeholder in TV Asahi, responded defiantly to Murdoch's scheme to exploit the company's program properties. With his takeover attempt thwarted, Murdoch reduced his stock ownership in TV Asahi in 1997. Frustrated, he made another attempt to launch JSkyB in 1998. This time he vied with only nine channels composed mostly of News Corporation's own stations, including Fox News, Sky Sports, and Star Movies. The second endeavor was called off when the proposed lineup proved unappealing to Japanese audiences, which are deeply habituated to programs congruent with national cultural sensibilities and specific to local social climates.

After these two failures, Murdoch finally entered Japan's CS arena successfully by launching JSkyB in 1999. The emergence of JSkyB is often regarded as the upshot of Murdoch's successful incorporation of Sony and Fuji TV. But it is hard to determine who incorporated whom given that the company's shares were equally distributed among the three participants. In the same vein, the popular representation (by mainstream media and scholars alike) of the birth of SkyPerfecTV as being indebted to Murdoch's absorption of Japan's indigenous PerfecTV lacks justification. In effect, my interpretation of the merger between Murdoch's JSkyB and PerfecTV runs contrary to the established account.

When the deal between JSkyB and PerfecTV was struck in April 1998, PerfecTV had already grown to one hundred channels with nearly half a million loyal subscribers. At that time PerfecTV was experiencing a minor slowdown in market share growth partly because its rival DirecTV had drawn off some prospective subscribers. Hence, PerfecTV invited JSkyB in via the mediation of Sony and Fuji TV, offering Murdoch an opportunity to take part in Japan's CS business. Things happened as planed, and a gargantuan empire of digital CS broadcasting was born, namely, SkyPerfecTV. Yet the power distribution among the four main players was not quite evenhanded. Murdoch assumed only 8.1 percent of the common stock whereas Sony, Fuji TV, and Itochu acquired 9.9 percent each. Given the uneven allotment of stock, it would not be sensible to claim that Murdoch held the upper hand in the formation and subsequent structuring of the conglomerate station. Speaking more liberally, the merger embodied the fusion of competition and cooperation between local and transnational media, a strategic symbiosis in which an unceasing strife for hegemony was waged.

It could be said of the postmerger state of affairs that Japan's Itochu, Sony, and Fuji blew their noses without getting their hands wet. As an amalgamation of Murdoch-led JSkyB and Itochu-led PerfecTV, SkyPerfecTV came to control a total of three hundred channels (television and radio combined) as of May 1998. After the merger there followed a barrage of advertising not only to boost public interest in SkyPerfecTV but also to oust its rival, DirecTV Japan. Although DirecTV was a veteran player in global digital CS broadcasting,[14] its branch in Japan could not weather the onslaught of SkyPerfecTV, and it went out of business in 2000. Absorbing 322,000 viewers from the now defunct DirecTV Japan, the total number of households subscribing to SkyPerfecTV rose to 2.4 million as of October 2000. In hindsight one can reasonably argue that the Japanese media dexterously harnessed Murdoch to oust another transnational media Goliath, DirecTV, and to quicken the national development of digital CS enterprise, which had lagged significantly behind its European and North American counterparts. In a way, the strategy employed by Sony, Fuji TV, Itochu, and other leading media companies in engaging Murdoch's JSkyB is akin to the feeding techniques of vampires. While complying with the imperative of transnationalization, Japan's media industry further solidified its toehold by devouring foreign media capital and programs.

A HYPOCHONDRIAC'S NARRATIVE

Why, then, did Japan's media industry respond to the arrival of Murdoch so hysterically? Did the advent of Murdoch's JSkyB in 1998 actually trigger disorder in Japan's broadcasting industry? Yes, perhaps. The entrance of foreign satellite broadcasters sparked intense rivalries and fleeting alliances between Japanese media capital and foreign media behemoths. The encounter between the two forces in the arena of Japan's digital CS has clearly subjected such sensitive issues as ownership, management, and content production/distribution to the whims of large scale mergers, tie-ups, and breakups. In light of the turbulent reorganization in broadcasting, Kaifu Kazuo, an executive researcher at Nippon Hōsō Kyōkai (NHK), states that internationalization and deregulation have proliferated market principles and will force a shift in Japan's public broadcasting-oriented systems.[15] In a similar vein, both Iida Masao and Hanada Tetsuro argue that advances in digital technology coupled with global media consolidation are testing the raison d'être of Japanese broadcasting.[16] They caution that indiscriminate liberalization policies would wreak havoc on the orderly landscape of Japan's broadcasting province.

Nevertheless, frenzied competition and mergers were the price Japan was willing to pay in exchange for making a leap forward in long-awaited multichannel broadcasting. PerfecTV, for example, showcased over seventy channels, immediately attracting some three hundred thousand subscribers between October 1996 and October 1997. To compete, DirecTV Japan introduced a new CS platform with a staggering 100 channels. With an additional 120 channels added by JSkyB shortly afterward, Japan's broadcasting industry found itself on a high plateau of channel superabundance less than three years after the introduction of digital CS. Aside from the exponential growth of channels, the unprecedented competition transformed Japan's CS topography in a rewarding way as far as the diversification of programs and the introduction of new services are concerned. Some even point out that the liberalization of Japanese broadcasting provided an opportunity to promote Japan's media products in international markets. Iwabuchi asserts that "what is at stake seems less a foreign invasion of Japan than [a] Japanese advance into global media markets and the enhancement of the competitiveness of Japanese TV software."[17]

There are more reasons to cast doubt on the view that portrays Japan's broadcasting en bloc as a victim of multinational media globalization and market liberalization. It should be noted that it was Japan (more precisely, the coordination between the Japanese state and its media industry) that methodically encouraged the wedlock between market-thirsty multinational media firms and momentum-hungry Japanese broadcasters. The self-victimization repertoire that proliferated on the eve of Murdoch's entry into Japan's digital CS, in this respect, can be interpreted as a hyperbolic defense mechanism of the vulnerable—either imagined or actual—whose melodramatic self-perception paradoxically manifested the will to keep its national media environment intact. Here the notion of the hypochondriac comes in quite handy.

Generally speaking, the hypochondriac is characterized by excessive attention to the microscopic symptoms of one's body in fear of illness. Hypochondriacs are, according to Freud, helplessly narcissistic in their obsession with physical functions and security. Caged in a fantasy of infection, these health diehards avail themselves of medical cures beyond necessity. On the other hand, one cannot overlook a paradox intrinsic to the mind-set of the hypochondriac. Always alarmed and busy heeding the workings of the body, hypochondriacs are usually healthy except for the habit of simulating the image of the ailing self. That is, hypochondria is a pseudo disease that can be therapeutically advantageous. This irony applies to the overall architecture of the hyperbolism Japan's media industry has shown. The excessive caution that the Japanese media circle exercised in response to

Murdoch's infiltration into the CS business is indeed a form of hypochondriacal obsession, a remedial sacrament that keeps its media habitat "sterilized." In a sense, the (collective) hypochondriacal mentality is a survival technique for Japan, as well as other local/national media, which is constantly anxious that it will be eradicated, ravaged, or bought-off by transnational "vultures."

VENTRILOQUISM IN LIBERALIZATION

This duality consistently surfaces in the legislative endeavors designed to stimulate the digital CS industry by inviting foreign investment. Deregulatory legislation often bifurcates, and it summoned up a series of countermaneuvers even before the influx of foreign capital began to look ominous to the integrity of Japan's broadcasting. The divestment of Murdoch from SkyPerfecTV epitomizes how legislative efforts to liberalize Japan's broadcasting industry have been offset by a strong undercurrent angled toward the renationalization of the domain. I shall call this duality, bifurcation, and schism within the same entity a ventriloquist plot. It is a scheme that transmits multiple voices (or signals) by discrete subjects or the same subject in different tones. Not only does Japan's ventriloquism utter multiple voices in heterogeneous tones; it also overlays plural articulations to the bewilderment of foreign media corporations. More specifically, internationalizing and liberalizing media entities, on the one hand, and renationalizing and reregulating them, on the other, is a case in point.

For instance, a number of Japan's major broadcasters hailed some amendments to the Broadcast Law made to lure foreign satellite broadcasters.[18] For example, NHK has been quite vocal in championing the internationalization of TV programs, and Fuji TV, Itochu, Matsushita, and Sumitomo have taken active postures toward the involvement of foreign media players in Japan.[19] Notwithstanding a series of legal relaxations and the creation of favorable environments for foreign investment, Japan's Broadcast Law (the master law that governs other subcategorical mandates) continues to police the traffic of foreign capital and its procurement of Japan's broadcasting license. Article 5 (paragraph 1, numbers 1–3), for instance, clearly bans more than 20 percent aggregate ownership of a Japan-based broadcasting company by foreigners (persons and corporations combined). When that limit is exceeded, the Broadcast Law decrees, the license of the company can be canceled by the MPT. Furthermore, Article 52-8, paragraph 1 requires that a public announcement be made when the cumulative ownership (entailing voting rights) of foreigners surpasses 15 percent of a Japan-based broadcasting company.

Using this restriction, SkyPerfecTV has profitably kept stock ownership by foreigners (the largest shareholder *was*, of course, Rupert Murdoch's News Corporation) below 20 percent and placed forewarnings that would deter further stock purchases by or registration of foreign investors. On 28 February 2003, for instance, the share (inclusive of voting rights) of SkyPerfecTV held by foreigners reached 19.7 percent of its total stock outstanding. In observance with the Broadcast Law, SkyPerfecTV had to post a notification in the morning edition of *Nihon Keizai Shimbun* on 12 March 2003 that deterred further acquisition of its stock by foreigners. Coupled with the defensive statute are subtler forms of barricade: cultural and psychological resistance, which would ultimately shipwreck multinational media titans. Owing to the austere legal watch blended with psychological impediments, the overall stockholding of foreigners has been on a decline lately. The percentage of stockholding by foreigners in SkyPerfecTV has ebbed from 19.7 percent on 28 February 2003 to 15.61 percent on 22 October.[20] As of 31 March 2003, Murdoch's News Corporation possessed only 8.13 percent of common stock outstanding,[21] and the only other foreign company with a comparatively high stake in SkyPerfecTV was the State Street Bank and Trust Company (4.84 percent), a U.S-based multinational financial corporation. Even though Murdoch was one of the chief architects of SkyPerfecTV, his foothold in the company steadily weakened to the point where he finally forsook his share in SkyPerfecTV completely. In the end, the new legal mandates promising foreign capital easy access to Japan's CS market have been constantly impaired by the apparatuses of censorship on foreign capital.

Schizophrenic as it may seem, the shifting balance between the reception of and resistance to multinational media capital forms an exquisite division of labor. Rather than resulting in sheer incoherence, the contrary orientations take on a rapport of supplement: coinciding, corresponding, and sometimes complementing each other. This is not to suggest, however, that the incoherence and disorientation produced by the ventriloquism were impeccably orchestrated by the Japanese state. Nor should this be taken to mean that the Japanese media industry in its entirety is a living organism with identical interests and a unitary goal. Quite the contrary, the very messiness, lack of coordination, and unorchestrated cacophony are sources of torment and bafflement among the multimedia troops. The ventriloquism in Japan's CS broadcasting is expressive of the overall contradiction inherent in the liberalization of Japan's media industry, which has generated (1) the shrinkage of the gateway that was initially designed to usher in foreign capital and broadcasters and (2) further tightening of jurisdiction over its national media landscape.

THE PAEAN OF RENATIONALIZATION: SEMIOTIC THIEVERY

On 29 August 2003, News Corporation announced that it had transferred its 8.13 percent shareholding in SkyPerfecTV to the three major Japanese stakeholders, Sony Broadcast Media, Itochu Corporation, and the Fuji Television Network. With 181,998 shares surrendered out of 182,000, News Corporation now holds only two symbolic shares in SkyPerfecTV, expressive of Murdoch's bitterness over the adverse business climate in Japan and his determination to come back. James Murdoch, a son of Rupert Murdoch and the executive vice president of News Corporation, commented, "We have enjoyed a close and profitable relationship with our partners, and together we have built a platform and a multi-channel market in Japan. News Corporation remains fully committed to this market, and we will continue to take part in this business as a content provider. . . . I am certain of SkyPerfecTV's future success and plan to continue to work closely with it."[22] The comment *"together we have built* a platform and a multi-channel market in Japan" is subtly coded. It expresses the resentment and frustration of the global media kingpin by reiterating the contributions that JSkyB has made to Japan's broadcasting industry.

In response to James Murdoch's remark, Shigemura Hajime, the president of SkyPerfecTV, said, "We are grateful for News Corporation's support in the establishment and consolidation of the pay television industry in Japan. . . . We will continue to consider ourselves a partner with News Corporation's global group of satellite platforms, and are planning to further enhance our relationship. We look forward to the continued exchange of information and programming cooperation."[23] This statement is, on the surface, a commendation of what News Corporation has achieved in Japan's CS industry. Beneath the facade, however, the adieu speech was something of a golden handshake, somewhat apologetic and yet long planned, meant to cheer up an ill-fated retiree.

The implication of News Corporation's withdrawal from the second-largest media market in the world is enormous. At the most transparent level, Murdoch's company has been relieved of the jewel in the crown. Unlike the individual broadcast channels that News Corporation owns in Japan, SkyPerfecTV is the country's foremost CS broadcasting platform and holds the key to the multichannel floodgate: it commands more than three hundred channels, transmits a giant collection of popular programs to over three million households in Japan, and interconnects simultaneously with numerous other essential media outlets, including digital BS (broadcasting satellite), cable, and Internet broadband service providers. Of course, News Corporation still retains a number of assets in Japan's media industry: 14.3 percent of JSky sports, 17.8 percent of Star Channel, 15.0 percent of Nihon Eiga, and 10.0 percent of the Space Shower Network in addition to its own Fox Channel and Fox News and the National Geographic Channel in Japan. Yet even the combined value of all these assets is no match for SkyPerfecTV.

From the standpoint of Japan's CS broadcasting, SkyPerfecTV has finally restored its "national purity" in ownership and management. The shares News Corporation released were transferred to the hands of the Japanese media victors—Sony, Fuji TV, and Itochu Corporation—each of which now holds 12.65 percent of the stock (283,058 shares) in SkyPerfecTV. The top ten investors in SkyPerfecTV, with the exception of the State Street Bank and Trust Company, are all Japanese firms: Japan Satellite Systems (JSAT), Nippon Television (NTV), Tokyo Broadcasting Station (TBS), Mitsui and Company, Matsushita Electric Industrial Company, and so on. Moreover, the board of directors does not contain a single foreign national or person affiliated with multinational corporations. Delegates from the Japanese shareholding firms occupy all the chief posts: two chairmen, an executive vice president, two managing directors, six non–executive directors, and even the five standing auditors.

Aside from the renationalization in financial and managerial terms, SkyPerfecTV also broke free from its tainted history as a crossbreed of Murdoch's JSkyB and Japan's PerfecTV. What seems noteworthy here is that the prefix *Sky*, a name bestowed by Murdoch's News Corporation, no longer evokes that company's foray into digital CS broadcasting in Japan; rather, it turned into a landmark "booty" that Japanese media firms seized from the hitherto indomitable multinational media giant. As a result, the Sky title has come into a semiotic aporia on a global scale: while Sky in other countries (BSkyB in Britain, ISkyB in Italy, and so on) remains the signatory banner of Murdoch's planetary satellite empire, in Japan it embodies the dethronement of the proprietor who gave life to it. The two divergent denotations undermine the transparency of the signifier Sky and, accordingly, suspend the mythical triumph of transnational media corporations. Consequently, the fractured ownership of the Sky trademark conjures up the fundamental ambivalence inherent in media globalization: the alterity of the dominant and the dominated, the aggressor and the defender.

Another example along this line is found in the emergence of Star Channel in Japan. Star Channel, not Star TV, is a company owned and run by Itochu, one of the principal shareholders of SkyPerfecTV. Itochu's Star

Channel was named after Rupert Murdoch's Star TV. Just like Star TV, Star Channel specializes in the provision of foreign movies to Japanese audiences via the diverse broadcasting venues of digital CS, BS, and cable television. In fact, Japan's Star Channel was an outcome of a bizarre negotiation between Itochu and Star TV's owner, News Corporation. Itochu asked for the right to expropriate Star TV's trademark and content. News Corporation demanded in return a large amount of stock from the local imitator, Star Channel. Through the tradeoff, Itochu came to possess copious content from Star TV while News Corporation grabbed a measly 17.8 percent of Star Channel's stock. Arguably, one can say that Star Channel in Japan lawfully purloined the identity, prestige, and content of Star TV without subordinating itself to Murdoch's media empire.

BEWARE THE LOCAL PREDATOR!

I have expressed my suspicion about the account that renders local/national media as an innocent prey to be devoured by transnational media carnivores. Beyond this suspicion, one has to be attentive to the similarity between local and transnational media companies. Some local/national media copy the predatory acts of transnational media to the degree that the label "performative proxy" of multinational media seems appropriate. The predispositions of local/national media, at least in Japan but possibly elsewhere, are gradually turning them into clones of the global media tyrants.

SkyPerfecTV, for example, has been no less belligerent and gluttonous than other transnational firms. It monopolized the digital CS television market after driving DirecTV, a subsidiary of General Electric, out of Japan in 2000. Since then, the company has exercised unobstructed control by clinching telecommunications markets, hoarding stock ownership of other businesses, and frustrating the emergence of new competitors. In effect, the latest steps SkyPerfecTV has taken are strikingly akin to the large-scale mergers and acquisitions now occurring around the globe. The formation of the world's largest media titan through the merger between Time Warner and Vivendi Universal runs almost parallel to SkyPerfecTV's advance into the realm of cable TV and telecommunications via a joint venture with the communications satellite operator JSAT and telecommunications giant Nippon Telegraph and Telephone (NTT).[24] Now that the cable industry is within a stone's throw, SkyPerfecTV is latching onto Internet services through a tie-up with Jupiter Telecommunications (J-COM Broadband), the largest broadband and cable service provider in Japan in terms of the number of customers served. This deal enabled SkyPerfecTV to absorb customers within reach of J-COM Broadband who were not yet incorporated to its digital CS broadcasting.[25] The outrageous expansion of SkyPerfecTV did not end there.

There are sufficient allegations that it attempts to obstruct the growth of competitors, as was demonstrated in the launch of Plat-One, a new digital CS platform set in motion in March 2002.[26] Plat-One initially drew much attention for its potential to give pause to the monopolistic practices of SkyPerfecTV in the digital CS market. Financed by a group of established Japanese media and other corporations—NTV, Mitsubishi, and WOWOW, among others—Plat-One was powerfully outfitted with a range of diversified programs: three free network channels, four pay-per-view WOWOW channels, seven NTV CS programs, twelve data network channels, and two radio channels. It even premiered an innovative service called "ep," which allows the downloading, storing, and retrieval of satellite television and radio programs. Nevertheless, its growth has not been as impressive as expected. Although analysts attribute this to a lack of satisfactory publicity, institutional backing, and originality in programming strategies, another factor also accounts for the sluggishness, namely, the commencement of SkyPerfecTV2. No sooner did Plat-One inaugurate its service, on 1 March 2002, than SkyPerfecTV launched its second CS platform in July 2002. What is curious about SkyPerfecTV2 is that it scarcely presents novel programs but instead duplicates a number of popular channels on SkyPerfecTV1.[27] Due to the blatant recycling of programs from its parent station, the market standing of SkyPerfecTV2 is pitiful. One might ask, did the Sky Perfect group rush the inauguration of its second platform without conducting thorough market surveys and laying the proper groundwork for program supply?

It is important to note here that the digital CS market in Japan has been overgrazed in a short span of time and is rapidly approaching a temporary saturation point. Despite the dazzling speed of CS's growth, Japanese audiences' disinclination to swing to digital satellite has remained strong since analog broadcasting will continue until 2011 when the nationwide conversion from analog to digital broadcasting concludes. Additionally, the introduction of digital terrestrial broadcasting in December 2003 began to cast a heavy shadow on digital CS. However, these are facts known even to laypersons in Japan thanks to continuous stories by mainstream newspapers, which have been troubled by the formidable leapfrogging of digital CS broadcasting over the last few years. It is highly improbable, therefore, that SkyPerfecTV embarked on another massive CS platform without conducting sufficient market analyses. One can infer, instead, that the chief function underpinning the impetuous launch of SkyPerfecTV2 had little to do with absorbing floating audiences; it was born as a straw man to hamper the smooth landing of its potential adversary, Plat-One.

Apart from the fact that it replicates a good deal of programming from its parent platform, SkyPerfecTV2 is appallingly understaffed, underfinanced, and ill-defined in its mission. Furthermore, it showed little enthusiasm for soliciting new audiences immediately after March 2002 when its competitor, Plat One, got off the ground. During its first fourteen months of operation, in October 2003, it attracted only a humble 56,000 subscribers. This figure stands in sharp contrast to the staggering 3.46 million subscribers held by SkyPerfecTV1 as of September 2003.[28] Yet the meager figure of 56,000 was substantial enough when it was used to slash the market that might otherwise have been tapped by Plat-One.

CONCLUSION

Discussions of globalization have gradually shifted away from the fixed conception of the global as an almighty, universal force and the local as either a noncompliant challenger to or a helpless victim of the global.[29] However, political-economic approaches to media globalization have remained rather impervious to the paradigmatic shift largely because media globalization has unfolded in a fashion that corroborates the binarism of the omnipotent, predatory global and the frail, besieged local.

It is true that new charters and mandates adopted by the G8, APEC, the World Trade Organization, the World Bank, and other international summits have shattered and overawed national/local media across the fields of ownership, management, and content production. Empowered by the new templates, transnational media corporations such as News Corporation, Time Warner, Bertelsmann, Disney, and Viacom have torn down local/national barriers in a frenzied sprint toward global media oligopoly. Nonetheless, local/national media groups do take action by forging flexible affiliations with various civil and state organizations.

Japan is not the only country that implemented controlled glasnost and ventriloquist tactics. Similarly, hypochondriacal reactions and the rise of local tyrants are relevant to other nations. Like Japan, South Korea has witnessed the spread of hypochondriacal attitudes, as well as the generation of incongruous ventriloquist speeches. In Korea, it was initially the Ministry of Culture and Tourism that called on News Corporation to invest in the country's CS market. When News Corporation finally decided to take part in the digital satellite industry in 2000, an official from the ministry commented, "We have nothing to be afraid of in Murdoch's entry. . . . The business [digital CS] requires hefty capital investment. So we hope domestic and foreign firms [will] form a harmonious consortium."[30] Murdoch's entry into the country seemed auspicious and failsafe given the enthusiasm a number of domestic corporations showed in developing a consortium with Sky TV. Yet Murdoch's venture into Korea's CS market encountered a major obstacle when a national coalition of fifty civic groups initiated a boycott against News Corporation. The leader of the coalition stated, "We welcome foreign capital into our country but not from Murdoch. . . . We also suspect Murdoch's investment here is aimed at securing a bridgehead for his attempt to move into China."[31] In effect, the latitude granted to Murdoch's Sky Channel in Korea was rather limited from the onset. Korea's Radio Law, like that of Japan, forbade foreign nationals from possessing more than 33 percent of the shares of local broadcasting businesses. Additionally, the Radio Law keeps foreign media firms under close scrutiny to prevent the transmission of either "contentious or culturally unbecoming" content, the elusiveness of which tightens the wiggle room for foreign content suppliers.

Compounding economic issues with cultural and political matters is not unusual in other countries. For example, the Indian government adamantly demanded that News Corporation, if it was to do business in India, sell 51 percent of Star TV India's equity to an Indian partner. This request was made amid raging civilian protests against Star TV India for airing culturally offensive content. To the exasperation of Murdoch, the Indian government skillfully transmuted a cultural issue into an ownership deal by mobilizing Indian citizens' animosity toward Star TV India. Many other countries employ similar strategies to cope with multinational media giants. Governments of these countries, sometimes hand in hand with civic groups or media entrepreneurs, are flying in the face of global media leviathans, outfoxing them and sometimes outlawing their maneuvers.

It is still hard to tell if Murdoch's departure from Japan will be followed by similar incidents. Almost concurrently with the divestment from Japan, News Corporation took a series of comparable actions, abandoning the New Zealand newspaper business and selling the Los Angeles Dodgers baseball team. Yet these withdrawals could have been based on a sheer managerial judgment. Nor did Murdoch's desertion of SkyPerfecTV deliver a decisive blow to his ambition to build a global satellite empire. News Corporation's recent launch of Sky Italia and its persistent attempts to procure DirecTV in the United States attests to this. The scattered footprints left by the global media mammoth are dizzyingly incongruous and make it too risky to predict the company's next move. The hazy outlook for News Corporation and other multimedia giants is quite revealing of the current state of affairs. It hints at the unfeasibility of adhering to a monolithic, static, and comforting interpretation of media globalization that has already outlived its utility.

I have critiqued two prevalent modes of storytelling about media globalization. First, one grieves over the dismantling of the local/national media by the wicked multinational media. I reject this melodramatic admonition not because it has a hue of self-defeatism but because it unjustly denies the agency of the local/national media while exaggerating the power of the multinational giants. The other paradigm exalts the potency of national/local agents in coping with the assault from multinational intruders. I also reject this view since it blindfolds us to the ever growing resemblance between the two entities, thereby leaving unproblematized the disquieting practices of local/national media.

The case of SkyPerfecTV palpably testifies to the fact that the outright binary opposition between the covetous, omnipotent, multinational giants and the innocent, emasculated, local media should be abandoned; the resemblance between the two antithetically imagined forces has increasingly outgrown the supposed polarity. Either pitying or lionizing local/national media simply because they are financial, organizational, and political underdogs is profoundly risky and untenable.

NOTES

1. Jaap van Ginneken, *Understanding Global News: A Critical Introduction* (London: Sage, 1998); Leslie Sklair, "Classifying the Global System," in Annabelle Sreberny-Mohammadi, Dwayne Winseck, Jim McKenna, and Oliver Boyd-Barrett., eds. *Media in Global Context: A Reader,* (London: Arnold, 1997), 37–47; Oliver Boyd-Barrett, "Global News Wholesalers as Agents of Globalization," in Annabelle Sreberny-Mohammadi, Dwayne Winseck, Jim McKenna, and Oliver Boyd-Barrett., eds. *Media in Global Context: A Reader,* (London: Arnold, 1997), 131–44.

2. Mike Featherstone, "Localism, Globalism, and Cultural Identity," in Rob Wilson and Wimal Dissanayake, eds. *Global-Local: Cultural Production and the Transnational Imaginary,* (Durham: Duke University Press, 1996), 46–77; Joseph D. Straubhaar, "Distinguishing the Global, Regional, and National Levels of World Television," in Annabelle Sreberny-Mohammadi, Dwayne Winseck, Jim McKenna, and Oliver Boyd-Barrett., eds. *Media in Global Context: A Reader,* (London: Arnold, 1997), 284–98; Georgette Wang, ed. *The New Communication Landscape: Demystifying Media Globalization* (New York: Routledge, 2000).

3. See Ministry of Public Management, Home Affairs, Posts and Telecommunications, Japan, *Major Aspects of Japan's Broadcasting Policy* (Tokyo, Japan: Ministry of Public Management, Home Affairs, Posts and Telecommunications, 2002), 3–4.

4. This department oversaw Japan's media industry in general. It was integrated with the Ministry of Home Affairs and the Public Management agency in January 2001 to become the Ministry of Public Management, Home Affairs, Posts, and Tele-communications. With this reorganization, the former MPT's Communication Policy Bureau, Telecommunication Bureau, and Broadcasting Bureau were combined to become two bureaus: the Information Communication Policy Bureau and the Basic Bureau for Integrated Communications.

5. This was a crucial agenda item during the summit between former U.S. president Bill Clinton and former Japanese prime minister Yoshiro Mori in April 2000.

6. J-COM was founded in 1995 as a joint venture between Japan's Sumitomo and cable provider Tele-Communications International (now Liberty Media). The company's major stakeholders include Sumitomo (36 percent), Liberty Media (35 percent), and Microsoft (15 percent). In contrast, TITUS was a subsidiary of the U.S. software giant Microsoft until it was purchased by Jupiter Telecom in September 2000. They both offered integrated services for cable, telephony, and the Internet.

7. SkyPerfecTV came into being as a result of merging Murdoch's JSkyB and PerfecTV Corp.

8. This, according to Iwabuchi Koichi, has been a consistent tendency except during the 1960s when programs imported from the United States flooded the Japanese broadcasting market. Iwabuchi also notes that more than 95 percent of all programs on Japanese TV have been produced domestically since the early 1970s. See Iwabuchi Koichi, "To Globalize, Regionalize, or Localize Us, That Is the Question: Japan's Response to Media Globalization," in Georgette Wang, Jan Servaes, and Anura Goonasekera, eds. *The New Communication Landscape: Demystifying Media Globalization* (New York: Routledge, 2000), 142–159.

9. See Kaifu Kazuo, "Digitization of Japan's Satellite Broadcasting," *Broadcasting Culture and Research* 3 (1998): 7–9.

10. Iwabuchi Koichi, "To Globalize, Regionalize, or Localize Us," 143–44.

11. George Gilder, *Life after Television* (New York: Norton, 1992), 11.

12. David Morley and Kevin Robbins, *Spaces of Identity: Global Media, Electronic Landscapes, and Cultural Boundaries* (London: Routledge, 1995), 148.

13. This precautionary move was, of course, an involuntary one. Many countries, including Great Britain, India, China, and South Korea, limit stock ownership by foreign investors to less than 50 percent.

14. As of July 2003, DirecTV had over twelve million subscribers in the U.S. market alone.

15. Kaifu Kazuo, "Internationalization, Market Deregulation, and Digitization: Restructuring Japan's Broadcasting Industry," *Broadcasting Culture and Research* 1 (1997): 9.

16. See Iida Masao, "The Digital Broadcasting Debate: How to Harmonize Public and Commercial Services," *Studies of Broadcasting* 34 (1999): 81–103; and Hanada

Tetsuro, "Digital Broadcasting and the Future of the Public Sphere," *Studies of Broadcasting* 34 (1999): 9–40.

17. Iwabuchi Koichi, "To Globalize, Regionalize, or Localize Us," 145.

18. The amendment promulgated in 1989, for instance, differentiated broadcasters as either facility supplying or program supplying, hastening the participation of foreign content providers in Japan's broadcasting market.

19. See Yasuma Sosuke, Kodaira Sachiko, and Hara Yumiko, "A Study on the Internationalization of TV Programs," *Studies of Broadcasting* 29 (1993): 125–50.

20. *Nihon Keizai Shinbun,* 22 October 2003, morning edition.

21. SkyPerfect Communications, "Press Releases: Notice Regarding Change in Major Stockholders and the Ratio of Foreigners' Stockholding," 29 August 2003, http://www.skyperfectv.co.jp/skycom/e/press/02-02/20030829_2e.html. (accessed July 1, 2004)

22. Ibid.

23. Ibid.

24. The satellite communications operator Japan Satellite Systems (JSAT) was the first private sector operator founded after the enactment of Japan's Telecommunications Business Law in 1985. Owning and operating a total of nine satellites, it is a leading satellite operator in the Asia-Pacific region. The other partner, Nippon Telegraph and Telephone Corporation (NTT), is Japan's premier telecommunications company.

25. J-COM Broadband commenced of its own digital CS broadcasting platform with approximately sixty channels at the end of June 2004.

26. Plat-One is often called CS 110 because it is controlled by satellite N-SAT-110, which is located at 110 degrees East. Another CS channel using this new satellite is SkyPerfecTV2. Those subscribing to digital CS 110 platforms can access both CS and BS channels via a single receiver with an antenna oriented toward 110 degrees.

27. There are some exceptions. The channel Takarazuka Sky Stage and some data network channels are new.

28. For details, see Sky Perfect Communications, Ltd., *Annual Report 2003*, http://www.c-direct.ne.jp/english/divide/10104795/ar2003/ar2003e.pdf. (accessed July 4, 2004)

29. Instead, the notion of *glocalization*, a popular term coined by the chairman of Sony and subsequently endorsed by many academicians, has enjoyed wide currency. The notion of glocalization rightfully attends to the inevitability of negotiation and enmeshment between the analytically split units of the global and the local. As reciprocal corollaries, the global actively incorporates and adapts itself to local vernaculars while the local becomes a site that embodies global idioms.

30. See C. W. Lim, "South Korea Shows Murdoch Who Has The Force", Agence France Presse, April 26, 2000. http://www.spacedaily.com/news/murdoch-00d.html. (accessed July 4, 2004)

31. Ibid.

"Ordinary Foreigners" Wanted: Multinationalization of Multicultural Questions in a Japanese TV Talk Show[1]

Koichi Iwabuchi

With the acceleration of globalization processes, cross-border flows and circulations of capital, people, and media have been considerably prompted, and the numbers of transnational organizations and institutions that promote such moves have proliferated. In this context, it has become commonplace to talk about the demise of the national. Instead notions that stress cultural transgression, such as hybridity, transnationalism, and cosmopolitanism, are highlighted. However, while the historical constructedness of "imagined communities" is widely recognized and no longer taken for granted, the national imagination paradoxically seems to have become even more strengthened.

We are witnessing, on the one hand, how the intensification of transborder flows and connections engenders the reactionary nationalism and ethnic absolutism that accompany the violent exercise of exclusion in many parts of the world. On the other hand, the upsurge of national feeling can take a less assertive, "banal" form.[2] While transnational flows and connections are increasingly becoming mundane in everyday life, this tends to work only to make the banality of the nation more solid and deeply infiltrated into people's minds. A significant role played in this development is the media spectacle of global events (especially sports) and inter-national gatherings of various kinds, which renders the national logo a highly marketable brand.

This chapter looks at how the pleasurable commodification of national belonging occurs by examining the representation of "ordinary foreigners" (*futsū no gaikokujin*) in a Japanese TV talk show, *Kokoga hen dayo Nihonjin*

(This Is So Bizarre, You Japanese). In the following, I will first discuss the paradigm shift in the discourse on Japanese national identity from international(ization) to global(ization) and briefly review how this shift is reflected in the media representation of "foreigners." Then I will discuss the ways in which the increasing presence and visibility of foreign national residents in the Japanese public space enhance the commercial value of "ordinariness." In this move, the boundaries between "us" and "them" are sharply redemarcated so as to subtly turn an intensifying multicultural situation into a multinational media spectacle.

FROM "INTERNATIONAL" TO "GLOBAL": THE SHIFTING PARADIGM OF ARTICULATING JAPANESENESS

There has been a strong interest within Japan in explicating Japanese uniqueness as evidenced by the popularity of Nihonjinron literature (discourses on Japanese and Japanese culture), which explains Japanese people and culture in essentialist terms. Many studies show that the Japanese national/cultural identity has been constructed in an exclusive manner through its conscious self-Orientalizing discourse, a narrative that at once testifies to subtle exploitation of and deep complicity with Western Orientalist discourse.[3] Japan is represented and represents itself as culturally and racially homogeneous and uniquely particularistic by way of a strategic binary opposition between two imaginary cultural entities, "Japan" and "the West".[4]

It was above all in the decade after Japan attained the status of an economic superpower that such discourses gained currency there. This was a period when the nationalist term *kokusaika* (internationalization) became prevalent in Japan.[5] The Japanese government and companies devoted themselves to furthering Japan's national interests through competition with their foreign counterparts in the international arena. This process accompanied a drastic increase in opportunities for the Japanese populace to encounter foreign (predominantly Western) people and cultures both outside and inside Japan. Backed by a strong Japanese economy and the relative decline of American power, the self-orientalist Nihonjinron literature became a popular commodity through which the Japanese populace could explain in a rather confident manner the distinctive characteristics of Japanese culture and society without undermining a definite demarcation between us and them.[6] Here culminated Japan's collusive exploitation of a Western Orientalist gaze in the 1980s, which marks "Japan's accession to the position of powerful nation-states."[7]

While this complicity has never disappeared, the collapse of the so-called bubble economy and subsequent social downfall of Japan since the early 1990s put an end to such internationalist Nihonjinron discourses. The last decade of the twentieth century, called "the decade of loss" (*ushinawareta jūnen*), witnessed the decisive structural breakdown of Japanese institutions such as the bureaucracy, corporate organization, the education system, and family relationships. In addition to a prolonged economic recession, a series of gloomy social incidents, such as the Kobe earthquake, an increasing number of brutal crimes by teenagers, and the nerve gas attacks in the Tokyo railway system perpetrated by the Aum Supreme sect, have further deepened the sense of crisis and pessimistic view of the future among the populace.

Along with this has come the rapid development of globalization processes in which transborder flows and connections among capital, people, and the media are accelerating at an unprecedented scale and speed. In this context, the key word in discussions of "Japan in the world" has changed from *international* to *global*.[8] The use of *global* in media discourse clearly reads as passive and lacking confidence, signifying the decay and crisis of Japan. Exemplified by the term *global standard*, Japanese discourses of globalization have most notably revolved around the urgency to readjust to the new, U.S.-led, global economic order.

While the lack of confidence in Japan's economic power and social harmony severely damaged the validity and usefulness of Nihonjinron discourses, this did not signal the end of Japanese nationalistic discourses. On the contrary, in this context nationalistic discourses have taken various forms but no longer claim cultural distinctiveness and superiority founded on economic power. Various attempts have been made to (re)discover the merit and virtue of Japan: nostalgia for past glory, reactive discourses that aim to revise history textbooks to counter the "self-tormenting" view of Japan's modern history of imperialism and colonialism in Asia, the state's emphasis on teaching Japanese children more about their traditions and instilling patriotic sentiments, and the excessive celebratory attention to Japanese people (sports players in particular) who succeed outside Japan. Indeed, the 1990s has been marked as the decade of the upsurge of neonationalism.[9]

This is suggestive of the common observation that while they erode national boundaries globalization processes also newly enhance the sense of belonging to a national community. Yet it should be noted that such nationalism does not necessarily take an aggressive or fervent stance. As Billig argues, the permeation of national feeling is more often than not facilitated and displayed by a mundane practice such as casually showing the national flag in the city.[10] Such "banal nationalism" is further promoted by an increase in encounters with people, goods, and images from many parts of the world. Rather than being perceived as a threat to one's national identity, it is interpreted and contained within the internationalized framework of global society in a highly commercialized and spectacular manner. As is clearly shown by the escalation of global sports events such as the Olympics and World Cup Soccer, there has been a rapid proliferation of global televised spectacles of various kinds in which people are asked to purchase a ticket to join the event by showing a particular national emblem.[11]

Likewise, during the FIFA World Cup Soccer championship in 2002, which was cohosted by Korea and Japan, some observed the rise of "petit nationalism" in Japan.[12] For the first time since their defeat in World War II, ordinary Japanese (and especially young people) cheerfully and innocently rejoiced at being Japanese: they waved the national flag, painted it on their faces, and sang together the national anthem that praises the emperor's everlasting rule. Such practices attracted much discussion in Japan; some saw it positively as a sign of open-minded cosmonationalism while others thought it a dangerous emotional expression that could easily lead to an exclusive ethnonationalism. In any case, this phenomenon cannot be interpreted as the rise of a zealous nationalism since the survey regularly shows that only small portion of Japanese youths are proud of their country.[13] Rather, significantly underscored in this event is the entrenched permeation of an assumption that the world is the congregation of various nations. The event testifies, I would suggest, to the increasing prominence of an Olympiad framework of multinationalism, a widespread perception that the nation is the local unit of which one is asked to display one's membership for participation in the global society is deeply internalized as taken for granted at an individual level. Through a spectacular international encounter, exchange, and competition, the uncanny ubiquity of the global is replaced not with a threatening enemy (them) but with a comfortable and enjoyable comradeship (us). In this process, the national flag becomes a most marketable brand logo and "banal nationalism" is reinforced by the pleasurable consumption of the sense of national belonging that ensures (pseudo) participation in the global society.

MEDIA REPRESENTATION OF FOREIGN RESIDENTS IN THE GLOBAL ERA

The shift in focus from international to global and the emergence of multinationalism are also discerned in the media representation of "foreigners" in Japan. On the one hand, the activation of people's border crossing has intensified anxiety about national communal security. The mass media have long tended to treat foreign residents as social problems and/or threats to the Japanese community. This became especially conspicuous in the 1980s when the number of temporary and permanent immigrants from Asian regions considerably increased. At that time, besides the exclusive view on the immigrants, how and whether Japan can be a multiracial nation was also one of the concerns if not the main one.[14] However, coinciding with a widely observed trend in many parts of the world, which became conspicuous especially after the 9/11, this inclusionist concern had been more clearly overwhelmed by that of exclusion by the late 1990s. In this context, (illegal) immigrants, especially from China, have attracted public attention in relation to an increase in crimes committed by foreign nationals.

This is exemplified by Tokyo governor Ishihara's racist comments on the rise of crime in Japan in 2000, which he attributed mostly to the increase in (illegal) Chinese migrants. The Japanese media also repeatedly report on the increase and viciousness of crimes committed by foreigners. While the number of such incidents is actually still insignificant compared to the total figure, the Japanese media uncritically play a collusive role in the recurring and manipulative dissemination of police data that stress the increase in foreigners' crimes.[15] Furthermore, in the news coverage it is frequently reported that a suspect is a foreigner or looks like a foreigner with no clear evidence of the nationality of the suspect besides his or her appearance and language. This racist inference lends itself to reproducing the image of foreigner = crime = dangerous.

It can be argued that the demonizing of foreign criminals effectively engenders and exploits the widely felt sense of social distress and insecurity, which is generated not just by the rise in crime but also by various kinds of worries in terms of unemployment, terrorist attacks, the breakdown of education system, and pensions after retirement. Instead of offering a comprehensive account for the complication of cause and effect of those globally shared social issues, the discourse of foreign crime easily attributes the cause of anxiety in a simplifying manner to palpable villains that threaten "our" national communities, which thus should be expelled to outside of the borders. In this way, a highly romanticized longing for a safe and caring community is provoked in an exclusive manner.[16]

On the other hand, the Japanese media have also been a strong impetus to represent foreign residents as consumable signs through which potentially disturbing transnational encounters can be translated into a pleasurable media spectacle. At least since the early 1960s, foreigners have appeared in the Japanese mass media as commentators and entertainers, but it was in the 1980s, the decade of "internationalization," that this tendency intensified and so-called *gaijin-tarento* (foreign celebrities) became media celebrities. They were mostly Caucasians from Western countries, predominantly the United States, and fluent in Japanese.[17] Their assigned task was, like the narrative in Nihonjinron, to mark the uniqueness of Japan in entertaining ways. They were repeatedly asked to comment on Japanese culture or current affairs with a particular emphasis on the difference between Japan and the "Rest/West."[18] *Gaijin-tarento*, on their side, subtly played their assigned role to satisfy the Japanese desire to be regarded as unique.

However, as Nihonjinron discourses declined so the value of *gaijin-tarento* decreased. The increasing number of foreign nationals residing in Japan who, to an even more considerable degree, acquired Japanese cultural competence in terms of language skills and insights into Japanese culture and society also undermined the raison d'être of *gaijin-tarento*. The favored Japanese media commodity became the "ordinariness" of foreign residents. There emerged, for example, TV programs in which unknown foreigners contested with each other in singing Japanese songs that included *enka* (a balladic music of Japanese popular song full of melancholy) and those programs that described the everyday struggles of foreign brides in Japan. There was also a public TV commercial by the Japan Advertising Council in 2002 that featured an American woman who successfully worked as a landlady in Yamagata. In the ad, she stressed the traditional virtues of Japan, which many Japanese people seem to forget, with a statement that the Japanese are short of "Japan" (Nipponjin niwa nihon ga tarinai). These examples demonstrate that the role of highlighting Japan's distinctiveness played by *gaijin-tarento* had been replaced by the "ordinary" foreigner's gaze and body. Testifying to this development, there appeared a new type of TV talk show, titled *Kokoga hen dayo Nihonjin* ("KHN", hereafter), which featured the outspoken voices and opinions of foreign residents about Japan. As I will discuss below, it displays an attempt to re-demarcate the cultural boundries of "Japan" through the representation of Japan in/and the global society. What is crucial here is the fact that ordinary foreigners are explicit about where they are from by showing their (non-Japanese) nationalities. A multinational spectacle is substituted for multicultural politics whereby the issue of inclusion/exclusion in the Japanese imagined community is rendered irrelevant.

"ORDINARY FOREIGNERS" WANTED

After a successful few trials as a special program, KHN was broadcast as an hour-long weekly program (at 10:00 P.M.) from October 1998 to March

2002. The program gained relatively high ratings in this time slot (around 15 percent on average). The show featured one hundred foreigners in a studio audience who were willing to utter their opinions on various topics. It usually began with foreigners' statements expressing their sense of anger and frustration and the oddness they felt about Japanese sociocultural matters such as racial discrimination, international marriage, school bullying, and animal abuse. On the Japanese side, concerned persons and commentators (comedians, intellectuals, social critics, and so on) appeared in the studio and in most cases agitated the discussion by refuting the foreigners' points in a confrontational manner. As the producer stated, the target audience of this program was those who did not have a critical awareness of the issues involved.[19] To appeal to such audiences, the program did not aim to offer rational, well-structured discussions but to provoke a quarrel through an exaggerated and simplified comparison between "Japan and the rest."[20]

The show apparently shares much with earlier media representations of foreigners in terms of the attempt to discursively construct an exclusive Japanese imagined community, but it also draws a clear line between them in some respects. In an interview I conducted at TBS on 19 January 2001, the producer told me that his idea for the show was originally inspired by Nihonjinron literature, which he had enjoyed reading as a university student.[21] He wanted to create a TV talk show that elucidated the distinctive traits of Japanese society and culture by comparing them to those of other cultures and nations. In implementing his idea, the producer stressed the significance of featuring nameless foreigners. According to him, the newness of the program lay in the review of contemporary Japanese society through the opinions of foreigners who were living as ordinary residents in Japan. This was necessitated by the steady increase in the number of foreign nationals residing there.

> I thought it was important to feature ordinary people from many parts of the world. There are now so many foreign-nationals living in Japan. The situation is much different from before. I want to give them a space to express their views on issues about Japanese culture and society as well as the sense of frustration they feel while inhabiting Japan, which is something we should not easily dismiss.

Yet representing ordinary people's voices is apparently commercially significant in making the show appealing to Japanese audiences. It is assumed that since foreign discussants appearing on the show are "ordinary" people, their comments will be regarded as genuine, not deliberately exaggerated and contrived performances as was the case with *gaijin-tarento*.[22] Moreover, convinced by the popularity of Nihonjinron, the producer was quite sure that "Japanese people would like to listen to how foreigners perceive their society and culture" to confirm Japanese distinctiveness. The ordinariness of enraged foreigners is believed to ensure the authenticity of their voices, which in turn helps their utterances about Japan sound radical and fresh to viewers. The talk show format is seen as a strategically appropriate way to represent such voices and reconfirm the symbolic boundaries of "Japan" in a stimulating way. Ordinary foreign residents are regarded as an attractive commodity of alterity in a televised multicultural "safari park" where Japanese audiences can safely enjoy the spectacle of (sometimes scary) intercultural encounters through the screen.

The minimum requirement for foreign participants in KHN is that they possess oral Japanese language skills fluent enough to allow them to discuss various topics with their Japanese counterparts. In addition, the producer seemed to be uncomfortable with the fact that the foreign discussants often make other media appearances, taking advantage of their participation in the program. However, this should not be taken straightforwardly. What ordinariness means to the producer is not at all self-evident. Whether or not the discussants are really nonprofessional, ordinary people does not seem to matter much to him; he is more concerned with making them look ordinary. Thus, the question to be investigated is how the program attempts to represent the ordinariness of foreign discussants to fit its commercial purpose.

While the talk show is expected to depict the spontaneous expressions of the discussants, the production side tightly controls the content of KHN. The topics of each program are entirely decided by the production team, and discussants are asked to report their views and opinions in advance. Then the production side considers what would be the desirable direction of the debate, who will make an interesting comment for the show, and what kinds of video images should be inserted, in order to make the show most enjoyable. In the studio, the master of ceremonies, Kitano Takeshi, is told who will make the most stimulating comments on the topic and should be picked.

The lifeline of KHN is how to secure foreign national residents who can make intriguing and stirring comments and compare Japan to their own countries. The program constantly inserts statements recruiting foreign discussants. According to the producer, some members of the foreign discussants are regularly renewed so the program will not get into a rut. Those whose presence and comments fail to enliven the discussion are apt to disappear from the program. Discussants who are able to make intriguing comments in the producer's favor continue to appear on the program, and some even become amateur media celebrities.

In relation to this, a talent agency, Inagawa Motoko Office (IMO) has played a significant role in the recruitment and management of foreign discussants. It has nearly exclusively handled foreign personalities and extras for the Japanese media since its inception in 1985, and it handles all of KHN's discussants. While this simplifies both payment and management, IMO does much more. It conducts the auditions and looks for foreign talent on the street.[23] Furthermore, contrary to the producer's stress on nonprofessional ordinariness, some discussants appeared in the media well before KHN aired. And it is those hidden talents that are purposely assigned to play key roles in heating up the debate on the program. A most infamous case in point is that of a Japanese American man who has worked as disc jockey. With his face suntanned face, he agitates the people in the studio by making offensive comments from the viewpoint of an American hard-liner. While audiences might not be aware that this is a media-manipulating performance, other foreign discussants know who the far from ordinary talents from IMO are. Some foreign discussants who have passed the audition are very sensitive to and frustrated by those who make provocative comments in the producer's favor. I will return to this point later. Suffice it to say here that the way the ordinariness of the discussants is so highly stage-managed works to marginalize the other discussants' presence on the show.

MULTINATIONAL REPRESENTATION OF THE GLOBAL SOCIETY

The commodification of ordinary foreigners on KHN is suggestive of two reasons for the end of the West-centered *gaijin-tarento* on Japanese TV. First is the substantial increase in foreign nationals who speak fluent Japanese, The second is the growing prominence of non-Western countries in the world and the increasing recognition that the Japanese people need to refute foreigners' (improper) views on Japan.[24] These changes need to be grasped in conjunction with the paradigm shift from internationalism to globalism discussed earlier. The phenomenon of KHN clearly shows the shift of emphasis in terms of the collusive othering from the (imbalanced) internationalist binary between "Japan" and "the West" to that of the globalism binary between the Japan and the Rest of the world nations. After the defeat in World War II, Japanese (post)colonial connections with other Asian countries were subsumed under its cultural subordination and rivalry with the West, especially the United States. Japan's peculiar position as the only modernized Asian country has long been be translated with a great skew towards Japan's relations with the West. The last decade, however, has witnessed the rise of non-Western players in the global economy, politics, and culture, as well as an increase in communication and exchange among the non-Western nations that overpass Western countries. These new trends have persuaded the Japanese media to pay more attention to non-Western countries and their perspectives, as is declared in one Japanese magazine that the world of *gaijin-tarento* on the Japanese TV is, though belatedly, entering the era of Asia and Africa.[25] This tendency is clearly demonstrated on KHN, in which the binary contraposition of "Japan" versus "the West" has given way to more representations of the global society. Many of popular discussants (and performers) are now actually from Asia and Africa, and their "non-Western" views are even more emphasized in the program.

Surely, the hitherto suppressed voices of Asian and African discussants might offer fresh insights into Japanese culture and society. They display critical views on Japanese racial discrimination from the perspective of the people concerned. Yet the program does not just aim to throw these insights into the limelight. No less important, underlining those voices is necessary to depict the global society in microcosm in terms of the contraposition of Japan and other nations. The producer consciously includes foreign discussants from as many countries and regions as possible so that the program can pretend to represent the whole world, as demonstrated by the program's claim that it features "foreign people from more than fifty nations."[26] To emphasize the picture of Japan versus the world, the studio set is organized in such as way that foreign nationals and their Japanese counterparts stand face-to-face and foreign discussants are required to wear the national flag of their countries on their chests. Furthermore, the production side regularly asks, if not compels, foreign discussants to make comments based on comparisons between Japan and their own nations. The most inflammatory comments on the program usually stress similarities between Japan and other nations. In my observation of the studio shooting, I heard some discussants complain that this black-and-white framework obscured the complexity of the issues concerned. Such views tend to be edited out, if they are successfully expressed at all, and the deviant discussant soon disappears from the program.

The global diversity represented on the program is thus fundamentally a one-dimensional composition of a nationalized binarism that eliminates ambiguity and multiplicity in the form of national belonging and ethnocultural identity. Although some discussants obtain dual citizenship and some have lived in Japan since childhood, they are all categorized as "foreign national residents." For example, one man wearing the South Korean flag was born in Japan and had lived in the United States, Korea and Japan, but he was categorized as a representative of Korea. He was lumped together with other Korea nationals, some of whom had come to Japan rather recently, and the national flag he put on all too easily reduced his opinions to Korean viewpoints. He insisted on his doubleness and "cosmopolitan identity" in his personal HP and expressed it in an interview in a Japanese-language magazine targeted at Korean residents.[27] His doubleness is never attended to on the program. All he is expected to do is act unambiguously Korean.

This is reminiscent of a familiar problematic associated with multi-culturalism. Multiculturalism is criticized for its underlying conception of culture as a coherent entity, which goes together with the conception of a multicultural society as a mosaic composed of clearly demarcated boundaries between ethnic cultures with the dominant group unmarked as such. More recently, the idea of multiculturalism has also been blamed for failing to take transnationalism into consideration; its obsession with multicultural situations "here," in a national society, for the purpose of socionational integration often tends to disregard immigrants' connections with "there," which is often regarded as a detriment to communal harmony in the multicultural nation.[28]

It seems premature to see the same multiculturalist trap in the Japanese context in which even the idea of multicultural symbiosis has not yet been widely embraced by the government and the populace, not to mention the need to adopt related policies to advance multiculturalism. Rather the issue at stake with regard to the cultural politics of KHN is, I suggest, multinationalism. The program's representation of the global society renders national belonging as even more taken for granted through the pleasurable consumption of a multinational spectacle. By suppressing foreign discussants' ambivalent (trans)national connections and sense of belonging to Japan, the program fixes them as foreign national others, essentially cutting them off from Japan. It is an attempt to control the implosion of difference within an imagined community by replacing it with a multinational situation that consists of a mob of temporary residents who will never be full members of the nation. They are allowed to express their difference in public only as long as they wear national flags that emphasize the division between us and them. Their differences are recognized and understood exclusively as "in but not of" in the highly commodified form of national branding.

THE MEDIA SPECTACLE OF A "WAR OF WORDS" IN A GLOBAL ERA

The program format of a "war of words" (*zessen*) between Japanese and ordinary foreigners makes KHN's multinationalism work more effectively. This is related to the second reason for the end of the era of the *gaijin-tarento*. In the age of internationalism, *gaijin tarento* pleasurably confirmed Japanese uniqueness to the Japanese people. However, thankfully accepting Western views on Japanese uniqueness is no longer satisfactory. As self-claimed cultural uniqueness has become associated less with the secret of Japan's economic power than with the shortcomings that account for its socio-economic decline, and as actual encounters with foreign nationals are becoming uncommon in everyday settings, the need to refute the improper views, criticisms, and misunderstandings about Japan that are uttered by foreigners has come to be stressed. Reflecting this trend, KHN presents not just foreign people's anger and criticism against Japanese society but also Japanese counterarguments (in a highly emotional manner in most cases). Provocative statements about Japanese bizarreness by a foreign discussant is followed by a studio discussion between other foreign discussants, who comment on the statement from their own national perspectives, and Japanese discussants, who often get excited and further stir up the quarrel. Extremely confrontational performances on both sides well work together to excitingly demarcate ethnocultural boundaries between Japan and other nations.

This picture overlaps with a new type of Nihonjinron appearing in the age of globalization. For example, Ishii Yoneo argues for the importance of acquiring "global literacy" in his coauthored book with Kawai Hayao, *The Japanese and Globalization* (2002).[29] To acquire global literacy, the mastering of basic communications skills in English, as the global lingua franca, is indispensable first of all, but this is just a means to an end. From his own experience in promoting international exchanges between Japan and the rest of the world, Ishii points out that it is not a dialogue but a one-way method of introducing Japanese culture to the world and vice versa. What is imperative in the age of globalization is, he argues, an international exchange that does not just sponsor superficial cultural exhibitions but promotes a dialogue that might be highly antagonistic in some cases. In the face of increases in the clash of opinions, values, and principles among people of different national backgrounds, a passive attitude toward defending and protecting Japanese culture or convincing oneself that Japan will always be incomprehensible to others, Ishii argues, must be discarded. Japanese people have to learn to actively express their own opinions, to maintain Japan's positions and interests, and even to be prepared for serious confrontation with other nationals in the global arena.

Conforming to this view, the Japanese media often appreciate KHN in terms of the representation of Japanese discussants' head-on back talk to those foreigners who assert their sense of anger and frustration with Japanese society without reserve. Their self-assertiveness can be seen as lopsided, but at the same time their ability to express their own opinions in a foreign language in public space is regarded as something Japanese people should emulate. No less entertaining to audiences is watching how Japanese people who are supposed to be unskilled at debate subtly refute such skillfully argumentative foreign discussants.[30] Watching KHN, Japanese audiences can release their pent-up emotions, which are heightened in the rather a stifling Japanese socioeconomic situation under the rough waves of globalization, and enjoy the spectacle of Japanese retorting to "ill-advised" foreigners in an exaggerated manner.

The nonfiction writer Hisada Megumi's comment that the program makes her head go round (*Asahi Shinbun*, 2 March 1999, evening edition) hits the mark in regard to how the Olympic-like war of words between Japanese and foreign discussants effectively distorts the public visibility and discussion of multicultural issues in the Japanese context.[31] In watching KHN, she was overwhelmed by the diversity of nationalities of people residing in Japan and their assertion, in fluent Japanese, of the anger and frustration they are made to feel living in Japan, so much so that she could not help but realize that Japan had become a multiracial society without her knowledge. This suggests that the public visibility and utterances of foreign residents with competency in Japanese might urge Japanese audiences to turn their attention to how the intensified transnational flows of people have made it untenable to believe in the homogeneity of the Japanese imagined community.

At the same time, however, Hisada also confesses that she was surprised to find a strong nationalistic sentiment evoked within her as she was annoyed by the foreigners' Japan-bashing and her inability to refute it. Here we can see how a multinational framework of the war of words operates to prevent public negotiation of incommensurable cultural differences within the society. Through TV's aptitude for entertaining simplification, such a chance is subtly replaced by the representation of a controllable confrontation of national-cultural diversity. The program reduces multicultural situations to a multinational spectacle by employing the framework of a global war of words between clearly demarcated nationalities whereby the potential to deconstruct the exclusive imagined communities from within are precluded and domesticated by the fortification of exclusive international diversity.[32]

THE CULTURAL POLITICS OF PUBLIC VISIBILITY

While multinationalism based on the distorted representation of multicultural situations in Japan should be critically examined, the fact that KHN makes foreign national residents visible and their hitherto suppressed voices audible in a mediated public space cannot be entirely dismissed. This point is suggestive of the argument concerning public participation in

American talk shows such as *Oprah* in terms of the possibility of construct-ing plural public spheres. Those shows are often criticized for the vulgar quality of debate among the studio participants, but they are also appreci-ated for underlining repressed issues and providing a forum for the voices of women, working-class people, homosexuals, and ethnic minorities in the mainstream media. Paulo Carpignano and his collaborators, for example, think highly of talk shows' role in democratizing the public sphere.[33] By intensifying the confrontation between the persons concerned and studio audiences, they argue, American talk shows make it possible for the hith-erto inaudible experience and voice of ordinary people to gain an advantage over intellectuals' pedagogical comments in the public sphere. Talk shows thus break through the limitation of a Habermasian bourgeois public sphere that is criticized for being elitist, male dominated, and racially exclusive in operation.[34]

Similarly, it can be argued that KHN contributes to making invisible foreign residents and their voices public matters. For example, many issues related to racial discrimination that have tended to be disregarded by Japa-nese TV are dealt with in the programs, if in an excessively sensational and superficial manner. Issues such as the bigoted comment of Ishihara Shintaro, the governor of Tokyo, that Chinese and Korean residents are associated with the increase in foreigners' crime and the discriminatory practices of a public bath in Otaru, Hokkaido, that forbade foreigners to enter it, were cov-ered and critically discussed from the point of view of those who were dis-criminated against. In the latter case, two foreign discussants flew to Otaru to cover the story on the program of 28 February 2001.[35] Their coverage was mostly from the viewpoint of a Japanese American man who is married to a Japanese and has Japanese nationality but was forbidden to enter the bath due to his "foreign" appearance. He brought a suit against the bath owner in order to let the Japanese public know how this kind of conduct, which is still not uncommon in Japan, is seriously discriminatory and racist.[36] In Japan, which lacks any penal regulations, a sign reading "no foreigners allowed" is openly posted at the door of some real estate agencies and bars. Yet such dis-crimination is, if pointed out at all in the media, rarely viewed as intolerable conduct. Following the journalistic principle of "objectivity and nonpartisan impartiality," the Japanese mass media tend to offer balanced coverage of such cases by hearing both sides of the story and pointing out the difficulty of multicultural symbiosis in a detached manner, ending with the clichéd suggestion that to maintain social harmony both sides should get together and discuss the issue.[37]

In KHN's coverage, nearly all foreign discussants condemned the pro-hibition of those who have "foreign" appearance to enter a public bath as racial discrimination, supporting the standpoint of the persons concerned. This created an unusual opportunity for the discriminated against to be heard in the mainstream media, and so it should not be easily dismissed as too subjective and biased. It exposed the fact that such objectivity is only beneficial to the majority of the Japanese populace. Foregrounding the minority's point of view, the myth of media objectivity and neutrality that is actually inclined to work for maintaining the status quo was debunked.

This should not, let me reiterate, divert attention from the fact that talk shows are highly stage-managed and controlled by the production side. We need to interrogate how supposedly spontaneous voices on the show are actually shaped under the production format of the talk show genre and whether a highly commodified and exaggerated debate on TV can be seen as a public forum. As Jane Shattuc argues, professional masters of ceremonies are apt to dissociate the issue under discussion from a wider social context and reduce it to a personal matter to be resolved at the individual level.[38] Despite the possibility of constructing an alternative public sphere, media gatekeepers' emphasis on sensationalism and personification deprives TV talk shows of a critical edge. Such criticism can be seriously applied to KHN, whose degree of stage-management and preclusion of the potential for creating a multicultural public sphere are not comparable to its American counterparts.

Rather, the point I'd like to bring up here is the limitation of posing a Manichean question of whether audience participation talk programs that foreground hitherto unenunciated voices of the marginalized create a new kind of public forum or are merely commodified TV spectacles. It would be more productive, I would argue, to analyze the multicultural politics of TV talk shows by acknowledging that both aspects cannot be considered separately but complement each other. Putting aside a bipolar view of spectacle or forum, circus or symposium, Joshua Gamson argues that, as they exist between two opposing poles, American talk shows blur the lines and redraw them at the same time.[39] With a particular focus on the issue of homosexuality, he empirically analyzes how boundaries between private and public and normal and abnormal are at once obscured and reconstructed by attending to the contradiction in the public appearance of marginalized people. Television talk shows highlight what he calls "paradoxes of visibility," which display

> democratization through exploitation, truths wrapped in lies, normalization through freak show. There is in fact no choice here between manipulative spectacle and democratic forum, only the puzzle of a situation in which one cannot exist without the other,

and the challenge of seeing clearly what this means for a society at war with its own sexual diversity.[40]

In exploring the paradoxes, Gamson attaches a particular importance to the examination of how marginalized people actively participate and, in some instances, collude in this media event. While admitting the significance of the analysis of the way in which the media production and representation "annihilate" and "deform" gay and lesbian people, he nevertheless points out its limitations in analyzing talk shows by posing a question about their agencies in the process.

> [W]hat happens to media representations of nonconforming sexualities when lesbian and gay men are actively invited to participate, to "play themselves" rather than be portrayed by others, to refute stereotypes rather than simply watch them on the screen? That is the twist talk shows provide."[41]

Gamson argues that public visibility through commercial media is something like "walking a tight rope" for the marginalized people. They cannot control the result of their public visibility though media entertainment shows, and there is no guarantee that it would lead to the deconstruction of their negative stereotypes. Nevertheless, "the struggle for self-representation is not one in which talk show guests are simple victims. . . . [T]hey have a strong hand in creating it."[42] Critical analysis of how talk shows represent and exploit marginalized people in terms of the democratization of the public sphere appears to take the side of the marginalized. Yet there is a risk that it eventually subsumes their active practices and performances of becoming visible under a big picture of the construction of the rational public sphere, a risk of disregarding the existing heterogeneous and contradictory practices of the marginalized within and behind the public sphere.

Likewise, I suggest that examining the active participation and performance of foreign discussants in KHN is imperative if we are to grasp the complexity and ambivalence involved in the multinationalist attempt to reconstruct national boundaries through media entertainment. While its symbolic violence to boundary demarcation cannot be stressed too much, we should also carefully look at various practices of the represented in the site of production and consumption in order to go beyond an oversimplified picture. This is not to uncritically celebrate the autonomy and active resistance of the marginalized to the mass media. Increased attention to those aspects, since they do not evidently appear on the surface of the mediated public sphere and thus cannot be grasped by representational analysis, I argue, would lead to a many-layered understanding of cultural politics and representational violence on KHN. A detailed field research analysis of how heterogeneous foreign discussants perform in various ways on the show is indispensable for this purpose, yet it is beyond the scope of this essay. In the remainder, I offer some findings and considerations drawn from my limited field research.

PERFORMING "FOREIGNERS" AND THE BURDEN OF REPRESENTATION

While it appears that foreign discussants tend to assert their differences in a nationalistic and ethnocentric manner on the program, once we meet those discussants who behave like nationalists on the screen it often becomes apparent that they are not nationalists at all. For example, a Chinese graduate student strongly defended China's position on the show, but she was critical of Chinese society and the government in an interview with me. Admitting that she tends to become nationalistic on the show, she told me, "I am not quite sure why I'd be [nationalistic] in the studio discussion, but perhaps I enjoy behaving that way. It is more enjoyable on that occasion [than being a rational thinker]. It is something like participating in the Olympics." She thus fully follows the intention of the producer and enjoys performing herself accordingly. Similarly a Japanese-Brazilian journalist states that while he tries not to be taken in, contrary to his initial intention, he often finds himself behaving in a manner that supports the aim of the producer, strongly defending Brazil's position vis-à-vis Japan in response to Japanese discussants' comments. In either case, the program's organizing format of war of words also induces foreign discussants to feel "you have no right to say that to me and my country" and respond nationalistically. Here too, we can see that multinationalism effectively works to generate the self-assertion of one's belonging to a particular nation.

However, foreign discussants' seemingly nationalistic performances are not just colored by their (often pleasurable) participation in the media show. They can also be seen as reflecting the burden of representation caused by their position as a marginalized citizen in Japan. Most foreign discussants apply for the audition of their own accord, and there are many practical reasons for their eagerness to participate. Some want to earn extra pocket money, some want to take advantage of their TV appearances to acquire better jobs in Japan, and some even want to become media celebrities. But there are also those who are motivated to contest widely held negative stereotypes of the country with which they (fully or partially) identify because such images strongly affect their identity formation and living conditions within Japan. Particularly, unlike people of Western origin, those from Asia and Africa, who suffer much more severe prejudice and discrimination in Japan, are apt to work hard to improve the images of their own countries. As the Chinese discussant mentioned above noted:

> I'd strongly argue against any criticism of Chinese society and culture on the show. Well, of course I know there are so many bad things in China that need to be reformed and changed. But that is another story. We do not have to show such bad aspects of China on Japanese TV. I'd rather wipe them out.

I was also informed that some Japanese-Brazilian participants deliberately refer to the positive sides of Brazil as much as possible in order to tear down unjustly spread images of their backwardness. And some participants from African countries take an opposite tack and enhance their images by representing a poor but "pure" Africa on the show. In this sense, even if they seem to be behaving like nationalists they do so for strategic reasons.

This kind of performance is sometimes forced on them by their expatriate communities in Japan. For example, the Chinese participant told me that there was strong peer pressure on Chinese discussants to make pro-China comments on the program. And if they do not meet this expectation their peers often condemn them. According to the Chinese woman, intense discussion occurred over several months concerning the comments made by Chinese participants on KHN in the readers' column of a Chinese-language newspaper published in Japan. It became the focus of criticism, as it was perceived as damaging to the image of China and themselves. My informant was the subject of much criticism over her failure to enhance the image of China. "If I cannot well respond to the criticism made against China or cannot well defend China's position on the show," she said, "I was blamed for my unsatisfactory performance by the people around me."

The case of a participant from Iran is more serious. An unknown Iranian man suddenly hit him in the face as he entered his favorite bar in Roppongi, where many foreign nationals gather for a drink. The person was angry over his performance on the show and the way he described Iran. He accused my informant of strengthening the negative images of Iranians in Japan. In both cases, the burden of representation put pressure on the foreign discussants to assume the multinationalistic strategy of the program.

In any case, participants can only have control of their representation during the off-air taping of the program Even if they get the opportunity to utter their comments in the studio, there is no guarantee that the scenes will be broadcast. Shooting the program usually takes more than three hours while the broadcast is around forty-five minutes, including the video coverage. Most of the discussion is cut in the postproduction process. It is in this regard, as mentioned earlier, that the presence of IMO talents on the show highly frustrates other participants. Their more frequent appearance in the program is perceived as unfair not simply because they collaborate with the producer but because the performance of their assigned roles on the show is thought to guarantee their frequent appearance on the screen. One participant expressed his sense of discontent that they are not really qualified to participate in the program.

> Their views of Japan are fundamentally different from ours. Their views of Japan are actually those of insiders, as they have been mostly brought up in Japan. I think this makes it difficult for them to see Japan "objectively" from outside. They are awkward, halfway foreigners, as it were. They just pretend [to be foreigners].

The sense of unfairness is also expressed in terms of language skills. Talk shows demand an instantaneous response with rhetorical sophistication, but those whose first language is not Japanese and who have not lived in Japan for long cannot easily do this. As my informant told me, "I often feel vexed since we cannot compete with pseudo foreigners in terms of discussion skills." Native language skills are also regarded as a sign of the lack of "foreignness."

Needless to say, it is questionable whether these views about "pseudo foreigners" are qualified and whether it is possible at all to distinguish the "real" view of foreigners from a false one expressed on a TV talk show. It might be the case that those who are mostly brought up in Japan and speak Japanese like a native also experience a strong sense of frustration since they are nevertheless treated as second-class citizens. At the least the above comments show how foreign discussants are sensitive to the way in which the commodification of ordinary foreigners in the TV production actually works to marginalize their presence and visibility on the show. And it should be considered as the negative effect of this commodification that the heterogeneous existence and experiences of people who are categorized as foreign in Japan are expressed in terms of an antagonistically demarcated boundary between authentic and unauthentic foreigners.

Moreover, the prevalence of some talent participants on the show pressures the other participants, overtly or covertly, to behave in accordance with the intentions of the producer to increase their on-air time on the screen.

> I try not to be a strong nationalist but often end up being like that.
> It is partly because the staff urges us to be so. You know, we do not
> want our comments to be cut, so we sometimes try to utter what
> will interest TV producers. Yes, we are conscious of the produc-
> ers' intentions, so we perform accordingly.

As this comment indicates, their collusion in a multinational spectacle is actually a necessary measure taken to maximize their visibility on the show. Such performances by foreign discussants tend to reproduce the demarcation of national-cultural boundaries as they highlight the image of ethnocentric foreigners who do not see the beam in their own eyes and simply attack Japan. In this sense, it can be argued that their "walking the tight rope" is highly precarious. Nevertheless, unless they get on the rope, they do not even have the chance to fall down, and no matter how much they are conscious of the danger associated with public visibility many still want to get on the wire. This precariousness is the price that foreign residents have to, and perhaps are willing to, pay for going public through KHN.

The desire to be visible, recognized, and heard in the public sphere is quite strong and serious for some marginalized people. In the case of KHN, I found that, irrespective of different personal motivations to join the program, most participants are keen to go public and have their say about Japan on a nationally networked TV program. It also gives them great pleasure to share the issues and problems they encounter in everyday life with those in similar circumstances. With this in mind, some, if not all, are determined to take on this risky business. As one participant told me:

> My friends often ask me why I am participating in a vulgar show
> like KHN, as this demeans me in public. . . . Well, I fully under-
> stand his comment. Nor do I think that participation in the pro-
> gram will make it easier to rent an apartment, to change the mind
> of the owner who turns us away at the door. I am not that naive.
> I know I am after all a foreigner here, even if I am a Japanese
> Brazilian. . . . But the studio is the only public space where we
> can complain [about Japan] and our say will be listened to. It is an
> exceptional occasion in a monotonous daily life. As we are always
> regarded as just foreigners no matter how long we have lived in
> Japan, our sense of resignation is so high. Yet those who partici-
> pate in the show do not resign themselves to the current situation,
> with a will to change the situation, to change Japanese society.

This comment urges us to realize how program participation is significant in satisfying, if just partly, some foreign residents' strong desire to go public *and* how the symbolic violence effected by the TV industry, which distorts and exploits such desires, is rough. This is the power-infused ambivalence we have to embrace in order to engage with the cultural politics of multi-nationalism on KHN.

Yet, to finish, let us be reminded that even such a humble desire for public visibility is at the mercy of the mass media. It is easily shut down due to the commercial logic that dominates the media industries. In March 2002, KHN went off the air. It reassured it audience that it would be back soon. A few special programs were broadcast, but nothing has happened since. As is the rule in the TV world, a drop in ratings is detrimental to the life of a program. Three and half years is not a short period for a weekly variety show, and the producer would say that KHN had exhausted its potential. This may be true for commercial purposes. But it is not true for a TV program that could expand the scope of the publicness of the Japanese media in an inclusive manner. We are compelled not just to consider the ways in which this deeply structured gap can be filled, a gap between commercialism and citizenship, pleasure and responsibility, but to consider how to implement it. Given that the Japanese media still repeatedly report increases in crimes committed by foreigners, this is an imperative issue for the creation of a more egalitarian and democratic public media space.

NOTES

1. The original version of this essay was published as "Multinationalizing the Multicultural: The Commodification of 'Ordinary Foreign Residents' in a Japanese TV Talk Show, *Japanese Studies*, Vol. 25, No. 2, September 2005: 103–118.

2. Michael Billig, *Banal Nationalism* (London: Sage, 1995).

3. See Naoki Sakai, "Modernity and Its Critique," *South Atlantic Quarterly* 87, no. 3 (1989): 475–504; and Koichi Iwabuchi, "Complicit Exoticism: Japan and Its Other," *Continuum* 8, no. 2 (1994): 49–82.

4. This is not to say that "Asia" has no cultural significance in the construction of Japanese national identity. While Japan's construction of its national identity through the complicity between Western Orientalism and Japan's self-Orientalism is conspicuous, Asia has also overtly or covertly played a constitutive part in Japan's construction of its national identity. While the West played the role of the modern other to be emulated, Asia was cast as the image of Japan's past, a negative picture that tells of the extent to which Japan has been successfully modernized according to Western standards. See Stefan Tanaka, *Japan's Orient: Rendering Pasts into History* (Berkeley: University of California Press, 1993).

5. Iwabuchi, "Complicit Exoticism."

6. Harumi Befu, *Ideorogii to shite no Nihon Bunkaron* (Nihon Bunkaron as Ideologies) (Tokyo: Shiso no Kagakusha, 1987).

7. Dorinne Kondo, *About Face: Performing Race in Fashion and Theater* (New York: Routledge, 1998).

8. According to *Asahi Shinbun*'s database, the number of articles using the word *international* dropped from 1,104 in 1990 to 436 in 2002 while the number of articles using *global* rose from 42 to 510 in the same period.

9. See Kiyoshi Abe, *Samayoeru Nashonarizumu* (Wandering Nationalism) (Tokyo: Sekai Shisosha, 2001).

10. Billig, *Banal Nationalism*.

11. See Maurice Roche, *Mega-events and Modernity: Olympics and Expos in the Growth of Global Culture* (London: Routledge, 2000).

12. Rika Kayama, *Puchi Nashonarizumu Shōkōgun* (Petit Nationalism Syndrome) (Tokyo: Chukoshinsho, 2002).

13. For example, in a recent survey only 15 percent of respondents feel this. See *Asahi Shinbun*, 16 March 2005.

14. For example, see *Bessatsu Takarajima*, no.106, *Nihon ga taminzoku kokka ni naru hi* (1990).

15. See, for example, Aiko Utsumi, Masataka Okamoto, Shigeo Kimoto, Nobuyuki Sato, and Shinichiro Nakajima, *Sangokujin hatsugen to zainichi gaikokujin* (*Sangokujin* speech and foreign nationals in Japan) (Tokyo: Akashi Shoten, 2000).

16. Zygmunt Bauman, *Community: Seeking Safety in an Insecure World* (Cambridge: Polity, 2001).

17. There were some nonwhite stars, such as Osmond Sanko from West Africa, whose performance of "primitiveness" and funny "Africanness" were much enjoyed by Japanese audiences. For the representation of black people in the Japanese mass media, see John G. Russel, *Nihonjin no kokujinkan* (The Black Other in Contemporary Japan) (Tokyo: Shinhyouronsha, 1991). Yet no person of Asian descent emerged as a TV celebrity. Marginalized groups such as resident Koreans have been treated until recently as taboo in Japanese TV programs.

18. Stuart Hall, "The West and the Rest: Power and Discourse," in S. Hall and B. Gieben, eds., *Formations of Modernity* (Cambridge: Polity, 1992, pp. 275–331).

19. *Asahi Shinbun*, 22 May 2001, evening ed.

20. This essay analyzes KHN with a focus on the drawing of boundaries between Japan and the foreign, but the cultural politics of its representation is by no means restricted to this. Particularly in its latter stages, perhaps to overcome the mannerisms of the content, the role of foreign discussants changed. Most commonly, the program foregrounds such queer and bizarre Japanese as motorcycle gangs, homosexuals, overweight people, and high school women in the sexual trades (*enjo-kousai*). Foreign discussants play the role of taking a stand against them. The foreign discussants' comments are sensationally represented as a substitution for the conservative

views against the marginalized that are assumed to be held by the majority of Japanese audiences so that the program can be subtly acquitted of the charge of showcasing degrading views by using foreigners' gaze as a safe filter. For the gender politics of KHN, see Hagiwara Shigeru, "'Kokoga hen dayo Nihonjin': Bunseki wakugumi to bangumi no tokushitsu" ("Kokoga Hendayo Nihonnjin": On the Analytical Framework and Characteristics of the Program), *Media Communication,* no. 53 (2003): 5–28; Kunihiro Yōko, "Gendai Nihon no jendaa hen'you to 'kokoga hen dayo Nihonjin'" (Changing Gender Relations in Contemporary Japan and *Kokoga Hendayo Nihonnjin*), *Media Communication,* no. 53, (2003): 29–48.

21. My field research was conducted in Tokyo between May 2000 and November 2001. In addition to the interview with the producer, I observed the program being shot in the studio and conducted informal interviews with some of the foreign discussants.

22. *Television,* 26 February 1999, 35–37.

23. Television production companies and talent offices play a significant role in choosing "appealing amateurs" for audience participation programs. See *Nikkei Trendy,* March 2003, 154–55.

24. *Housou Bunka,* November 1996.

25. Ibid.

26. See, e.g., *More,* July 1999.

27. *Senuri,* no. 51 (2002).

28. Steven Vetrovec, "Transnational Challenges to the 'New' Multiculturalism," paper presented at an annual conference of Association of Social Anthropologist (ASA), University of Sussex, 30 March–2 April 2001.

29. Kawai Hayao and Ishii Yoneo, *Nihonjin to gurōbarizeishon* (The Japanese and Globalization) (Tokyo: Kodansha and ∝-shinsho, 2002).

30. See, e.g., *Sapio,* 10 March 1999, 96–97.

31. *Asahi Shinbun,* 2 March 1999, evening ed.

32. Homi Bhabha, "The Third Space," in J. Rutherford, ed., *Identity: Community, Culture Difference,* 207–21 (London: Lawrence and Wishart, 1990).

33. Paolo Carpignano, Robin Andersen, Stanley Aronowitz, and William DiFazio, "Chatter in the Age of Electronic Reproduction: Talk Television and the 'Public Mind,'" *Social Text,* 25/26 (1990): 33–55.

34. Sonia Livingstone and Peter Lent, *Talk on Television: Audience Participation and Public Debate* (London: Routledge, 1994).

35. In the latter period of the show, some discussants were assigned video coverage of the issue of the week and the film was shown in the studio for discussion.

36. For details, see Debido Arudou, *Japanizu onrii* (Japanese Only) (Tokyo: Akashishoten, 2003).

37. See, e.g. TV program, *NHK News 11,* 9 February 1999.

38. Jane Shattuc, *The Talking Cure: TV Talk Shows and Women* (New York: Routledge, 1997).

39. Joshua Gamson, *Freaks Talk Back: Tabloid Talk Shows and Sexual Nonconformity* (Chicago: University of Chicago Press, 1998).

40. Ibid., 19.

41. Ibid., 22.

42. Ibid., 215.

The Uses of Routine:
NHK's Amateur Singing Contest
in Historical Perspective

Shuhei Hosokawa

Nodojiman, we can say, has made the postwar history of Japanese popular music.

—Yabe Okihiko

Repetition as a form of transmitting sound and image is basic to television.[1] By displaying a repetitive world onscreen in a domestic space, television sustains the social order of everyday life, embedded in quotidian patterns and habits, providing the focus of our daily rituals and a frame for limited transcendence, extending our reach and security, locking us into a network of time-space relations (both local and global, domestic and national), and finally offering peace and reassurance through the repetitive transmission of quasi-fixed genres and formats.[2] In its "ordinariness," or "the more or less secure normality of everyday life, and our capacity to manage it on a daily basis," television regulates and guarantees the spatial, temporal, affective, and physical continuity of our not so dramatic lives.[3] Whether we switch it on or off, television as object, medium, and imagination occupies some kind of place in our private and public lives. Its primary role is to make the extraordinary ordinary as opposed to Brechtian Verfremdung (estrangement), which makes the ordinary extraordinary. Unprecedented catastrophes, spectacles, and dramas are "domesticated" through television. The banality of any cultural product, however, is an aesthetic effect of repetition. Banality is brought about when the salience of an aesthetic object begins to sink into the commonplace and becomes taken for granted.[4] What is at stake in this process of banalization is time allocation programming, seriality, and genre rules, all of which make transmissions highly predictable. This predictability, however, should not be confused with replication.

Weather forecasts, for example, are different every day but are presented in a totally predictable format even during natural and human catastrophes.

One Japanese television and radio program, shown at Sunday lunchtime, *Shirōto Nodojiman Taikai* ("The Laypersons's Singing Contest," hereafter *Nodojiman*, literally "boast of throat"), on NHK (Nihon Hōsō Kyōkai, the Japanese Broadcast Association), is a good example of the way television visibly and invisibly makes our everyday lives orderly. It is an amateur singing contest that has been broadcast since 1946 from all corners of Japan. It is integrated in many people's Sunday routines so perfectly that few have reflected on it seriously. This essay aims to reconstruct the process of the banalization of *Nodojiman* by questioning how a symbol of postwar democracy became one of the most routinized, most lingering, but least examined programs on Japanese television and radio. The received obsolescence of *Nodojiman* is well illustrated by an awkward coinage of the term *nodojiman-na*, translatable as *nodojimanic*, which was used in the newspaper *Asahi Shinbun* to refer mockingly to the government's irrelevant long-term economic provisions.[5]

I will examine *Nodojiman* as an intersection of three program genres: audience participation show, popular music show, and home place show. Without of these three specificities, *Nodojiman* would not have been so successful, as is confirmed in the epigraph that opens this essay. Viewing *Nodojiman* from historical, social, and political angles, I will venture to understand it with reference to the changing relationship among the radio, television, and the music industries; the mediated formation of "audience," "public," and "the nation"; the institutional tension between "public" and "commercial" stations and between amateurism and professionalism; and the negotiation between local and the national identities. Finally, my argument will touch on how the "home place" is significant for NHK's "publicness" (*kōkyōsei*).

THE INCEPTION OF NODOJIMAN

Nodojiman, originally *Nodojiman Shirōto Ongakugai* (Throat Boast Amateurs' Concert), was launched on 19 January 1946.[6] On the morning of the first audition, the NHK building in Hibiya, Tokyo, was so crowded with about 900 contestants that the studio and its surrounding streets were in chaos. Only the first 300 would have a chance to audition, and as few as 25 succeeded in singing on the air.[7] One of the planners of the program, Maruyama Tetsuo (elder brother of the thinker Maruyama Masao), whose pro-democracy tenet was manifested in the same month,[8] believes that its overnight success may have derived from the "combination of the microphone with the mass" and the "democratic" procedure of application (anyone who came to the audition was eligible). The "layperson" in the title, he thinks, was especially attractive for the "democratic" ethos of the age. Until May of the same year, they held auditions four times, and, surprisingly, a total of 3,500 candidates appeared in studio.[9] Several months later the program fixed its Sunday lunchtime slot.

The program's success can be easily explained by the general scarcity of recreation after World War II. Two days after the inauguration of *Nodojiman*, *Asahi Shinbun* deplored the "musicless" life of the distressed masses: "[E]ven during the war we could hear people singing, but today this has completely disappeared. It seems that the masses hardly know what music is."[10] Giving musical enjoyment to these people was an initial intention of the producers. Liberated from wartime control, music programs were expected to entertain the nation by way of new devices such as the listener's request, guess-who-sings quizzes, satirical song shows, and so on.[11] *Nodojiman* was the most popular among them, as is shown by the publication of a how-to book in August 1946 that celebrated the program as "the first step in the democratization of broadcast."[12] The program was adopted in the recreational events organized by neighbors, shopping arcades, factories, offices, cities, and villages by record companies searching for new talent.[13] *Nodojiman* functioned as an important incentive for the reconstruction of the music industry immediately after the war.

The participants of *Nodojiman* included children, students, office workers, merchants, housewives, craftsmen, and war returnees among others. Some came from distant provinces.[14] Many sang contemporary and prewar popular songs, but school songs, concert songs, and traditional and folk pieces were also performed. Although NHK provided an accordionist and a pianist in the studio, some of the participants brought their own accompanists or accompanied themselves on guitar, *shamisen* (a three-stringed instrument), and other instruments. The same songs were sung again and again, and a singer could sing a third verse only if he or she liked it. In other words, the rules were much looser than they are today.[15]

Staff members at NHK assumed the role of judges and continue to do so today. This contrasts with other audition programs in which judges are drawn from a pool of showbiz professionals, celebrities, or the general public. This judging system clearly distances the program from show business. It creates the notion of "wholesome recreation," one of the most persistent NHK slogans since the 1930s. Another rule, frozen from the beginning, is that singers must introduce themselves by number (in order of appearance) and the title of the song. This rather rigorous and impersonal procedure makes the program more serious, imposing the authority of NHK on the singers.

In the first several months of transmission, the results of the judging were verbally reported by the announcer, who called out "Good!" or "Sorry!" This brusque verbal announcement was replaced with the sound of tubular bells in April 1947 when *Nodojiman* was broadcast for the first time from a theater as a radio drama attraction.[16] The system of bell scorings is very clear: one ring means "not good," two rings mean "regular," and three rings mean "good." The singers must stop performing when the bells are rung. The three-rings signal in fact sounds more like a fanfare than the plain rings. The sound of tubular bells has become the most vivid symbol of *Nodojiman*.[17] By 1947 the program had been gradually and solidly formalized.

AUDIENCE PARTICIPATION AND POSTWAR DEMOCRACY

In many countries, the phrase "Radio Days" is associated with the 1930s. Yet this was not always the case in Japan. A 1941 poll reported that 89 percent of the respondents found radio "unentertaining."[18] Since the beginning of radio broadcasting in 1926, NHK, the only station licensed by the Ministry of Communications, has kept the strong posture of "guiding the people" and "encouraging good manners and morals".[19] Entertainment programs were often in conflict with the enlightened policies of NHK because popular taste did not necessarily coincide with "wholesome recreation." After the Great East-Asian War, the American occupation's General Headquarters (GHQ) intervened in radio programming, aiming to establish new programs and even new stations that would advocate the coming age of democracy.[20] The transmission of the people's voice was one of many measures meant to liberate the mass media from militaristic control.

The earliest program reflecting this direction was *Gaitō Rokuon* (Street Recordings), which began broadcasting in September 1945.[21] On the street, the announcer conducted impromptu interviews, asking curious bystanders questions such as "How do you make a living?" and "About what are you concerned most?" The GHQ intended to uncover social problems through these spontaneous statements. However, the interviews were perceived as "directed" (predetermined) because the same interviewees appeared again and again and many passersby were reluctant to be approached by the announcer.[22] As the film critic Satō Tadao notes, the voices in *Gaitō Rokuon* were so stiff that they were ineffective in persuading the public of the new political reality.

In *Gaitō Rokuon*, the respondents had difficulty expressing what they wanted to say with logic and emotion. Their voices became inaudible in the mix of variegated voices and the opportunity for serious discussion was lost. That the people's voices were put on the air, I think, was one advantage of democracy. But the program treated the people's opinions merely as a mélange of fragmentary voices addressed to a vacant audience. This made me feel hollow; the people's voices were simply insignificant, even in a democracy.[23]

The more a respondent tried to talk seriously about his or her unsatisfactory life, the more Satō detected the powerlessness of an individual to resolve the problem. It is probable that the awkwardness was caused by the inexperience of both the interviewers and interviewees in the sense that neither was able to negotiate not only the optimal distance (authority) and closeness (intimacy) between them but also the relationship between the interview location and the imaginary public across the country.[24] The program was too close to social reality and the American intervention too explicit to be appealing to Satō. The program understandably was canceled within a year.

By contrast, *Nodojiman* gave him the "pleasure of deviating from order or of subverting the order."[25] Transmitting singing out of tune itself was totally new to Japanese radio.

It shifted the listeners' attention from the quality of the performance to the "people's singing voices" themselves. In other words, poor performers were welcomed for their participatory—not aesthetic—worth. Satō associated *Nodojiman* with *engeikai*, or a sort of vernacular talent show held in shrines, parks, factories, army camps, and other public places.[26] This mixed performance event (often held at banquets) derived from folk festivities, popular religious ceremonies, amateur theater, vaudeville, wartime recreational activities, and other theatrical practices. In case of *engeikai*, farmers, workers, and soldiers could show their "hidden" talents. In Satō's words, *Nodojiman* was a nationally extended version of such recreational events and it successfully combined vernacular performance with the democratic mass media and the ideological notion of "the people."

> [In the wartime engeikai] there was a tacit feeling among us that the hierarchy [order] in the workplace and the military was but temporary and that *naked humans are all equal*. This notion was certainly very far from democracy. But that was a feeling we could share. Only when we do silly things, can we become equal regardless of our positions and status. At the end of war, they said "it's

time for democracy" and we could very quickly convert our attitude [from militarism to democracy]. This was probably enabled by a sense [of equality] that could somehow become an ersatz for the idea of democracy.[27]

Here Satō's naive yet strong faith in the populace is evident. Certainly, the question of why the Japanese so quickly converted to democracy is hard to answer. Even more difficult is determined whether the Japanese understood the term *democracy* the same way as the occupation forces did (remember Ruth Benedict's satirical spelling *de-mok-ra-sie* for Japanized democracy). According to Satō, the new idea of democracy smoothly penetrated Japan because of a vernacular sense of "equality" that governed and continues to govern daily life. It was not the occupation that planted the seeds of democracy in new soil because people's lives had already been democratic before the war. It is easy to note that he confused egalitarianism (social form of equality) with democracy (its political form thereof) and romanticized the pristine Japanese lifestyle. But his populism may explain, at least in part, the instant popularity of *Nodojiman*. The producer of *Nodojiman*, Saegusa Kengō, in fact revealed later that his idea had come from an *engeikai* held in a military barracks.[28]

The emotional continuity from vernacular recreation to *Nodojiman* is based on the persistent sense of equality in amateur performance. In *engeikai*, the performers showed their "true" personalities. Their inner selves were usually more playful, drunken, emotional, and "human" than their bureaucratic, sober, rational, and "inhuman" masks. This sense of equality, as Satō notes, is closely tied to an alleged equality among individuals who were otherwise differently positioned in a hierarchical society. In Japan, as well as many other societies, egalitarian and hierarchical time and space are interlocked and alternate with each other in the micropolitics of everyday life. Both *engeikai* and *Nodojiman* are egalitarian in their participatory framework. What differentiates one from the other is the significance of egalitarianism in the politics of prewar and postwar Japan. (It is suggestive that Satō regarded the later routinization of *Nodojiman* as "pseudo-democratic").[29]

Another difference between the two kinds of amateur performance is the nationwide simultaneous transmission of *Nodojiman* in contrast to the community-based space of *engeikai*. Different from a "live" space, where the performers and the public are mostly known to each other, the radio-phonic space of *Nodojiman*, like to the nationwide penchant for reading the morning newspapers, is inhabited by fellow listeners and performers who imagine themselves expanding over the national geography.[30] The success of audience participation programs owes much to the plebian facade, which gives them easy access to the imagined totality of the nation. Every audience member knows that he or she is eligible to participate in the program and that the participants this week will be listeners next week. The permeable boundaries between the performer and the listener make the audience feel integrated in the program. People on both sides of the radiophonic space complicitly form an egalitarian space associated with nationhood. Just by switching on the radio, one can join a domesticated national community.[31]

What makes *Nodojiman* distinctive in the audience participation genre is the competitive use of popular songs. How does the audience musically participate in the technological community by listening to a commonplace performance? Popular song is more effective than other types of music in establishing affective alliances among audience members because the vocal expression is often tied to the notion of subjectivity in the sense that it embodies the meaning of lyrics as well as the interior self of the performer by means of musical structure, emotion, character roles, and bodily perception.[32] The subjectivity embedded in the vocals of amateur singers is different from that of stars, whose aura—superb musicianship, noteworthy biography, distinguished looks, mass-mediated omnipresence, and so on—is essential to creating a "vocal personality".[33] *Nodojiman* participants usually fall short of these criteria for aesthetic appreciation; furthermore, because they, unlike recording artists, perform in mass media only once, most listeners and viewers perceive their personalities as anything but "sincere."[34] The effect of the vocal and performative sincerity of *Nodojiman* singers is related to the belief that amateurs do their best because they are not yet jaded by a corrupt show business. This is their one, unrepeatable, grand occasion. Sympathetic audiences, possibly future participants themselves, value their courage and effort more than their final results. Their collective sincerity produces a benevolent atmosphere as good as a Sunday lunch appetizer.

FROM EQUALITY TO COMPETITION

From the beginning, *Nodojiman* was in conflict with the machinery that is show business. The above-mentioned how-to book indicates that singing well on the program might attract the attention of a record company.[35] In opposition to NHK's amateurism, many earnest participants were lured by the dream of turning professional. According to Maruyama Tetsuo, the first objection to the program took place in December 1947 when members of the NHK programming department tried to stop the show because some participants, they felt, had utilized it as a stepping-stone to a professional career. The "would-be professionals," according to the anti-*Nodojiman* faction, were spoiling the "wholesome recreation" policy and infringing on its "publicness" by exploiting the airwaves for private profit.[36] The program was thus pressured to cancel in 1948.

As a farewell gala, the All-Japan Nodojiman Contest was held on 21 March 1948 in Tokyo, where twenty-six singers were selected from eight provinces. The spatial move from studio to public hall made the event more like an *engeikai*. As one newspaper described it:

> The rushing crowd was so overwhelming that the main entrance of the Kyōritsu Hall was closed to keep out gatecrashers. Only a slit of 60 centimeters was open. . . . All the participants were nervous because they believed the event could influence their whole lives. Some were eating raw eggs [a folk remedy thought to improve the vocal cords]; others were gargling or practicing in the WC. This is usual backstage behavior for the *Nodojiman,* but the singers were glaring at each other, conscious of the competition between them.[37]

The success of this performance allowed the program to stay on the air. The closing show was the beginning of the next phase, one of emphasized competitiveness. As this essay suggests, rivalry attracted audiences as well as participants. To respond to this new demand, *Nodojiman* intensified its competitiveness by establishing a pyramid system of contests that ranged from town rounds to prefectural, provincial, and finally the national one, and NHK began broadcasting from local public halls. The site of transmission often looked like a local carnival with a festive atmosphere akin to that of *engeikai*.

> The popularity of *Nodojiman* in regional locales is enormous. In front of the hall can be found candy stands, *oden* [popular food] stands, bicycle racks, and so on. The audience rushes into the hall from early in the morning. They take lunch boxes and big bottles of water with them. But not all of them can enter, so electric speakers are set up outside and the festive mood is in full swing.[38]

Each broadcast was defined as an elimination round; winners were promoted to superior levels, and the finals were always held in March in Tokyo. The timing and place are significant because March is the last month in Japan's business and school calendars (a time for the settlement of accounts and graduation) and Tokyo is the centralized capital. Therefore, this all-Japan meet was easily recognized as the ultimate goal of every *Nodojiman* singer.

This new structure utilized Japan's cultural and geographic hierarchy, connecting local participants with national aspirations and thus stimulating interest among amateurs all over the country.[39]

The advent of a nationwide organization led to the formalization of the program. New rules stipulated that participants must send applications by postcard (with information such as age, profession, gender, and title of song) and their accompaniment had to be performed by NHK musicians. Furthermore, singers could not be under fifteen years of age (a children's singing contest has been irregularly broadcast since the 1950s). Candidates were auditioned on the day before the broadcast. This preselection system enhanced NHK's control and enabled it to exclude undesirable songs and keep the spectacle as serious as possible. Self-penned songs have become ineligible because the NHK musicians cannot play them.[40] Another measure of formalization was the appointment of a regular master of ceremonies (MC). Around 1949, Miyata Teru, one of the most eloquent symbols of the postwar NHK, became responsible for the program's flow. As much as the tubular bells, his smooth talk incited the national passion for *Nodojiman*.

AMATEURISM, WHOLESOME RECREATION, AND PUBLICNESS

If one considers the wide popularity of *Nodojiman*, it is no surprise that corporate-run radio stations (*minpō*), when they were launched in 1951, also broadcast singing contests. In 1956, it has been reported, a certain radio station broadcast singing contests as many as fourteen times a week. The *minpō* contest deployed entertaining devices such as "mimickists," duets, tournaments, and interfamily competitions, among others, and the sponsors offered attractive prizes in order to differentiate the show from its serious counterpart on NHK.[41] By doing so, the *minpō* singing contest came closer to the genres of game and play.[42] It was important for *minpō* not only to raise audience ratings but also to show a commercial populist policy that contrasted with the moral and educational focus of NHK. With more and more singing contests on *minpō*, a "*Nodojiman* tribe," a group of frequent or regular participants, came into being and grew in numbers. The NHK *Nodojiman* was also inhabited by them. The majority of all-Japan singers in the early 1960s were already known to the audience due to their previous appearances. For example, the 1961 winner of the *kakyoku* (concert song) section had been elected seven times a prefectural representative and four times an all-Japan singer in his eleven consecutive appearances on the program.[43] One old man even auditioned 170 times over seven years.[44] They were, so to speak, the "pros of lay competition."

Some of them expected talent scouts to listen and sign them with a record company. As noted above, these "preprofessionals" were not welcomed by NHK. In the words of the head of its Music Section, "*Nodojiman* should be 'a hobby of laypeople,' never a gateway to professional musicians."[45] He wanted the program to be as healthy and wholesome as amateur sports. By the 1950s, only a few winners of the NHK All-Japan *Nodojiman* got contracts with record companies and only one singer, Arai Keiko, had a minor hit and appeared regularly on NHK. Interestingly, many losers became famous singers, as one article ironically noted: "Better to Lose [If You Want to Be a Pro]."[46] The label "NHK singer" did not have a good reputation in show business. According to the forgiving words of an NHK employee, Kondō Tsumoru:

> The NHK *Nodojiman* is concerned with musicianship. We have different criteria than those of record companies. They value personality (*kosei*) more than singing. For example, Hashi Yukio [a popular young star in the early 1960s] is not a good singer and would not make it as a three-bell singer in our *Nodojiman*. Ours is not a mimicry show. We admit that singers who start out in our event don't always appeal to the masses as some of the pros do. But producing pros is not our purpose. ("Nodojiman ga Puro ni Naru Shunkan")[47]

In this quote the amateurism and anticommercialism are as self-explanatory as the difference in the programming policies of NHK and commercial stations. Kondō's characterization of the commercial stations as vulgar is standard rhetoric for NHK. The opposition between wholesome recreation and vulgar mass taste, inherent to Japan's broadcast history from the beginning,[48] overlaps with that between public service stations and commercial ones, between education and entertainment. Kondō was proud that NHK presented "quality" singers rather than popular yet unmusical singers or mimickists.

The beginning of NHK and commercial television in 1953 drastically changed the way audiences perceived transmitted voices and personalities. Television doubtlessly reshaped popular culture as listening to amateur singing alone did not satisfy the audience. Visual appeal was especially important in audience participation shows on commercial stations such as the *Sokkuri Show* (Impersonators Show, 1965–69) and *Kachinuki Eleki Gassen* (Electric Guitar Band Contest, 1965–67). *Star Tanjō* (A Star Is Born, 1971–83) was another program diametrically opposed to the amateurist ideology of *Nodojiman* since its attraction was a public "auction" of the participants by record companies and artists'.[49] Probably due to the increase in stations and entertainment programs on television, and the limited repertoire and participants, the 1960s saw a gradual decline in popularity of the NHK *Nodojiman*. The exit of Miyata, the master of ceremonies, in 1966 was perhaps symptomatic of its demise. Along with the diversification of television music programs, a great shift in youth music in the mid-1960s—the rise of the electric guitar band, self-accompanying guitarist-singers, and singer-songwriters— led to the steady fall of *Nodojiman*, a show restricted to solo artists who sang professionally written songs accompanied by NHK musicians. They could not keep up with the changing trends in pop music.[50]

Kondō's stance against professionalism draws on the concept of "publicness." Publicness (*kōkyōsei*) is an ambivalent concept derived from a hard to translate Japanese word, *kōkyō* (public). As the critic Uryū Tadao notes, the notion of *kōkyō* has strong ties to the state and government since the word was invented by some Meiji intellectuals involved with the nation-state project who believed that no exact counterpart of the public-private basis of Western society existed in.[51] Furthermore, *kōkyōsei* is a magic word that can mean any desirable attribute of NHK: fairness, impartiality, neutrality, wholesomeness, morality, sobriety, and democracy among others.[52] This publicness justifies NHK's monopoly over the monthly dues each household pays to support the service.[53] The supporters and detractors of this argument have never fully agreed who the public are and what the public interest is.[54] Insisting on presenting an ideally all-encompassing national and public character, NHK makes every effort to cover the least populated islands and villages, disregarding the cost of doing so. This inclusiveness is constitutive of the publicness conceived by NHK. Its programs, it states, reflect the widest range of opinions of the audience as nation. If audience ratings do determine commercial programming, NHK's programming department, in addition to the objective measurement of audience, seriously consider wholesome recreation and public service.

Why *Nodojiman* was not canceled despite intermittent declines in audience ratings can be explained by the way it meets the goals of wholesome recreation and publicness. It is wholesome because in theory the participants are fond of singing for its own sake (regardless of showbiz aspirations and prizes), and it is public because it presents and represents the people's voices. The concept of wholesome recreation is closely tied to the ideal of family auditions and viewing; these programs should be neither harmful to children nor infantile to adults. They are expected to reinforce the affective bond among family members and members of the nation as an extremely extended family. This notion of continuity from family to nation is basic to NHK's publicness.

BACK TO THE MASS-MEDIATED GRASS ROOTS

To recover from the slump in ratings toward the end of 1960s, the format of *Nodojiman* was revised from 1970 on in several ways. First, duets, choreography, and other entertaining elements were permitted. Second, the all-Japan meet was withdrawn (although it was resumed later) so that the shows became less competitive.[55] Third, professional singers were invited to make shows more attractive. Fourth, a new master of ceremonies, Kaneko Tatsuo (1970–87), was appointed. Kaneko, and his successors Yoshikawa Seiichi (1987–93), Miyakawa Yasuo (1993–2005), and Miyamoto Ryūji (2005–2007) have ordinary looks. In praise of Kaneko's modesty, one article frankly stated, "A not-so-handsome MC is good".[56] In accordance with the loosening of the rules, the selection of the MC implies NHK's intention to reintroduce the "ordinary" and "commonplace" into the program. Kaneko, aware of his role, brought a "performed sincerity" to the program.[57] The concept of the "MC next door," in fact, fit well with the presentation of "singers next door."

To make the program entertaining, the program director, during the Saturday audition, must be careful to select a diversity and balance of singers in terms of musicianship, personality, age, gender, repertoire, and other aspects. In a broadcast, none of the twenty singers on the air sings the same song, and the twenty songs range from folk and old songs to the latest pop hits. Some of the contestants are always engaged in occupations characteristic of their home regions (agriculture, fishing, forestry, crafts, tourism, and so on). By saying a few words about them, the MC can introduce some features of local industry to national viewers.

Participants who mimic guest professional singers always please the audience as much as the mimicked professionals. Conversing and shaking hands with the star, the admirers often get so nervous that the audience bursts into laughter with a tinge of jealousy. The professionals do not participate in the judging but add glamour to the show by communicating with the amateurs and presenting a karaoke performance after all the contestants sing. Contrary to shows in which the stars talk with their fans from the central position of the program, in *Nodojiman* professionals are invited to a layperson's show. Therefore, in the NHK view, they do not interfere with the amateurism.

One comical moment comes with the self-consciously out-of-tune singer who appears in an overly showy costume or overacts. For example, a firemen's group sang in their traditional *happi* uniforms the 1990s hit "Burn!" pretending to put out a fire. In another case, a gray-haired female duo sang a new pop song dressed in shocking orange costumes, telling the MC after their breathless performance that the old should not concede to the young. Such disharmony between age and appearance (and the act) is usually sniffed at in Japanese society, but in the program their "youthfulness" of heart sent a generational message to the public. Generational and gender harmony is visible in the hand waving of all the waiting participants in unison to encourage the other singers.

One participant noted that the two-day event from the Saturday audition to the Sunday broadcast gave rise to solidarity among the singers.[58] In many cases, the participants organize a fraternal group and get together once a year or so. In this way, they celebrate and remember a once-in-a-lifetime event. Sometimes this becomes an occasion for matchmaking. It is easy to see that the rivalry characteristic of the first decades of the show was almost gone. In his characterization of *Nodojiman*, a previous MC, Miyakawa Yasuo, invoked an oft-quoted maxim, *ichigo ichie* (once in a lifetime encounter), which implies that a trivial meeting will not happen twice and life never repeats itself.[59] This saying is still constitutive of the everyday philosophy by which we live. Underlying the program is less Andy Warhol's motto "Everyone can become a star for fifteen minutes" than Dean Martin's hymn "Everybody loves somebody sometime." To paraphrase this, everybody is somebody, a singular person with a favorite song that is worth listening to and singing along with.

An emotional moment on the show is when a qualified singer names himself or herself. This is the important transition from anonymous individual called by number to a person with a name and story. The most crucial moment comes when he or she declares to whom the performance is dedicated: to my beloved mother, to my late grandmother who loved that song, to my sick father watching me from the hospital, to my fiancée working far away in Tokyo, to my old classmates, to my baseball team, to my newborn granddaughter, and so on. The success of Izutsu Kazuyuki's film *Nodojiman* (1999) comes from the smooth, Robert Altman-like flow of the mini-story of each ordinary singer. The audience now knows the "addressee" of each successful performance, and the singers are happy in expressing their gratitude. *Nodojiman* thus transforms an individual performance into a narrative of family or friendship portrayed through popular song. No personal story is too dramatic for the audience, yet each one has a special meaning for the singer. No audience can know the sentimental value of the performance to the life of each singer beyond his or her thirty-second declaration. Personal stories are suddenly, momentarily, and nationally known. What the audiences are interested in is not the details of each personal story but the ordinariness of each human relationship with reference to the song presented.

The performance is thus "signatured" but not sentimentalized as the next performer is already waiting to take over the microphone. The MC has to maintain the balance between the tears and the laughter, the sentimental stories and the upbeat feel, the slow and the fast tempo. What underlies the seemingly simple structure of *Nodojiman* is the equilibrium between spontaneity and management, ordinariness and extraordinariness, the mechanical procedures of the performance and the affective personification of it, the unchanged mold and individually differentiated content, and the nationwide broadcast and local interests.[60]

It should be also noted that *Nodojiman* is almost the only program in which a shared sound track is simultaneously broadcast on radio and television. With the salient exception of *Kōhaku Utagassen* (a popular singers' grand gala on New Year's Eve), it is the only such transmission in Japan. Large sports events, for example, are usually broadcast live both on radio and television, yet the content is strikingly different because radio commentators verbalize the visual facet of the game in real time whereas television commentators can dispense with the details and instead make dramatic and analytical comments on instant replays and other types of visual devices. *Nodojiman* has made a smooth transition from the radio format to this audiovisual apparatus. Its static camera work in coordination with the static format makes for a sharp contrast with the dynamic audiovisual techniques used in other music programs.

While other music shows exhibit the spectacular in all senses, *Nodojiman* sticks with the ordinary. It is an unspectacular spectacle whereby the audience can easily identify with the participants or at least can have the illusion that they do. This is, of course, the basic rhetoric of the program genre, "audience participation program," but *Nodojiman*, while downplaying visual techniques, secures the "household flow" of particular time and space. The notion of household flow, as it is used by Rick Altman, refers to the continuity of the television (and radio in our case) experience for the intermittent viewers who are the majority of the audience.[61] The goal of the programming department, he notes, is not to persuade audience members to watch the program but to keep them from turning it off. People tune in while doing something else in a room next door or chatting with someone else. The distracted contact with TV is essential for the integration of the media experience in the real lives of viewers. Altman suggests that the significance of television sound tracks lies in way they sustain the household flow. Good programming should have a flow—what Raymond Williams called "programming flow"—in harmony with household flow.[62] The sound track of *Nodojiman* is self-contained, and the visual is somehow redundant. In other words, the "embeddedness" of domestic media in everyday life depends on how well they mesh with household flow. *Nodojiman's* shared sound track may indicate that one will lose nothing if one does not watch it. In the *Nodojiman* transmission on television, a "sound hermeneutic" does not exist since any sound source can be clearly identified and located. That transmission is a visual supplement to the simultaneous radio broadcast.[63]

FROM HOME PLACE TO NATION

So far I have analyzed the aspects of *Nodojiman*: audience participation and popular music. In this section, I will discuss its third face, what I call the "home place show". This is loosely defined as a genre that depicts small town and village life featuring local people. Its purpose is broadly to present and represent provincial life nationwide. One of its subgenres is the travelogue, which began with *Shin Nihon Kikō* (New Japan Travels, 1963–82) on NHK. It spotlights ordinary people, traditions, and folk lifestyles with a tinge of geography, history, ethnology, and other educational elements. This combination of entertainment and education is proper to the NHK notion of wholesome recreation. Another subgenre is the folk song and dance show, which is usually broadcast from a public hall featuring the local singers and troupes.

The precursor of this latter subgenre is without doubt *Furusato no Utamatsuri* (Song Festival of the Home Place, 1966–74). Not by coincidence, it was Miyata Teru, from *Nodojiman*, who assumed the role of *Utamatsuri's* master of ceremonies in 1974. (Just after quitting *Utamatsuri* and NHK, he was elected senator with the highest number of votes in the election. *Utamatsuri* presented local preservation societies of folk song and dance, grassroots institutions of amateur devotees who allegedly inherited authentic melodies and choreography.[64] The performers were mainly senior amateurs. Miyata often displayed instant knowledge about the local dialect, preaching as to how rural folkways were important even for hastily urbanized Japan. Here linguistic difference, far from being an obstacle to communication and a deviation from the canon, was treated as a source of local pride. The use of dialect certainly created as much intimacy with local spectators as the presentation of local color did for the national audience. Miyata recognized the effect of local parlance in national broadcasts as early as in 1951 when his fame was about to be established, saying, "The use of the local dialect is much better [in creating intimacy with the participants and the public]. Local color is especially effective for national broadcasting."[65] This statement shows how *Nodojiman* and *Utamatsuri* were continuous in the art of hosting. The fact that *Utamatsuri* was broadcast during prime time seems to have had an intrinsic association with rising nostalgia for rural Japan and to anticipate the extensive campaign of the Japan National Railroad called "Discover Japan" in the early 1970s.[66] *Furusato no Utamatsuri* was literally the re-creation of a home place for everyone. As William Kelly succinctly concludes, "the Furusato 'boom' has appropriated the individual's home place as the nation's heartland."[67] *Utamatsuri* was an important part of this "boom" because it not only provided concrete images to go along with the emotional content in terms of the folk songs and dances but it also diffused and fixed home place stereotypes through Miyata's apparently benign conduct. By doing so, the program accelerated the process of "nationalizing" the home place.

The contemporary successor of *Utamatsuri* was *Dontokoi Min'yō* (Here Comes a Folk Song) on NHK, the only *min'yō* (folk song) program broadcast regularly (although it went off the air in 2004). It consists of performances by local preservation societies and professional *min'yō* singers (not always from the region), as well as the vignettes featuring the local cuisine, spas, tourist landmarks, historic places, and so on. Borrowing the style of numerous talent shows, a pair of masters of ceremonies mediate: a middle-aged man and a young woman. The former assumes the role of interrogator and explainer while the latter's role is to "experience" and "witness" local things as a sort of substitute for spectators. This device makes local ways of life more accessible because the audience identifies with the visitor's point of view. The expected audience, however, is the elderly, as is seen in the light calisthenics inserted in the middle of the program.

The different ways of depicting local life in *Dontokoi* (and *Utamatsuri*) and *Nodojiman* can be best summarized in the dual face of rural life in Japan: *furusato* (the home place) and *chihō* (the provinces). The former is charged with affective value and emphasizes continuity with the past whereas the latter is used in a geopolitical hierarchy topped by *chūō* (the capital, the center) with emphasis on continuity with modernity and urbanity.[68] In other words, *Nodojiman* represents "popular" culture made in the metropolis while *Dontokoi* and *Utamatsuri* represent a "folk" culture tailored locally. The distinction is not very clear-cut, however, since *Nodojiman* has a brief video introduction of the spotlight area's geography and some sing *min'yō* of the province. Yet the show's emphasis is placed on a popular repertoire shared nationwide (the lineup of songs in *Nodojiman* shows little local particularity). Locality in *Nodojiman* is less concerned with the expression of local color than with the placelessness of *furusato*, the homogenization of provinces in a coercive cultural industry operating from the metropolitan *chūō*.

CONCLUSION

In this essay, I have analyzed how *Nodojiman* provides a series of micro-dramas surrounding popular songs and ordinary lives. Banality and singularity are easily mixed in a particular performance. In this context, it is worthwhile to recall Billig's concept of "banal nationalism," which designates ideological habits that enable established nations to be reproduced.[69] Habits by definition appear to be "natural." The banalization of *Nodojiman* implies (or runs parallel to) the naturalization of "democracy" in Japanese common sense and ideology. It is "endemic" because these habits are embedded in the lives of the citizenry.

The viewers and listeners of the program can extrapolate the peace of the self-contained provincial public hall to the whole of Japan because of its ordinariness. The Japanese nation is not only an abstract collective, as in political discourses, but a cohort of "somebodies" next door or in the next town. *Nodojiman* turns a nation into a people and a people into a congregation of somebodies. Every Sunday it brings to the home a nationally extended family and village. The banality of *Nodojiman*, in this context, quietly celebrates the ordinary and orderly lives of people. Unnoticed yet always underlying its context, *Nodojiman* demonstrates that NHK's publicness and its related notion of nationhood are well integrated in postwar Japanese habits. Given the quick alteration of Japanese television programming, the longevity of *Nodojiman* is exceptional. Its uniqueness lies in its presentation of nationally known songs by anonymous individuals from neglected towns. By virtue of this particular combination of repertoire, performance, and place, the program clearly fits NHK's grassroots nationalism, which is based on publicness and wholesome recreation.

NOTES

The author is thankful to Carolyn Stevens and Christine Yano for their comments on earlier versions of this essay.

1. In the epigraph, Yabe Okihiko, the producer of *Nodojiman*, is quoted in Kamata Kiyoshi, "Minna de Utatta Nichiyōbi" (On Sundays We Sing Together), *Sankei Yomimono*, 12 February 1956, 29. This essay is revised from Shuhei Hosokawa, "Utau Minshushugi: 'Nodojiman' to Chinpusa no Kōyō" (The Singing Democracy: *Nodojiman* and the Uses of Routine), in Tōya Mamoru, ed., *Popyurā Ongaku eno Manazashi*, 181–205 (Gaze on Popular Music) (Tokyo: Keisō Shobō, 2003).

2. Roger Silverstone, *Television and Everyday Life* (London and New York: Routledge, 1994), 19.

3. Ibid., 166.

4. Shuhei Hosokawa, "Fascinating Banality of the Hit Parade," *Onetwothreefour* 4 (1987): 66–73.

5. *Asahi Shinbun*, 25 February 1999.

6. The title of the program has changed several times in accordance with minor changes in format, but I use the abbreviation *Nodojiman* throughout this essay. During the 1930s, there were occasional programs on NHK that featured amateur musicians auditioned by the network. Since their repertoires were heavily inclined toward art music (e.g., *nagauta* and Western piano pieces), they hardly merited public attention.

7. Maruyama Tetsuo, "Chūshian Kara Kon'nichi no Ryūsei" (From the Plan of Closing Came Today's Popularity), *Shūkan Tokyo*, 9 March 1957, 30–31 (interview).

8. Maruyama Tetsuo, "Ongaku Bunka no Saiken" (The Reconstruction of Music Culture), *Ongaku Bunka* 4 no. 1 (1946): 6–10.

9. Maruyama Tetsuo, "Taishū Ongaku Hōsō Tenbō" (Reviewing the Popular Music Programs), *Hōsō Bunka*, June 1946, 11–13.

10. *Asahi Shinbun*, 21 January 1946.

11. Maruyama Tetsuo, "Taishū Ongaku Hōsō Tenbō."

12. Anonymous, *Nodojiman Shirōto Ongakuka Tebiki* (A Guide to Lay Singers) (Tokyo: Taki Shobō, 1946), 1.

13. Shimizu Takiji, "Rekōdo Kaisha Karamita Shirōto Nodojiman Fūkei" (Layperson *Nodojiman* Seen from the Record Company), *Hōsō Bunka*, October 1948, 18–19.

14. *Asahi Graph*, 25 March 1946, 12–13; *Asahi Shinbun*, 3 February 1946.

15. In its heyday, *Nodojiman* was used as a narrative device at least for two comedy films in the 1950s: Watanabe Kunio's *Enoken no Sokonuke Daihōsō* (Enoken's Funny Broadcast, 1950) and Watanabe Takashi's *Nodojiman Sanbagarasu* (The Three in *Nodojiman*, 1951).

16. Maruyama Tetsuo, "*Nodojiman*," *Hōsō Bunka*, May 1958, 54–55.

17. The bells had and still have a Christian connotation in Japan. They symbolized peace and purity in the immediate postwar era, probably because of their association with a 1946 best seller by Dr. Nagai Takashi, *Nagasaki no Kane* (Bells in Nagasaki), the true story of a Christian doctor who died of radioactivity poisoning after his dedicated care of atomic bomb victims. A highly acclaimed radio drama, *Kane no Naru Oka* (Bells Ring on the Hill, 1947–50), an everyday story of children in a small town with bells on a tower used as a time signal, might also resonate with the peace symbolism of bells. There were several bell songs in that period, including "Francesca's Bells" (1948), "Bells of Nagasaki" (1949), and "Nicolai's Bells" (1951), that have exotic—and Christian—lyric references.

18. Gregory J. Kasza, *The State and the Mass Media in Japan, 1918–1945* (Berkeley: University of California Press, 1988), 256.

19. Nihon Hōsō Kyōkai, ed., *Nihon Hōsōshi* (History of Japanese Broadcasting), 2 vols. (Tokyo: Nihon Hōsō Kyōkai, 1965), 1:79ff. See also Kasza, *The State and the Mass Media in Japan*, 88ff.

20. The legal reformation of postwar broadcasting has been well analyzed in Hiroshi Matsuda, *Dokyumento: Hōsō Sengoshi* (Document: The Postwar History of Broadcasting), 2 vols. (Zushi: Sōshisha, 1980–81); and Hōsō Hōsei Rippō Katei Kenkyūkai, ed., *Shiryō: Senryōka no Hōsō Rippō* (Documents: Broadcast Legislation under the Occupation) (Tokyo: Tokyo Daigaku Shuppan, 1980). Both works discuss the repugnance of NHK to licensed commercial stations and the intervention of GHQ in demonopolizing broadcasting entities.

21. The initial title was slightly different: *Gaitō Nite* (On the Street). Later *Gaitō Rokuon* was changed to *Rokuon Kōsei* (Recorded Arrangement), a forerunner of the radio documentary genre in Japan. Satō Tadao, *Terebi no Shisō* (Thoughts on Television) (Tokyo: San'ichi Shobō, 1966), 61ff.

22. Sakaedani Heihachirō, Honda Teruaki, Hayashi Fumiko, Furuya Eikichi, Igarashi Kiyoe, Uda Michio, Komori Seiji, "Zadankai: Chikagoro no Hōsō wo Hihansuru" (Dialogue: Criticizing the Recent Broadcast), *Hōsō Bunka*, 12 January 1947; Asanuma Hiroshi, Aoki Kazuo, Kobayashi Toshimitsu, Fujikura Shūichi, Nagashima Kingo, Miyata Teru, Takahashi Keizō, "Zadankai: Zoku anaunsumento to Imamukashi" (Conversation: The Announcements Yesterday and Today), *Hōsō Bunka*, January 1955, 46–51; Iijima Yōzō, "Gaitō Rokuon," *Hōsō Bunka*, August–September 1946, 23.

23. Satō Tadao, *Terebi no Shisō*, 60–61.

24. Paddy Scannell, "Public Service Broadcasting and Modern Public Life," in Paddy Scannell, Philip Schlesinger, and Colin Sparks, eds., *Culture and Power: A Media, Culture, and Society Reader*, 317–47 (London: Sage, 1992), 333.

25. Satō Tadao, *Terebi no Shisō*, 56.

26. Fujihisa Mine also notes the association between vernacular festivities and the egalitarian character of *Nodojiman*. Fujihisa Mine, "Kotoba Bunka to shiteno Rajio" (Radio as Verbal Culture), in Tsuganesawa Toshihiro and Takeshi Tamiya, eds., *Hōsō Bunkaron* (On Broadcast Culture) (Kyoto: Mineruva Shobō, 1983), 24. Yet her highly idealized vision of democracy, the masses, and egalitarianism should be read with caution.

27. Satō Tadao, *Terebi no Shisō*, 57, emphasis added.

28. "Shiroto Nodojiman Daiikkai Gōkakushatachi" (The Singers Who Passed the First *Nodojiman* Audition), *Shūkan Shinchō*, 5 January 1974, 50.

29. This feeling of equality can be seen as later developing into a "middle-class consciousness." Many surveys since the 1970s indicate that 90 percent of the Japanese people identify themselves as middle class in spite of the economic differences

among them. This result is often cited as evidence of the homogeneity of the Japanese nation. On the critique of the relationship between the "middle-class phantasm" and the homogeneous self-portrait, see Marilyn Ivy, "Formations of Mass Culture," in Andrew Gordon, ed., *Postwar Japan as History*, 239–58 (Berkeley: University of California Press, 1993).

30. Benedict Anderson, *Imagined Communities: Reflections on the Origin and Spread of Nationalism* (London: Verso, 1983), 35.

31. David Morley and Kevin Robins, *Spaces of Identity: Global Media, Electronic Landscape, and Cultural Boundaries* (London and New York: Routledge, 1995), 67.

32. Richard Middleton, *Studying Popular Music* (Milton Keynes [Buckinghamshire] and Philadelphia: Open University Press, 1990), 249–67.

33. Simon Frith, *Performing Rites: On the Value of Popular Music* (Cambridge: Harvard University Press, 1996).

34. Ibid., 197.

35. Anonymous, *Nodojiman Shirōto Ongakuka Tebiki*, 1–3.

36. Maruyama Tetsuo, "Chūshian Kara Kon'nichi no Ryūsei," 31.

37. *Asahi Shinbun*, 22 March 1948.

38. Kamota Kiyoshi, "Minna de Utatta Nichiyōbi" (On Sundays We Sing Together), *Sankei Yomimono*, 12 February 1956, 28.

39. In January 1949, NHK Tokyo launched *Mittsu no Kane* (Three Bell Rings), a short-lived program that featured "three-rings" singers. When these talented amateurs signed with record companies, they often appeared on *Uta no Myōjō* (Morning Stars of Song), a music show that featured professionals. These programs for "advanced" singers show how NHK, in the precommercial television period, tried to shrink the distance between amateurs and professionals.

40. In its early years, *Nodojiman* accepted songs by anonymous composers. The most famous was "Ikoku no Oka" (Hill in a Foreign Country, 1948), a song first broadcast by a war returnee who had learned it in a Japanese camp in Siberia. No one knew who wrote it until Tadashi Yoshida, after his return from Siberia, claimed authorship. He later became one of the best-known melody makers in postwar Japan. Even today about 10 of every 250 or so candidates sing wartime songs in the off-air audition, although none has been lucky enough to perform one on the air (*Asahi Shinbun*, 23 August 1995). The songs are censored probably because NHK believes that wartime songs, even if they are sentimental and evoke antiwar feelings in the hearts of the old singers, do not meet the criteria of wholesome recreation.

41. Within the framework of wholesome recreation, NHK broadcast music and game programs, such as *Mittsu no Uta* (Three Songs, 1951), in which participants were asked to sing correctly the first strophe of three songs announced on the spot.

42. Quiz programs were a genre that NHK appropriated in the immediate postwar period, copying American programs such as *Information Please, Twenty Ques-*

tions, and *What's My Line?* The contestants on the early quiz programs were mainly celebrities.

43. *Shūkan Kōron,* 3 April 1961, 47.

44. Anonymous, "7 Nenkan ni 170 Kai mo Chōsen" (170 Trials in Seven Years), *Shūkan Heibon,* 30 August 1973, 150.

45. Miyake, Zenzō, "Daisankai Nodojiman Zenkoku Konkūru wo Oete" (After the Third All-Japan *Nodojiman* Concours), *Hōsō Bunka,* April 1950, 33.

46. "Nodojiman ga Puro ni Naru Shunkan" (The Moment When an Amateur Turns Pro), *Shūkan Kōron,* 3 April 1961, 47.

47. Ibid., 48.

48. Kasza, *The State and the Mass Media in Japan,* 81ff.

49. Carolyn S. Stevens and Shuhei Hosokawa, "So Close and Yet So Far: Humanizing Celebrity in Japanese Music Variety Shows, 1960s–90s," in Brian Moeran, ed., *Asian Media Productions,* 223–46 (Richmond [Surrey]: Curzon, 2001).

50. To respond to the increase in young songwriters, NHK launched *Anata no Melody* (Your Melody), a competition for amateur composers (1964–85). The singers and musicians were usually professionals, and the judges always were. This program was much less successful than *Nodojiman* and never produced a hit song.

51. Uryū Tadao, *Hōsō Sangyō* (The Broadcast Industry) (Tokyo: Hōsei Daigaku Shuppan, 1965), 229–39.

52. Tsuganesawa Toshihiro and Takeshi Tamiya, eds., *Hōsō Bunkaron* (On Broadcast Culture) (Kyoto: Mineruva Shobō, 1983), 229–63.

53. The argument concerning what kind of entities should be licensed started with the birth of the Japanese broadcast history. One should note that the Tokyo-based NHK successfully established its monopoly when the Communications Ministry rejected a petition of some Osaka entrepreneurs for establishing a local station (Kasza, *The State and the Mass Media in Japan,* 72–88).

54. Scannell, "Public Service Broadcasting and Modern Public Life."

55. Today the all-Japan *Nodojiman* is broadcast every March with some twenty singers who represent the provinces and a panel of judges consisting of composers, lyricists, singers, and other celebrities. It appears as merely an appendix to the weekly routine but with a showier stage set. The only time an all-Japan meet was reported on the front page of a newspaper in last twenty or thirty years was when an ex-professional singer who hid her former career became the grand champion. See "NHK Nodojiman Yūshō Kashu wa Puro kashu Datta" (The Winning Singer of NHK *Nodojiman* Was a Pro), *Tokyo Supōtsu,* 18 March 1999.

56. Uemura Kenzō, "Shikaisha ga Binan de Nainoga Ii" (The Not So Handsome MC Is Good), *Kurashi no Techō,* October 1980, 159.

57. Shaun Moores, "Broadcasting and Its Audiences" in Hugh Mackay, ed., *Consumption and Everyday Life,* 213–46 (London: Open University Press, 1997), 224.

58. http://www.coara.or.jp/~ike/pasto/nhk/, access date: 5 February 2005.

59. Miyakawa Yasuo *"Nodojiman" ga Yuku* (*Nodojiman* Travels) (Tokyo: Mainichi Shinbun, 2000), 182.

60. For the local town halls, hosting *Nodojiman* is a great stimulus to revitalization. Some use it to celebrate the anniversary of a town or village while others use it as the opening event for a new or renovated public hall. Satō Yoshio, *NHK* (Tokyo: Asahi Shinbun, 1992), 86–89. *Nodojiman* is thus part of an important political and cultural agenda for the provinces to such an extent that local politicians routinely petition NHK to host it and the itinerary of the *Nodojiman* caravan is usually determined years in advance.

61. Rick Altman, "Television/Sound," in Tania Modleski, ed., *Studies in Entertainment: Critical Approaches to Mass Culture* (Bloomington: Indiana University Press, 1986), 43.

62. Raymond Williams, *Television. Technology, and Cultural Form* (London: Routledge, [1975] 1990), chap. 4.

63. Altman, "Television/Sound," 46.

64. David. W. Hughes, "'Esashi Oiwake' and the Beginnings of the Modern Japanese Folk Song," *World of Music* 34, no. 1 (1992): 35–56. see also David W. Hughes, *Traditional Folk Song in Modern Japan: Sources, Sentiment and Society* (Folkestone (Kent): Global Oriental), chap. 3.

65. Miyata Teru, "Sutēji Shikai" (The Master of Ceremonies Onstage), *Hōsō Bunka*, December 1951, 6.

66. Marilyn Ivy, "Tradition and Difference in the Japanese Mass Media," *Public Culture* 1 (1988): 21–23.

67. William W. Kelly, "Rationalization and Nostalgia: Cultural Dynamics of the New Middle-Class Japan," *American Ethnologist* 13, no. 4 (1986): 613. See also Jennifer Robertson, *Native and Newcomer. Making and Remaking a Japanese City* (Berkeley: University of California Press, 1991), chap. 1.

68. Kelly, "Rationalization and Nostalgia," 611–13.

69. Michael Billig, *Banal Nationalism* (London: Sage, 1995), 6.

Scaling the TV Station:
Fuji Television, Digital Development,
and Fictions of a Global Tokyo

Stephanie DeBoer

The first episode of Fuji Television's 1998 drama *Love Generation* features a montage sequence set over nighttime views of Odaiba, the "urban resort" and waterfront entertainment district that surrounds the Fuji TV station in Tokyo. Beginning from the overpass walkway of an everyday nighttime street, the drama's soon-to-be romantic popular couple suddenly walks along the walkway of the Rainbow Bridge, which connects the mainland Tokyo landscape to the site of the Fuji station itself. They ride the glass-encased tube escalator that leads to the station's fifth-floor Studio Promenade (a journey that would otherwise, outside this TV narrative, take visitors to tours of sound studios and exhibits of Fuji programming) and then stand on a waterfront observation deck to gaze at the vast Tokyo cityscape across the bay. The sequence ends on a stretch of beach beneath the bright lights of the bridge, the couple seen this time against the lights of the Odaiba playground that surrounds the Fuji headquarters they had just scaled.

Media and architecture critics have highlighted television's role in mediating the promise of the city as it promotes "encounters between stars [of TV programs] and buildings by star architects" as an everyday experience.[1] My own encounter with Odaiba had also been inspired by TV. During my first visit, I found myself following the same paths, ending up in the same places as the stars of *Love Generation*: from the Rainbow Bridge to the tube escalator and the interior of Fuji's massive television station. The Fuji TV station had loomed large in accounts of not only the urban development of Odaiba but also the development of television technologies themselves.

From well before its construction in 1997, the station had been promoted as a central node of access to the surrounding bay area. Its futuristic titanium-clad structure was to be a staging ground for the promise of Tokyo, intimately connected to the latest lifestyles and soon to be broadcast through the building's support of emerging digital technologies. *Love Generation*'s fictional incorporation of the station is thus only one instance of television's central place in imagining and constructing Tokyo's potential contours. As I joined the thousands of urban tourists visiting Odaiba, I intersected with a range of lived responses to this convergence between urban and technological development. Tokyo's popular press, for example, is filled with not only celebratory accounts of connectivity and romance across the environs of Fuji TV, but also complaints about the difficulty of traversing its material landscape as the coherence of the area is disrupted by entertainment venues and malls too vast and far apart to be comfortably spanned on foot.[2] Indeed, it is against a recognition of both the possibilities and problems of mobility, within television's relationship to Tokyo, that popular discourses have reflected on the nature of how one lives, works, and moves about in a city whose spectacular development engenders experiences and interactions that can appear increasingly thin.

This essay approaches the Fuji TV station as a nodal point for interrogating the links among fiction, media technologies, and urban renewal in the context of its mediation of Tokyo as a place of promise and development. Here I am primarily concerned with intersections between mobility and connectivity as they interweave with both popular and theoretical debates surrounding the relationships between communications technologies and the perceived nature of urban life. For geography and media studies at the very least, such debate has largely centered around the question of vision—the ways in which media technologies and their linking of seeing to the geography of the city constitute one way in which its lived experience is carved into an ideologically charged domain. As Michael Dear has argued, this intersection between the built environment (the city) and technologies of seeing (media technologies) is one field "whereby meanings of place are made, legitimized, contested and obscured."[3] This essay extends this argument to focus on the structures of feeling that are carved out of this intersection of urban space and vision. Here the potential for connectivity promoted in advertisements for Fuji's media technologies and the resonating possibilities of intimacy and romance produced in fictions set around its TV station together constitute a field across which bodies are imagined to traverse the mediated landscapes of Tokyo. This intersection between new technologies and new relationships, however, is also a place where the spatial and temporal ideologies that undergird these structures of feeling must be unpacked.

The romantic take on Tokyo in the TV drama with which I introduced this essay thus inflects a history of technologies of connectivity throughout the city. Indeed, the television station itself has often functioned as a central nexus for negotiating this intersection between broadcast technologies and Tokyo's urban development. The completion of NHK's "mammoth" station complex in the late 1950s, for example, was hailed as signaling the public broadcaster's central place in predictions of Japan's participation in the promise of global broadcasting that was popularized at the time. Its massive architectural stature fit neatly into a Tokyo rapidly restructuring to the scales deemed necessary for hosting such global events as the 1964 Olympics, which was broadcast via a landmark cross-Pacific satellite link partly enabled by the station's infrastructure and staff. The intense promotion and urban renewal that have surrounded Tokyo's commercial television station buildings since the mid-1990s, here accompanied by an industrywide refiguring toward digital broadcasting, are only the latest in a long series of station reforms to be linked to the promotion of the city as a setting for cosmopolitan lifestyles. Against developments that have centered around newly built and technologically refitted station buildings—TBS's station renovations against Akasaka's nightlife and broad consulate buildings, TV Asahi's upgrade in the "urban culture center" of Roppongi Hills, and Nihon TV's more recent transfer to the high-rise centers of communication in Shiodome, for example—Fuji Television's 1997 placement in the popularly promoted "future city" of Odaiba is only one illustrative facet of this entwining of technological and urban development to center around the waterfront districts of Tokyo.

Yet the matrix of contexts through which this version of Tokyo has been produced in and across the television station—not only discourses in the popular press but also television fictions, industry practices, and tourist routes—suggest that place is not simply reduced in these contexts of urban renewal and technological progress. Rather, the Fuji TV station provides a locus for thinking through the ways in which such often "thin" experience is better explained by way of what media scholars Nick Couldry and Anna McCarthy have termed "increasingly complex entanglements of scale."[4] As we attend to the matrixes that surround the urban television station, the problems of mobility and connectivity at stake in this entwining of urban experience and media technologies reflect a "power geometry" of spatial promotions, ideals, and experiences.[5] It is here that we can interrogate the often "global" or developmental promise implicit in the technological ideals that have been associated with Tokyo (and Japan) over the last several decades or more.

ODAIBA: URBAN CONNECTIONS/TEMPORAL STAKES

Popular accounts of the television station in Tokyo have underscored the importance of temporality in envisioning the close relationship between TV technologies and urban experience. The transfer of two remaining major commercial TV stations into newly developed urban centers of Tokyo's bay area Minato ward in 2003 was heralded by the *Asahi* newspaper as completing a broadcasting trend that had been inaugurated six years earlier when Fuji Television first moved its headquarters to the still developing area of Odaiba. The more recent construction and technological refitting of station buildings for Nihon TV and TV Asahi coincided with an industrywide promotion of the fiftieth anniversary of Japanese television (locating its beginning with NHK's first public broadcast in 1953), all of which was simultaneously heralded as marking the partial "inaugural year of digital broadcasting" in Japan.[6] This latter event had been predicted by industry promotions and corresponding media histories since the first successful test of a Japan-owned satellite in 1984 had paved the way for Japan's realization of worldwide satellite coverage by the end of the decade.[7] The latest configuration of television's broadcasting, and now digital, future was to be linked to the spaces of Tokyo with the hope that TV would work to enliven a "new" kind of interconnected city living in the urban environment surrounding these stations.[8]

Fuji Television's transfer of its headquarters to Odaiba in 1997 also placed it at the forefront of predictions of the connective possibilities that television could enable across the city. Waterfront developers in particular have cited the television station's central role from the late 1990s in popularizing images of Odaiba, as its scripted programming and live public events were utilized—along with Tokyo's formidable tourist print and media industry—to promote it as an entertainment area filled with themed shopping and future wired environments.[9] One prominent developmental model for the waterfront district has promoted it as an "urban resort," a site of so-called location-based entertainment where visitors can stop by for an afternoon of leisure that, in the phrasing of Sony Urban Entertainment, "integrates both real and cyber experience" into the patterns of Tokyo urban life.[10] Cultural and urban critic Yoshimi Shunya's examination of Tokyo *sakariba*—a term indicating main stages of urban culture, gathering, and amusement—argues for the "contemporariness" of media technologies for entertainment centers in Tokyo over the last few decades of the twentieth century. While, for example, the youth culture that surrounded the suburban train terminal of Shinjuku in the 1960s was concerned with a kind of anti-urban (and often anti-Western) impetus for gathering and performing in its city streets—a series of political and avant-garde activities that brought people to publicly gather for unscripted events—Shibuya in the 1970s came to characterize Tokyo's increasing commercialism. The Seibu Company's 1973 "Parco" building and redevelopment of the Park Street district was accompanied by a highly successful ad campaign that produced a new, commercially scripted image of this transportation hub that appealed to contemporary youth. From the late 1970s on, then, going to Shibuya became an "act of confirmation about the information people have received of the mass media." It was a place wholly dependent on performance and its viewing in an increasingly mass-mediated city where "new consumable styles of [an ever elusive and disappearing] 'now' are to be presented by pedestrians."[11]

View from Odaiba looking back toward the Rainbow Bridge and the rest of Tokyo from the perspective of the Fuji TV station.

In contrast to the "now" of 1970s Shibuya or the futuristic tone of more recently constructed television stations, the development of Odaiba over the course of the 1990s—and Fuji TV's place within it—instead reflects what we might call a desire for "yesterday's future."[12] Disparaged by at least one critic as a "dreg of the bubble era" economy, Odaiba was part of an urban development project conceived and then transformed from 1980s economic and urban optimism.[13] Urban planners and developers imagined Tokyo's then industrially bleak waterfront as a place that could potentially be on a par with other world urban centers (Manhattan, for example) in its fluid weaving together of leisure attractions and the global economic interests the site was also expected to draw. This area of the Tokyo Bay, from its 1984 inception, was to be a "city of the future" (*mirai toshi*), part of an increasingly decentralized Tokyo intricately connected with global media and entertainment trends, information technologies, and twenty-first-century cosmopolitan lifestyles.[14] By the early 1990s, however, the still largely empty landfill came to controversial public and media attention. The bayfront project had been slated to be the site for the massive World City Exposition, which was to inaugurate the waterfront project as well as showcase Tokyo on a world stage. With the bursting of Japan's prosperous bubble economy of the 1980s, however, the extreme expense of the project was criticized as one more financial burden Tokyo could ill afford. Television personality and author Aoshima Yukio was elected governor of Tokyo on a campaign promise to cancel the exposition, killing what had been billed as an urban and global event to rival even Osaka's 1970 sponsorship of the World Expo.

As a scaled-down version of the waterfront project continued into the early 1990s, Odaiba has often been construed as representative of a Tokyo without history. Today's version of Odaiba was built on a larger span of reclaimed land that incorporated two offshore gun emplacements hastily built in 1853 after Commodore Perry's first visit and attempt to force Japan to open itself to world markets. Against this global past, and over the course of the latter half of the twentieth century, much of the area came to feature industrial warehouse districts—a dark and empty setting, as it was characterized by its later urban developers, perfect for its frequent use as a bleak shooting location for detective and gangster genres in television and film.[15] Yet in the following decades Odaiba continued to be reported as the optimal backdrop—a surface imbued with "zero memory of land" against which creators and artists could set disillusioned urban narratives.[16]

When Fuji TV moved its station headquarters to the bay area in 1997, it was set against a built environment that promised a conglomeration of global trends and scales in urban entertainment. It was a seeming simulacrum of past and future sites constructed to attract visitors to this Tokyo location from across the city, Japan, the region, and the globe. Odaiba sites included Palette Town, which features shopping for women in the reconstructed and indoor streets of old Venice (a construction based on Las Vegas Forum Shops concepts in malled architecture); Daiba Little Hong Kong, set on the seventh and eighth stories of the Deck's Tokyo Beach shopping mall as it simulates the feel and sound of the city's alleyways of the 1980s; Sony Entertainment "urban resort" amusements constructed through screen experiences—state-of-the-art digital movie theaters and the indoor Sega Joypolis amusement center; the Oedo hot spring spa, the interior of which re-creates the street life of early Edo Japan; and a variety of museums set against the Telecom Center and the Tokyo Big Sight (the Tokyo International Exhibition Center), at the time of its construction the largest convention facility in Japan. A more recent development includes an as yet uncompleted casino and hotel complex intended to attract capital from high rollers across the region—from Shanghai, for example, as it is to be more closely linked to Tokyo via the Haneda airport's expansion and focus on Asian travel—on the model of what the developer notes are entertainment trends apparent in other cities across the world.[17]

SCALING STATION ROUTES AND VIEWS

Not simply repeating the spectacular sense of the entertainment city emerging around it, Fuji TV also worked to contain the fictions of emptiness and alienation through which the popular press often disparaged these surroundings. The station building—a massive retro-futurist construction of aluminum, glass, titanium, and steel columns—is easily recognized against the skyline of Odaiba's surrounding Minato district waterfront. It consists of two blocks of massive frame columns rising from the same base connected by three levels of girderlike pedestrian sky corridors and a titanium-paneled ball thirty-two meters in diameter. The imaginative visitor might see the building's high-tech exposed structure as an erector set replica of a hi-vision wide-screen television set, as its "cathode globe" public observatory deck and windowed walkways offer panoramic views of the surrounding landscape.[18] Fuji TV's 1997 transfer of its headquarters to this building's futuristic and technological proportions provided an impetus for both technological and image refashioning. It offered not only an advantageous jump into a structure that would support its future digital broadcasts but also new interior sound studios and tourist routes that were to revitalize the station's popular image.[19] Yet Fuji TV also produced promotions reminiscent of the ways in which the 1998 Fuji Drama *Love Generation* opened, as the then famous Kimura Takuya and Matsu Takako walked over the infrastructure of a nighttime Odaiba and scaled the Fuji Television station itself. Here Fuji TV offset the spectacular developments of its surrounding entertainment district with station routes that cultivated a sense of intimacy with—and nostalgia for—the kinds of connections that "only" television could engender.

The Fuji TV station building, with its tube escalator leading visitors to exhibitions of Fuji TV programming and views of sound studios.

Promotion of the station building as a tourist destination—an architectural draw for its interior views as much as its public staging of events in Odaiba—has worked to establish the structure's place in the city through Fuji TV's recent history of recycling urban imaginaries for Tokyo. Well before the transfer of its headquarters, Fuji featured a series of programs in

1996 to inaugurate its move, showcasing TV events at its future setting in Odaiba. On the one hand, celebrating the "youthful" and "energetic" image of Fuji through hip rock concerts, fireworks, and television programming, it also promoted the formidable presence of Fuji in recent TV history through a series of rerun variety shows and playbacks of previously popular Fuji dramas.[20] This marked the beginning of a long line of programming— specials, news events, variety shows, and dramas—that combined a media spotlight on the area with the use of Odaiba as a narrative backdrop. The 1998 drama *Kamisama mō sukoshi dake* (God, Please Give Me More Time), for example, featured scenes of its romantic couple attempting, and failing, to meet at the base of the Madame of Liberty, which still stands as a land-mark on the beachfront before the Fuji TV station. Donated to the island as part of Odaiba's support of festival events for the 1998 Year of France in Japan, this same drama also featured a documentary-style sequence detail-ing the statue's transportation and establishment at its beachfront site. Since 2000, an 11.5-meter replica of the popular statue has stood before the Fuji TV building, floodlit and erected less than a year after its original was returned to France in 1999.

The television station is thus situated at a nexus between its TV pro-grams and the contours of the city that surround its architectural location. At this juncture, television constructs urban space not only in its (often live) broadcast of Tokyo and the entertainment center of Odaiba but also in the structures of feeling it produces in these same spaces. Indeed, the establish-ment of Fuji TV's importance to the past half century of Japanese television goes hand in hand with nostalgia for television's presence in the everyday life of the city and its inhabitants. The scene of (here momentarily failed) romance exemplified in the 1998 *Kamisama mō sukoshi dake* is also reminis-cent of the invitation for televisual encounter that has been promoted in tourist routes through the TV station. Accessed through the glass-enclosed tube escalator used by the TV drama protagonists introduced at the begin-ning of this essay, its fifth-level Studio Promenade affords a view of the sta-tion interior as a site of reruns, and of revisiting one's past through televi-sion. Alongside corridors and windows that look down into sound studios featuring live and on-air Fuji television productions, there are set displays of popular TV shows that offer the opportunity to be photographed on the site of Fuji TV. Encased behind glass and pasted along corridor walls are also broadcasting schedules, picture promotions for current programming, and quizzes and games linked to television shows. All of this is interspersed with histories of popular Fuji TV genres: lists of the talent and stars featured over the twenty-year span of a popular variety show, celebrations of the scale of Fuji's TV news coverage of Tokyo and Japan, photograph collections and collectors' goods linked to drama series, accounts of Fuji's first 1969 airing of a popular TV animation show, and the town set used for a recent live-action remake of that show reconstructed in miniature before the display.[21]

This material display of television—its physical presence in the tourist routes of the station—has also been starkly contrasted by Fuji TV against its recent investment and thus renewal in new technologies. A 2001 *Asahi News* article featured a photo of urban tourists exploring the Fuji headquarters in Odaiba. The story that accompanied this image highlighted the station's tactics in drawing viewers closer to not only see but also touch the very site of TV production. Here visits to interior soundstages and purchases of Fuji tourist goods were contrasted with the station's ongoing development into a multichannel digital platform. Digital technologies had long been promoted by Fuji as the future of television broadcasting as they engender a more expansive and spectacular view of the world. Yet these same new technologies, according to this article, held a simultaneous danger—the potential to empty the TV station, as well as its surrounding environment, of any "real" experience. In response, the more tangible contours of the station's interior theme park and tourist routes were figured as compensation for television's potentially virtual (read here as "unreal" or "global") experience.[22] Urban and architectural critic Akira Suzuki has suggested that, with all its "shopping centers, game arcades and hotels of a Coney Island daydream," Odaiba is "not the real city, but its Net equivalent."[23] In his recognition of the resonance between digital and theme park virtualities, Suzuki's statement does not simply argue for the ways in which the "Net city" drains its pathways of meaning or a significant sense of place. Less opposing a "real" city to a "false" one, his statement instead provides insight into the ways in which Odaiba became a stage over which discourses of "virtuality" and "emptiness" were conflated. This was a problem that the more tangible experiences linked to television were to solve.

The external views offered to the public from the TV station's interior—images and pathways structured by the building's various corridors, windows, panels, and screens—also reveal this nexus between TV and Odaiba to be constructed in close relation to the transnational problematic that has recently accompanied emerging media technologies in Japan. The Fuji Station was designed, according to its developers, to be "an open information broadcasting center offering public spaces with high human and cultural content . . . relat[ed] to other public urban spaces in the area."[24] Yet these relations simultaneously extend across a dynamic of urban, national, regional, and global imaginaries. The high view provided by the promenade decks that occupy the "digital ball" situated at the center of the structure is a 270-degree panorama of the Tokyo Bay area from a height of 123 meters. It offers views of the central landmarks of the Tokyo skyline—maps along its windows help the visitor to identify the Rainbow Bridge, the Tokyo Tower, and the Tokyo Municipal Government building—as well as glimpses of the boxlike malled exteriors that edge the landscaped waterfront of Odaiba directly below. Scholars and critics of urban tourism have argued that any city that "tries to build an economy based on tourism must project itself as a 'dreamscape of visual consumption,'" one that "coaches" visitors on how to travel and cues them in how to look, as well as what to look for, in its contours.[25] This panoramic tourist view, however, is by now a mundane and even nostalgic experience in Tokyo, for nearly every high building wishing to establish a name for itself boasts a public viewing platform. Yet here, from within the Fuji TV Station, what visitors are directed to look at is not only the wide cityscape that is labeled and encased in glass before them but also the global imaginings and technological intersections that are its implicit underpinning. A stroll through the station building's sky-level corridors might just as easily bring the visitor past screened views differently scaled and multiplied. Against a backdrop of the Tokyo skyline one might also encounter interactive computer touch screens displaying interface after interface of the Fuji playground: details of its interior mall attractions, entertainment technologies, and dreamscape world environments of Venice shopping, Hong Kong dining, and strolling under the shadow of France's Madame of Liberty.

In this invitation to interact with, even touch, the station's entertainment environs, concerns for technology that have long been a locus of debate for Japan and its cultural products come into play. Yoshimi Shunya has outlined what he terms the "structurally different 'techno-nationalism'" engendered by recent electronics and television in Japan. As opposed to earlier domestic imaginings that emphasized the particular "Japaneseness" of 1960s technologies, in the 1980s "images of electronic appliances in Japan became more and more hybrid, transgressional and diasporic." Here, against images that utilized foreign locations, bodies imagined as "putting on a new electronic technology" could travel across and beyond all kinds of borders of nation, culture, or race.[26] This outline of the transnational dynamics inherent in everyday technologies in Japan may be productively extended to Fuji TV's cosmopolitan environment of the 1990s. As the station mobilized emerging technologies to rework the future imagined for the area in the 1980s, similarly global, and here networked, landscapes are brought to the visitor's fingertips at the touch of a screen.[27] Within this problematic of so-called cross-border transgression, however—and as the station links up with the "global" dreams promised by the entertainment city around it—the possibility of disillusionment with this environment is compensated in promotions of intimacy and connectivity.

LOCATING FICTIONS OF A GLOBAL TOKYO

What is significant in this account is that Fuji's youth-oriented and urban dramas of the 1990s are themselves situated at an intersection between television's transnational presence and the station's engagement with the unevenly accessed city. One of the most widely watched of Japan's internationally traveling TV genres, post-1980s versions of Fuji TV's so-called trendy dramas are frequented by popular young talent set against locations in Tokyo. These urban scenes have drawn not only local but also regional tourists and fans throughout the Asia-Pacific region to the architectural site of its station.[28] Television's production of urban space is often figured as a history of technological achievements and a set of innovations in media technologies that repeatedly rejuvenate TV's importance to the city. Particularly from the mid-1970s on, developments in video made location shooting outside the soundstage interior more of an economic and aesthetic possibility for Japanese TV dramas. The 1977 TBS drama *Kishibe no arubamu*, for example, marked a sentient transition for outdoor shooting as it engendered a sense (and marketing point) of direct engagement with places beyond the studio—a kind of "landscape attraction" that was later capitalized on in the broad views of Hokkaido featured in the first season of Fuji's 1981 award-winning drama *Kita no kuni kara* (From the North Country).[29] By the late 1980s, at the height of Japan's bubble economy, Fuji's introduction of the trendy drama brought its viewers to the most fashionable areas of Tokyo as part of its mission to attract a younger and more affluent pool of viewers. Yet these urban images are not simply an archive of static achievements in capturing architecture, outdoor scenes, or TV stars but also a testament to spatial relations, accounts of Tokyo that imagine, mediate, and narrate possibilities for navigation through the intensified commercial spaces of the city.

Recent urban dramas have also frequently set their protagonists to walking across the city's most recently developed facades—the new commercial centers of Roppongi Hills and Shiodome, themselves accompanied by the transfer of commercial TV stations in 2003, for example—and linking them, by way of editing techniques, to other parts of the city. The 1998 drama *Love Generation* with which this essay began ends its montage journey through Odaiba and the Fuji TV station with a final perspective from the Tokyo mainland. This area supports the less spectacular overpasses, apart-

A scene from *Love Generation*, as Kimura Takuya and Matsu Takako walk over the Rainbow Bridge that connects Odaiba to the Tokyo mainland.

ments, and routes through which the drama's hopes and dreams will play. Its central romantic protagonists (again, played by the then popular Kimura Takuya and Matsu Takako) had both come to the city from the outskirts of Tokyo with the hope of discovering in its landscape a hint of who they truly can be. And who they truly can be will be intricately linked to the gendered concerns of romance and connectivity, to discovering whom they *can be with* in its urban contours. Here scenes of their journey through the nighttime locations of Odaiba are overlain with a voice-over track of the couple's conversation: despite Tokyo's smog-filled sky, its small apartments and mundane occupations, the city still, in the words of Matsu Takako, "seems to hold out some promise for the future" for them. In many ways, there is nothing new in this scenario as Tokyo has long served as a setting for narratives of hope or despair in the big city. Urban youth TV dramas of the 1970s certainly imagined the metropolis as a place of potential monetary gain against the hometowns from which its protagonists had often recently moved.[30] Yet the city to which the figures of *Love Generation* are drawn, as with many urban dramas of the 1990s, is not one that will necessarily engender societal success. Rather it offers a promise similar to the romantic sentiment expressed in their montage-inspired exploration of the entertaining sites of Odaiba, the realization of one's place in the city (and by extension the world) that can only be played out in their search for companionship through the streets and communications routes of Tokyo.

Following its opening promise in the future city of Odaiba, the remaining episodes of *Love Generation* (culminating, of course, in the realization that love can overcome all obstacles) feature this romantic couple in chance encounters before a busy train station, office building episodes set against windowed views of a wide cityscape, and strolls over nighttime street overpasses. These scenarios are reminiscent of cultural critic Michel de Certeau's suggestion of the narrative function and possibilities imbued in the very act of walking through a city, and notions of the flaneur that have long been associated with cultural and entertainment centers throughout Tokyo (the Ginza of the 1930s or Shibuya of the 1970s, for example).[31] Similar connections have also been made explicit in a central model for many urban dramas of the 1990s, Fuji TV's hugely popular 1991 drama *Tokyo Love Story*. Its opening montage sequence, of which the opening scenes of *Love Generation* (and, indeed, of many urban dramas) are also reminiscent, begins with two silhouettes kissing before a sunset-lit cityscape. The sequence then cuts to a montage of city trains leaving terminals, crowds of pedestrians walking the streets, lines of people using public telephones, street traffic, and passing buildings. The careful viewer would also notice the drama's main protagonists walking among the largely professionally classed and suited urban crowd.

Yet these dramas lead the viewer not only toward exterior urban pathways but also to the function of the city's interior spaces, a refraction of the one-room studio block apartments around which lifestyles for single living in 1990s Tokyo revolved. The "one-room mansion," a place for living that emerged against the dramatic rise in Tokyo's population over the second half of the twentieth century, is a central location from which these romantic protagonists navigate the city. Its implications were captured in a 1993 contribution to the English-language newspaper the *Daily Yomiuri* in Tokyo.

> The cover story of the November 1992 issue of the magazine *anan* was about living alone as an adult woman. I bought the magazine; I live alone. I live in one of those ironically labeled "one-room mansions." . . . Actually, it might be better to say that I don't live alone at all. I live alone with countless others who must be much like myself. . . . I know that a sizable number of the young, single population must live in one-room mansions because they are the source of the major decorating problems in a huge number of magazines. . . . The one-room mansion is not exclusively a magazine topic. It appears in television drama as well. In "Tokyo Love Story" Rika and Kanchi [the drama's main romantic couple]

sit alone in their respective one-room mansions (better furnished than mine) and talk to each other on the phone.[32]

In contrast to the city's crowded walkways and open public plazas, the private spaces of these dramas are small and confined. Yet they are also an experience of Tokyo living that is mediated and shared through television and popular media. As opposed to the long tradition of Japanese "home dramas"—narratives that still appear in daytime slots on Japanese TV in which the house remains the (unstable) icon of stability—home here is a temporary site used only for sleeping and necessary domestic activities as its small size dictates that all social life must occur beyond its confines.[33] Such single-resident abodes are also often places of loneliness, of "empty" single living, a message both verbally and graphically displayed in scenes of its residents looking out of their stark apartment windows onto dark nighttime scenes of the city. *Tokyo Love Story* featured its romantic protagonists escaping such alienating constrictions through a network of phone lines and calls. This landscape of connectivity was also rendered through cell phones and public phones in the later *Love Generation*. For Fuji's recent urban dramas, then, the places of possibility lie in not only its street-level transportation but also its communications routes, where the desolation of urban living as a single person exacerbates the need to literally "look out" for romance over its streets and technologies.[34]

Even as these dramas point to the crises of urban living, at the same time they offer street-level romance and communications technologies as compensation, a sense of personal connection and proximity that demands our looking properly (and dialing correctly) through the contours of the city. In the urban dramas of the 1990s, romance thus becomes the urban attraction pursued over the Fuji-imagined landscapes of Tokyo. Indeed, the idea of love as an "event" was a central component of Fuji Television's reconfiguration of the late 1980s version of the trendy drama in response to its decline in popularity by 1990. Earlier configurations of this genre were primarily concerned with displaying popular stars in the most stylish and enviable contexts throughout Tokyo.[35] One of Fuji's first trendy dramas to be labeled as such, the 1988 *Kimi no na o taiho suru*, centered its action around the fashionable Dogenzaka section of Shibuya, a popular area of Tokyo that provided a stage for the display (and here the detective pursuit) of bubble economy fashions and hip urban lifestyles. *Tokyo Love Story*'s successful revitalization of the genre was central to transforming Fuji TV's Monday night nine o'clock time slot into a weekly event for young, especially female, viewers.[36] This spot in the Fuji schedule was later to feature such popular high points in drama ratings as *Long Vacation* (1995) and *Love Generation* (1998), to date the highest-rated drama of its time slot. Yet the new brand of love first marked in *Tokyo Love Story*, as characterized by one of its producers, was to be an "event for which anyone can be the protagonist."[37] After Japan's economic bubble burst in the 1980s, what was needed, it was asserted, was an "everyday kind of love . . . and lifestyle" that its viewers could feel able to attain. This was a production strategy to which shooting everyday (though no less developed) urban locations throughout Tokyo was also central.[38]

Fuji Television's central concern with location shooting in its production of a TV genre more in tune with contemporary (1990s) urban lifestyles and possibilities underscores the connections among fiction, the changing face of urban development, and television's presence in 1990s Tokyo. Indeed, the station's own imaginings and promotions also intersect with the inevitable books and publications that feature and locate the places of these dramas throughout the city, rendering the less spectacular spaces of Tokyo a destination and fiction for tourism as well. Such urban landscapes, of course, continue to be layered with the global dynamics and imaginaries inherent in the everyday technologies of Japan over the past century. In Taiwan, for example, Japanese TV programming has inspired such publications as *Cinderella's Tour in Tokyo* (1999), a fan-inspired journey through the trendy drama shooting locations of the city, from the public telephone used in one episode to the monumental return to the site of the Fuji TV station itself.[39] Yet what is discovered and promoted in these accounts is not simply a pursuit of TV's mediated spaces, of simply returning to the site of where television has been. For the couples (or single urban residents) who also stroll along the waterfront decks and entertainment arcades of Odaiba, experience in the information city is figured and intertwined with a hopeful nostalgia for a technological future of possibility. In this future, its inhabitants and visitors remain intimately connected even as they make their way through the city's often precariously alienating spaces.

ROUTES TO THE STATION

By the time of this essay's publication, the once "future city" of Odaiba is already yesterday's news. More recent Tokyo developments such as Roppongi Hills and Shiodome—the environs for TV Asahi and Nihon TV—have reportedly replaced it as centers for living, working, and navigating the city. Yet, even as they continue to be promoted through predictions of digital convergence and urban development, the recent refitting of commercial television stations in the bay districts of Tokyo are also places for unpacking the technological ideals that have often been associated with Japan's facade. Television's role in the production of urban experience is not simply, as the rhetoric of TV (as well as urban development) might imply, about its power to mediate and direct the experiences of its viewers. Engaging with television in this context also requires recognition of the ways in which imaginaries produced at the intersection of media technologies and urban space intersect with a complex geometry, a geometry that revolves around ideologies of mobility and connectivity. While it is beyond the scope of this essay, this becomes especially important when we consider Tokyo's increasing significance as a landscape over which a wide range of national, classed, sexed, and economic figures from across the Asia-Pacific region navigate the developmental terms through which Tokyo and its technologies continue to be constructed. In his discussion of Tokyo Disneyland, Mitsuhiro Yoshimoto explains what Tokyo's frequent label as a "theme park" might imply. No longer simply a place for people to get ahead in the world, Tokyo is now increasingly a global image imbued with fantasy and fun.[40] Arguing for the ways in which television intersects with "complex entanglements of scale" is to situate it at a dynamic of transnational experiences, environments, and technologies. This essay is only one step toward opening a space for recognition of the ideologies that impact their place in the city.

NOTES

1. Ernest Pascucci, "Intimate (Tele)visions," in Steven Harris and Deborah Berke, eds., *Architecture of the Everyday* (New York: Princeton Architectural Press, 1997), 39.

2. Mizoue Yukinobu, "Odaiba būmu no kachigumi makigumi" (The Winners and Losers of the Odaiba Boom), *Gekkan keizai juku*, May 2000, 54.

3. Michael Dear, "Film Architecture and Cityspace: The Politics of Representation," in *Postmodern Urbanism*, quoted in Sarah Matheson, "Televising Toronto from Hogtown to Megacity," PhD diss., University of Southern California, 2003, 25.

4. Nick Couldry and Anna McCarthy, "Orientations: Mapping MediaSpace," in Nick Couldry and Anna McCarthy, eds., *MediaSpace: Place, Scale, and Culture in a Media Age* (New York: Routledge, 2004), 7.

5. I have found such theorists of critical geography as Doreen Massey helpful in parsing a more dynamic sense of the global space of Tokyo. Her argument for a "global sense of place" is particularly insightful in its conception of local space as always intersecting and interweaving with global interchanges that include concerns not simply of economy (as terms such as *space-time compression* might suggest) but also of gender and ethnicity. Doreen Massey, *Space, Place, and Gender* (Minneapolis: University of Minnesota Press, 1994).

6. "Zai kī kyoku Minato ku ni shūketsu: Atarashi machi no kasseika ni kitai" (The Massing of Key TV Stations in the Minato Ward: Hopes for a Reactivated City), *Asahi shinbun*, 19 February 2003, 12.

7. *Broadcasting in Japan: The Twentieth-Century Journey from Radio to Multimedia* (Tokyo: NHK, 2002), 243, 249.

8. "Zai kīkyoku Minato ku ni shūketsu," 12.

9. Hiramoto Kazuo, *Rinkai fukutoshin monogatari: Odaiba o meguru seiji keizai ryoku gaku* (The Story of the Waterfront Subcenter: The Political Economy of Odaiba) (Tokyo: Chūkō, 2000), 11–12.

10. Sugiyama Totomu, "Riaru to saibā no yūgō o nirami: Rokēshion bijinesu o honkakuka saseta Soni no kigyō senryaku—San Furanshisuko, Berurin, Odaiba no sekai mikkasho ni tanjo" (The Fusion of Real and Cyber: Industry Strategies Realized by Sony's Location Business—the Birth of the Three World Locations of San Francisco, Berlin, and Odaiba), *Reja sangyō* (Leisure Industry) 406 (June 2000): 20–25.

11. Yoshimi Shunya, "Urbanization and Cultural Change in Modern Japan: The Case of Tokyo," in Steffi Richter and Annette Schad-Seifert, eds., *Cultural Studies and Japan* (Leipzig: Leipziger Universitatsverlag, 2001), 98.

12. Although I use it in a different context and to different implications, I am indebted for the phrase "yesterday's future" to Lynn Spigel's insightful exploration of the "home of the future" in her "Yesterday's Future, Tomorrow's Home," *Journal for the Study of Media and Composite Cultures* 11, no. 1 (May 2001): 29.

13. "125 mannin o mikomu odaiba 'Dai bijutsukan' keika no saisan" (1,250,000 People Expected in Calculations for Odaiba's 'Big Art Museum' Plan), *Shūkan Shiōhō* 46, no. 29 (2 August 2001): 40.

14. Hiramoto Kazuo, *Rinkai fukutoshin monogatari*, 31, 40. Indeed, the initial plan for the then termed Tokyo Teleport project (*tele*communications plus sea*port*) imagined a beachfront district filled with communications capabilities that would promote Tokyo as an ideal model of twenty-first-century cosmopolitanism intimately linked to worldwide information networks and lifestyles.

15. Ibid., 2.

16. "Umi miwatasu: 'shima' no kaihōkan" (Looking Out over the Ocean: an 'Island' Sense of Freedom), *Asahi shinbun*, 16 August 1996, 12.

17. "Ajia goraku toshi yume mite" (Viewing the Dream of an Asian Entertainment City), *Asahi shinbun*, 27 June 2002, 10.

18. Stephen Mansfield, *Insight Pocket Guide to Tokyo* (Singapore: Insight Print Services, 2000), 58. This is how one English-language travel guide to Tokyo describes the station building.

19. Indeed, even as I wrote an early draft of this essay from my Tokyo apartment (or one loaned to me by a friend) in September 2003, Fuji TV broadcast a variety spe-

cial featuring television personalities being quizzed on the identity and attractions of Odaiba.

20. "Honsha iten ni chinande ibento to tokubetsu bangumi" (Events and Special Programming for the Move of the Head Office), *Asahi shinbun*, 6 August 1996.

21. This description is based on several visits to the Fuji Station from June 2002 to September 2003. I also visited Odaiba in August 2004 and August 2007.

22. "Shichosha o kakoikome: Terebi kyakkyoku, tachyaneru ni sonae" (Encircling the TV Audience), *Asahi shinbun*, 2 July 2001, 14.

23. Akira Suzuki, *Do Android Crows Fly over an Electronic Tokyo? The Interactive Urban Landscape of Japan* (London: Architectural Association, 2001), 72.

24. Watanabe Hiroshi, *The Architecture of Tokyo: An Architectural History in 571 Individual Presentations* (London: Axel Menges, 2001), 100.

25. Susan S. Fainstein and Dennis R. Judd, "Global Forces, Local Strategies, and Urban Tourism," in Dennis R. Judd and Susan S. Fainstein, eds., *The Tourist City* (New Haven: Yale University Press, 1999), 7.

26. Yoshimi Shunya, "'Made in Japan': The Cultural Politics of 'Home Electrification' in Postwar Japan," in Steffi Richter and Annette Schad-Seifert, eds., *Cultural Studies and Japan* (Leipzig: Leipziger Universitatsverlag, 2001), 117–18.

27. Here I am confronted with the difficulty of describing the changing face and developments of both the city and the TV station itself. My description of these screens is based on a visit to the Fuji Station in June 2002. When I visited in September 2003, these particular screens were no longer standing in its passageways. Instead, the observation deck was filled with flat-screen televisions promoting Odaiba as the site of the big-budget film *Odoru daisōsasen II* (Bayside Shakedown II), a detective drama that pursues its criminals over the district's wide concrete blocks. As these and following screens have displayed a similar rhetoric of scale, I have decided to retain my original description.

28. There is some debate over whether the trendy drama genre established in the 1980s actually continued into the 1990s. (Hirahata, for example, has called the 1990s refashioning of this genre "pure drama.") As the 1990s versions are popularly labeled trendy dramas in the contexts I am considering, and due to the continuing urban nature and setting central to the dramas I discuss, I have decided to retain this label.

29. Komatsu Katsuhiko and Office 21, eds., *That's terebi dorama '90s* (That's TV Drama '90s) (Tokyo: Daiyamondosha, 1999), 12–14.

30. This scenario is closely linked, as Lisa Leung has argued, to the central mantra of *gambaru*, to "keep on fighting," prominent in many Japanese dramas. Lisa Yuk Ming Leung, "*Ganbaru* and Its Transcultural Audience: Imaginary and Reality of Japanese TV Dramas in Hong Kong," in Koichi Iwabuchi, ed., *Feeling Asian Modernities: Transnational Consumption of Japanese TV Dramas* (Hong Kong: Hong Kong University Press, 2004), 90.

31. Michel de Certeau, *The Practice of Everyday Life*, trans. Stephen Rendall (Berkeley: University of California Press, 1988), 129.

32. Quoted in Akira Suzuki, *Do Android Crows Fly over an Electronic Tokyo?* 23.

33. Hirohata, Hideo, "'Home Drama' and Rapid Economic Growth," in Masunori Sata and Hideo Hirahara, eds., *A History of Japanese Television Drama* (Tokyo: Japan Association of Broadcasting Art, 1991), 112.

34. While I have a slightly different interpretation—one that incorporates imaginaries around communications technologies and urban development into a reading of their streets—Lisa Leung's reading of Japanese drama in terms of public and private urban space in *"Ganbaru* and Its Transcultural Audience" has been extremely helpful to my account.

35. Komatsu Katsuhiko and Office 21, *That's terebi dorama '90s*, 14.

36. Ibid., 19, 34.

37. Akiyama Shinobu, "Fuji ren'ai kyo" (Studies in Fuji Love), *Shinchō* 45, no. 11 (January 1992): 112.

38. Kami Akira, "Torendī dorama ni naku wakushatachi" (Young People Crying for Trendy Dramas), *Purejidento* 30, no. 6 (June 1992): 256.

39. Lee Ming-tsung, "Traveling with Japanese TV Dramas: Cross-Cultural Orientation and Flowing Identification of Contemporary Taiwanese Youth," in Koichi Iwabuchi, ed., *Feeling Asian Modernities: Transnational Consumption of Japanese TV Dramas* (Hong Kong: Hong Kong University Press, 2004), 152. Zheng Xiujuan's recent essay on the disillusionment felt when confronted with the "real" site of Fuji TV (and the "real" Tokyo) is an important contrast in this context. Zheng Xiujuan, "'Suppin no Tokyo' ni deau: Nihon būmu no atosaki" (Encountering Tokyo Unmasked: Following the Japan Boom) in Yoshimi Shunya and Wakabayashi Mikio, eds., *Tokyo sutadīzu* (Tokyo Studies) (Tokyo: Kinokuniya, 2005), 199–208.

40. Yoshimoto Mitsuhiro, "Images of Empire: Tokyo Disneyland and Japanese Cultural Imperialism," in Eric Smoodin, ed., *Disney Discourse: Producing the Magic Kingdom* (New York: Routledge, 1994), 198.

The Dramatic Consequences
of Playing a Lover:
Stars and Televisual Culture in Japan

Eva Tsai

There is something inspiring about an individual who is simultaneously an object of public adoration and an agent of love in a media text. Television and film stars, whose careers develop within myriads of fictional narratives, often exemplify such affective figures. Portraying a lover is no guarantee of instant or everlasting fame. Yet playing a lover seems to be an en/acting ritual and, in some cases, a process arousing public empathy and adoration. The mode of articulation within this intertwining play of affectivity is stimulating and central to an inquiry about stars' contemporary meanings.

This essay explores the importance of lover-subjects in Japanese fictional media who are also the beloved icons of Japan's contemporary media culture. It sees stars as an industrial-cultural phenomenon whose meanings are situated within specific historical, cultural, media, and dramaturgical conditions. Japanese stars can easily be dismissed as one-dimensional figures because of their conspicuous habitation of a supposedly postmodern image culture.[1] Popular representations of lovers are treated as shoddy copies of Western ideals or noticed only when positioned as the exotic object of Western spectatorship in film and cultural writings.[2] Nevertheless, the lovers in pulp *manga* and TV dramas have been, for a long time, the shared cultural intake of women and men in Japan and, more recently, of young, middle-class, urban dwellers throughout East Asia.[3] Fans and audiences often address the heroes and heroines as intimate acquaintances and are inspired to reflect on their own vigor as human beings.

The Japanese lovers I focus on in this essay are not exotic, timeless, or sacrificially terrific. They are ordinary, short-lived, and capricious. They are from the prime-time TV dramas of the 1990s, an era in which dramaturgical lovers were most passionately generated by the Japanese culture industries. Being onscreen lovers in this context shaped the experience of many celebrities in an interesting way. Stars who emerged and stayed remembered in the 1990s were in a crucial aesthetic development on Japanese TV known as *ren'ai dorama* (love stories) whose narrativity and durability also provided relatively secure economic conditions for average actors seeking continuous and intertextual exposure.[4] *Ren'ai dorama* is an important melodramatic vehicle through which stars are humanized, celebrated, and thereby constructed in Japan. The vehicle's televisuality and dramaturgicality invite rumination on the relationship between media representations and the authenticity of the characters. After all, the lover is one of the most engaging characters one can en/act because loving itself is a prized capacity of human beings.

Why dramatize love through television and stars? Why humanize stars through television and drama? These two questions state this essay's theoretical curiosity. In the discussion that follows, I shall relate the structural emergence of lovers in the 1990s to (1) Japan's star history and culture, (2) televisual fictions' melodramatic narratives and genres, and (3) the recent cultural production of love in the culture industries. Using the 1998 drama *Kamisama, Mō Sukoshi Dake* (God, Give Me Just a Little More) as an exemplar, I hope to illustrate *ren'ai dorama* as a dynamic nexus on which stardom, lovers, and the culture industries conflate and privilege the experience, stylization, and humanization of love.

HISTORICAL AND CULTURAL MEANINGS OF STARS IN JAPAN

One place to begin our historicization of stars in Japan is the language used to denote them, words such as *tarento* (talent), *suta-* (star), and *aidoru* (idol). The emergence of this lexicon of celebrity was contingent on the dynamics of the overlapping culture industries in Japan. *Tarento*, the all-purpose entertainer, entered the popular lexicon during the "era of television" between 1954 and 1964. *Aidoru* reached its height of recognition in the 1970s and 1980s owing to the booming pop music and TV industries. A review of the stars featured on the covers of *Myōjō* (Stars)—an entertainment monthly published since 1952—reveals a broad shift in the industry's perception of stars. In the 1950s, those who graced the magazine's covers were mostly film actresses who embodied the new bourgeois ideal of femininity.[5] Forty and fifty years later young male idols and talents under the management of

Johnny's and Associates, such as SMAP, V6, and Arashi, dominated the covers.[6] The following section illustrates television's ascendancy as the primary culture industry in Japan to create stars.

Problematizing "Film" Stars

In light of the proliferation of multitalents—a star concept that breaks down genre and media boundaries—John Ellis's thesis of "stars as a cinematic phenomenon" seems to ring true only in particular histories.[7] Certainly, Japanese actors continue to appear in films, but the Japanese film industry has lost its legitimacy to create stars. Yoshinaga Sayuri, who has made over one hundred screen appearances in the past fifty years, may embody the idealized Japanese "film star." As Nikkatsu Studio's most precious star-actress in the 1960s, she established her graceful screen presence through numerous dying-for-love roles.[8] The appearance of a kimono-clad Yoshinaga promoting liquid crystal TVs in Sharp's campaign in the 2000s may startle those who read it as a film actress's capitulation to the small screen. But Yoshinaga was never just a film star. Her dramatic and commercial roles in the televisual media gave her a concrete presence in Japanese popular culture and destabilized the absolute star-inscribing role of the cinematic apparatus.[9]

The same can be argued for Yoshinaga's contemporary, Ishihara Yūjiro. In his discussion of the phenomenal *taiyōzoku* (the "sun tribe" and the ultimate signifier of angry young men in the 1960s) star, Michael Raine calls attention to Yūjiro's status as a "multimedia star whose celebrity exceeded any particular medium."[10] In his early career, the *taiyōzoku* film narratives and the surrounding parallel texts popularized his sexual physique and defiant attitude. Later, suggests Raine, it was music that brought Yūjiro to broader and more enduring fame. Within this otherwise very sophisticated treatment of the media-celebrity relationship, television is regrettably overlooked. During this period in Japan, television became a common household item and a novel source of entertainment, a development that apparently upset Yūjiro's attempt to revive his film career in the mid-1960s. Despite his initial contempt for TV dramas, he gave memorable performances in detective serials such as *Taiyō ni Hoero* (Howl at the Sun!).[11] His role as a reticent, heavy-built police chief who quietly nurtures and disciplines his hot-blooded subordinates made him a prototypical police chief in the age of television. The serial also made him a common cultural icon across generations.[12]

Although it seems logical to blame the disappearance of film stars in Japan on the ascendancy of television, this structural diagnosis grounded to an assumed industrial totality lacks a holistic sensitivity to how stars in Japan have historically been a construction of multiple cultural and media narratives. In other words, the industrial totality surrounding stars is not a zero-sum game between film and television. There is a need to acknowledge that star formation takes on new trajectories and meanings in the changing media culture.

The Idolization of Tarento

Tarento is a distinctive manifestation of the Japanese TV culture. The term was first promoted by magazine weeklies and monthlies in the 1960s to describe personalities in television shows, commercials, and politics.[13] Yoshimoto has suggested that *tarento* functions as a money sign whose circulation sustains the cultural economy of contemporary Japan.[14] *Tarento*, which derives from *talent* in English, is an eerily appropriate word choice for image labor in late capitalism. As a monetary and weight measure in ancient Greece, the talent was routinely used to calculate the value of a person's service, property, and income. The quantifiable nature of *tarento* marks the beginning of a star's worth in the televisual age. To grasp the way contemporary stars in Japan are organized economically and symbolically, we must turn to the intertextual modes of star making in an era in which the Japanese television industry commands leadership in the presence of other competitive culture industries. In this context, the rise of the *aidoru* (idol) as a commodified *tarento* in the 1980s was significant.

If *tarento* is a fundamental labor component of the Japanese entertainment and televisual industries, *aidoru* can be considered its exemplary commodified form. Japan's idol boom, argues Inamasu in *Aidoru no kōgaku* (Manufacturing idols), developed against the backdrop of an accommodating and strengthening televisual medium.[15] Yamaguchi Momoe and Matsuda Seiko—the iconic female idols in the 1970s and 1980s, respectively—are phenomenal figures that entered into the formation of a Japanese TV culture that was beginning to exercise powerful modes of incorporation. Yamaguchi was "born on" NTV's talent-scouting show, *Star Tanjo!* (A Star is Born!). The show represents Japanese television's earliest attempt to generate its own talents to compete with the major talent agencies, which at the time had a firm hold on the generation of both entertainment content and artists.[16] By televising the frantic talent audition, *Star Tanjo!* challenged talent agencies' dominance while at the same time capitalizing on the effect of authenticity from the program's live publicity.[17] Like most idols of her generation, Yamaguchi was a singing idol. But during her glorious eight-year idol career she also became a heroine in what would be seen today as prototypical idol dramas. An important dramatic illusion that sustained Yamaguchi's idol legend was the *Akai* (Red) television series, in which she played a leukemia-stricken young woman who faces one mind-boggling tragedy after another. Yamaguchi's desire to return to a life less extraordinary and her resolute abandonment of her career at age twenty upheld the fairy tale of stardom gracefully.

It would not be until the 1980s that television and the idol's mutual reflexivity reached the effect of full-blown commodification. The media and culture industries seized the power to define idols through an increasingly self-conscious style of production. Japanese television was populated, quite literally, with *tarento* or amateurs "playing" idols. Matsuda Seiko, in particular, embodied television's reflexive figure to flaunt the fictionality of idols. She exemplifies a career idol whose multiple and interweaving narratives on and off the screen, such as her permanent *burikko* (a woman who acts cute) image, her fairy tale marriage in 1985 to actor Kanda Masaki, and her whirlwind romances around the globe fractured the coherent idol legend familiar to a previous generation.[18] Rather than preserving the front- and backstage distinction in her personae, Seiko proudly embraces her life character as a permanent cute idol.[19]

The Industrial Reembodiment and Disembodiment of Tarento

Japan in the 1980s experienced a heightened awareness of idols in its popular culture thanks to the promotional power and everyday presence of the television industry and its close interactions with other culture industries (talent agencies, recording companies, advertising agencies, and so on). A variety of television genres now contended to exhibit talents, making way for a new breed of idols in the 1990s that arose from predominantly visual materials intended for mass consumption. They ranged from fresh-faced models to erotic teen girls posing and smiling in sports and entertainment weeklies, magazine spreads, print ads, personal photo albums (*shashinshū*), and commercials.[20] Symptomatic of image societies, the so-called gravure idols often turned to the familiar institution of television to generate real-life resonance.[21]

The phenomenal superidol musical group Morning Musume aptly illustrates the materiality of Japanese idols as they are assembled and fragmented by television's cultural and economic processes. Nicknamed "citizens' idols" (*kokumin no aidoru*), the members of this polymorphous girl group dutifully play their role as the nation's surrogate daughters (*musume*) by crooning therapeutic songs, staging spectacular extravaganzas, and serving as marketing role models.[22] Their ongoing proliferation in the televisual space is more than display though. As Stevens and Hosokawa argue, it has become a common practice for music stars to sport pseudo-private and "normal" lives on TV for a knowing audience.[23] Japanese stars who maintain huge popularity over the years, such as Sanma Akashiya and Masami Hisamoto, are dubbed personalities because they deploy an identifiable persona across genres and situations.[24] Even the pretty boy (*bishonen*) talents of Johnny and Associates have, starting from SMAP in the 1990s, dropped the usual princely act of idols and vigorously transformed themselves into stock characters in comedies, variety shows, and genres that are more intimately synchronized with the compartmentalized everyday rhythms of the viewers.[25] The televisual space as a whole in Japan constitutes an indispensable arena of star exhibition that also requires performers to engage with reembodiment (personality making and authenticity building) and disembodiment, which involve a versatile presence, plural membership identities, and role playing in fantastic scenarios.

In the historical contexts of Japanese televisual media, talents and idols manifest stars' cultural as well as economic subjectivities. No matter how famous they become, their role as talent and/or idol will not disappear into a hierarchy of positions but will be compounded by more professional titles such as actress, singer-songwriter, and comedian. In *manga* artist Catherine Ayako's humorous caricature columns, all celebrities—from Matsuda Seiko and SMAP to Julia Roberts—are shrunk to the same cute size and commented on in a tongue-in-cheek style.[26] When transposed to the televisual context of Japan, foreign stars from the West undergo instant miniaturization and banalization by appearing in advertisements for everyday consumer goods such as canned coffee (Winona Ryder), jeans (Brad Pitt), and plum spirits (Meg Ryan). The mystique ascribed to film stars thus requires rethinking, for media celebrities are not the prerogative creation of any one medium or industry. In fact, along with the new product identities stars can now be associated within an intertextual, decentralized cultural environment, and television emerges as both a modern social institution and a postmodern image corridor. The televisual media in Japan encompass an alluring environment in which stars—not just television stars—can be constituted.

THEORIZING STARDOM
THROUGH THE MELODRAMATIC VEHICLE

Here I wish to challenge the "personality" thesis, which creates a "separate but equal" identity for television stars out of an assumption that television is ideological because of its accessibility, familiarity, and celebration of individuals.[27] I find it important to locate a shared vocabulary between film and television in star criticism because, first of all, noncinematic intertextual materials (for example, public appearances and celebrity journalism) sustain—along with film narratives—a star's authenticity. Second, Japan's postmodern media culture deserves a constructive rather than imitative voice in the general development of star criticism. Both film and television deploy narrative economies for the construction of star authenticity or the make-believe discourse of a star's appeal.[28] Coupled with a particular structure of viewing, such as the privatized spectatorship and disjointed glances in the mundane everyday, the narrative vehicles address the viewers intimately through what Margaret Morse calls "the fiction of discourse."[29] Well-established characters in soap operas, for example, bond with the popular culture and audience through parallel and interweaving narratives.[30]

The melodramatic imagination of soap operas, in particular, has been central to various feminist claims to subjectivities.[31] While soap opera has matured into a cultural institution in television studies and feminist media studies, it has remained relatively quiet on the possible relationship among characterization, genre, and the making of public subjectivities. Dramatic characters are rarely given the "star treatment" not only because they are assumed to exist only "grammatically" within the tragic narrative structure but also because they are played by actors who are rarely known outside their roles. Projected unproblematically to soap operas around the world, this teleological paradigm precludes precisely the search for the subject of enunciation in melodramatic televisual representations rooted in a different modernity.[32] In Roland Barthes's structural analysis of narratives, characters are defined not as "being" but as "participants" who are permitted by the narrative structure to undertake a limited range of actions such as love and communication.[33] In the world of literary analysis, Barthes turned to linguistics to identify such agency. In dealing with Japanese televisual texts, the production of the romantic genre mediates the material and symbolic structure for idols and their figural enunciation.

During what was termed the "idol recession," television dramas in Japan became *aidoru*'s lifeline.[34] Trendy dramas in the late 1980s emerged as a conspicuous program type to command a large pool of idols. Originally coined by a television weekly in the late 1980s, "trendy drama" as a generic label has gained popular currency outside the Japanese television industry. Trendy drama is known for its excessive use of idols, fashion, pop music, narrative formulas, and emotionality. Such excess resonates with Japan's burst bubble economy, the imploded boundaries in popular culture, and the aesthetic pursuit of overstatement typical of the period. It makes Japanese trendy drama melodramatic and historically specific even though the story unfailing tells of the search of love and friendship in settings characteristic of the bubble economy, that is, metropolitan Tokyo and the sites of its chic lifestyles. While dramas today can still aim for the trendy style with the right mix of elements, the effect is nostalgic rather than realistic. On several occasions, a famous television producer known for his successful involvement in trendy drama underlined the obsolescence of the term.[35] This points to the need to go beyond ephemeral program types and search instead for a generic vocabulary rooted in enduring cultural and television production.

Trendy drama's capacity to stage enchantment demystifies the assumption that television is a more mundane than spectacular medium. Particularly relevant to my concern is the fact that the emergence of trendy dramas set an important precedent as narrative economies that not only commanded the *tarento* workforce across generations but also transformed them in visually and narratively dazzling display windows. It is difficult to imagine trendy dramas without idols. Even the "post–trendy dramas" have become cast-centered, star-driven productions. The writers in my research[36] and the fieldwork of Gabriella Lukacs (see her essay in this volume) have confirmed the growing consciousness of the influence of stars on stories and characters.

It is here that I wish to foreground the love story (*ren'ai dorama*) as a generic umbrella to address the inadequate category of trendy dramas as well as the vagueness of post–trendy-dramas. One reason to turn to love stories as a genre is that they break the urban-rural divide assumed in trendy dramas and allow an articulation between stars and characters by introducing the recurring lover as the subject of enunciation. Romance has been a major theme in Japanese television dramas, but it was not until the 1990s that its discursive value was fully discovered and exploited as a cultural commodity. The *ren'ai dorama* (love story) is characterized by its distinctive televisual storytelling, which, under the industrial logic of television production, has yielded—season after season—substantial modern tales inspiring, moving, and arousing journeys to love. The *ren'ai dorama* of the 1990s entered Japan's popular discourse of love, often serving as a benchmark of or manual for romantic experiences. In the history of Japanese television drama, there is no shortage of memorable love stories dating back to the afternoon melodramas for housewives known as *hiru mero* in the 1950s. While carrying on the familiar narrative of love, *ren'ai dorama* was shaped through a historical-industrial process that took place within contemporary Japan's self-reflexive culture industries.

THE CULTURAL PRODUCTION OF LOVE

The "turn to love" in Japan's television industry in the late 1980s and early 1990s is best understood in conjunction with the commodification of scriptwriters. As the leading production bodies of this period, television networks, notably Fuji TV and TBS, facilitated a dynamic milieu in which writers could develop a professional identity hinged on the success of love stories. Through contests and social networking, the networks recruited young writers and offered them opportunities to work with a core creative team consisting typically of a producer and, occasionally, a director. As they were courted, the writers' creative intentionality was molded through constant negotiations of shared cultural tastes and professional histories and knowledge. For example, writers and producers of this period drew on trendy drama's experience in the portrayal of group romance.

Still, the input of young writers changed the implications of love stories. They foregrounded the emotional and psychological interiority of the main heroines and heroes so that the story is not mere formulaic execution of, say, a love triangle or adultery. Writers, producers, and audiences share an understanding of narrative tricks and shortcuts. Emotional love confessions—such as crying and yelling *"suki da"* (I love you), running to reach the beloved, the juxtaposition of deep gazes, and the calculated use of background music—are some of the common dramaturgical techniques employed. They are over the top by today's standards, but they establish the materiality of *ren'ai dorama* by helping the creators tackle the craft of story making. Drama workers routinely reproduce and subvert trade skills and professional knowledge, thus adding a reflexive dimension to what seems to be an uncomplicated methodological question.

Few writers see scriptwriting as uninhibited work. As often as writers and producers talk about heroes and heroines as fiction, they never work with empty ideals. Experienced writers, in particular, internalize this production reality and generate stories and characters in a reflexive, messy, and intertextual environment. While knowing that they reproduce and commodify experiences and emotions, writers and producers have sought to confirm the practicality and authenticity of love stories. Writers who have been lionized by the media constantly express the exigency to pursue a larger and more humanistic goal rather than aiming for the ideological effect of a love story. The producer Kurihara Miwako, for example, emphatically called love "a big deal" to back up her unrelenting search for the ideal male lead in a production.[37] The writer Mizuhashi Fumie approaches love stories as human stories rather than stock formulas.[38] Even for Kitagawa Eriko, whose unparallel *ren'ai dorama* track record in the 1990s has led her to mock herself as the "authority originator" of cute heroines and desirable heroes, representing love via lovers commands hard work and conviction in the lover's subjectivity.[39] These creators seem to be making a distinction between a melodramatic and a poignant love story. The former is devoid of an empathetic view of the lover as a subject and mocks the lover's subordination to the text's discursive control. The latter, while still as likely to trigger the "false consciousness" criticism, deserves a closer look because it connotes a different set of concerns about love stories as a specific form of expression in Japan.

The Lover as a Reflexive Creation and Role

How is poignancy—defined here as respect for subjective human emotions—constructed in *ren'ai dorama*? It begins with the creation of a subject capable of love. In *ren'ai dorama*, drama workers have developed a narrative and visual language for representing a lover's birth and rebirth. A star's name is quite enough to trigger a story conference between the writer and producer, leading to a character and scenario. This is because the name evokes a history of roles and performances that inform their current project. Drama creators are conditioned to research star representations and images in order to locate new character and narrative possibilities. The cultural reality that gives lover ideals any meaning at all is thus the intertextual discourse of the *tarento*.

Commenting on sources of inspiration for her dramas, Kitagawa suggests that the *tarento* discourse is at least as important as the received cannon of age-old fairy tales in providing examples of model lovers.

> Come to think of it, the first love stories that touched us were movies and television dramas. The stories that were read to us when we were little—the sleeping beauty who wakes up to a prince's kiss, for example—are standard texts. A model of love naturally involves a prince and a princess. In a drama, it would be Ishida Ayumi, Furuya Ikko, and Yamaguchi Momoe and Miura Tomokazu. . . . We grow up to anticipate a handsome man and a beautiful woman falling in love in a dazzling, rosy world.[40]

In the production of *ren'ai dorama*, the search for the "golden couple" has become the foremost concern of both producers and writers. While social bonds and work history allow certain drama creators to demand the labor of a particular star, the schedules of individual *tarento*, the result of delicate negotiations between talent agencies and the conditions of the performance, are more likely to dictate the performers' availability. Drama creators must therefore quickly learn to make the evolving *tarento* discourse their creative resource.

Developing the lover-subject is arguably one of the drama creators' most important jobs. But lovers in *ren'ai dorama* are not always big celebrities, at least not at first. Memorable lovers are works of collaboration that help move the story to its end in a closed narrative structure. Celebrity discourses, which fuse talents' continuous "life movies" with their performances in fictional television, can impact a love story's direction.[41] Creating a character capable of love is a common undertaking among scriptwriters. Given the importance and values accorded to a script in drama production, the search for tomorrow's lover takes shape first in a script.

In some cases the distinctiveness of a particular role becomes a vehicle for stardom. The rise of Fukada Kyōko, for instance, has been credited to her first dramatic role on *Kamisama, Mō Sukoshi Dake* (1998) as a sixteen-year-old schoolgirl who contracted HIV through a specific kind of prostitution problem among youth in Japan known as *enjokōsai*. In situations in which the *tarento*'s public image history has just begun to evolve, sudden stardom is easily attributed to the ingenuity of the creators or to natural-born star quality. The point is not to make a distinction between "star-making roles" and "role-carrying stars" but to notice how the tension between the celebrity and the character is naturalized.

Ren'ai dorama foregrounds lovers as individuals who experience inner growth as they develop the capacity to love another individual. The "emergence of the lover" is at the heart of *ren'ai dorama*'s reflexive narrativity. Anthony Giddens has raised an interesting point regarding romantic love, which he sees as encouraging "self-interrogation."[42] Questions such as "How do I feel about the other and vice versa, and do we have a future together," he argues, offer individuals an alternative sphere of integration that can outcompete societal and familial definitions of an individual. His view on romantic love places the individual in a creative new space. It helps us locate *ren'ai dorama*'s aesthetic and narrative concern: the process of becoming a lover.

In *ren'ai dorama*, the lover traverses a great emotional distance to confess his or her love and embraces the risks accompanying the new journey. This syntagmatic process also drives the character relationship (a paradigmatic dimension) to change for the sake of the lover-subject. The power of this genre lies precisely in its insistence on storytelling and on its irreducibility, two conditions that allow an individual to develop a distinctively private, creative, and bold sense of existence.

CASE STUDY: "GOD, GIVE ME JUST A LITTLE MORE . . ."

The Japanese culture industries have a systematic method for making lover-subjects. Within the narrative economy of love stories, drama creators fashion love into a self-righteous state of existence and a lover into an ideational and idealized human being. Using the drama *Kamisama, Mō Sukoshi Dake* as both an intrinsic and general case study of *ren'ai dorama*, I will elaborate the televisual construction of the lover and the relationships between the lover and the beloved, which can be interpreted at two levels: one within the dramatic performance of the heroine (Masaki) and hero (Keigo); and the other within the popular culture performance of the actress, Fukada Kyōko. In a way, this 1998 drama about a high school girl who contracts HIV represents a typical love story surrounding ordinary characters in contemporary Japanese society in search of a meaningful life. The premise of the story draws on a long melodramatic tradition in Japan's television history, containing sickness, accidents, bullying, the breakdown of the family, and other tragedies. Its predictability, however, does not undercut its capacity to celebrate love. On the contrary, the premise of mortality serves to intensify the primacy of love.

A Character in Production: The Sick and Troubled Schoolgirl

First, let us consider how the protagonist was framed during the initial stage of the production at Fuji TV, a commercial network known for its youthful and trendy image. In-house producer Koiwai Hiroyoshi came to writer Asano Taeko with the request to create a pitiable heroine who not only dies of AIDS but also catches the HIV virus through an *enjokōsai* (escort service), a social problem that was receiving much media attention at the time. Asano turned to books, documentaries, and investigative reportage to create a composite of a believable troubled schoolgirl of seventeen. In melodramas, characters are often ideological, compelled to play the cards they are dealt. Masaki's character belongs to this tradition even though the writer strove for a touch of social realism. Even the character's decision to engage in casual prostitution speaks of inevitability because it justifies her need to see her idol in live concert. While other—possibly more tragic—plots such as contracting HIV through a blood transfusion were considered, using *enjokōsai* lends a sense of social urgency given its association with unruly femininity and sexuality.[43]

Masaki embodies multiple social roles—bad student, reckless teen, unruly child in a well-off, middle-class, suburban family—and is subjected to a variety of moral beatings. Throughout the drama, these roles are played out in her relationship with her parents, particularly with her conservative father, who painfully comes to realize that Masaki has a mind of her own outside the authority of school, parents, and doctors. Such forms of social power provide the grounds for her to unflinchingly proclaim, "I troubled no one to replace the lost tickets to my idol's concert, and I made the decision to have unprotected sex with a stranger."[44] Hereafter the drama provides room for the development of the heroine's viewpoint. The story prioritizes the empathic question, "What is important to Masaki now that her days are numbered?"

Recentered Subjectivity: Becoming a Lover

The subject articulated through the drama's televisual representation is the subjectivity of a lover. *Kamisama* is a complete love story in the sense that what is told televisually in the drama's twelve episodes is the birth and death of a lover rather than a social commentary on schoolgirl prostitution or living with AIDS. Without discounting the social resonance, its overall inattention to the problem of AIDS and *enjokōsai* is precisely why it is problematic for some. The story is told of the young heroine's dreary school life in which the only fun seems to take place after school in the public restroom, on street corners, and with a karaoke box.

Like millions of young girls, Masaki finds hope in the music by pop producer Keigo. When she spots him after a concert, she dashes for a chance to meet him by running after his van in the rain. When the van stops for a traffic light, she runs up to a nearby skywalk and dramatically (with the help of pouring rain, slow-motion editing, and Luna Sea's wailing *I For You*) unfolds a handmade cloth banner that reads "I Love Keigo." Masaki's stereotypical behavior means little to the indifferent Keigo, who makes a habit of mocking his fans backstage for their hysteria. Before their one-night stand, he questions Masaki about the sincerity of her banner message, saying, "You don't know the first thing about me; how can you say 'I love you?'"[45] Expressing her belief in the authenticity of his music, she says, "I may not know what you are like every day, but I know that you are searching for a place of belonging in your music."[46] Keigo denies it, but he sits submissively on the bed and lets her caress his head, assuming the place of a hurt child in need of maternal healing. Their initial encounter is simultaneously dreamy and honest. In the beginning, Masaki's love for Keigo is an excessive and unconditional kind of worship that expects nothing in return. The direct engagement with him produces a new subjective experience that changes the quality of her existence. For instance, her best friend notices her suddenly chirpy behavior at school. The change is not a reaction to the HIV-positive condition. The difference begins from the interior world of Masaki, a lover-subject in the making through her reflexive development of a new awareness that there is an alternative place of being or belonging. As she puts it passionately to Keigo, "It's true. It's true that I didn't know anything about the feeling of liking someone . . . not until I met you. I took my life for granted. Then I met you, and I risked everything to love you."[47] The confession marks the birth of Masaki as a lover.

Narrative techniques such as narration and conversation and plot devices such as confessions and fights consistently allow articulations of the lover-subject as in other *ren'ai dorama*. In *Kamisama*, this is reflected in Masaki's evolving relationships with Keigo, her family, and her friends, though not so much in the sense that she must win approval from the people around her. Rather, it is the significant people in her life who must learn to see her in a new light. And, since the new self as the lover isn't self-apparent and is metamorphosing through everyday realities, the new understanding must be negotiated through a wide array of communicative actions with individuals other than the couple in love. An example from *Kamisama* is a conversation between a disheartened Masaki and her mother, whose own extramarital love affair has given her the rare perspective to see Masaki as a lover in progress rather than merely a wayward daughter.[48]

> MASAKI: A [sick] kid like me probably shouldn't ask for more, even if I've got someone dear to my heart . . .
>
> MOTHER: I think it's great that you found someone to love. That alone is a wonderful thing, don't you think? You may run into all these dreadful troubles. But as long as you remember that you love someone, won't you feel encouraged by it?

Creating Reflexivity through Montage

In *ren'ai dorama*, the unfailing action to take for the evolving lovers is to express, declare, and utter their love. These enduring efforts constitute a different constellation of a "lover's discourse," which, in Roland Barthes's conception, is a collection of descriptive utterances that render visible the structuring of the amorously speaking "I."[49] *Ren'ai dorama* commands a different lover's discourse because of its heterosexual mode of address and the televisual representation of the lover-subjects. The central involvement of writers in a *ren'ai dorama* production is one reason why "verbal" lovers appear in each story, other reasons being television's orality and ordinariness and the strong presence of writers in the history of Japanese television. They speak reflexively, rhythmically, colloquially, poetically, silently, and philosophically. For analytical purpose they speak visually, musically, and verbally. Words and pictures are powerful building blocks for meaning making in this world and, by the same token, for human reflexivity. The standard montage editing in *ren'ai dorama* has been an effective device in visualizing *omoi* (feelings and thoughts). Although the camera can convey a character's emotion with a still shot of the face, a montage takes the spectator into the lover's interiority and allows the viewer to experience a dimension situated squarely in the lover's subjectivity. One of the montages in *Kamisama* illustrates Keigo's *omoi* for Masaki, triggered by a note she left after their one-night stand. The visual and audio encoding are summarized in table 1.

The fragments and scenes used in this montage to express Keigo's personal thoughts of Masaki come from a finite source of dramatic scenes presumably shared by the fictional characters, the creators, and the audience. The flashbacks are not Keigo's alone because as a character he is a dramaturgical construction whose thoughts and activities are not possible outside the drama. However, as a routine and affective device to jog the memories of the audience, montage also provides what Raymond Williams

TABLE 1. Montage sequence in *Kamisama, Mo Sukoshi Dake*

Visual Track	Audio Track
Medium shot of Keigo reading the note in his study.	(Voice-over Masaki): Thank you for last night. I know you weren't serious about it when you said that you picked me out of two-thousand-some girls. But I was still flattered.
Cut to slightly slow-motioned flashbacks: (1) Masaki running in the rain (2) Masaki unfolding the "I Love Keigo"banner (3) Masaki standing on her hands against the wall in his room (4) Masaki caressing Keigo's head like a mother hugging a child	(Theme song, "I for You," instrumental, orchestra version)
Close-up of Keigo reading the note.	(Voice-over Masaki): Why do you look so sad? (from the scene of their one night stand)
Cut to another slow-motioned flashback sequence: (1) Masaki revealing her feelings after finding out she is HIV positive (2) Masaki running on the street with a stolen poster of Keigo (3) Masaki's HIV speech at her high school	(Voice-over Masaki): To me, falling in love with you is a big event in my life! (from the scene where she finds out about her HIV condition)
Cut to Keigo in the study.	(Voice-over Masaki): Every moment in life has become meaningful . . .

calls "dramatic mobility," a representation capable of carrying emotions and unspoken thoughts across time and space.[50] For example, family rooms and domestic relationships are made public through sitcoms and soap operas. Williams considers the private experience to be the major structure of feelings in television dramas. In Japanese *ren'ai dorama* like *Kamisama*, the "private" feelings exposed through televisual techniques rest on the indispensable construction of the lover. Whether it is a confession of love or a flashback montage, the televisual tactics employed in this genre externalize and prioritize a lover's intentionality. Each gesture demands a unique effort and has a corresponding dramaturgical manifestation. The lover makes constant statements about his or her selfhood through expressions permitted by the convention of *ren'ai dorama* and the Japanese cultural context. The enactment is always more significant in itself than the availability of reciprocation. Even gestures of reciprocation (such as a phone call or a gift) are quickly absorbed into the process of the lover-subject's reflexivity toward a new phase of understanding of the relationship. Although *ren'ai dorama* provides copious happy endings, it confirms Barthes's observation that the lover's discourse is one of "an extreme solitude . . . spoken, perhaps, by thousands of subjects, but warranted by no one."[51]

From Lover-Subject to Beloved Idol

The relational transformation between the couple in *Kamisama*—from idolization as a fan to mutual commitment as lover-subjects—bears an elaborative association with the making of idols in Japan. The drama made sixteen-year-old Fukada Kyōko one the most promising *tarento* in 1998 along with the reigning "fresh face," Hirosue Ryoko, who was well recognized as a translucent, untainted teen idol.[52] It is worth mentioning that *Kamisama* was also the big break for the Taiwanese-Japanese actor Kaneshiro Takeshi, whose image in Japan at the time had been constructed as a Hong Kong film star with a whiff of pan-Asian exoticism. The fact that both actors took a chance playing roles of extraordinary circumstances was the result of measured decision making at the executive and production levels of Fuji TV. Making a drama with elements of AIDS and *enjōkosai* could generate media attention because they were topical and forbidden. But they were perceived as risky publicity by Fuji TV, which was promoting its futuristic new headquarters in Odaiba. Compared to other established *tarento*, Fukada (a newcomer) and Kaneshiro (a foreigner) had little to lose. In fact, because the drama succeeded, Fukada went on to become a regular and major presence in prime-time dramas, showing a capacity early in her career to work collaboratively and cross-culturally with other Asia talents.[53] *Friends* (with

Won Bin) and *Fighting Girl* (with Yoon Son Ha) heralded her facile and much-needed contribution to Japan's embrace of Korean media and popular culture commonly known as "Korean Wave" since the early 2000s.

While the ability to act or sing is not typically privileged in the making of idols, it has emerged as a differentiating niche in the complex idol typologies in Japan. Being in dramas can initiate, sustain, and resurrect stardom. One of the recurring comments on Fukada since her portrayal of Masaki in *Kamisama* is her contemporary and larger than life presence (*sonzaikan*).[54] She plays a convincing high school girl of her times—pragmatic, bold, and raised in a well-off family. What makes her larger than life is her assertive embodiment of a lover-subject culminating in life and death. In many of the dramas she starred in subsequently, notably *To Heart* (1998), *S.O.S* (2001), *First Love* (2002), and *Friends* (2002), she typifies young women (for example, OL, high school student) of her times while articulating, still and evermore, lover-subjects whose radiant and throbbing aliveness is *ren'ai dorama*'s most material output. What I am arguing is that it is possible for an idol to be everywhere in the media culture and yet insubstantial. The larger than life presence of Fukada and other idols turned actresses such as Suzuki Honami, Matsushima Nanako, and Tokiwa Takako has particularly been aided by their representations of lover-subjects in contemporary Japanese televisual fiction. In each individual love story and *ren'ai dorama* as a whole, these stars are the unambiguous heroines and heroes. Engaging in story after story with a refreshed search for one's place and finding it in the embodiment of lover-subjects humanize the stars and earn them indispensable places in Japanese mass culture.

THE LOVER AS THE BRICOLAGE

The work of character reading is a postmodern and political project. It is postmodern because the unitary subjectivity is no longer obtainable. It is political—or at least should be—because a politicized sensitivity liberates the singular desire by allowing readings to proliferate, juxtapose, and contest each other. Japanese television is both a spectacular and ordinary site where one can reflect on questions of humanity. Stevens and Hosokawa have argued that music stars use the chit-chat formats on the music shows to promote their humanity and ordinariness.[55] In this essay I make the claim that Japanese televisual love stories (*ren'ai dorama*) in the 1990s became a crucial cultural vehicle through which talents could be humanized. In the star-studded *ren'ai dorama*, they articulated a unique and common cultural figure: the lover-subject.

The lover-subject is always situated in a private narrative engendered through reflexivity and actions. Thus, no two lovers (especially in relation to each other) make quite the same televisual statements, echoing Barthes's contention that the fragments of a lover's discourse are "distributional" rather than "integrative."[56] Despite the possibility of deducing a narrative formula from the heap of love stories, the practice would only uncover the lover function rather than the lover-subject. It might locate the ideological pulse of the genre, but it will miss the qualitative transformation within the character, thus never seeing the ethical implications of "becoming a lover."

In her work on an ethical gender relation, the French philosopher Luce Irigaray attaches great importance to love. By critiquing Georg Hegel's theory of labor of love and French sociolinguistics, she suggests that "I love to you" may elucidate a more nonreductive relation between man and woman, for the *to* mediates what was originally a subject-object relation and encourages communication, not consumption, between two singularities. She further situates this relation in our global context:

> [W]hen this globality and universality [of culture] are now ungovernable and beyond our control, making us divided and torn between differing certainties, opinions, dreams or experiences, it seems appropriate to return to what is governable by us here and now: love.[57]

"Here and now" deserves particular emphasis because it obliges us to qualify the particular temporalities and spatialities to which we are committed. In most advanced industrialized locations, the question of how to participate in a unified project such as modernization or globalization is becoming increasingly difficult to answer or refuse. But what remains an attainable goal may just be that of the lover-subject.

Why is Japanese television, and not Japanese film or American television, the site of such inspiration? Having researched the influence of the American prime-time soap opera *Dallas* during its peak in the world, Ien Ang is only too aware of the decline of the melodramatic imagination in the West, especially when the imagination is juxtaposed with popular Japanese love stories that demonstrate the unwavering pursuit of romance and love.[58] Despite the abundant output of contemporary romantic comedies and television series in the American television and film industries, there is little analysis of love as a serious and philosophical issue. Mark C. Henrie's *Doomed Bourgeois in Love* attempts to take up the subject of love in the films of Whit Stillman within the knowing sensibility that the only way to represent love meaningfully in popular films these days is through self-aware ironies and comedies.[59] Stillman certainly knows the degeneration of love, for the characters in his films use irony as a way to deal with the passing of their class (the urban haute bourgeoisie) and values such as happiness and duty in love.

The postmodern ennui since the bubble economy burst has left ample room for the pursuit of new—even cynical—narrative flights in Japan. In the final analysis the persistent construction of lover-subjects may have its roots in the professional, commercial, and competitive Japanese culture industries. This is not to say that the drama creators made it a goal to realize the "lover project" in each production. Quite the contrary, the drama writers, producers, and actors could only have been spinning new stories from a shared discourse with elements from Hollywood films, old Japanese television dramas, other popular cultural texts, and their own familiarity with and involvement in the making of popular entertainment. Relatively free of the educational burden of public television and the film industries' financial fiasco, commercial productions provided a place for young creators to foreground love. In *ren'ai dorama*, we see fragments of Hollywood's romantic comedies, manga-like acting, poetic self-confession, and nuanced scenes reflecting irreducible experiences. Creating lovers was probably not the collective goal of TV drama creators when they first entered television production, but lover-subjects have emerged as a practical and unique solution— a bricolage—to their "here-and-now" problem.

NOTES

1. Roland Barthes, *Empire of Signs,* trans. Richard Howard (New York: Hill and Wang, 1982); William Gibson, *Idoru* (New York: G. P. Putnam's Sons, 1997).

2. Kenji Sato, "People Who Can Only Play at Love," *Japan Echo* 20, no. 4 (winter 1993): 69–76; Nicholas Bornoff, *Pink Samurai: Love, Marriage, and Sex in Contemporary Japan* (New York: Pocket Books, 1991).

3. Lisa Leung, "Romancing the Everyday: Hong Kong Women Watching Japanese *Dorama,*" *Japanese Studies* 22, no. 1 (April 2002): 65–75; Ming-tsung Lee, "Traveling with Japanese TV Dramas: Cross-Cultural Orientation and Flowing Identification of Contemporary Taiwanese Youth," in Koichi Iwabuchi, ed., *Feeling Asian Modernities: Transnational Consumption of Japanese TV Dramas*, 129–54 (Hong Kong: Hong Kong University Press, 2004); Fabienne Darling-Wolf, "Virtually Multicultural: Trans-Asian Identity and Gender in an International Fan Community of a Japanese Star," *New Media and Society* 6, no. 4 (2004): 507–28.

4. Such stars included Suzuki Honami, Suzuki Kyōko, Oda Yūji, Kimura Takuya, Yamaguchi Tomoko, Tokiwa Takako, and Matsushima Nanako.

5. The inaugural cover featured Tsushima Keiko. Others included Hara Setsuko, Wakao Ayako, Kishi Keiko, and Yamamoto Fujiko.

6. Myōjō Henshubu, *Myōjō 50nen 601mai no Hyoshi* [50 Years and 601 Covers of *Myōjō*] (Tokyo: Keieisha, 2002).

7. John Ellis, *Visible Fictions* (London: Routledge and Kegan Paul, 1982).

8. Mark Schilling, *The Encyclopedia of Japanese Pop Culture* (New York: Weatherhill, 1997), 306.

9. Since 1957, Yoshinaga has been building a continuous repertoire of television drama performance. She has appeared in long series (*Maboroshi Tantei* [1959–60], *Ayu no Uta* [1979], and *Kaze to Kumo to Niji to* [1976]) as well serials and single plays. J. Shinshi, "Yoshinaga Sayuri Home Page," http://homepage3.nifty.com/fwhj5337.

10. Michael Raine, "Ishihara Yūjirō: Youth, Celebrity, and the Male Body in Late-1950s Japan," in Dennis Washburn and Carole Cavanaugh, eds., *Word and Image in Japanese Cinema* (Cambridge: Cambridge University Press, 2001), 203.

11. Schilling, *Encyclopedia of Japanese Pop Culture*, 75.

12. Yoshikawa Kenjiro, ed., *Terebi Dorama Besuto 100* [Best 100 TV Dramas] (Tokyo: Enterbrain, 2001).

13. Okuyama Masuro, *Gendai Ryukōgo Jiten* (Modern Dictionary of Popular Usage) (Tokyo: Tokyodo Shuppan. 1974), 155.

14. Mitsuhiro Yoshimoto, "Image, Information, Commodity: A Few Speculations on Japanese Televisual Culture," in Tang Xiaobing and Stephen Snyder, eds., *In Pursuit of Contemporary East Asian Culture*, (Boulder: Westview 1996), 123–38.

15. Inamasu Tatsuo, *Aidoru Kōgaku* [Engineering Idols] (Tokyo: Mitsumatsudo, 1989), 136–209.

16. Ibid, 137.

17. From 1971 to 1983, *Star Tanjo!* was aired every Sunday as an audition show. From 10:00 A.M. to 6:00 P.M., the show "processed as many as 120 young hopefuls an hour—thirty seconds for each" (Schilling, *Encyclopedia of Japanese Pop Culture*), 296.

18. Ibid, 118.

19. Sharon Kinsella, "Cuties in Japan," in Lise Skov and Brian Moeran, eds., *Women, Media and Consumption in Japan* (Honolulu: University of Hawai`i Press, 1995), 234.

20. Nishino Akihiko, "Nikutai wo Ushinatta Aidoru Tachi," [The Idols who Lost Their flesh] *Hōsō Hihan*, 16 April 1993.

21. Such gravure idols from the 1990s included Miyazawa Rie, Mitsuki Arisa, Tanaka Rina, Yūka, and Shaku Yumiko.

22. Asano Kouyou, *"Mo-Musume" no Keizaigaku* [The Economics of Morning Musume] (Tokyo: OS Shuppansha, 2002); Morinaga Tetsuro, "Mo-musume ga Nihon Keizai wo Sukuu!" [Morning Musume will Save the Japanese Economy!] *Shūkan Hoseki*, 15 June 2000, 47–49.

23. Carolyn S. Stevens and Shuhei Hosokawa, "So Close and Yet So Far: Humanizing Celebrity in Japanese Music Variety Shows, 1960–1990s," in Brian Moeran, ed., *Asian Media Production*, (Surrey: Curzon, 2001), 223–46.

24. "Favorite Male and Female Talent in 2002," NHK Web site, http://www.nhk.or.jp/bunken/book-en/b4-e.html, accessed 1 December 2003, page now discontinued.

25. Yazaki Yoko, *Jyani-zu Rinneron* [The Theory of Reincarnation about Johnny's] (Tokyo: Tada Shuppan, 1996), 143; Komatsu Katsuhiko and Office K., *That's Terebi Dorama '90's* (Tokyo: Daiyamondosha, 1999).

26. Catherine Ayako, *An-an Suta Meikan* [An-an Directory of Stars] (Tokyo: Magazine House, 2001).

27. John Langer, "Television's 'Personality System,'" *Media, Culture, and Society* 3, no. 4 (1981): 351–65; David Lusted, "The Glut of the Personality," in Christine Gledhill, ed., *Stardom: Industry of Desire* (London: Routledge, 1991), 251–58; David P. Marshall, *Celebrity and Power: Fame in Contemporary Culture* (Minneapolis: University of Minnesota Press, 1997).

28. Richard Dyer, "'A Star Is Born' and the Construction of Authenticity," in Christine Gledhill, ed., *Stardom: Industry of Desire*, (London: Routledge, 1991), 132–49.

29. Margaret Morse, "Postsynchronizing Rock Music and Television," in Leah R. Vande Berg and Lawrence A. Wenner, eds., *Television Criticism: Approaches and Applications* (New York: Longman, 1991), 289.

30. Chris Rojek, *Celebrity* (London: Reaktion, 2001).

31. See Tania Modleski, *Loving with a Vengeance: Mass-Produced Fantasies for Women* (New York: Routledge, 1982); Janice Radway, *Reading the Romance: Women, Patriarchy, and Popular Literature* (Chapel Hill: University of North Carolina Press, [1984] 1991; Ien Ang, *Watching Dallas: Soap Opera and the Melodramatic Imagination* (London: Methuen, 2004); Mary Ellen Brown, *Soap Opera and Women's Talk: The Pleasure of Resistance* (Thousand Oaks: Sage, 1994); E. Graham McKinley, *Beverly Hills, 90210: Television, Gender, and Identity* (Philadelphia: University of Pennsylvania Press. 1997).

32. Robert C. Allen, ed., *To Be Continued: Soap Opera around the World* (New York: Routledge, 1995).

33. Roland Barthes, "The Death of the Author," in *Image, Music, Text*, trans. Stephen Heath, (New York: Hill and Wang, 1977), 142–48.

34. Marume Kurōdo, "Mo-musume de Wakaru Gendai" [Understanding Modern Times through Morning Musume]. *Da Ka-Po*, 6 February 2002, 44–67; Kurosumi Hikaru, "90 Nendai Dorama Ga Unda Aidoru Tachi," [Idols Made in 1990s' TV Drama] in Ishida Yoko, ed., *TV Dorama All-File* (Tokyo: Asupekuto, 1999), 16–19.

35. Ōta Toru, *Hittoman: Terebi de Yume wo Uru Otoko* [Hitman: The Man Who Sells Dreams Through Television] (Tokyo: Kadokawa Shoten, 1996); "Producing (Post-) Trendy Japanese TV Dramas," in Koichi Iwabuchi, ed., *Feeling Asian Modernities: Transnational Consumption of Japanese TV Dramas*, trans. Nasu Madori (Hong Kong: University of Hong Kong Press, 2004), 60–86.

36. Eva Tsai, "Empowering Love: The Intertextual Author of *Ren'ai Dorama*," in Koichi Iwabuchi, ed., *Feeling Asian Modernities: Transnational Consumption of Japanese TV Dramas* (Hong Kong: University of Hong Kong Press, 2004), 43–67.

37. Kurihara Miwako, "Kurihara-tisuto wa 'Rabu and Hyuman' kongo wa Hito no Chikara wo Karita Ue de, Watashi ga Shimidereba" [Kurihara Style is built on the power of love and human], in Koiketa Shichimi, ed., *Getsuku Dorama Seishun Gurafiti* (Tokyo: Dobun Shoin, 1999) 218–223.

38. Mizuhashi Fumie, interview with the author, 4 July 2001, tape recording, Shinagawa, Japan.

39. See Tsai, "Empowering Love."

40. Kitagawa Eriko, *Ren'ai Do* [Path of Love] (Tokyo: Kadokawa Shoten, 1996), 11.

41. Neal Gabler, *Life, the Movie: How Entertainment Conquers Reality* (New York: Vintage, 2000).

42. Anthony Giddens, *The Transformation of Intimacy: Sexuality, Love, and Eroticism in Modern Societies* (Cambridge: Polity, 1992), 44.

43. Asano Taeko, interview with the author, 17 April 2001, tape recording, Kamakura, Japan.

44. *Kamisama, Mo Sukoshi Dake* [God, Please Just a Little More], VHS, written by Asano Taeko and produced by Koiwai Hiroyoshi (Tokyo: Fuji TV, 1998).

45. Ibid.

46. Ibid.

47. Ibid.

48. Ibid.

49. Roland Barthes, *A Lover's Discourse: Fragments*, trans. Richard Howard (New York: Penguin, 1977).

50. Raymond Williams, *Television: Technology and Cultural Form* (New York: Schocken, 1974).

51. Barthes, *A Lover's Discourse*, 1.

52. Kitagawa Masahiro and T. P. Rankingu, eds., *Nippon Aaidoru Ttanteidan, 2001* [Japan Idol Detective Team 2001] (Tokyo: Takurajimasha. 2001).

53. She appeared in *Oni no Sumika* (1999), *To Heart* (1999), *Imagine* (2000), *Food Fight* (2000), *S.O.S.* (2001), *Fighting Girl* (2001), *Friends* (2002) *First Love* (2002), *Remote* (2002), *Minami's Girlfriend* (2004), and *My Life After Her Death* (2004).

54. Kitagawa Masahiro et al., *Nippon Aidoru Tanteidan, 2001*.

55. Stevens, and Hosokawa, ""So Close and Yet So Far.""

56. Barthes, *A Lover's Discourse*.

57. Luce Irigaray, *I Love to You: Sketch for a Felicity within History*, trans. Alison Martin (New York": Routledge, 1996).

58. Ien Ang, ""The Cultural Intimacy of TV Drama,"" in *Feeling Asian* Koichi Iwabuchi, ed., *Feeling Asian Modernities: Transnational Consumption of Japanese TV Dramas*, 303–9 (Hong Kong: Hong Kong University Press, 2004), 303–309.

59. Mark C. Henri, ed., *Doomed, Bourgeois in Love: Essays on the Films of Whit Stillman* (Wilmington, Delaware: ISI Books. 2002).

Kind Participation:
Postmodern Consumption and Capital
with Japan's Telop TV

Aaron Gerow

The cultural philosopher Azuma Hiroki has helped rekindle debates on postmodernity in Japan through the publication in late 2001 of his book *Dōbutsukasuru posutomodan* (Animalizing Postmodernity). There he argues that forms of textual production and consumption evident in recent anime and computer texts (games, Web sites, databases, and so on), ones he ties to *otaku* or fan cultures, not only well represent the age of the simulacra and the end of metanarratives postulated by such theorists of postmodernity as Jean Baudrillard and Jean-François Lyotard but also point to a fundamental cultural shift in Japan, finalized in the mid-1990s, which he calls the "age of the animal" (*dōbutsu no jidai*).[1] The argument that present-day *otaku* are no longer "human" in the Enlightenment sense, but essentially animal-like, is both a provocative (though not necessarily negative) statement about contemporary Japanese popular culture and an attempt to historically periodize the contemporary. Azuma's text is aligned with a proliferation of other discourses, both popular and academic, that are attempting to delineate and define the difference of the contemporary moment in Japan using its popular culture, particularly its popular texts, as markers.[2] A number of works, including Azuma's, delineate the contemporary era especially through a particular intersection between textuality and consumption. In such discourses, present-day Japan is defined by a fundamental change in the relation of reception to the text. While Azuma's book does not specifically discuss the television medium (computers are of more interest to him, although television anime is a crucial intertext), other texts do. Ōta Shōichi's

Shakai wa warau (Society Laughs), for instance, concentrates largely on television when discussing how transformations in *manzai* comedy since the 1980s reflect basic shifts in the relationship between textuality and reception and in Japanese society as a whole.[3]

In this essay I will examine a specific televisual intersection of textuality and reception that I believe illuminates some of the issues of power, commodification, and postmodernity involved with present-day Japanese popular culture. I will investigate what, to many observers, is television's most prominent textual trend in the last decade: the use—or to some the overuse—of words and images superimposed on the primary image. The practice is most prominent in variety programming (such as comedy, music, and game shows), but it is also evident in commercials and news, "wide show" or tabloid TV journalism, and educational and even sports programs. It is most often represented by the textual device of rendering visual the words spoken by a performer onscreen, mostly in the form of subtitles. Given the dominance of the variety format in evening programming and the wide show in morning and afternoon schedules, it is safe to say that the majority of programs on Japanese broadcast network television engage in this practice in one form or another. The technical term for such superimposed items is *telop* (in Japanese, *teroppu*), short for "*tel*evision *o*paque *p*rojector," which generally refers to all items, from words to other images, that are superimposed on the main image. I will use the term *telop* here, despite its lack of familiarity, instead of such terms as *subtitle* or *chyron*, because recent television's tendency to combine the use of titles with other superimposed images all over the screen renders such words imprecise.

The use of *telop* itself is not new. It is a basic feature of news and documentary programming, where superimposed titles provide names for news anchors and other figures onscreen, explain the place and time of an event, summarize the basic points of a story, and even sometimes reiterate a statement made by an interviewee, especially if that person speaks Japanese considered difficult to understand. The use of *telop* in such programming has increased in recent years, as even statements made by those speaking standard Japanese are reproduced as words onscreen. International news venues such as the Cable News Network (CNN) and Fox News also offer information other than that conveyed by the anchor through ticker scrolls, but in Japanese television news telop mostly reiterates the words being spoken by the person onscreen. In variety programming, this phenomenon has become even more central. For instance, the late evening variety show *Kibun wa jōjō* (Feeling Good, TBS network), starring the comedy duo Utchan Nanchan (Uchimura Teruhiko and Nanbara Kiyoteru), even went to the extreme of having every single word spoken in its recorded segments—down to the *unhs* and *ahs*—appear on screen in a barrage of words that was not only hard to follow but completely redundant from the standpoint of conveying information.

A critical discourse has already emerged that blames telop for oversignifying, for effectively treating Japanese viewers as "idiots" by repeating what is already obvious.[4] At the same time, observers such as Ōta have tied the increase in telop to a general shift toward viewer participation in television comedy. This vision of participation, coupled with a playful textuality in which television images are always supplemented and reinscribed, intersects with new discourses on postmodern consumption by Azuma and Ōtsuka Eiji that allow telop to potentially be included under the rubric of what Azuma terms "database consumption," in which, after the postmodern loss of metanarratives, reception is fundamentally a factor of retrieving and reshaping data stored in a text that is nothing more than a database. Such conflicting views suggest that telops are not merely a problem of production practice but of the power relations between production and consumption and the shaping of televisual reception itself. Telop, I would argue, complicates the often apolitical and aeconomic analyses of Japanese postmodernists by reminding us of the operations of capital on the processes of signification and the viewer's gaze. In this, telop is only one, perhaps ephemeral instance in larger televisual strategies to commodify the gaze and enlist the viewer in the production of television capital itself.

KIND TELOP

I will first sketch the historical background of telops and some of the functions they perform in contemporary television. Since telops have become a prominent feature of televisual textuality only recently, there is little precise literature on changes in their usage over time. The television critic Sakamoto Mamoru, citing telops as one of the major changes in television in the last fifteen to twenty years, ties their proliferation in variety programming to Nippon Television (NTV) shows from the early 1990s such as the quiz show *Majikaru! Zunō pawā!!* (Magical Brain Power, premiered 1990) and *Susume! Denpa shōnen* (Advance! Electric Youth, premiered 1992) and to their powerful producers, *Majikaru!*'s Gomi Kazuo and Tsuchiya Toshio of *Denpa shōnen*, each of whom has gone on to produce other hit shows that prominently use telops.[5] Yet, while it is true that 1980s programs such as *Oretachi hyōkinzoku* (We're the Clown Tribe, Fuji TV, premiered 1981), arguably the most important comedy variety show of that decade, feature very few telops, it is not as if they were absent in pre-1990 programming. For instance,

119

there is the long-standing practice in fiction programming of using titles to denote characters' and even actors' names on their first screen appearance in a narrative, a usage evident especially in Nihon Hōsō Kyōkai (NHK) period pieces or foreign-made dramatic series or movies. What unifies these and other uses of telops, such as in news programming, is the project of clarity: telops are mobilized to ensure viewer comprehension by summarizing important information, identifying characters, and clarifying what is difficult to understand. They served this function in *Majikaru! Zunō pawā!!* and *Denpa shōnen.* Sakamoto explains that the telops in *Majikaru!* were in effect "kind" (*shinsetsu*) because they picked up muttered and overlapping adlibs by the show's large group of personalities, in effect singling out the funny gags. *Denpa shōnen* was notorious for sending second-rate comedians first into situations without an appointment (for example, when Matsumura Kunihiro visited the Gaza Strip to get Arafat to sing a Japanese kids' song) and later on colossal treks (such as Saruganseki's hitchhike across Asia), but this mixture of reality television and the *tarento* (talent personality) system featured handicams as well as frequent long or voice-off shots. Telops were needed, explains Sakamoto, to supplement the poor sound and the fact that it was not always clear who was speaking and what.

In the ensuing decade, this "kindness" has taken many forms through an expanded range of telop. The most extreme form renders every utterance into telops, confirming it visually through writing on the screen. Such diligence in documenting speech can border on the "unkind" for at some moments there are just too many words to be read completely. That is why the majority of telop programs do not record everything that is said but selectively emphasize only what is deemed important. Such kindness assists viewers not only when several *tarento* talk at once but in underlining what is important narratively or in terms of humor. The degree of selection can vary according to the program; the music and talk show *HEY! HEY! HEY!* (on Fuji) or *Gakkō ni ikō!* (Let's Go to School! on TBS), the latter a variety show starring the teen idol group V6, actually cut out very little, while *Nainai saizu* (Ninety-Nine Size), featuring the comedy duo Ninety Nine, can have thirty seconds of conversation without a dialogue telop. With the former two shows, one can say that the process of emphasis is evident less in what is reproduced as a telop than in the kinds of telops used. Unlike *Nainai saizu,* which sports uniform, staid, if not "tasteful" telops, those in *HEY! HEY! HEY!* or *Gakkō ni ikō!* audaciously stress important words through telops of different colors, sizes, or fonts or even through animation (certain dramatic words wiggle or shake on the screen).[6] Although such varied uses can establish trademark stylistics for a show (both visually and in terms of its humor or mood), selection and emphasis underline how telops more broadly digest and process televisual information. It is not rare to see a television screen on which in one corner there is the show's title, in another the name of the section of the show, and in a third the current topic of conversation in that section, all apart from the dialogue telop. At a glance, one can determine the show and one's place in the narrative. Such digestive telops are an accommodation to channel zapping, working to arrest the viewer's gaze with suggestive topics while enabling him or her to enter the flow of information quickly and with little difficulty.

Telops also facilitate and reward continued viewing by predigesting the program. It is not unusual for telops to prepare the viewer for a turn in the conversation or a gag that will take place several seconds later, thus drawing the audience into the flow.[7] Telops, therefore, do not just exist synchronously with the dialogue but operate diachronically to facilitate the construction and pursuit of the narrative. As such, they are freed from the speech of performers in the show's space to function on behalf of what seems to be a separate, narrative-enunciating presence. This is partly evident through the use of telop images or aberrant graphology. In one episode of the music talk show *Utaban* (Song Show, TBS), for instance, the cohost and comedian Ishibashi Takaaki kids the idol singer Nakazawa Yūko about her dream of marrying, having children, continuing to sing, and pursuing the hobby of glassblowing by standing up and pantomiming doing all at once.

Utaban: Visual telops augmenting the humorous narrative.

Not only do the dialogue telops emphasize the joke he is making, but an animated baby, microphone, and glassblowing pipe are superimposed on him to visually "illustrate" what he is acting out. The narrative enunciation adds visual absurdity to his verbal gag, expanding and amplifying it. As part of this enunciation, dialogue telops can occasionally take on lives of their own, using symbols (such as @, &, =, ÷, and § or あ" and ～, evident in examples from *Gakkō ni ikō!* and *Utaban*) to playfully visualize speech in ways that are both unconventional (the voiced [*dakuon*] あ" does not exist in Japanese phonetics, although one can find it in *manga*) and call attention to the telops as elements not completely tied to speech. A transcendent narrator is most apparent when telops literally function as footnotes to conversation. When Okamura Takashi of Ninety Nine is talking to a chef in an episode of the variety show *Guru guru Nainti Nain* (Round and Round Ninety Nine, NTV), for instance, he blurts out that the cook looks like "Kuwanan." Telops assist not just by picking out Okamura's comment, which was half-buried among other comments by the show's *tarento*, but also by showing a picture of the *tarento* Kuwano Nobuyoshi complete with his full name and nickname, Kuwanan, alongside the close-up image of the chef. This not only explains who Kuwanan is for the uninstructed but visually makes the comparison obvious. One is reminded of an editor producing a concordance of explanatory footnotes to help us read a text. Telops not only add extra text to the program but arch over the show, connecting it to other works in an intertextual network. Especially when much Japanese variety humor is comprised of ad-libbed in-jokes or references to other or past shows, telops, especially image telops, are frequently brought in to present a slice of that other text, both explaining the gag and firmly placing the show in its context. Thus, in a show from 1997, *Mechamecha motetai* (I Really Wanna Be Popular, Fuji), when the diminutive Okamura, asked what his height is, incomprehensibly mumbles the answer, his partner, Yabe Hiroyuki, blurts out "That brings back memories!" The reference by itself is unintelligible to anyone but the most devoted Ninety Nine fan, but a black-and-white image of the two when they were younger is "kindly" placed in the bottom right corner accompanied by the telop "Gag from when they debuted." In a glance, we understand the gag and are inserted into a certain comedy history and intertextual knowledge that allows us to enjoy the inside joke. Telops do not simply render the obvious more obvious; they actively engage in digesting what is hard to read. Their kindness even extends to assisting viewers in constructing the image and, in some ways, themselves (as part of an in-group).

It is the kindness of telop that bothers some observers, however. Too much effort to clarify information, it is argued, treats viewers like children unable to read the scene independently. Such complaints tie into discourse on TV as the idiot box, something that degrades the mental abilities of the populace and, to quote Ōya Sōichi's famous phrase, "turns all 100 million Japanese into idiots" (*ichioku sōhakuchika*).[8] This is not a criticism exclusive to the use of the telop. The television scholar Kitamura Hideo, for instance, writing in the mid-1980s, complained of the excessive amount of commentary (*kaisetsu*) on television, especially in sports programming. While stressing that such explanation is part of the codifying process, turning a live event into a televisual phenomenon, he expressed concern over its function as an "agent for processing information." Such processing may be helpful in an age of overabundant information, but it could also result, he argues, in a sort of "abandonment of subjective semiotic behavior" in which coding and decoding are entrusted to another.[9] Critics of telop in fact express fears that its overuse will "rob viewers of the ability to sense the delight of turns in conversation or figures of speech" or eliminate forms of "thinking humor" with the audience itself left stupid.[10]

Such expressions of fear over popular culture often say more about those who are uttering them than about the culture itself. Yet "explanation" has been a center of contention in Japanese image media ever since the rise of a mass culture industry. In the era of silent film in the 1910s and 1920s, for instance, one could hear similar complaints being directed against the *benshi*, the figure who stood next to the screen and explained the movie to the audience. Intellectual film critics who valorized cinema as a visual medium with no need for words, resolutely rejected *benshi*, seeing in the effort to explain a Japanese film to a Japanese audience an insult to an intelligent audience or a pander to vulgar, ignorant taste. My research on these debates has shown how much of the discourse criticizing the *benshi's* explanation involved cultural struggles over control of the medium that were deeply entwined with questions of class and politics.[11] At the same time, the fact that intellectual critics often favored a form of cinema that sufficiently explained itself—that did not allow for the audience's own discretionary production of meaning—and that police and education authorities actually favored *benshi* as a means of controlling dangerous meanings and promoting positive ones, indicates the degree to which explanation could also become a technology of power in the political struggle over meaning.[12]

Such conflicting views of explanation warn us that, while criticism of telop as an excessively kind digestion of meaning certainly participates in the demonization of popular culture, it would be simplistic to reduce the debate to that. It is because telops mediate the relationship between textuality and reception that they can potentially become the site for struggle over the determination of meaning and textual technologies of power. When complaints about telops usurping the spectator's ability to read the text prove incomplete is when they do not fully understand the complex role the viewer still plays in the process. In a word, they don't fully take into account the postmodernity of this phenomenon. It is to this problem I turn next.

THE TELOP AS THE STRAIGHT MAN

Consider again the example of *Kibun wa jōjō*. While there is a section taped in front of a live audience that uses few telops, the centerpiece of this comedy variety show was when the duo Utchan Nanchan did various tasks outside the studio with guest personalities and regular people. These sections, usually taped using small cameras set up in rooms and cars like surveillance equipment, as a rule presented all the dialogue spoken by the various *tarento* in the form of horizontal telops at the bottom of the screen; nothing was left out, so there was no obvious digestive process. As if this were not enough, occasionally an additional set of vertical telops appeared in the middle of the screen, sometimes superimposed over the performers, to bring a further dimension to the text. In one show, for instance, Nanbara, Golgo Matsumoto (of the comedy team TIM), and the actor Ihara Tsuyoshi take part in a real bartending competition. Ihara, after a pretty good performance, comes back

Kibun wa jōjō: External commentary on the narrative.

to the waiting room visibly relieved and begins happily chattering about how well he did. A vertical then appears over the image: "The winner's interview already." Since Ihara did not win the competition, this telop neither digests the narrative nor necessarily explains what is going on. One could say it is interpreting the scene, making clear Ihara's psychological state, but this is less a telop working with the narrative flow than one externally commenting on it.

This is actually one of the major functions of telops in contemporary Japanese television. Ōta Shōichi describes these telops as *tsukkomi* in light of the division of labor in Japanese *manzai* comedy between *boke* (the clown) and *tsukkomi* (the straight man). Classically, if the *boke* is supposed to generate laughter through absurd actions or comments, the role of the *tsukkomi* is to amplify this humor by pointing out how stupid it is. *Tsukkomi* can thus be rather conservative, regulating the disruptive comedy of the *boke* through rhythm and reminders about normalcy; nonetheless, *tsukkomi* itself cannot exist without *boke* (and visa versa).[13] *Tsukkomi* in some ways defines what comedy is by providing a frame for the *boke*, both protecting normal society from its force and giving the *boke* a context in which it can go crazy without being condemned as insane. *Tsukkomi* telops function as one of the primary means by which contemporary Japanese television comedy shows define themselves as comedy. A famous example of this is *Denpa shōnen*, which was never funny just for the antics of Matsumura Kunihiro and others but for the narration and the telops that resonated with it. The narrator, Kimura Kyoya, developed a unique voice style that through brash shifts in intonation almost self-parodically overemphasized his commentary. Telops graphically augmented that overemphasis. So when the comedian Nasubi, consigned by the show to "live" only on what he could win through write-in lotteries, actually won something, the narrator's excessive exclamation "JOY!" was accompanied by a large pink telop "JOY!" and a heart symbol.

Telops can function like a straight man external to the space of performance, prodding and defining the clowns onscreen. This extra presence is obvious when it is accompanied by a voiced narration, but in many cases *tsukkomi* telops operate silently or, at best, with aural Mickey Mousing. *Utaban* again provides an interesting example. In addition to the colored dialogue telops at the bottom center of the screen, the program uses more inconspicuous white telops on the right side that have no relation to the spoken dialogue. For instance, in one show, when the singer Fujiki Naoto mentions that he did something naughty in his youth, one such telop appears, asking, "Hey, hey! Just what did you do?" a phrase neither host used. Fujiki confesses that he pocketed some of the cram school tuition his parents gave him, something he has never told them. "Don't put this on air," he pleads half seriously, but the white telop comments, "Sorry! We've already aired it!" The hosts, Ishibashi Takaaki and Nakai Masahiro, are experts at *tsukkomi*, constructing their singer guests, who are in no way professional comedians, as *boke* for the audience, but the telops add another *tsukkomi* presence that at one remove further defines the scene as comedic.

Ōta closely relates the increased use of telop in comedy (*warai*) programming to changes in the relation between *tsukkomi* and *boke* over the last thirty years. Since these changes are intimately connected to shifts in the relation between text and spectatorship, I would like to review his argument in detail. Ōta's work argues a connection between a fundamental disengagement between *tsukkomi* and *boke* in recent comedy and a shift in viewership, one in which viewers straddle a new division between being an audience member (in the same space as the performer) and being a spectator (in a different space), between participating in the comedy and objectively observing it from a far.[14] With the *manzai* boom in the 1980s and the success of teams such as the Two Beats, Yasushi-Kiyoshi, and Shinsuke-Ryūsuke, not only did traditional *rakugo* humor (Japan's "sit-down" comedic storytelling), which exhibits a clear division between the professional performer and the listening audience, give way to a *manzai* world in which amateurs and audiences had more of a role, but the close relationship between *tsukkomi* and *boke* weakened. *Boke* became more and more independent of *tsukkomi*, a trend exemplified by the *boke* Beat Takeshi's climb to fame as his Two Beats *tsukkomi* partner Beat Kiyoshi gradually faded away. *Tsukkomi* in TV comedy became such a weak presence that it barely seemed to exist. This, on the one hand, helped create a wild, playful, and fantastic performance space in which barely any *tsukkomi* existed to recall the rule of reason and sensibility. As in *Oretachi hyōkinzoku*, comedy became more and more centered on a space of "friends" (*nakama*), with humor itself based on inside jokes and keeping up the momentum (*nori*).[15] On the other hand, it fostered the entrance of the audience/amateur into the comedic space. If *tsukkomi's* role was not simply to control the *boke* by framing it in but also to enable it, the decline of onstage *tsukkomi* had to be supplemented by another force or comedy would cease to exist. To Ōta, this was the audience members, who now no longer waited to be led to a well-structured punch line by a professional but began to find humor in even supposedly straight drama.[16] The audience, in part, became the *tsukkomi*, but one that was still weak. This is evident in changes in impersonation (*monomane*) comedy. If imitations of celebrities or politicians once had a critical or parodic edge, contemporary impersonation, argues Ōta, merely aims to cite the object either faithfully or with simple exaggeration.[17] Without the performer's critical *tsukkomi*, the humor merely stems from the audience recognizing the "tracing" of the object (e.g., "I know who that is!"). This "tracing" (*nazoru*) humor is, to Ōta, one of the central forms of contemporary comedy, and it depends in part on the audience providing the minimum degree of *tsukkomi* through recognizing the tracing.

With the audience supplying the *tsukkomi* essential for comedy, it is not too great a step for it to begin actively engaging in the comedic performance itself. With in-joke humor becoming central through the *nakama* space of *boke*-led comedy, more and more shows began featuring the staff behind the camera and the private lives of the performers in the comedy. This, to Ōta, helped break down the walls between not only professional and amateur but between performer and audience, becoming the model for a new kind of humor based on amateurs (*shirōto*) from the audience. Audiences were invited into the group of "friends" by being given information necessary to understand the in-joke humor or by citing their shared experience (say, of old TV shows, which are then less parodied than traced). They then became performers themselves as more and more shows like *Tensai Takeshi no genki ga deru terebi* (The Genius Takeshi's Enlivening TV, NTV, 1985) began to feature amateurs either in the form of noncomedians such as singers or other *tarento* or just people off the street. If these people were funny, it was not because they had any talent for humor but because they conformed to the new ideal for the humorous individual: *tennen-boke*, the "natural clown." *Tennen-boke* are funny not because they have humorous intent but because they are read as funny when just being themselves. All of everyday life can thus become part of this humor, which invades reality, especially in the form of such "reality" variety shows as *Denpa shōnen* and *Urinari* (NTV). Ōta reminds us, however, that even with the *tennen-boke* the amateur never has a natural existence external to television codes; in the end, the *tennen-boke*, if not the *nakama* space of comedy itself, is a matter of self-tracing, a figure coded as a noncoded existence.[18] *Tsukkomi* helps make such individuals funny, but, as Ōta notes, the *tsukkomi* of Tamori or Tunnels with amateurs is, far from reining in the *boke*, rather encouraging it.[19] It traces over and encodes the amateur while remaining weak partly in order to make the *boke* seem natural and less obviously coded. In the end, the audience must again be there to help read the performers—who are now audience members "tracing" themselves—as funny. In this way, Ōta sees the contemporary TV audience as being both audience members and performers, part of the space of friends and outside it, subjectively engaging in *boke* behavior and looking at it objectively as *tsukkomi*. This exemplifies the ambiguous boundaries of the new space of friends: it can include everyone in Japan with shared knowledge of popular culture while presuming an outside from which the audience observer traces a comedic space.

Ōta sees telops in variety programming as representative of such changes in television comedy if not their essential outcome.[20] Telops definitely function as *tsukkomi*, but they are rarely the critical *tsukkomi* of yesterday; they often serve as footnotes providing information on inside jokes that audiences need to join the space of friends. When they stand out beyond the function of recording and clarifying, acting almost like a third comedian on the scene, theirs is a largely weak *tsukkomi* that often aids rather than corrals the *boke*. When Tamori is in a hurry, with no time to deal with Okamura and his pals on *Mechamecha iketeru* (What a Cool We Are, Fuji), the telop *kyu* (「急。」), which simply means "in a rush," only stands out as *tsukkomi* through its brevity and the graphic (and grammatically unnecessary) use of the full stop (*kuten*). Ōta argues that the weakness of contemporary *tsukkomi* is epitomized by telops that don't appear as *tsukkomi* at all: the dialogue telops that merely "trace" what is being said. *Tsukkomi* has become so weak, so invisible, that it is the mere tracing of what is already visible or audible, the repetition of what is there; at best, it only enters into the graphic choice of fonts or colors or, at the most basic level, Ōta argues, into the gap between speech and writing.

Ōta also argues that telops represent to a degree the divided position of the television viewer. By being placed on the screen and in effect tracing one text onto another, they reinforce the spectator's perspective outside this comedy space. At the same time, they provide the information necessary to join the space of friends, to in a sense be on the scene. The role of the telop, if not the participation of audiences themselves, is actually visually and spatially rendered in some variety shows by dividing the performers into those who engage in some activity (often involving amateurs) and those who watch this on monitors in a different space. The latter's comments directed at the television not only approximate the role of the telop, explaining and commenting on the scene (comments that are often reproduced as telops), but reinforce how such distanced "audience" participation is a central aspect of variety programming. Such internal spectators, along with the telops, can also serve as models for how viewers should read the text.[21]

Ōta's account is powerful both because it is based on a close reading of numerous televisual and even nontelevisual texts and because it formulates suggestive conclusions from those readings. Telops, by existing on the ambiguous boundary of the space of friends, if not of the televisual text itself, seem to bridge the text and its viewer, its production and consumption. As such, they can be said to mark profound changes in the relations between textuality and consumption that can distinguish the contemporary moment.[22] Ōta's account of telop, for instance, aligns with certain arguments about postmodernity. The weakening of *tsukkomi* easily reminds one of Lyotard's decline of master narratives or Fredric Jameson's account of the disappearance of parody in favor of pastiche. The resulting comedy of tracing can be seen as merely a proliferation of intertextuality, texts reading texts but without pursuing any deeper meaning. It is in this empty space that reception—the ability of viewers to help construct the text—becomes crucial to the televisual experience. Telops become emblematic of the lack of textual closure and the need of readings to (literally) be laid on the surface of the text. In fact, one could align telops with the *tarento* system itself, which Mitsuhiro Yoshimoto has argued functions as a sort of low-cost, post-Fordist system of audience participation (in which viewers help create the text by identifying and following the *tarento*).[23] The telop could thus be a post-Fordist means of consumption producing the text, one of Japanese television's solutions to how to construct the image in an age of postmodern image economies. What I want to investigate next is how telops specifically intersect with some contemporary Japanese discourses on postmodernity.

TELOP AS *SHUKŌ*

As with theories of postmodern culture elsewhere, much ink has been spent in Japan discussing the phenomenon of rereading, sampling, and other forms of textual appropriation. The most famous example has been the Comiket (Comic Market) and the *dōjinshi* (coterie journals) central to that market, which present *manga* by noncommercial artists that, far from being original, largely borrow characters from popular comics but in alternative stories (such as homosexual romances). This has been elevated as a kind of ideal in which consumers appropriate mass-produced commodities for their own subcultural and sometimes resistive uses.[24] In this practice, the original *manga* become merely a basic set of patterns and structures that the readers, now producing their own work, reread and rework in numerous variations.

Despite the interest of some scholars in the political potential of this practice, the dominant discourse in Japan defending it, which one can call *otaku* discourse, has often been a-political, defining the phenomenon through recourse to such tropes as national tradition.[25] The culture critic Otsuka Eiji, for instance, has explained the Comiket example through the Kabuki concepts of *sekai* and *shukō*. Just as Comiket *dōjinshi* artists produced small stories (*chiisana monogatari*) out of the large story (*ōkina monogatari*) of such popular *manga* as Takahashi Yōichi's *Captain Tsubasa*, so Kabuki playwrights produced inflected plot elements (*shukō*), or specific Kabuki plays, out of a shared set of story and character elements called *sekai* (literally, "world"; an example would be that of Chushingura). Since no one owned the communal *sekai*, nothing produced from it was an original creation; each *shukō* was rather a specific reading or interpretation utilizing contemporary fashions and other individual touches.[26] Okada Toshio, a self-proclaimed *otaku* whose "otakology" has latched on to such elite institutions as Tokyo University (where Okada has taught part time) as a means of cultural legitimization, has enthusiastically appropriated the concept of *shukō* to argue that *otaku* culture is the only legitimate successor to Edo culture and thus the proper representative of Japan both at home and abroad. In an example of such conservative cultural nationalism, Okada uses *shukō* not only to explain the activities of Comiket artists but also to define the *otaku* reader-viewer in light of Edo *iki* (stylishness) as an elite cultured eye who takes pleasure not in original stories—which are less important in anime, *manga*, or TV hero shows—but in knowledge of the main pattern and appreciation of small variations in that pattern in individual texts.[27]

Azuma Hiroki, for one, has criticized such ascriptions of traditional Japaneseness to *otaku* culture as an effort to repress the trauma of postwar Americanization through the reconstruction of a pseudo Japan, one that allows *otaku* to forget their debts to American culture.[28] While I can second such criticism, I want to note the potential homologies between telops and the discourse on *shukō*. Contemporary variety programming is certainly not a televisual version of the Comiket, but, as Ōta argues, it does crucially depend on audience participation. What is important here is that the telop, like contemporary accounts of *shukō*, value the rewriting of the text over its original state; the television image, it seems, is defined as insufficient in itself and in need of reinscription. Perhaps this relates to the undeniable reality that much variety programming lacks originality and follows basic patterns from program to program. One could say that contemporary Japanese variety comedy resembles *shukō* in its emphasis on ad-libs in these conventional situations over original, scripted skits. Telops both underline these ad-libs and add their own interpretations of the basic pattern. In reference to Okada's *shukō*, telops can also appear to promote a form of *iki* spectatorship but without the labor needed to become a connoisseur. Telops can enable the easy consumption of expert learning, providing viewers with the illusion of instant knowledge of the fundamental formulas and intertextual citations that allow for greater appreciation of a show's version of the basic pattern. At the same time, the telops themselves follow the same essential rules with only small variations, thus encouraging a spectatorship across individual shows that appreciates these minute permutations.

What interests me here is less how well telops suit the Kabuki concept of *shukō* than how they align with the contemporary trend toward discoursing on *shukō*. That discourse reveals a fundamental concern with the instability of textuality and redefines textual pleasure from an enjoyment of closed narrative into delight in the processes of rewriting and reinterpretation. Neither Okada nor Ōtsuka, however, fully pursue the historicity of such a shift or of their own interest in that phenomenon, especially how both issues relate to transformations in capital and power. Their discussions of the contemporaneity or postmodernity of such popular phenomena as telops may in fact serve only to obfuscate such shifts. As with many scholars of subculture in Japan, neither considers the problems raised by Sarah Thornton, who shows how subcultures, in their effort to find recognition in a society that does not acknowledge them, can sometimes simply reproduce in a different space problematic hierarchies of power and discrimination evident in the dominant society.[29] It is some of these issues of power that I would like to pursue in my discussion of televisual textuality and consumption. I would therefore like to critically address one discourse that, more than those of either Ōtsuka or Okada, pursues the specificities of contemporary forms of textuality and consumption: Azuma Hiroki's theory of database consumption.

TELEVISION AS A DATABASE INTERFACE

Azuma argues that recent trends in *otaku* culture such as database consumption represent the epitome of postmodernity in Japan. In claiming this, he begins with Ōtsuka's notion of "narrative consumption" (*monogatari shōhi*). As with the Comiket phenomenon, but also in cases like the "Bikkuriman Chocolate" craze of 1987–88, Ōtsuka focuses on instances where consumers are no longer consuming the product but rather the narrative behind it. Bikkuriman Chocolate was candy sold with cards that, if sufficiently collected, told an elaborate story fascinating enough for some to buy it only for the card, and throw away the chocolate. Since Bikkuriman was not a known character marketed here through tie-ins, it was the desire to appropriate the story that fed this consumption. Ōtsuka sees in *dōjinshi* the result of such consumption: once the story had been completely appropriated (that is, Bikkuriman cards had been purchased), there was nothing stopping consumers from using the larger story to produce their own smaller versions it. Narrative consumption is thus the attempt not only to purchase a larger narrative but to use it once it has been appropriated.

Azuma first relates this phenomenon to Baudrillard's simulacrum, arguing that, as in the case of *dōjinshi*, none of the producers of these new versions sees the initial *manga*/story as the "original" but rather as only another version of the real story that lies behind it. Thus, none of the actual texts, from the first *Captain Tsubasa* to its "imitators," can be called the original; all are equally simulacra. Yet, unlike Baudrillard, Azuma does not want to ascribe a fundamental flatness to the simulacrum; he rather claims that such cases of secondary creation (*niji sōsaku*) can only be understood by postulating another level behind the simulacrum.[30] Azuma argues that this other level is no longer a larger story but, citing Lyotard's declaration of the end of master narratives, rather a "large non-narrative" (*ōkina himonogatari*).[31] He posits a history behind this. If the 1980s was the "age of fiction" (*kyokō no jidai*) defined, as Ōsawa Masachi argues, by a cynicism in which a society that no longer believed in overarching truths still acted as if it did, the *otaku* of that era didn't really believe in the large narratives behind their anime and *dōjinshi* but still felt a strong need to construct one.[32] Yet if those *otaku* could still feel compelled by the greater world evoked by numerous versions of, say, the *Gundam* story, *otaku* at the time of his book, Azuma argues, no longer had such concerns. Contemporary *otaku*, he says, consume anime with little regard for the larger narrative, concentrating instead on isolated elements in the text, especially characters. What they then see behind those texts is not a coherent narrative but a more amorphous, though still bordered, collection of elements amenable to different combinations—in other words, a database. Characters are similarly no longer beings with coherent personalities but just a collection of "cute elements" (*moe yōso*) that can be combined in different ways.[33] Both characters and individual stories in anime and *manga*, then, are mere readouts of particular databases. Azuma focuses on such phenomena as role-playing games as illustrations of his point: such games can have multiple progressions and multiple endings, and thus *otaku*, while not abandoning their interest in the "small" stories an individual play creates, are ultimately consuming the database, not the narrative, the total range of data elements that be read out into different stories. Some *otaku*, in an extension of the Comiket phenomenon, he notes, even begin taking these games apart so they can create yet other combinations of the same database elements.

Telops in variety programming do not at first seem analogous to such database consumption. Shows are not directly interactive and do not exhibit multiple endings. Yet there is much about telops that intersects with discourses about databases and consumption. First, as I have noted, much variety programming is based on various patterns, with individual shows becoming interpretations of those patterns. The narrative coherence of these patterns, however, is often loose, being based mostly on a situation that then develops through the somewhat haphazard logic of ad-libs and the tenuous relations between *tsukkomi* and *boke*. Conversation and physical pratfalls could be considered the basic structural forms of variety comedy, neither of which exhibits strong linearity or closure but nonetheless follows some basic rules and patterns. If actions on the set can be seen as readouts of a database of patterns of *tsukkomi*, *boke*, and other comedy formulas, telops foreground and double this readout by picking up, arranging, interpreting, and in effect processing a text that now, in the spirit of Lev Manovich, can be considered only a collection of data.[34]

What is interesting is that not a few shows actually construct their telops, if not their overall image, on the model of a computer monitor. Shows such as *Mechamecha iketeru*, *Guruguru Nainti Nain*, or *Dauntaun DX* (Downtown DX, Yomiuri TV) often introduce new corners, comedy situations (especially games), and even characters with readout screens containing multiple windows and telop boxes full of data on the relevant subject. A show like *Kokoriko no Mirikaru Taipu* (Cocorico's Miracle Type, Fuji) consciously utilized the computer interface as a formative schema for its design. Composed of skits that re-create humorous incidents sent in by viewers via e-mail, the show introduced each skit with a huge telop giving the gist of the e-mail. Some of the skits could themselves be distinctively computerlike. Every single word uttered by one recurrent character, Tanaka-kun (played by Cocorico's Tanaka Naoki), appears in the form of a telop, similar to *Kibun wa jōjō*, but since his diction is extremely fast the telops appear character by character on the screen accompanied by computer beeps as they are "scrolled" out. After the skits are completed and the performers talk in the studio, huge telops appear, covering the entire screen in multiple color fields. Most are dialogue telops, but some, more obvious, *tsukkomi* telops literally take over the screen. For example, when Lily Franky, a writer–illustrator and avid Yomiuri Giants fan, unabashedly asks for the autograph of Nagashima Kazushige (a former Giants player and the son of Giants legend Nagashima Shigeo), the screen is covered with a semitransparent color field, except for one small opening showing Franky on which the telop "A Failed Adult" appears in monstrous type. Telops as a whole treat the image not as a window onto the world but as a flat surface on which telops are to be overlaid. *Kokoriko no Mirikaru Taipu* consciously aligns this with the computer screen. The dominant aesthetic of the variety show is, then, one of overlapping windows and flat fields that can shift from foreground to background throughout the show. *Puchi marijji* (Petit Marriage, Fuji), a "reality" variety show featuring groups of male and female *tarento* who comment on a real couple living together on a trial basis, could have multiple layers at once. The primary level is the surveillance camera

Puchi marijji: Computer-like multiple windows and layers of commentary.

views of the couple's lives, but these are occasionally literally "paused" and placed in the background over which the male or female *tarento* comment, superimposed, of course, by telop.

Telops clearly intersect with the computer aesthetic. One could even relate them to the superflat, the aesthetic term originated by the pop artist Murakami Takashi, and developed by Azuma in part by citing the layered windows and dimensions of the computer screen.[35] Certainly the viewer is not engaging in the interactive selection of different windows, but some television shows with telops have effectively developed a low-technology interactive system of windows. With shows offering multiple telops or image texts on the same screen, in addition to the "original" image, it is difficult to take in all this information at once. Viewers, as a matter of necessity, must select through their gaze which items they will process. Telops, then, by multiplying the layers and windows of information onscreen, are not simply a readout of the televisual database; they become a data amplification device between television and the viewer that encourages the spectator to become an information-processing interface, sorting out which bits of information are necessary for that viewer's needs.

Following Lev Manovich's theorization of new media, one could say that the telop, if not much of Japanese televisual style, belongs to an "aesthetic of density." Borrowing from Walter Benjamin, he argues that there is a connection between the experience of work and the aesthetics of entertainment, which, with the computer dominating the workplace with its rapid overflow of layered information, is generating a new aesthetics of dense information in the arts.[36] Telops in variety programming do have definite antecedents in *manga*, sometimes utilizing the coded expressions, mostly familiar to a Japanese public, found in *manga* dialogue bubbles (in a few cases, one can even see telops in the form of dialogue bubbles). Yet Tsuchiya Toshio, the producer of the telop-rich shows *Denpa shōnen* and *Urinari*, has cited video and computer games as telops' most relevant intertext, claiming that they have trained a viewership used to quickly processing such words onscreen.[37] This aesthetics of speed and density extends in television beyond the telop into even set design. While classical Hollywood set design used lighting, color, focus, and other devices to render the background subservient to narratively important characters in the fore, a show such as *Dauntaun DX* features a very busy set design, with many background items in bright, splashy colors competing with the performers for attention. Spatial depth is lessened, and the eye seemingly must roam over the image, much like the motion of the gaze Murakami locates at the center of the superflat experience. The gaze in variety television is constantly stimulated and must excitedly process the overflow of data.

THE VIEWER AS ANIMAL

This leads us to two questions. What is the politics of this gaze and what does the consumption of databaselike telops imply about the construction of power in contemporary television if not new media itself? Azuma's answer centers on his theorization of the age of the animal. When describing the *otaku* experience of role-playing games, he notes a shift from the modern pleasure of narrative. What is enjoyed is less the registers of narrative closure and identification with the hero than experiencing multiple stories with different endings. Azuma says that users may temporarily identify with the hero, but that attachment always presupposes subsequently abandoning it to enjoy another hero in another play of the game. This trying out of different possibilities is, then, more the pleasure of the database than the narrative. Azuma calls this postmodern form of consumption "dissociative" (*kairiteki*) because essentially the player dissociates his or her experience of individual play (the small story) from the pleasure of the database, leading to the separation of and equality between enjoyment of the individual plays and the database.[38] Azuma finds this kind of consumption fundamentally animal-like because it no longer draws meaning from the text but experiences it as a means of satisfying needs. He cites Alexandre Kojève's famous footnote in his *Introduction to the Reading of Hegel*, which states that, at the end of history, "man" will become like either the animal Americans or the Japanese snobs. To Azuma, Kojève's ascription of snobbism to the Japanese is quite prescient because the snobbish act of maintaining the form of an action or belief even when one knows it lacks content is simply another way to describe the cynicism of the 1980s.[39] Yet, since Azuma argues that such cynicism ended in the late 1990s in Japan, American consumerist animalism is all that remains.

Azuma's logic and his use of Kojève has many dubious points, but his conclusion is that the fundamental terms used to define the human— conflict with the environment and the ability to desire, especially to desire the other's desire—are no longer fully applicable in postmodern Japan. He distinguishes between "needs" (*yokkyū*) and "desire" (*yokubō*): while the latter can never be fulfilled because it involves the social interaction of desiring the other's desire, the former can be satisfied individually merely by supplying the object of need. The advance of consumer society, goes the argument, has enabled the fulfillment of needs and eliminated the exigency to conflict with the environment. Azuma sees *otaku* as no longer desiring what they cannot have (that is, the larger story) but only requiring small stories or "cute" elements, needs easily fulfilled. Their mode of consumption resembles that of an animal eating food or, to use a more extreme expression, that of a drug addict.[40] Azuma, however, does not completely eliminate the human from the *otaku* picture. *Otaku* consumers still desire the database, which itself cannot easily be acquired, and so they, Azuma says, maintain social connections in order to exchange information on the database (although, he cautions, such connections are not necessary).[41] In a repetition of his structuring trope of doubled yet separate layers, he pictures the *otaku* as being animal-like in needing small stories and pseudo human in desiring the larger database, two aspects that remain so distinct that the dissociative becomes in *otaku* culture the equivalent of multiple personality disorder. This is the age of the animal, an age that Japan has achieved first, but one that is not restricted to Japan.[42]

Dōbutsukasuru posutomodan is a slippery if not chameleonlike text. Azuma's self-proclaimed objectivity renders it difficult to nail down his position, making the book appear critical or laudatory depending on one's perspective. Calling *otaku* animals and equating their pleasure mode to that of drug addicts certainly appears critical, but the book's rigid teleology, its emphasis on Japan as leading the world in postmodernity, and Azuma's unequivocal praise for many *otaku* cultural phenomena lead one to consider his objectivity as less neutrality than praise through lack of critique. The book's last lines seem to confirm this. When concluding his discussion of the computer "girl game" *YU-NO* as an allegory of the postmodern he has described, he concludes:

> This book was written in order to create an era in which this kind of superlative work can be freely analyzed and freely criticized without such distinctions as high culture/subculture, academic/ *otaku*, adult/childish, or artistic/entertainment. What develops after this is left up to each individual reader.[43]

Perhaps in a good poststructuralist spirit he is seeking the eradication of binaries and an era of free reader participation. However, he sets up this elimination of binaries in order to freely discuss not this "work" but rather this "superlative work." Its value is presumed, and therefore the vanquishing of binaries removes boundaries not to critique but to the recognition of the work's excellence. Read in this light, Azuma's text is ultimately less an effort to describe an era than a manifesto to create one, a polemic that, while more theoretically sophisticated than Okada's blundering *otaku* nationalism, attempts to neutralize the theories and methodologies that restricted the *otaku*, thereby legitimizing it as the dean of the new age if not the end of history.

Reader participation is, then, action on behalf of the work, one lacking a negative critical stance. This could only be so in the age of the animal. Allan Stoekl reminds us that the end of history in Kojève, because it represents the conclusion of man's dialectical opposition with nature, can only constitute the lack of such opposition and thus the rule of nature. (Man thus becomes natural—an animal.) The Book (Hegel's book explaining history) remains important because its self-consciousness must be recognized for history to end, yet at that point of conclusion it must be a true, universal text separate from any individual and thus one that can never be worked on or interpreted.[44] Azuma's conception of reading the *otaku* text is, despite his discussion of secondary creation and use of "cute" elements, essentially no different from this. When he discusses the computer games produced by the Key company, for instance, he claims, "Key's games have been made less to provide the consumer with erotic satisfaction than to thoroughly combine the cute generative elements popular with *otaku* and efficiently make them cry—providing a sort of exemplary response for generative creation."[45] His repeated use of the word *efficiently* (*kōritsu yoku*) only underlines a vision of the *otaku* reader/player as an animal-like being who both consumes and produces texts in a mechanical, almost reflexlike manner, absent critique or interpretation. By reducing the consumption and production of texts to mere animalistic behavior and failing to ask what ideological conditions have precipitated *otaku* becoming, for instance, "used to perverse images,"[46] he effectively naturalizes a contingent condition and eliminates issues of ideology and politics as irrelevant to *otaku* culture. Ultimately, Azuma has perversely succeeded in sheltering the *otaku* both from the effects of ideology and from political criticism. *Otaku*, by definition, can no longer engage in critical or even creative reading, and presumably neither can we.

Power, if not the operations of capital itself, is painfully absent from *Dōbutsukasuru posutomodan*, which only underlines how apolitical—or sometimes reactionary—many "*otaku*" theoreticians are. Ōtsuka is more conscious of these phenomena. Consumers may be the "pseudo creators of the story," but to him they never have a "free hand" because such forms of consumption usually involve a "game master" who directs the way the consumer creates the stories.[47] Azuma also speaks of limits to secondary creation, but he ascribes these not to controlling forces but to consumer needs, thus failing to connect these phenomena to the operations of consumer capitalism.[48] In fact, by obfuscating or even naturalizing these operations he effectively legitimizes them. If we are to achieve a greater consciousness of these operations, as well as perhaps imagining alternatives and resistances, we need to think more critically about the contemporary state of reading/consumption in relation to power and capital.

COMMANDING THE TELOP GAZE

Analyzing telop, I believe, can help us to both problematize Azuma's conception of consumption and better outline the contemporary conditions he fails to recognize. It should first be said that Azuma's age of the animal and its concomitant forms of consumption do have parallels in the use of telop. In particular, the dominance of what Ōta calls "tracing telop" (*nazoru teroppu*) can be said to exemplify a mode of reading defined by pure repetition of the same, one similar to Azuma's animalistic encounter with the text, which only traces what is already there. Repetition, one can say, is one of the most prevalent textual devices in contemporary Japanese television and not simply in the way certain textual formulas are endlessly repeated. It is not unheard of to see the identical commercial repeated in the same commercial break. In fact, it is during the commercial break that one encounters one of the more common forms of repetition. Much variety programming often returns from the commercial break by repeating, sometimes with slight alterations, the half a minute or so of the program that was shown before the ads. Perhaps, as with tracing telop, this aims to help viewers who have lost the narrative thread during the commercial, but it also underlines the fact that the model of televisual reception offered by the texts themselves is mostly one of repetition not interpretation or critique. The question for us is how this model functions.

First, it is apparent that telops, though aligned with trends in Japanese comedy that encourage audience participation and approximating, in a low-tech fashion, a mode of database consumption, do not necessarily allow the viewer a free hand. When not just repeating the image and sound text, telops mostly condense and digest the information given, kindly rendering it easy to consume. If telop can function as *tsukkomi*, it is usually, as Ōta notes, in a weak form that less critiques and corrals the *boke* than renders it more palatable. Even when there is an excess of telop and other information on the screen, prompting the viewer to interface with and process this set of data, there is usually a clear hierarchy between the data defined by size, placement, use of sound, and duration. Some telops stay on the screen for minutes, giving viewers multiple information windows while also allowing them to focus on briefer windows that are deemed more narratively important. Telops thus guide and shape reception, acting like prompters in shows with studio audiences, getting audiences in the mood (*nori*), and telling them when to laugh or applaud.

The cinematic style of classical Hollywood was also an efficient means of guiding the spectator's gaze and interpretation, but usually in an unobtrusive way. Telops are clearly visible, but that does not make them a Brechtian means of critically exposing the artifice behind naturalism. In a sense, they acknowledge the processes of directing viewing but without necessarily criticizing it. In an age of postmodern irony, Ōta's viewer/spectator both participates in the comedy and ironically views it objectively from afar. Yet if viewers are going to make fun of serious television shows, as they famously did with *Suchuwadesu monogatari* (Stewardess Story, TBS, 1983), telops self-ironically acknowledge, if not duplicate, this parodic gaze while working to reinsert it in the text. They can poke fun at the show and expose its manipulative artifice while also rendering such pleasures part of the program, essentially co-opting them. Telops reproduce the *tsukkomi* many viewers engage in when commenting on TV in their brightly lit living rooms with family and friends but in effect relieve them of the need to actually do it themselves by rendering it a televisual object of consumption. It is the combination of *tsukkomi* and the ease of having it done for you that is part of the pleasure of Japanese variety programming.

Telops thus remind us that in most forms of role-playing games and participatory, database textuality there are preferred plays and readouts, ones that offer the most points and the most pleasure. Participation is often less consumer creation than repetition of prepared paths and interpretations. For viewers no longer content to passively receive the text, new forms of textuality offer positive interactivity and a vision of dynamic intertextuality but usually within a system of guidance in which interactivity produces prepared results and cynicism allows viewers to accept the manipulation they are aware of. Azuma may idealize game users who take apart the program and reconstruct it in different ways, but, as with some scholars of subculture, he focuses too much on the minority of avant-garde creators of subculture and not enough on the majority who follow more than create.[49] It is with these participants that one can see the operations of subtler yet also more enticing modes of power controlling meaning and defining the commodity.

What of these idealized, truly creative consumers? Telops also caution us about celebrating them too soon. Remember that television has always been confronted with the problem of its own distractiveness. Unlike the cinema, with its dark theaters demanding the viewer's attention and concentration, television viewing in lit rooms is subject to distractions. For an enterprise such as NHK, which supports itself on receiver fees, this is not necessarily a problem: as long as a household owns a set and is paying the required fees, it is not crucial for it to actually watch NHK programs. The story is different for commercial stations (in Japan, called *minpō*), which must support themselves by selling advertising. What is bought by advertisers is not commercial time but viewers (as reflected in the ratings) and especially their attention. But how can the attention of viewers be sold when television, almost by definition, is a distractive medium? The most common tactic has been to ensure attention through the use of strong narratives, but, given commercial breaks and the now ubiquitous remote controller, there are too many obstacles to linear narration. Another solution is spectacle, as sports programming and now reality shows promise visual pleasures that demand that the viewer at least gaze at the tube; with popularity of the hard disk recorder and other devices, even commercials must become unprecedented spectacles if they are to stop the viewer from pressing the fast-forward button. Televisual aesthetics have always been a sort of compromise, working on the one hand to attract attentive viewing while also acknowledging the essential impossibility of commanding the undivided attention of the audience. Television's style has thus been called "glance aesthetics," as opposed to the "gaze aesthetics" of classic cinema, one in which fragmentation is acknowledged and the glance directed less through contemplation of the text than through kinetics.[50]

Telops are in some ways an extension of glance aesthetics. By offering much of the essential information on the current stage of the program at a glance in the form of several telops, the variety show creates a textuality that is easy to pick up and follow, a convenience also supported by the formats of conversation and multiple topic corners. One need not have watched the show from the start and can enter at any time after switching from another channel, watching a video, or looking up from a magazine. In this sense, variety and telops accommodate distraction more than dramatic series do and perhaps can even be said to enable channel surfing because the viewer always knows he or she can switch to another channel and still return with ease. Yet telops provide something that variety programs do not: a reason to watch the screen even without the spectacular goings-on of a *Fūun Takeshi-jō* (Takeshi's Castle, TBS). Telops increase the spectacular value of the program even when the show is composed of talking heads. In fact, by rendering the image incomplete in itself—in need of *tsukkomi* and viewer participation— telops make themselves necessary and thus direct our attention toward the screen. So while they accommodate the distractions of television they capture viewer attention through spectacle and quickly consumable information about the narrative flow. Telops, in a way, solve the contradiction of television by requiring attention without the need for intense concentration, enabling distraction while preventing the viewer from straying from the set.

Telops and other devices are rigorously used to maintain viewer attention at the crucial moment: the commercial break. Just before going to the commercial, telops appear, often supported by a narrator, proclaiming some unexpected or dramatic turn of events and urging the viewer not to change the channel. Narrative structures, sometimes in conjunction with telops, are used to the same effect as many shows will build a mininarrative but delay the conclusion until after the commercial. *Urinari*'s famous ballroom dance competitions, in which *tarento* couples competed in real national dance tournaments, always had the camera scan down the posted competition results, the tension amplified by telops, only to cut to the commercial just before the score of the couple in question appeared.[51] It is in part because of this breach of linear narrativity that shows repeat about a half a minute of the program after the break in order to recoup the narrative momentum that was lost. In that sense, the show does not abandon narrative continuity altogether, but by so obviously rupturing it the show acknowledges that narrativity—if not the telop as well—exists for these breaks not for what comes in between. Narrative continuity becomes defined as continuity not of story but of attention during the commercial.

Telops certainly play a generic role in new forms of television comedy and news programming, but such functions must be linked to television's overall efforts to commodify the gaze. Television is producing a product for sale, and that commodity is the viewer's attention. The fact that NHK uses telops to a lesser degree, especially in variety programming, does suggest their commercialized nature. However, the fact that *tsukkomi* telops could be found in NHK variety shows such as *Yume miru tamago* (Young People with Dreams) or children's programs such as *Tentere waido* (Tentere Wide) reminds us that telops are both an overwhelming fashion in contemporary television and a dominant mode of shaping viewership and interpretation, even if that viewership is not directly commodified. The NHK network does "sell" its viewers in its own fashion, since ratings do justify its existence and funding, and it certainly must package texts and their interpretations as national, unified entities. Telops help ensure that. As the heavy use of explanatory telops in NHK news programming reminds us, processes of shaping viewership inextricably link commercializing the gaze with processes of authorization and power, as summoning the gaze is also a means of controlling it, regulating a product and its viewing even if that product is a "public" not a commercial one.

TELOPS AS LABOR POWER

Commodifying or controlling the gaze is neither new to television nor peculiar to Japanese programming. What strikes me as significant about the process of commodification in recent Japanese TV is its openness. It would be an insult to viewers to assume they do not recognize that the blunt attempts to build up attention before the break are an effort to ensure viewing of the commercial; ad breaks are far too intrusive to be invisible. We could dismiss these attempts as simply the product of a crude, low-budget, commercial mentality, but that would divert our attention away from the real issue: the viewers. Ōta interestingly comments that telops promising earth-shaking revelations after the commercial create a viewership whose attention is placed less on the content of what is revealed than on whether the prediction is correct. Ōta sees this as a process by which television creates tension only to alleviate it, thus proving that the world is predictable, a realm in which viewers can experience set and coded emotional reactions. He argues that the fact that many of these "predictions" prove to be excessive threatens to dull the viewer's perceptions, but I would take that as proof that such promissory telops themselves become a sort of game with the gaze, one in which the viewer remains conscious of the other player in this sport, the commercial.[52]

This is a viewer who is conscious of the manipulation, if not the commodification, of his or her own gaze. Telops are a medium of televisual self-consciousness, one in which the program and the viewer recognize that this is a text, one that is constructed, maneuvered, re-read, and sometimes ridiculed. This self-consciousness, however, is less radical than cynical because, even if the viewer is aware of these manipulations around the commercial, he or she still scans through the advertising if only to see how the game of prediction pans out. This has profound implications for all sorts of interactive or participatory media. Jonathan Beller has theorized a "cinematic mode of production" in which the spectator, by watching a visual text, is engaged in labor that produces the work in a way that, under a sort of "attention theory of value," more value is created than the spectator is actually "paid" for.[53] This is also true of much in the digital world, where in blatant cases, such as the Internet Movie Database, the product of the voluntary, interactive efforts of users is sold for colossal sums and continues to generate income through unpaid labor. Much of the Internet is based, like telops, on the use of written and visual texts to grab the user's attention for advertising, thus transforming the interactivity of the Net into a product for sale. Role-playing games may offer players the opportunity to create a text on their own terms, but players must pay for that chance to complete the product for the producer.[54] Azuma's database consumption or the Comiket thus should not be easily conceived as instances of consumers expropriating the commodity from the producers. Even if the database or large story is appropriable, the user's own creations or interpretations generate more value for the database and its constitutive elements such as characters. The user can create new meanings around the product but, as both Azuma and Otsuka admit, only within certain bounds; the meanings are inevitably accumulated around the primary commodity and augment its value. One could argue that the use of "cute" elements (*moe yōso*) can allow characters to morph and transform, possibly changing the product beyond "ownership," but in an age of flexible accumulation flexible commodities can still produce profit for their copyright holders. *Otaku* users, one could say, are the unpaid laborers of the digital age, even more so if one accepts Azuma's "age of the animal." Following that, *otaku* may have become Pavlovian workers who buy or produce products as if reflexively reacting to the appropriate stimulus.

Telops, as some of the elements through which audiences produce their own attention for sale, are not the fixed capital of narrative that is acquired through absorption but part of a flexible accumulation of intertexts, repetitions, distractions, and viewer participation. On the whole, they can represent a shift in the center of televisual value creation from the sphere of production to that of post-production, from expensive *tarento* to cheap, anonymous editors and viewers, from the profilmic to off-screen.[55] Telops are significant to the degree that they, in their "kindness," make the labor of creating television's value seem quite easy. If producing a *dōjinshi* for the

143

Comiket or taking apart a "novel game" to produce a new version requires time and effort, telops seemingly only require the work involved in reading and processing them (though that often hides the underpaid labor of the show's editors). As a whole, they take over much of the labor viewers should engage in on their own (from understanding and analysis to interpretation and ridicule) and in effect support and guide the viewer in doing so. It is so simple that it does not seem like work at all. One could argue this is the reason to fundamentally distinguish reading telops from more participatory forms of consumption; the latter involve "real participation" (real labor) while the former does not. I would argue that the difference, if there is one, is more quantitative than qualitative and that telops help reveal crucial aspects of the operations of capital and power in contemporary consumption. First, consumption labor is often conscious and voluntary, paid for in part by pleasure but usually in an unequal exchange. Second, the ease and pleasure of such labor, to the point that it does not appear to be work at all, represents less the obfuscation of labor (given self-consciousness) than the flexible nature of contemporary production and the increasingly ephemeral nature of capital in a postmodern age. With telops, labor in television viewing has practically been reduced to pure attention devoid of the labor of concentration, thus becoming perhaps the most appropriate form of labor in the society of the spectacle. Third, in the digital age the value of the database or information commodity lies less and less in the labor it takes to construct the information than in the labor it takes to read, interpret, or simply look at it (and the ads on the same web page). Thus, in order to control the production of the product, and thus the commodity itself, capital must render the user/database interface more and more pleasurable and easy to use. Fourth, and finally, these coordinated efforts to shape the reading of the database, efforts that I argue are well exemplified by the use of telops, represent the process of appropriating labor value itself.

While I contend that telops provide an important case study in this regard, we should be careful not to fall into a formalist essentialism. While they signal significant changes in televisual textuality and the value of attention, telops less constitute these processes of power and capital than represent just one of the strategies—though a prominent and at this time persistent one—that exist to commodify the gaze and appropriate viewer labor. One of the reasons I emphasize the analogic similarities between such activities as *dōjinshi* and the telop is precisely to underline the variety and range of these strategies. Although telops have remained a strong element in Japanese television for nearly two decades, it is conceivable that in the fashion-led world of popular culture they may soon disappear or significantly alter in form. Yet, as long as the structures of capital and power that define the contemporary moment remain, telops will disappear only when their functions have been taken over by other devices, some of which, such as voice-over narration, spectacle, and mininarratives, I have already mentioned. This is one reason why the fact that dramatic television programming in Japan generally refrains from the use of the telop does not disprove my argument. Telops are absent from dramatic shows for a number of reasons, primarily the nature of the genre and the need to maintain the diegesis.[56] Yet I would argue that the increasingly self-consciousness acting and directing in *dorama*, as well as the excessive use of style and narration, especially near the commercial break, evinces some of the same operations performed by telops in variety shows.

In painting this broad picture, I intend neither to wholly condemn telops nor conceive of Japanese television as a monolithic entity with viewers hopelessly lashed into servile labor relations. Telops exist in part because this is an age when viewers are more skeptical about media representations; the role of the telop, I have argued, is to corral this criticism and appropriate it into added value for the program and its advertising time. This operation may backfire, however, because telops thus recognize critiques of television, if not the critical value of television itself. It is convenient when such derisive laughter actually produces a hit like *Suchuwadesu monogatari*, but telops, it must be emphasized, operate less to foster compliant readings than to appropriate existing readings in an already volatile struggle over meaning. The use of telops sometimes exemplifies this by transcending the realm of tracing or even weak *tsukkomi* and entering into pure criticism. One broadcast of *News Station*, Asahi TV's popular 10:00 P.M. news program, for instance, reported Prime Minister Koizumi Jun'ichirō's general policy speech for 2003 with a most interesting use of the telop. Several times, as Koizumi was shown delivering major points of his speech, the telop "Generalization" (*ippanron*) was superimposed over his image on the screen. This was, of course, neither an explanation nor a tracing but a critical commentary on a speech lacking details and full of vague generalizations, one *tsukkomi* that would be unthinkable on NHK or much American network news. This use of the telop, which was supported by editing showing Diet members sleeping, reflects the fact that commercial network news programs in Japan, as well as the so-called wide shows, have long enjoyed a relative freedom to engage in criticism and commentary of the news they report. What is new about the telop is that, instead of having the anchor or guest comment after the clip, they can provide viewers a model of critically evaluating the image as an image, destabilizing it from within. In that, one can see the potential for a kind of critical media literacy, one that is both involved and detached from the images, writing over them with alternative and sometimes resistive meanings. At the same time, such openly critical telops can fall into their own trap. With them, not only could the source of criticism become an anonymous, omniscient force, but telops again can take over the labor of criticism, the role the critical faculties of the viewer should play on their own.

The example thus shows that in the contemporary relations between consumption, power, and textuality, in both television and other potentially interactive media, it is appropriation that is the site of contestation. For whom and for what ends is the labor of the viewer being appropriated? One can conceive of some forms of textuality that refuse such appropriation[57]— I still hold out for the possibility of viewers appropriating their own labor and their own interpretations—but I doubt this can be done without making viewing an issue of collective agency, if not the public sphere itself. It is significant that Azuma, in his concluding remarks to *Dōbutsukasuru posutomodan* leaves interpretation up to the *individual* readers. In an age of atomistic reception of television and computers, it remains difficult to organize and collectivize reception and appropriate the fruits of one's own labor, especially when "participation" can seem so easy in comparison. When telop can make consumption so effortless, we have to begin thinking about the politics of less kindly forms of participation.

NOTES

1. Azuma Hiroki, *Dōbutsukasuru posutomodan* (Animalizing Postmodernity) (Tokyo: Kōdansha, 2001). This book has recently appeared in translation: *Otaku: Japan's Database Animals*, trans. Jonathan E. Abel and Shion Kono (Minneapolis: University of Minnesota Press, 2009). I refer only to the original Japanese text in this article and all translations are my own.

2. Much discourse, for instance, has been generated around sarin gas attacks committed by the apocalyptic cult Aum Supreme Truth in 1995, seeing in that either the end of an era or the polar opposite of a new youth culture better able to deal with contemporary existence. Other incidents, such as the burst of the economic bubble, the end of the cold war, or the death of the Shōwa emperor, have also served as milestones for arguing for a distinctly different contemporary moment through popular culture. On the end of an era, see Ōsawa Masachi's *Kyokō no jidai no hate* (The Edge of the Age of Fiction) (Tokyo: Chikuma Shobō, 1996) and *Sengo no shisō kūkan* (The Philosophical Space of the Postwar) (Tokyo: Chikuma Shobō, 1998). On the new youth culture, see Miyadai Shinji's *Owarinaki nichijō o ikiro* (Live the Endless Everyday) (Tokyo: Chikuma Shobō, 1998).

3. Ōta Shōichi, *Shakai wa warau: Boke to tsukkomi no ningen kankei* (Society Laughs: The Human Relations of Boke and Tsukkomi) (Tokyo: Seikyūsha, 2002). *Manzai*, a form of stand-up comedy that originated on the vaudeville stage, features two

performers: a straight man (*tsukkomi*) and a clown (*boke*). Many of the major stars on Japanese television, such as Beat Takeshi, Shimada Shinsuke, Utchan Nanchan (Uchimura Teruyoshi and Nanbara Kiyotaka), Tunnels (Ishibashi Takaaki and Kinashi Noritake), Downtown (Matsumoto Hitoshi and Hamada Masatoshi), Ninety Nine (Abe Hiroyuki and Okamura Takashi), and Cocorico (Endō Shōzō and Tanaka Naoki), are either *manzai* comedians or strongly influenced by *manzai* comedy.

4. Such complaints can be found on Web sites that discuss TV and entertainment such as Uozumi Akira's "Gokuraku TV shinan: Tōku baraeti, dai 1-kai" (Paradise TV Instruction: Talk Variety, Part 1) (http://tv.nifty.com/column/talk/010605.htm, accessed 30 January 2003) or Suzuki Yumi's "Engeki no senden" (Theater Publicity) *Butaiura dayori* (Backstage News) (http://www.kinokuniya.co.jp/05f/d_01/back/no16/essay/essay09.html, accessed 31 January 2003).

5. Sakamoto Mamoru, "Hanransuru jimaku bangumi no kōzai" (Plusses and Minusses of Shows Overflowing with Subtitles), *Galac*, June 1999, http://www.aa .alpha-net.ne.jp/mamos/tv/jimaku.htm, accessed 31 January 2003.

6. Telops in Japanese television are as much visual as linguistic texts. Jagged fonts can be used for yelling or "dripping" letters for eerie statements (in the tradition of the horror film) such that the graphic codified representation of the word itself visually embodies what is being said. Telops can also be aided by or substituted with sound effects that perform similar functions.

7. Consider, for example, a moment in the variety show *Nakai Masahiro no kin'yōbi no suma-tachi e* (Nakai Masahiro's "To the Friday Sumas," TBS). When a *tarento* panelist in the studio, speaking of the male participants in one of the show's corners, says the words "Speaking from my preference," Nakai, the show's host, kids him on his use of the word *preference* (*konomi*), jibing him about the implied homosexuality. This jibe, however, was prepared for by a telop of the *tarento*'s initial phrase, which singled out the word *preference* with a different color. The telop thus analyzed the flow of the dialogue across narrative time and laid the groundwork for both Nakai's comment and the audience's reading of it.

8. Uozumi, "Gokuraku TV shinan."

9. Kitamura Hideo, *Terebi media no kigōgaku* (Semiotics of TV Media) (Tokyo: Yūshindō Kōbunsha, 1985), 140–48.

10. Sakamoto, "Hanransuru jimaku."

11. In my forthcoming book *Visions of Japanese Modernity* (University of California Press), I argue against previous attempts to account for *benshi* through essentialist claims that the Japanese "prefer" explanation. See, for instance, Joseph L. Anderson and Donald Richie, *The Japanese Film: Art and Industry,* expanded ed. (Princeton: Princeton University Press, 1982), 23.

12. See my essay "Kankyaku no naka no benshi: Musei eiga ni okeru shutaisei to kazoku kokka" (The Benshi inside the Spectator: Subjectivity and the Family State in Silent Cinema) in Abé Mark Nornes and Aaron Gerow, eds. *In Praise of Film Studies: Essays in Honor of Makino Mamoru,* 130–38 (Yokohama: Kinema Kurabu, 2001). For

an account of post-1980s debates over "explanation" in television and film, see my *Kitano Takeshi* (London: British Film Institute, 2007).

13. Ōta Shōichi, *Shakai wa warau*, 69–70.

14. Ibid.,14–17.

15. Ibid., 41–51.

16. Ibid., 96–99. Ōta uses the example of *Suchuwadesu monogatari* (Stewardess Story, TBS), a romantic drama so conventional that it became a hit when people began tuning in to laugh at it.

17. Ibid., 81–83.

18. Ibid., 92–96.

19. Ibid., 54–59, 74–76.

20. Ibid., 103–11, 162–64.

21. Showing the reaction of *tarento* to other performers is a central aspect of variety programming: it augments the space of friends, guides viewer reactions, and when used in previews, shapes expectations regarding upcoming images.

22. It is thus unfortunate that Ōta, in making an essentially historical argument, ultimately undermines that historicity by relating the above-mentioned trends to an ahistorical rendition of Japanese culture as defined by *amae* (dependency) and the group. He argues, not necessarily uncritically, that shifts in *boke* and *tsukkomi* work to preserve the shreds of Japanese culture at its limits yet without detailing the transformations in power and capital that shredded "Japanese" culture in the first place or articulated the transformations of comedy he outlines.

23. Mitsuhiro Yoshimoto, "Image, Information, Commodity," in Xiaobing Tang and Stephen Snyder, eds., *In Pursuit of Contemporary East Asian Culture*, 123–138 (Boulder: Westview, 1996).

24. See, for instance, Sharon Kinsella, *Adult Manga: Culture and Power in Contemporary Japanese Society* (Honolulu: University of Hawai`i Press, 2000), 102–38. Similar practices abroad have been described as "textual poaching" by Henry Jenkins in his *Textual Poachers* (London: Routledge, 1992).

25. By *otaku* discourse I mean statements that aim to justify or culturally valorize the *otaku* phenomenon. *Otaku* generally refers to a fandom of mostly *manga* and anime that in the 1990s was considered excessively if not abnormally attached to its object of affection.

26. See Ōtsuka Eiji, *Teihon monogatari shōhiron* (Standard Edition: A Theory of Narrative Consumption) (Tokyo: Kadokawa Shoten, 2001), a revised edition of *Monogatari shōhiron* (Tokyo: Shin'yōsha, 1989). The cautious Ōtsuka goes on to historicize this analogy by arguing that today's process of interpretation involves even greater participation by the audience, one that is implicated with the desire for a *sekai* that has largely been lost in today's atomistic society.

27. Okada Toshio, *Otakugaku nyūmon* (Introduction to Otaku Studies) (Tokyo: Ōta Shuppan, 1996).

28. Azuma Hiroki, *Dōbutsukasuru posutomodan*, 14–38.

29. Sarah Thornton, "The Social Logic of Subcultural Capital," in Ken Gelder and Sarah Thornton, eds., *The Subcultures Reader*, 200–209 (London: Routledge, 1997).

30. Azuma Hiroki, *Dōbutsukasuru posutomodan*, 40.

31. Ibid., 54–62.

32. See Ōsawa Masachi, *Kyokō no jidai no hate* and *Sengo no shisō kūkan*.

33. Azuma Hiroki, *Dōbutsukasuru posutomodan*, 62–70.

34. See Lev Manovich, *The Language of New Media* (Cambridge: MIT Press, 2001).

35. See Murakami Takashi, *Superflat* (Tokyo: Madra, 2000); and Azuma Hiroki, *Dōbutsukasuru posutomodan*, 144–61. Azuma tries to distance himself slightly from Murakami's concept by using the kanji term *chōheimensei* instead of the katakana *sūpāfuratto*.

36. Manovich, *The Language of New Media*, 326–30.

37. Quoted in Sakamoto, "Hanransuru jimaku."

38. Azuma Hiroki, *Dōbutsukasuru posutomodan*, 122–23.

39. Ibid., 98–100.

40. Ibid., 126–129.

41. Ibid., 136–37.

42. Ibid., 132, 140.

43. Ibid., 174–75.

44. Alan Stoekl, "'Round Dusk: Kojève at 'The End,'" *Postmodern Culture* 5, no. 1 (September 1994). (http://muse.jhu.edu/journals/postmodern_culture/v005/5.1stoekl .html, accessed 20 February 2009)

45. Azuma Hiroki, *Dōbutsukasuru posutomodan*, 114.

46. Ibid., 130.

47. See Ōtsuka Eiji, *Teihon monogatari shohiron*, 33–40. Far from critiquing this, Ōtsuka urges corporations to further pursue this kind of marketing and urges us to reject academism and embrace consumerism (54).

48. Azuma Hiroki, *Dōbutsukasuru posutomodan*, 88.

49. For a forceful presentation of such a critique of subculture studies, see Gary Clarke, "Defending Ski-Jumpers: A Critique of Theories of Youth Subcultures," in Ken Gelder and Sarah Thornton, eds., *The Subcultures Reader*, 175–80 (London: Routledge, 1997).

50. See, for instance, Timothy Corrigan's discussion of glance and gaze aesthetics in relation to recent cinema in *A Cinema without Walls: Movies and Culture after Vietnam* (Bloomington: Indiana University Press, 1991), 26–33.

51. This, of course, emulates the structures of serial films or television but in a fashion that not only puts the cliffhanger inside a single episode but often refuses even the provisional textual closure of the classic cliffhanger, which uses such devices as

"To be continued" to confirm that episode's conclusion. Many variety shows will cut to a commercial, interrupting the action or narration, without such provisional closures.

52. Ōta Shōichi, *Shakai wa warau*, 153–54.

53. See Jonathan Beller, *The Cinematic Mode of Production: Attention Economy and the Society of the Spectacle* (Hanover, N.H.: Dartmouth College Press, 2006).

54. In an interesting parallel in variety programming, many shows from *Urinari* to *Kuizu! Hekisagon II* (Quiz! Hexagon II, Fuji) have made viewer purchasing activity part of the show. A famous example is when *Denpa shōnen* locked the unsuccessful pop group Something Else in an apartment with an ultimatum: either produce a single that debuts in the top ten or break up. The resulting song, fed by the show's drawn-out narrative of the group's struggles, debuted at number two on the charts. In such cases, television is practically celebrating its manipulation of consumer behavior by making the viewer's labor, which the viewer herself pays for, central to the narrative.

55. Telops shift the center of textual creation from pre-production and production to post-production, as it is the considerable effort by unknown personnel after the show is taped that shapes the core of the program. Telops can help maintain the *tarento* system by removing that much of the burden of creating entertainment from overworked performers who can appear in up to a dozen shows a week (one even sees the occasional *tarento* on air joking that they hoped some mediocre gag they just said would be "fixed" through telops), but they also reduce the importance of performer labor, taking away control of the value they may produce and concentrate it in the production company or network. Such shifts in both the temporality and the economy of television align Japanese variety programming with American reality shows, which reduce the role of pre-production (scriptwriting), render performers dispensable and exchangeable, and place considerable emphasis on the processing of recorded footage after production is completed. The fact that it has been variety shows that have most taken up the reality format, by recording *tarento* undertaking various "real-life" tasks, confirms the parallel and suggests again how transformations in modes of production link with changes in program content.

56. Telops, when they do appear in dramatic shows, such as in the outtakes section of the last episode of *Kimochi ii koi shitai* (I Want a Feel-Good Romance, Fuji, 1990), function in part to designate a distance from a diegetic world.

57. In my book on *Kitano Takeshi* and elsewhere, I have argued that some contemporary Japanese filmmakers consciously oppose the overexplanatory style of television with a form of cinema that refrains from forcing an explanation on spectators, instead encouraging them to provide the meaning on their own. This could be considered a strategy of nonappropriation but one that only succeeds through audience consciousness.

Revolutionary Girls:
From Oscar to Utena

Noriko Aso

More thrilling and stylish than a beruffled princess, more noble and beautiful than a muscle-bound knight, the heroic young woman who adopts a masculine identity and triumphs in a male world of adventure is a recurring figure in postwar Japanese popular culture. Eyes flashing, locks flowing, sword or fist raised to defend the defenseless, her dashing image has inspired deep and enduring fan devotion. Significantly, she is often portrayed as an agent of "revolution." In this essay, I examine a particular trajectory for this archetype that traverses three television animation series: from Oscar François de Jarjayes in Ikeda Riyoko's *The Rose of Versailles* (*Berusaiyu no Bara*) through Fujinami Ryūnosuke in Takahashi Rumiko's *Those Obnoxious Aliens* (*Urusei Yatsura*) to Tenjō Utena in Be-Papas's *Revolutionary Girl Utena* (*Shōjo Kakumei Utena*).[1] All three series have left their mark on television animation history. *The Rose of Versailles*, shown on Nippon TV from 1979 to 1980, was a pioneering entry in the development of animation for a female audience. *Those Obnoxious Aliens*, shown on Fuji TV from 1981 to 1986, constituted a key moment of expansion for Takahashi Rumiko's creative empire, which continues to break down audience gender, generational, and national barriers. *Revolutionary Girl Utena*, shown on TV Tokyo from 1997 to 1998, gained a certain notoriety for the outrage that some viewers expressed regarding the dark skin color of one of the main characters.[2] However, in this essay, rather than discussing these works in terms of general television history, I explore the distinctiveness of the medium by tracking how these stories were "translated" from their original comic book (*manga*) form into weekly animated series.[3] In particular, I focus on the televised incarnations of Oscar, Ryūnosuke and Utena because their animation brought out new dimensions of their characters in more than movement and sound. The spotlight on these figures was adjusted for the new stage they occupied, new story lines were created, and the link between their unconventional behavior and "revolution" was made all the more emphatic. Nevertheless, what was meant by "revolution" differed in each work. Indeed, the very strength of the lineage that links these characters provides us with an opportunity to assess some of the limits, as well as possibilities, of conceptualizing "revolutionary" gender identities from the 1970s through the 1990s.

FIRST TIME AS TRAGEDY

The author and artist Ikeda Riyoko was a revolutionary girl herself, one of a remarkable group of female artists that transformed young girls' comics (*shōjo manga*) in the late 1960s and early 1970s.[4] Her work, *The Rose of Versailles*, which ran in the weekly *Margaret* from 1972 to 1973, played a central role in this deepening and darkening of themes explored within the genre.[5] Inspired by the work of Stefan Zweig on the doomed life of Marie Antoinette,[6] Ikeda threw herself into meticulous historical research for this "great adventure" (*taihen na bōken*).[7] Meanwhile, to win support from her skeptical editors, Ikeda swore to keep the story easy to follow even as she dealt with such topics as death, adultery, and revolution. Ikeda's foolhardy guarantees of success, given to convince her editors, were more than fulfilled; *The Rose of Versailles* was not only an instant hit, it went on to spark a national sensation. As soon as the series concluded, Shūeisha published a ten-volume special edition. Sales quickly reached twelve million, a first for a work in the girls' comic genre. Teachers assigned it as a supplementary text in history classrooms, and school libraries added it to their shelves. French language and literature classes enjoyed a surge in enrollment, while Japanese tours of France were organized around landmarks from the series.[8] With Ikeda's work, girls' comics reached a new level of social acceptance and even respect.

While *The Rose of Versailles* basically begins with Marie Antoinette's arrival at the French court and ends with her execution at the hands of the French people, Ikeda also develops a number of subplots populated by a broad range of both historical and fictional figures. Through clashes between the various perspectives she introduces, Ikeda explores the dramatic tensions of the prerevolutionary era—and her own. Indeed, from very early on it was clear that Marie Antoinette was not the one who was inspiring unprecedented numbers of readers to rush to buy each issue of *Margaret*, write enthusiastic letters. and form fan clubs. The readers vastly preferred the fictional character of Oscar François de Jarjayes, the strong, handsome, daring, and dashing head of Marie's royal guards. A stock character for a historical romance, except that Oscar is a woman raised as a man in order to fulfill her aristocratic father's need for an heir. Oscar's struggles to shape her own destiny—to transcend social boundaries and forge her own gender and class identity—obviously struck a chord.

As Ikeda's work was translated into other media, such as the hit Takarazuka musical, Oscar began to occupy an increasingly dominant role in the narrative.[9] By the time the story was turned into an animated series for television in 1979, the "Rose" of the title had been redefined as a reference to Oscar.[10] In the process, the rose became a symbol not only for a showy, exotic kind of beauty but for a beauty that was noble and born of great pain. Each week, the first image impressed on the viewer in the opening credits was that of Oscar's naked body bound in thorny vines. The viewer was then swept up as wind rushed through a forest of thorns, over grassy plains, and up to the stark silhouette of Oscar kneeling, rose petals scattering from her hand. The wind flows into a uniformed Oscar standing alone on a pinnacle. A white rose fills the screen and turns red. Finally, the sequence ends with Oscar's body bound again in thorns. This time, however, she holds a sword and has apparently succeeded in partially setting herself free. The song lyrics accompanying these images further underscore the elements of valiance and adventure: "I was born under the rule of the rose, born to live brightly and to the extreme / A rose blooms proudly, a rose scatters beautifully." Marie Antoinette is literally nowhere in sight. Yet she is by no means excluded from "rosehood." Indeed, she is often portrayed in the series with a rose tucked in her hair. Marie even occupies the foreground in her portrait with Oscar in the closing credits, which features stills of the main characters. In the course of the series, rosehood is redefined through Oscar to be a *sisterhood* composed of strong, exceptional women—good and bad—who share knowledge of pain. The importance of pain is underscored by the melancholy lyrics for the closing credits: "If love is pain, however much [it hurts], let us suffer together . . . / The more we suffer, the more our love will deepen."

For Oscar, pain and conflict are intrinsic to her condition as a woman raised as a man. In the first episode, flashes of lightning and roaring thunder provide a dramatic backdrop for Oscar's father when, with a wild light in his eyes, he decrees that his newborn daughter, latest in a long succession of daughters, will be raised as a son to be his heir. A stormy future for Oscar is similarly augured by the weather the night she wrestles with her father's demand that she accept a position commanding the palace guards of Marie Antoinette. Oscar protests that she has no interest in such a girly assignment, but her reluctance is gradually revealed to stem from an internal "struggle between [being] a woman and a man" (*otoko to onna no tatakai*). Oscar knows that this decision marks a point of no return: femininity will be forever barred to her once she agrees to perform masculinity not just at home, in play, but in the public eye, as her job. After a gloomy night of contemplation and a bracing fistfight with her best friend the next morning, Oscar's decision is revealed when she appears resplendent in her commander's uniform at the top of a towering staircase. Yet sacrifice and dark resolve, as much as or more than triumph, marks this moment in which she embraces her destiny as a hero.

What was sacrificed at this crossroads? Oscar's father, who undergoes a very belated change of heart in episode 30, pleads with Oscar to turn away from masculinity by accepting a marriage proposal from a fellow aristocrat: "Please forgive your father . . . for not being able to raise you in happiness as a woman. . . . My greatest failure in life was to not think of your true happiness as a gentle (*sunao*), natural (*shizen*) woman." Yet for much of the series Oscar appears to have little interest in romance let alone marriage and childbirth. Indeed, the still teenage Oscar adopts an absurdly mature—both disapproving and compassionate—attitude toward the illicit love growing between Marie Antoinette and the Swedish noble Hans Axel von Fersen. Acting as a reluctant go-between, however, seems gradually to sensitize Oscar's heart to romance. As Fersen becomes a close friend, then rescuer, Oscar finds herself in love as well. For Fersen, Oscar attempts once and only once to play the conventional woman. In episode 25, she attends a ball in an elegant gown and styled hair, "disguising" herself as a foreign aristocrat by preserving a graceful silence. Stunned by her beauty, Fersen asks her to dance. As they whirl around the ballroom, Fersen murmurs that she reminds him of a very dear friend. Realizing that Fersen will never be able to think of her everyday self as an object of romance, Oscar breaks away in tears. Alone outside, she brings herself to accept the situation with the thought, "With this [time in his arms], I can give up [my dreams of Fersen] (*kore de watashi wa akiramerareru*)." Dressed as a woman, Oscar acts like a stereotypical woman, which, based on the examples of her mother and sisters, means being weak, submissive, and practically invisible. So Oscar's eventual response to the Fersen interlude is to become more masculine: "I want to live even more as a man (*yori otoko to shite*)." And her reply to her father's suggestion of marriage in episode 30 is first to laugh and then to thank her father for teaching her to live with strength and courage.

In the end, however, Oscar learns to transcend the binaries that threaten to rend or perhaps worse, calcify her. Her transformation, moreover, is inextricably intertwined with the French Revolution looming on the horizon: the series opens with a reference to the blindness of the aristocrats to the poverty of the people and climaxes with the storming of the Bastille. Oscar's instinct to cross boundaries is evident from her childhood when she befriends the stable boy André and makes him her boon companion. In episode 10 Oscar begins to become conscious of the disastrous implications of, and therefore the need to bridge, the gap between the aristocrats and the common folk through an encounter with Rosalie, a young girl who begs Oscar to "buy" her so that she can get some medicine for her dying mother. Oscar gives the girl money and tells her never again to think of prostitution as an answer. Moreover, Oscar gradually comes to see that individual acts of kindness to those weaker than herself are not enough; a more systemic response to the problems facing French society is needed. She warns Marie repeatedly that to be a great queen her generosity needs to be extended to the French people, not just to her immediate friends. While Marie will not listen, Oscar's political reeducation proceeds apace, bringing her into contact with none other than Robespierre.

In the final episodes, Oscar's personal and political trajectories become increasingly entangled. To avoid further contact with Fersen after confessing her love, she leaves the palace guards to command a regiment of commoners. Their hostility to her aristocratic background forces her to physically prove her merit as a leader rather than simply relying on her elite connections. Her position as their commander then leads her to strike a deal with revolutionary acquaintances to save a number of her men from execution. Finally, the social and political revolution becomes identical with the personal when Oscar realizes at last that her one true love has been André, a commoner, all along. Significantly, for this love Oscar does not dress or act as a woman. Quite the contrary. André has been clear all along that he loves Oscar exactly as she is and without limits, "everything, to the end of my life (*subete o, inochi aru kagiri*)." Their romance is explicitly configured as one of equality, class and gender lines blurring in the friendship that underpins their love. Thus, in episode 37 their lovemaking is conveyed in large part through the movements of fireflies reflected in still water, symmetrical patterns tracing a tender dance of complementary partners.[11] With André, Oscar casts her lot with the commoners and revolutionaries, bidding a firm though melancholy farewell to both her father and Marie Antoinette.[12] The scene with the latter is particularly wrenching, as Marie looks abandoned and betrayed.

At the moment of the storming of the Bastille, Oscar and the revolution are glorious. However, Oscar is targeted and killed as she issues commands to fire on the prison. Meanwhile, as explained in the final episode, the revolution soon loses its noble ideals as it descends into individual ambition, political factionalism, and terror. The conclusions we draw from this tale of transgression are thus mixed. Oscar is the hero of the tale, without question. Yet she dies sui generis, without leaving a legacy. The aristocracy is not redeemed by her example, nor is there anyone to follow in her footsteps. Oscar, in the early stages of tuberculosis, and André, slowly going blind from a head wound, were doomed even before their social rebellion. Was a second generation forbidden to their bonding? Even the young girl Rosalie, for a while cultivated as a successor to Oscar's manly ways, reverts to her social class, her femininity, and heterosexuality once she leaves Oscar's protection. In sum, while Oscar was far more fascinating than her queen, challenging and crossing various social boundaries, her adventures came at a forbidding price, and her fate was, if anything, more tragic than that of Marie Antoinette. While Oscar at least ended up on the "right" side of social history by participating on the side of the people, she remained an exception rather than an example.

SECOND TIME AS FARCE

Takahashi Rumiko overturned a few assumptions about the possibilities for female comic book artists herself. She began as an amateur in a college club but broke into the professional world by winning a Shogakkan competition for new artists with "Those Selfish Aliens" (*Katte na Yatsura*). This piece was reworked into the classic and award-winning series *Those Obnoxious Aliens* (*Urusei Yatsura*), which ran in *Shōnen Sunday* from 1979 to 1986.[13] What was so unique about her success? Takahashi was a pioneer for women working in—and reworking—the broader and more lucrative field of comics aimed at boys (*shōnen manga*), not the relatively specialized market for girls. Her popularity has only continued to grow both in Japan and internationally with such hit series as *Ranma 1/2* and *Inuyasha*.

The main story line of the comedic romance *Those Obnoxious Aliens* centers on the tumultuous relationship between Ataru, a high school boy with "the life strength of a cockroach" (*gokiburi no seimei ryoku*) devoted to chasing girls, and Lum, a girl from outer space with electrifying powers that she uses to try to make him settle down. A huge cast of characters—stereotypes pushed to their absurd limits, such as the aforementioned Ataru, who resembles a Prince Genji gone mad, or figures defined by ludicrously mismatched character traits, such as Sakura, the glamorous Shinto priestess with an appetite that would put lumberjacks to shame—pitches in to maintain a constant state of chaos. One such recurring character introduced midway through the series is a clear parody of Oscar François de Jarjayes. Like Oscar, Fujinami Ryūnosuke is handsome, dashing, and brave and was raised by her father as a "male" heir. However, the father's legacy is not an aristocratic title but a ramshackle and bankrupt snack hut at the seaside, and instead of the exotic splendors of the eighteenth-century French court Ryūnosuke's stage for action is an at least superficially ordinary Japanese high school. Like Oscar, Ryūnosuke is torn between pride in her self-sufficiency and accomplishments as a fighter and awareness that her masculine upbringing has cost her the ordinary joys of girlhood. However, Ryūnosuke is not a noble commander but a hotheaded hooligan. Meanwhile, the femininity to which she is drawn is not the romantic grace of tragic queens but the cloying cuteness of teddy bears and fruit parfaits. Thus, Ryūnosuke evokes laughter, not sorrow, with her catchphrase "[But] I am a woman!" (*ore wa onna da*).

The animated version for television, which ran from 1981 to 1986, capitalized on Fujinami Ryūnosuke's possibilities and fan appeal.[14] It expanded her story lines and rounded out her characterization through sound, movement, and a ratcheting up of intertextual references that range from the boxing classic *Tomorrow's Joe* (*Ashita no Joe*) to Herman Melville's *Moby Dick*.[15] In particular, *The Rose of Versailles* connection was celebrated all the more openly as the animators exploited the crossover audience possibilities that the television medium offered. A number of the male readers of the comic book version might have easily missed the various subtle and not so subtle girls' comic references that cropped up from time to time. However, savoring the absurdity of the scene in episode 88 when Ryūnosuke's sexual orientation is debated by her classmates demanded, not simply hoped for, cross-gendered television literacy. Spectacle sports and historical drama meet head on as Megane (who fancies himself an intellectual and the class conscience) intones, "Fujinami Ryūnosuke, who, as we know has been raised all these years as a boy, could well have an anima and libido as twisted as the spine of a luckless pro-wrestler trapped in Antonio's 'Special Destruction Hold'." All the while, the aqua-tinted screen is filled with the image of Ryūnosuke's naked body bound in thorns as rose petals flow around and up in spiraling columns.

Such intertextual referencing was also the way the television version of a particular episode could extend a scenario that only took a few pages to play out in the original into a full half hour of entertainment. This was certainly the case in the transformation of the chapter "Hard Work, the Way of Women!" (Doryoku, Onna no Michi!) into episode 113, "Lady Ryūnosuke"

(Redii Ryūnosuke).[16] What starts out in the manga as a brief interlude in which Ataru offers to teach Ryūnosuke how to be more feminine balloons in the anime version into a group project involving most of the major characters in a not unsophisticated discussion of gender. Into this are woven parodies of, to begin with, teacher tearjerkers, the volleyball comic book classics *The Sign Is V* and *Attack No. 1*, and Robert Louis Stevenson's *Treasure Island*. Events are set in motion when Ryūnosuke's homeroom teacher, Mr. Onsen, asks her if she would like to become a woman (*onna ni naritai to omowan ka*). Insulted, Ryūnosuke responds by beating Onsen up. Onsen approaches her later with a slightly more thought-out proposal: would she consider one week's worth of concentrated training (*tokkun*) to make her into the kind of girl that would look natural in a sailor suit school uniform, pleated skirt and all? He challenges Ryūnosuke to look into her heart and honestly answer whether it was only her father who oppressed the girl inside. Has it not been easier to just go on acting like a boy? Borrowing from Simone de Beauvoir, he presses his point: "A woman is not born, she is made." As his earnest speech gains intensity, strong winds pick up and lightning flashes, sly references, no doubt, to the wild weather of Oscar's times of crisis. Ryūnosuke looks shaken by this speech. It is, however, the promise of looking good in a sailor suit that ultimately inspires her to cry out, "I WILL become a woman!"

The first stage of training involves taped lectures to drum into Ryūnosuke's brain what are, according to Onsen, the two cardinal principles of femininity (*onna rashisa*): do not engage in violent behavior and do not use rough language. When Ryūnosuke's classmates learn of the project, they compete to offer advice of their own. Tireless girl chaser Ataru begins by observing that he is far more qualified than Onsen or Ryūnosuke to comment on the essence of womanhood based on his long study of the subject. He goes on to prove himself an uncanny female impersonator by employing a series of stylized expressions and gestures, somewhat reminiscent of the tradition of Kabuki *onnagata*, to conjure up a surprisingly old-school version of "woman." On the other hand, two of the most popular girls in class, Lum and Shinobu, insist that *real* girls ought to be the ones to impart femininity, though they fall into squabbling among themselves over what should be considered "normal." The cloyingly cute Ran is then brought in as a special coach to teach Ryūnosuke the secrets of flirting and eating a parfait in a ladylike manner. Taken aback at the depths of Ryūnosuke's social backwardness, Ran suggests that perhaps she should first aim at being a little softer (*yawarakai*). However, special coach number two, the drop-dead gorgeous Sakura, says flatly that there is no such thing as femininity (*sonna mono wa nai*)—or masculinity either. The most "essential" thing for humans is to eat![17]

Despite being pulled in so many different directions, Ryūnosuke doggedly pursues her training in subjects ranging from cosmetics to cooking, though she looks miserable all the while. Indeed, it hard to say who looks more incongruous going through these paces, Ryūnosuke or the middle-aged male Onsen, who accompanies her each step of the way. But her hard work seems to have paid off when she appears for her final trial looking fabulous in the white and black gown and oversized hat and veil that Eliza Doolittle wore to the Ascot Races in a delirious reference to the film version of *My Fair Lady*. The test is to remain calm and ladylike amid the excitement of a professional wrestling match. Poor Ryūnosuke is, of course, doomed to fail. When a wrestler inadvertently tears her dress, Onsen pleads with her to endure this offense. However, Ryūnosuke's other friends insist that defending herself is perfectly womanly; Lum sums it up by observing that a real woman fights for what is important to her. Chaos ensues as Ryūnosuke takes on the entire wrestling establishment, aided and abetted by her comrades.

What is there of revolution in Ryūnosuke's tale? The key seems to lie in the frenzy of concern around her sexuality. It is significant that in "Lady Ryūnosuke," Onsen's initial question "do you want to become a woman?" is preceded by a scene in which schoolgirls scrabble for possession of a volleyball handled by Ryūnosuke. Everyone knows that Ryūnosuke is a girl even though she acts like a boy, which is also the case for Oscar François de Jarjayes. Ryūnosuke particularly excites a great deal of admiration from other females for her distinctive style, as does Oscar. Some of her fans sigh, "if only she were male." But others clearly love her precisely because she is not. Herein lies the problem from the perspective of the males in Ryūnosuke's high school. Homosexuality is explicitly raised as an issue in the anime version of *Those Obnoxious Aliens* in a way that contrasts with the anime version of *The Rose of Versailles*, where it is at best a latent possibility in the "masculine" aspects of Oscar and André's coupling. From the first episode in which Ryūnosuke appears, her male classmates are jealous of all the attention she receives from the girls and mutter about such relations being "improper" (*tadashiku nai*) and "unhealthy" (*fukenkō*).[18] This—together with the fact that Ryūnosuke raises the bar for the boys since she is described by her fans as epitomizing the good side of masculinity without any of the drawbacks of real males—provides the boys with a powerful motivation to bring Ryūnosuke under the sign of the feminine. Until this is accomplished, girlish libidos will continue to be stimulated by the presence of this masculine female while males will be judged inferior. The masses will not be contained.

For her own part, Ryūnosuke seems unaware of the excitement she generates and largely steers clear of romance, once again much like Oscar. Yet in the regular run of the animated series her closest brushes with the dating scene are in fact encounters with other women.[19] While most of these scenarios are based on multiple and colliding sets of "misrecognitions," Ryūnosuke comes closest to finding her soul mate in the form of a cute biker chick. Episode 135, "Benten and Ryūnosuke: Run Facing Tomorrow!" (Benten to Ryūnosuke Asu ni Mukatte Hashire!)—an original story for the television series—depicts the teaming up of Ryūnosuke with Benten, one of Lum's friends from outer space and the only other girl in the series to evenly match Ryūnosuke in such "masculine" traits as rough manners, tough language, and a readiness to rumble. What unfolds is an extended send-up of buddy movie conventions as the two set off on a quest to save a little girl's lost kitten. Their relationship is delicately sexualized, as is so often the case with buddy movies. This is underscored in the final scene when Ryūnosuke is kissed by the little girl in thanks for getting her kitten back. Benten comments, "Cute girlfriend." When Ryūnosuke shouts back, "I'm a woman!" Benten slyly smiles and says, "I know."

In the end, however, Ryūnosuke's revolution is not in her flirtation with lesbianism, although it certainly rattles the complacency of most of the males around her. As seen in "Lady Ryūnosuke," her constitutional inability to act in a manner socially constructed as feminine suggests that the central upheaval contained within Takahashi's work is the implication that gender is a matter of performance rather than essence. Thus, the eventual romantic resolution Takahashi provides for Ryūnosuke in her inimitable fashion is one in which this revolution is made permanent, as in a perpetual motion machine. Who might constitute an ideal mate for a young woman who thinks, feels, and acts like a man? None other than a young man, Nagisa, who thinks, feels, and acts like a woman (introduced for animation in a video feature issued after the regular series had ended).[20] While complementarity is achieved, gender norms remain forever distanced and divorced from biological sex.

REFLECTION AND REFRACTION

In the late 1990s, Be-Papas, a creative collective anchored by comic book artist Saitō Chiho and animation director Ikuhara Kunihiko, produced *Revolutionary Girl Utena* (*Shōjo Kakumei Utena*), a story in comic book, animation,[21] and movie form that pays clear tribute to the now iconic Oscar.[22] The members of Be-Papas belong to a generation for which comics and animation have "always" been dominant and mainstream vehicles for popular culture. As readers and viewers, growing up has been intimately intertwined with both individual and collective consumption of these narratives.[23] As artists, their way has been paved by the likes of Ikeda and Takahashi. Saitō Chiho, for example, was known for her reproductions of images from *The Rose of Versailles* while still an amateur in school clubs.[24] Her special affinity for Oscar is further revealed in the title of her first published piece, "The Sword and Mademoiselle" (*Ken to Madomoazeru*). For his part, Ikuhara Kunihiko laments having had to suppress his imagination during the transition from fanciful youth to dreary adulthood, even as he carved out a respected (perhaps too respected?) position within the creative field of animation.[25] Ikuhara has, moreover, a particular association with action heroines: he is best known for directing the international hit series *Sailor Moon* (*Bishōjo Senshi Sērā Mūn*), which features "pretty knights" in school uniform. Although a sense of ennui—what can be said that is new?—clouds the beginning of Ikuhara's account of his initial search for a suitable subject for Be-Papas, he finds inspiration in the end by returning to the past, both of his youth and of the genre of girls' comics.[26] Nevertheless, the homage to *The Rose of Versailles* that is woven through *Revolutionary Girl Utena*, though loving, is hardly slavish. Oscar's tale is ruthlessly pulled apart and pieced together again for a significant rereading. Reminiscent of much fan fiction, while favorite elements are retained, disappointing developments are rewritten to fan satisfaction and latent, especially sexual, possibilities are explored in greater depth.[27]

Once again, the central character is a dashing teenage girl who dresses and acts in a masculine manner, Tenjō Utena. She is beautiful, brave, and much admired by boys and girls alike. Utena spends most of the series trying to protect her friend Himemiya Anthy, the "Rose Bride" (*bara no hanayome*), from the attempts of other characters to take possession of her. Again we have twin roses: if Utena is Oscar, then Anthy is Marie Antoinette, the romantic queen who must be defended against a hostile world.[28] The setting is a fancy European-style boarding school up on a hill, self-enclosed, and completely separated from ordinary society, replicating the aristocratic isolation of Versailles. Proud to the point of arrogance, the top students of Ohtori Academy immerse themselves in intrigue and power plays, often resolving their conflicts through sword duels. In addition to such broad structural similarities, small details insistently remind the viewer of the relationship between original and revision. Roses and rose tints serve as ubiquitous design elements, from blossoms in the background, to the rose signet rings of a "revolutionary" secret society, to the pink of Utena's hair. Meanwhile, the alternate, or "translated," title of the series is provided in French: *La fillette revolutionnaire.*

However, *Revolutionary Girl Utena* does not simply replicate the *The Rose of Versailles* experience for a later generation. Oscar's identity as a masculine female sets her on the path toward a series of tragic sacrifices that culminate in the loss of her life and legacy. Ryūnosuke furiously insists on her womanhood even as she is repeatedly confronted with the fact that she is constitutionally incapable of performing femininity. In contrast, Utena breezily shrugs off any suggestion of gender conflict within herself. In the first episode, she is introduced calmly responding to an irate teacher's demand that she dress in a girl's uniform: "There's no rule that says a girl can't wear a boy's uniform. Guess there's no problem." In the next scene, Utena outplays the boys on a basketball court. At the end of the game, her female fans gather around to offer towels and drinks and the captain of the basketball team invites her to join. Utena's reply? "Excuse me, but I happen to be a girl (*boku wa joshi*)! I'd hate to get covered with smelly boys' sweat." When the captain presses his case, saying that Utena acts like a boy anyway, she claims to be insulted. Why, then, the captain asks, does she wear a boy's uniform? Utena explains that her desire is not to be a boy as such, but "rather than be a protected princess (*mamorareru himesama*), I want to be a dashing prince (*kakko ii ōjisama*)." Utena seems unconcerned with, and therefore will not be sidetracked by, social conventions regarding biological sex and gender in relation to power. This is not to say, however, that *Revolutionary Girl Utena* joins *Those Obnoxious Aliens* in lightheartedly poking fun at the tragic conflicts of *The Rose of Versailles*. If anything, *Utena* distills the themes of pain, betrayal, and sacrifice into an even more concentrated cocktail. Oscar's internal "struggle between man and woman" is redefined or clarified as Utena's choice of power in the structural position of protector rather than submission as the protected.

Power—what it is, how one gains it, and how one wields it—is in fact one of the organizing principles of the series. The central relationship between Utena and Anthy is explicitly developed to provide opportunities to think through not only the defining poles of power but also its limits. That is, if, on the one hand, we can identify Utena with action and mastery and Anthy with passiveness and obedience, on the other, their friendship begins and ends with a questioning of the inevitability of the master-slave dynamic. In episode 1, Utena is inadvertently drawn into a secret world of intrigue in the academy when she challenges Saionji Kyōichi, vice president of the Student Council, to a duel over his cruel mockery of her friend Wakaba. It turns out that fighting with a member of the council means more than a brawl in a back lot: there is an elevated stadium, an elaborate set of rituals, and a rock opera soundtrack for such duels. Ordinary students are not allowed in this sanctum, but Utena happens to wear a special rose signet ring that gains her entry. She is shocked to find that the stakes in the duel are higher than she supposed: the victor wins Anthy as his or her fiancée to do with as he or she pleases. As unusual as Utena in her own way, Anthy represents an extreme version of "femininity" understood as both desirability and submissiveness. In fact, in her first appearance she is being abused by her "fiancé," Saionji. Since Utena is only seeking to avenge her friend Wakaba, she attempts to release Anthy from this bond of servitude as soon as she puts the unpleasant Saionji in his place. However, Anthy smilingly refuses this freedom. She insists on serving Utena both in ordinary life by cooking and cleaning for her and in the fighting arena by producing a special sword from her breast that Utena can use in subsequent duels. Though repulsed by this unequal relationship, Utena continues to fight to protect Anthy from falling under the power of more ruthless duelists. Meanwhile, she keeps trying to convince Anthy that a more egalitarian relationship, a friendship, is possible.

As the series comes to a climax, we find that the protector-protected relationship between Utena and Anthy is not quite as it seems. Anthy's steadfast though passive resistance to Utena's suggestions that she break loose, make some friends, and lead a normal life provides the first clue that she is not quite "without will." We then find that Anthy has been hiding an incestuous sexual relationship with her older brother, Akio, the charismatic director of the academy. It is finally revealed that Anthy is one of the most powerful and manipulative figures in the story, a "witch" (*majo*) who has been quietly but inexorably leading Utena and the other duelists to their doom at the behest of her brother. Meanwhile, Utena becomes increasingly feminized in the later episodes, temporarily seduced into playing a "princess" with Akio as her dark "prince." This arc culminates in Anthy's *piercing* Utena with a sword, saying, "You can't become my prince, because you are a girl" (watashi no ōjisama ni wa narenai, onnanoko dakara), just as Utena finally confronts Akio directly in a duel. Not so incidentally, this is the first time in the series that a duel results in a direct, mortal wound rather than being settled symbolically through the taking of one's opponent's rose.

As in *The Rose of Versailles*, we have two strong women who end up at odds. In *Utena* this relationship is recentered and reworked so that it is both more complicated than that of Oscar and Marie and yet more optimistic about the possibilities for female friendship. As part of the fan revisionism that gives us the relationship we would like to have seen, the story of the relationship in *Utena* does not end at the moment of tragic betrayal, as when Oscar must reject Marie's request for protection against the people's uprising. Instead, Utena's ongoing efforts to introduce friendship to Anthy turn out to not have been in vain: subtly they begin to wean Anthy from the brutal affections of her brother. We find, in the final episode, that the story may actually have been about Anthy all along, as in the final frames she takes center stage and learns to accept the possibility of female friendship and love. Anthy had to learn to choose Utena, just as one might wish Marie had transcended herself to choose Oscar.

Power is pursued by many of the main characters because they see it as the means to effect revolution. Whenever members of the Student Council meet in their chambers, they open their sessions by reciting "If it cannot break its eggshell, a chick will die without being born. We are the chick, the world is our egg. If we don't crack the world's shell, we will die without being born. Smash the world's shell! For the revolution of the world!" Yet the content of this revolution is never specified beyond a vague association with eternity. Do the council members wish to enslave or liberate the world? Do they represent particular constituencies? Do they have programs or policies to implement? None of that seems relevant to "revolution" in the eyes of the major players. They prove incapable of imagining a world beyond Ohtori Academy; the school is closed in to the point of claustrophobia. Indeed, it becomes clear in the final episodes that this world is much like, or may literally be, a coffin. As Akio silkily but sinisterly reveals in episode 22, "As long as he or she stays in this garden we call the academy, a person will never become an adult." The Student Council members do not understand that the "eternal thing" (*eien na mono*) they think they will gain with revolution is in fact already all around them. Eternity and immortality are nothing more than death. Eternity is the opposite of revolution.

In contrast, Utena is free from the obsession with revolution that absorbs the other duelists. She is initially drawn in to their secret world because of her desire to protect her friends; this desire is also what eventually frees her from it. The ability to think of others allows Utena to reach beyond herself, beyond the school, beyond the fabric of reality. In the last episode, "Someday Together We'll Shine" (Itsuka Issho ni Kagayaite), Utena finally is able to consciously recall what first motivated her to choose "princehood" and come to Ohtori Academy, pushing aside the weight of time and social convention that had warped her memories of a pivotal moment when she was a young girl. Having just lost her parents, the child Utena also lost hope and lay down in a coffin to wait for death. A beautiful young prince—Dios, the better half or twin of Akio—came by just then and "rescued" her by giving her a reason to live. However, unlike the distorted version of events given as an origin story at the beginning of several episodes in the series, this reason to live was not the clichéd romantic dream of meeting the perfect prince once more. Rather, it was to liberate the prince's sister, Anthy, who had been sentenced to eternal torture by being pierced with swords for trying to protect her brother, the prince, from the world's incessant demands for rescue. In the final duel, Utena is betrayed by this same sister and brother and left for dead. Akio turns to the Rose Gate, behind which lies the power to revolutionize the world. He hacks at the gate with a sword forged from Utena's spirit, but to no avail. As Anthy is targeted once more by a mountain of shining blades, Utena drags herself to the gate to pry it open with her bare hands. Though beyond hope, Utena will not give up for Anthy's sake. Her sweat and tears transform the gate into Anthy's coffin, which she succeeds at last in opening enough to clasp hands with her friend. Then the world crumbles, the two are torn apart, and Utena disappears. The next scene reveals that a month or so has passed, routine has been reestablished, and memories of Utena are fading. Akio makes plans to start the whole cycle of dueling over again with Anthy's help. This time, Anthy refuses. "You don't know what happened, do you?" she says. "It's all right. Please continue playing "'prince'" within this coffin forever. But I have to go." Anthy explains that Utena has not disappeared, she has just left Akio's dominion. In the final scene, Anthy takes a fateful step outside the school gate to follow Utena's lead.

In this way, Utena is the one who achieves and inspires revolution in the series finale. What is the content of her revolution? We might begin with the first two words in the title of the series, *shōjo kakumei*, which literally translate as "girls' revolution." There is certainly a feminist aspect to the "change of regime" that eventually takes place. Utena, of course, is the poster girl for testing boundaries from the very beginning. Her example strengthens a number of girls along the way, culminating in Anthy's declaration of independence from her brother. Rather than solely being about biological girls, however, this revolution needs to be understood as one in which masculine power, epitomized by the twinned dark and light princes Akio and Dios, is ultimately set aside, even by Utena herself. It is not her power or her "sword" that breaks open the Rose Gate but her love for and friendship with Anthy that finally budges the coffin lid. What is more, it is clear particularly in the animated version of the story that the male characters in the series are as trapped, isolated, and deformed by masculine power as any of the female characters. Ultimately, revolution in *Utena* is to choose to live in the "real" world where one does not have perfect control, in fact where one is often powerless. It is to live in a world that is constantly changing, for good and ill, rather than a fantasy world of artificially preserved youth and beauty. And it is to choose friendship over the illusion of mastery in negotiating an uncharted future. The king is dead! Long live the people!

ASO

POSSIBILITIES AND LIMITS

It is likely apparent from the above that this essay on Oscar François de Jarjayes, Fujinami Ryūnosuke, and Tenjō Utena does not begin to exhaust the individual and joint analytical possibilities they raise. At this point, however, I would like to venture a few remarks to tie up some threads introduced in the previous sections.

First, we see in all three examples discussed above that the process of turning comic books into television animation opened up a creative moment for revision and reinterpretation. This act of "translation" not only allowed the creators to reassess their work in light of fan response but also forced them to work in conjunction with a new set of collaborators. In the case of Ikeda Riyoko's work, this resulted in refocusing the spotlight on Oscar, the young woman who flouted convention and pursued adventure in a masculine mode, at the expense of Marie Antoinette, the more stereotypical romantic heroine. In the case of Takahashi Rumiko's work, the Oscaresque Ryūnosuke was similarly given a larger presence in the animation series, along with a husky voice and fluid martial arts movements. We also see a subtle transformation of sensibility that emerged through Takahashi's collaboration with directors Oshii Mamoru and Yamazaki Kazuo and others involved with the animation series. In particular, the additional layers of freewheeling intertextuality and zingers aimed at the political and philosophical currents of the day reveal a new degree of direct influence from the university student counterculture of the 1970s. Finally, in the case of Be-Papas, their work in *Revolutionary Girl Utena* suggests the power of postwar fandom through its structural continuities with fan fiction. We see this, for example, in the way in which the revival of themes and characters from *The Rose of Versailles* in *Revolutionary Girl Utena* did away with the bothersome "excess" of accurate historical detail in order to concentrate on atmosphere and to rework to fan satisfaction the more familiar terrain of personal relationships. In the translation of the *Utena* story line from comic book to television animation and finally to movie form, we further see each representing a distinct level of intensity in the tale's tendencies toward psychologism and sexualization. The fragility of the construction of individual identities, for instance, is explored through identity switching in the comic book only as a completely separate short story, "The Curry Transformation" (Karee Naru Henshin).[29] Later this anecdote is not only integrated into the main body of the animated series, but the potential for characters to trade identities is repeatedly suggested through such scenes as the merging of the *identical* shadows of Utena and Anthy on the wall of their shared bed-

166

room. We should also note that, in contrast to *The Rose of Versailles* and *Those Obnoxious Aliens*, *Revolutionary Girl Utena* was from the very first a product of collaboration among well-known figures in the world of Japanese comic books and animation. The development of different versions of the story for distinct media and audiences was carefully planned from the beginning. The multidimensional potential of such professional collectives is quite exciting.[30] Yet there may be a downside in the diminishing temporal gap in translation, six years in the case of *The Rose of Versailles*, two years for *Those Obnoxious Aliens*, and concurrent planning for *Revolutionary Girl Utena*. With less time and fewer holes, fans will have to exert pressure in new ways to shape how such stories will be retold for later audiences.

Second, by tracing the trajectory of these three narratives we can limn imaginative possibilities and limits as they changed shape over the final decades of the twentieth century. In the late 1970s, Ikeda unexpectedly tapped into female desires and concerns with Oscar's action hero lifestyle and romance on equal terms. While Oscar was not the first female figure in Japanese popular culture to challenge gender conventions, she appeared at an important juncture.[31] Her immense popularity further fueled trends in girls' comics toward greater experimentation with a darker atmosphere, broader subject matter, and more explicit sexuality. Nevertheless, Oscar's life is tragically conflicted and all too chaste until her final days. Moreover, when she does wear a dress or is placed in the structural position of a woman she quickly reverts to rather stereotypical womanly ways. Her masculinized self is thus presented as not "natural" and the love she acknowledges in the end is heterosexual. In the early 1980s, Takahashi poked fun at the somberness of Oscar's saga and in the process suggested that masculine traits in female figures may not be uncommon or unnatural at all. Ryūnosuke is incompetent at playing a woman according to socially accepted conventions; meanwhile, the attempts of her friends to help her gain such skills reveal cracks in their own gender facades. *Those Obnoxious Aliens* also openly plays with the possibility of a homosexual relationship for its masculinized female, although its eventual resolution matches her with a feminized male to maintain a form of heterosexual pairing. In the late 1990s, Be-Papas redefined the conflict in their gender-bending protagonist's life as one centering on the attractions and perils of power. Utena wears a boy's school uniform not because she wants to be a boy but because she wants to be a "prince" or protector of the weak. *Revolutionary Girl Utena* is also far more sexually explicit than either *The Rose of Versailles* or *Those Obnoxious Aliens*. The relationship between Utena and Anthy takes center stage, delicately eroticized in the television series, tense, hot, and heavy in the movie. Indeed, sexuality in *Utena* is most often depicted as a weapon for the constant power plays between the main characters rather than as part of a sweetly romantic relationship. Much of the sex is portrayed as punishing, not liberatory.[32]

The kind of revolution touted by the three animation series also changes shape over time. In *The Rose of Versailles*, we see Oscar go through a process of political education, meeting and interacting with a broad range of individuals, to eventually leave behind her heritage of aristocratic privilege in order to assist the French people in their attempt to create a new, more egalitarian society. Painful as her parting is with longtime friend and benefactor Marie Antoinette, Oscar knows she must go beyond herself and her immediate circle in order to do what is right. In *Those Obnoxious Aliens*, revolution basically means the ruthless deconstruction of social platitudes. The end result is chaos with the characters kept in perpetual motion. Ryūnosuke still longs for but will never achieve "femininity" even, or especially, in her relationship with Nagisa. *Revolutionary Girl Utena* sloughs off any direct reference to society or collective action to concentrate on the transformative effect of honest and open personal relations. When Anthy leaves her brother to follow in Utena's footsteps, the message is that the "prince" (dominance or power) must be forsaken to free the self. Only Anthy takes action, however. Everyone else quickly forgets that Utena ever existed. No *social* movement looms on the horizon. Thus, the arc traced by these iterations of the masculine female hero mirror a trajectory away from collective and confrontational engagement with politics toward a more personal approach to social change that numerous scholars and social critics have linked to the rise of consumerism in postwar Japanese society.[33] The revolution led by Oscar, Ryūnosuke, and Utena can be seen as narrowing down from a call for political engagement to personal consciousness-raising, Yet this formulation risks undervaluing the progressive movement across the series to portray hybrid gender identities and sexualities in terms of choice and as part of a spectrum. Given the fluid political as well as cultural landscape of the twenty-first century, it will be interesting to see how the next incarnation of this iconic figure meets the challenge to better (or best?) the world.

NOTES

This essay was written in 2002; the genealogy and texts that I discuss have continued to expand and evolve over the past few years. I would like to thank the students in the various incarnations of my Japanese popular culture classes at the University of California, Santa Cruz, both for letting me test some of these ideas in lectures and for energetically responding with interpretations of their own. In particular, Connie Kotkin's enthusiasm for the topic was infectious, and her generosity in first lending me the comic book version of *Revolutionary Girl Utena* is greatly appreciated.

1. The first postwar incarnation of this figure is generally traced back to Tezuka Osamu's 1953 comic book *Princess Knight* (*Ribon no kishi*), which was recently republished in a bilingual edition as Tezuka Osamu, *Ribon no Kishi/Princess Knight*, trans. Tamaki Yuriko, 5 vols. (Tokyo: Kodansha International, 2001). It was developed into an animated series by Mushi Productions and broadcast from 1967 to 1968.

2. Jonathan Clemens and Helen McCarthy, *The Anime Encyclopedia: A Guide to Japanese Animation since 1917* (Berkeley: Stone Bridge Press, 2001), 425.

3. For a brief but useful account of animation and television history, see Susan Napier, "Anime and Global/Local Identity," in *Anime from* Akira *to* Princess Mononoke (New York: Palgrave, 2001). For a more detailed account, see Misono Makoto, *Zusetsu Terebi Anime Zensho* (A Complete Guide to Television Animation, Illustrated) (Tokyo: Harashobo, 1999).

4. Ikeda Riyoko began her career in Japanese comics by creating works aimed at young girls distributed through the book rental (*kashihon'ya*) market of the early postwar period. She continues to be known for her epic historical romances set in Europe such as the award-winning *Orufeusu no Mado* (*Orpheus' Window*). For further biographical details, see Nagatani Kunio, ed., *Nippon Mangaka Meikan* (Japanese Comic Artists Directory) (Tokyo: Deeta hausu, 1994), 42.

5. For an account of the dramatic changes in girls' comics in the late 1960s and early 1970s, see Frederik Schodt, *Manga! Manga! The World of Japanese Comics* (Tokyo: Kodansha International, 1983), 97–105.

6. Stefan Zweig, *Marie Antoinette*, trans. Eden Paul and Cedar Paul (London: Cassell, 1960).

7. Ikeda Riyoko, "Preface," in *Berusaiyu no Bara, Aizōban*, 2 vols. (Tokyo: Chūōkōronsha, 1992), 1:2.

8. Mark Schilling's entry on the *Rose of Versailles* effectively conveys the excitement of this instance of fan power through such details. Mark Schilling, *The Encyclopedia of Japanese Pop Culture* (New York: Weatherhill, 1997), 206–9.

9. The first performance of the *Rose of Versailles* by the Takarazuka Revue was in 1974. It was a smash hit and added fuel to the fire of the story's popularity. A new generation was hooked with a revival production in 1989. All told, the *Rose of Versailles* has been performed about twelve hundred times for three million viewers. Umehara Riko and Otohara Ai, *Takarazuka* (Tokyo: Gendaishokan, 1994), 38–40.

10. *The Rose of Versailles* (*Berusaiyu no Bara*), DVD, created by Ikeda Riyoko, directed by Nagahama Tadao and Dezaki Osamu, 1979–80 (Tokyo: Shūeisha, 2005).

11. In the comic book original, this scene is more explicit in terms of both the love-making and the key role played by equality and shared experiences in shaping their love for one another. In this, Ikeda participated in and contributed to the trend toward *shōnen ai (boys' love)*, which has since become a staple genre in girls' comics.

12. Oscar does so in an alarming turn toward submissiveness, declaring it her duty as André's wife *(tsuma)*. However, André insists once more that Oscar remain the leader she has always been, and her troops look to Oscar, not André, until the very end.

13. Nagatani Kunio, *Nippon Mangaka Meikan*, 200–201.

14. Takahashi's second hit series, *Ranma 1/2*, can in this light be seen as an expansion of the possibilities of the character of Ryūnosuke. The play with gender roles, the father-son relationship, and the dynamics of the romantic pairing of Ranma and Akane are all carried forward.

15. *Those Obnoxious Aliens (Urusei Yatsura)*, DVD, created by Takahashi Rumiko, directed by Yamazaki Kazuo, 1981–86 (Tokyo: AnimEigo, 2001).

16. See chapter 12 of volume 7 of the "wide" version of Takahashi Rumiko, *Urusei Yatsura* (Tokyo: Shonen Sunday Comics, 1990), 179–94.

17. While Ryūnosuke exhibits the densest collection of character traits usually associated with the opposite gender, it should be noted that many of Takahashi's characters are "mixed up," albeit to a lesser degree, in this way. We can see Ryūnosuke not just as an incidental character but as a key to the importance of gender play in the series as a whole.

18. Episode 86, "Enter Ryūnosuke" (Ryūnosuke tōjō).

19. Ryūnosuke goes on actual dates with Ran in episode 88, "The Great Date Strategy of Miss Ran" (Ran-chan no Deeto Daisakusen), and with Shinobu in episode 119, "Shine! The Bra of Desire" (Kagayake! Akogare no Bura).

20. The feature is entitled *Nagisa's Fiancée (Nagisa no Fianse)*. In the original comic book, the story line is further developed so it is fairly clear the two will remain a couple.

21. *Revolutionary Girl Utena (Shōjo Kakumei Utena)*, DVD, created by Be-Papas, directed by Ikuhara Kunihiko, 1997–98 (Tokyo: Wea Corporation, 2003).

22. According to Saitō Chiho, the overall "boss" at Be-Papas was Ikuhara Kunihiko ("the 'Komuro' of the animation world"), Saitō was in charge of the comic book version, Enokido Yōji ("the model for Miki") wrote the scripts, "Sweetie" Hasegawa Shin'ya was in charge of the animation designs, and Oguro Yūichirō (also known as "Mr. Bear") was in charge of publicity and planning. Saitō Chiho, *Shōjo Kakumei Utena*, 6 vols. (Tokyo: Shogakkan, 1997-98), 3:166.

23. For an insightful account of this process, see Matt Thorn, "What Japanese Girls Do with *Manga* and Why," paper presented at the Japan Anthropology Workshop, University of Melbourne, 10 July 1997.

24. Saitō Chiho claims that as a child she wanted to be both a stewardess and a comic book artist. She is a great fan of the Takarazuka Revue and theater in general. Nagatani Kunio, *Nippon Mangaka Meikan*, 152–53.

25. Ikuhara Kunihiko, "'Saitō Chiho' and 'He'" ("Saitō Chiho" to "Kare"), in Saitō Chiho, *Shōjo Kakumei Utena*, 5:180.

26. Ibid., 180–84.

27. In the movie, in particular, relationships are taken to a new level of sexual explicitness.

28. Both names, not coincidentally, are flower related. Utena refers to a receptacle for flowers, while Anthy means "flower." Saitō Chiho, *Shōjo Kakumei Utena*, 5:52.

29. Saitō Chiho, "Karee naru Henshin" (The Curry Transformation), in Saitō Chiho, *Shōjo Kakumei Utena*, 2:153–89.

30. CLAMP, the collective author of such popular works as *Tokyo Babylon*, is another example.

31. In addition to Tezuka's *Princess Knight*, mention must be made again of the Takarazuka Revue. For a wide-ranging and thought-provoking account of this theatrical tradition, see Jennifer Robertson, *Takarazuka: Sexual Politics and Popular Culture in Modern Japan* (Berkeley: University of California Press, 1998).

32. Depictions of experimentation in gender identity should not be conflated with depictions of homosexuality in Japanese popular culture. While the two are linked in some instances, as in *Revolutionary Girl Utena*, they are not in productions such as *The Rose of Versailles*.

33. The essays in Andrew Gordon, *Postwar Japan as History* (Berkeley: University of California Press, 1993), provide a useful and wide-ranging introduction. The long-standing debates in Japan on the generational character of the so-called *shinjinrui* (new humans) and subsequent iterations are grounded in this understanding of postwar social trends.

Dream Labor in Dream Factory: Japanese Commercial Television in the Era of Market Fragmentation

Gabriella Lukacs

Although the television industries of advanced capitalist countries have been struggling with dwindling prime-time ratings since the early 1980s, the Japanese television industry was revitalized by a new genre, the trendy drama (*torendii dorama*) commercial broadcasters developed in the late 1980s.[1] This was a curious development. Long predating the HBO show *Sex and the City*, trendy dramas targeted young women by entertaining them with images of well-heeled young sophisticates enjoying consumer-oriented lifestyles and managing their love lives. In parallel with the development of trendy drama, a growing number of young female scriptwriters entered the television business, a phenomenon that has been discussed in the popular media as the "young female scriptwriter boom" (*wakate josei kyakuhonka būmu*). Interviews with young female writers have been collected and published, and many of these television writers, in turn, became celebrated columnists of weekly and monthly magazines, ready to give advice to women on such various themes as dating, falling in love, and conflicts in marriage and at work.[2] In the 1990s, hundreds of individual interviews graced the pages of women's magazines with accompanying images posing the scriptwriters as celebrities clad in pricey designer fashions. In this period, television writing was one of the top five most coveted professions among young women.

This essay will suggest that the young female scriptwriter boom was emblematic of how commercial television networks struggled in the 1990s to reinvent their system of mass production in an era marked by the demise of mass middle-stratum society (*chūkan taishū shakai*) and the declining importance of mass consumption. I will argue that young female writers played a crucial role in reconciling the conflicts between a mass-oriented television industry, viewers who were less and less interested in programs having mass appeal, and advertisers who demanded either audience maximization or more precise demographic targeting. The Japanese television industry has remained a highly capital- and labor-intensive system of production, with significant costs of operation covered for the most part by prime-time advertising.[3] Unlike in most fields of manufacturing, where automation can reduce the demand for human labor and the cost of the goods produced, television production entails creative labor that cannot be automated. Given these conditions, advertisers are charged astronomical fees for commercial time, for which they, in turn, demand high ratings, preferably 15 to 20 percent or more.[4] On the one hand, this expectation forces networks to produce prime-time programs that appeal to broad cross-segments of the audience. Viewers, on the other hand, increasingly demand entertainment tailored to their age, gender, and taste. The challenge for Japanese commercial networks, then, was how to readjust their system of mass production to cater to new demands in an era in which the traditional balance between mass and niche marketing had been fundamentally upset.

Media economists have noted that concentrating on wealthy audience segments has always been a fundamental strategy to fall back on in volatile business conditions.[5] In this essay, I contend that the young female scriptwriter boom was an effect of the trend that networks started seeking out new "wealthy" audience segments that fetched top dollars from advertisers. In the wake of the growing tensions between advertisers, viewers, and networks, Fuji producers identified a new demographic: single women between the ages of eighteen and thirty-four who had become the most dynamic consumers by the mid-1980s. In the 1980s the fashion-, cosmetics-, and leisure industries primarily relied on magazines to reach young female consumers. In the second half of the 1980s, however, these sponsors became interested in advertising on television and it was in response to this new interest that television producers began developing the trendy drama to attract young women to the medium.

While the new target audience was young single women holding non-career-track clerical and secretarial positions (referred to as "office ladies," or OLs, a term adopted from English), the producers and directors— overwhelmingly male—were career-track employees of elite media corporations.[6] Because of their social proximity to the new target audience, young female writers could serve as translators between male producers and the young female viewers the networks considered such a valuable demographic. This translation, however, was not a smooth process, and the conflicts between these female freelance writers and male producers were enduring. According to scriptwriters' accounts, producers were frequently perceived to violate the scriptwriters' authorship and pride in their work. Producers, meanwhile, blamed scriptwriters for "being unprofessional." By this, the producers meant that the young women writers did not understand that the ultimate goal was to win the "ratings game" with other networks. In other words, they accused young writers of not sharing the corporate identity. Indeed, corporate identity was exactly what was denied to them, for they were not on the corporate payroll, as were the producers.

I suggest that these conflicts shed light on an important characteristic of the shift in the television industry toward niche programming, for such specific targeting calls for new forms of mediation between production and reception. In the fields of media studies and cultural anthropology, television has been dominantly analyzed as a mass medium; as a corollary, television production and reception have been treated as separate analytical categories, and agency has been analyzed in terms of how viewers negotiate or resist the meanings proposed to them by the culture industries. In this essay I do not question viewers' ability to decode televisual texts in ways unintended by their producers. Rather I aim to highlight the fact that in the era of post-Fordist[7] televisual production the crucial site of conflict over meaning ("semiotic warfare"), previously located between producers and viewers, has moved to the realm of program production, which has in turn become a primary ground where notions of identity and womanhood—of particular interest in this essay—are negotiated.[8]

TRENDY DRAMA: ENTERTAINING AFFLUENT CUSTOMERS

Fuji producer Yamada Yoshiaki explains the launching of the new drama.

> Until ten years ago . . . there were no dramas addressing young women from eighteen to twenty-five. We realized that it was a precious market, and we did not understand why it was not covered. . . . In the beginning many people argued that in the bubble period young women actually did not return home to watch television. Audience research concluded that young women were more likely to hang out with friends after work; they went to discos, attended English-language classes, and pursued hobbies. We started producing new dramas (later labeled trendy dramas) in the midst of this general pessimism suggesting that young women were simply not interested in watching television.

> We decided to make dramas that would gratify young women and persuade them to return home early so that they could watch the dramas. . . . It was important that these dramas be *a source of information* to the viewers.[9]

By "information" Yamada meant not so much that commercials targeting young women would air during the broadcast of the trendy dramas but rather that information on consumer trends would be integrated into the dramas to make them more appealing to young women. Fuji producer Ōta Tōru is more unequivocal in explaining the connection between consumerism and trendy dramas.[10]

> We came up with the basic concept for trendy dramas, but we didn't know how to get young women to watch them. I leafed through women's magazines to learn about popular trends among young women, and we've adopted all of them in the new dramas so that they will attract young female viewers. It seems ridiculous now to recall how meticulously I discussed the fashion sections of women's magazines with my staff (stylists, hair and makeup artists, and so forth) in order to craft characters that would be appealing to young women. In the early trendy dramas we paraded around protagonists with fancy, foreign-sounding professions and reconstructed the latest trends in cuisine, fashion, and interior design. We measured the success of our dramas by the number of phone calls we received inquiring about fashion and other items featured in the dramas.[11]

Fuji producer Yamada (cited above) argued that the trendy drama had been launched in order to "gratify young women and persuade them return home early so that they could watch the dramas." Somewhat naively, he expressed surprise that television networks had not produced dramas for young women earlier. What surprised him was not the simple discovery of a heretofore uncolonized territory but rather the discovery of an uncolonized *rich* territory. The lack of recognition of the distinction between young women and *affluent* young women is important. It sheds light on how slowly Japanese television was transforming itself from a system of mass production to one of niche targeting. In the late 1980s, networks began to realize that they did not have much chance of appealing to viewers if they failed to offer more customized entertainment. The shift to niche programming, however, had a crucial precondition, namely, that the income-earning potential and purchasing power of particular target segments had to be great enough to attract sufficient advertising revenue. (Young single women ideally fit this bill.) In 1987 Fuji introduced a program slot called *getsuku* (*getsuyōbi kuji* meaning Mondays, 9:00 to 10:00 P.M.) in which only trendy dramas were broadcast. One year later, the Tokyo Broadcasting Network (TBS) responded by introducing its own trendy drama slot (Fridays, 10:00 to 11:00 P.M.).

Television responded to young women's privileged position in consumer culture in the late 1980s—much later than magazines—when this segment of the population was already compartmentalized into clearly distinguishable marketing categories. The fashion and leisure industries then perceived it safe to invest in television advertising. To recapitulate, television drama production is capital intensive, and producers try to avoid high-risk financial investments. The risk in launching a trendy drama was that it would cater to a demographic that had not been committed to the medium previously. Initially producers could not predict whether young women would incorporate television watching into their leisure practices. This is why Fuji producers decided to embed the first dramas in the consumer culture with which young women felt so familiar. Fuji producer Ōta explained above that the first trendy dramas were geared particularly toward consumption. In industry slang, they were called "catalogue dramas" because they had very loose story lines. The focus was on brandishing images of luxurious lifestyles and portraying urban professionals working in the mass media and living in spacious, flamboyantly designed, downtown apartments.[12] The male producers imagined that this was the lifestyle young women craved.

Ōta's comment quoted above illustrates the pains male producers took to make the new dramas appealing to viewers. To tie the new dramas to consumer culture was their first strategy. In the first phase of trendy drama, young female writers were not yet part of the scene. It was more established male scriptwriters who wrote the catalogue dramas. The dramas achieved good ratings, but the ratings did not increase, and the overall viewer response was that the dramas had nothing to do with reality (*rearitī no nai yumemonogatari*). On hearing such responses, producers recognized that *realism* was something they could cash in on. To that end, they engaged young female writers in the production, scriptwriters who could help them portray women's culture, aspirations, and fantasies in a more down-to-earth, realistic manner.

CINDERELLA AS A POSITIVE ROLE MODEL: THE PRODUCERS' STORY

By the early 1990s, it had become clear that mediation was needed between female viewers and male producers. This is not surprising; while the new audience was composed of young, non-career-track office ladies, the drama producers were high-flying, career-track males. In other words, these two groups occupied starkly different spaces in the social geography. Male producers tended to believe that it was the Cinderella myth, and ever-new configurations of it, that female viewers wanted to watch. In this section, my aim is to explore the producers' positions in order to understand why they held this perception, as well as to analyze the degree to which they had the power to impose their ideas on other drama professionals, mainly the writers.

Most producers and directors come from top private universities (for example, Keio and Waseda), but many are graduates of the most prestigious national universities, The University of Tokyo and The University of Kyoto. In the television business this means that producers and directors-to-be are not graduates of professional schools but start their careers as assistants assigned to older colleagues under whose guidance they master the profession. Particular to Japanese enterprises,[13] this method of in-house training serves to secure the loyalty of employees to the network that launched their careers. This is why it is highly unlikely that producers or directors would seek reemployment at a network other than the one that trained them. This said, most television employees do not retire from the section in which they began their careers. Even though it takes years to learn the craft of producing a particular televisual genre such as dramas, news, or variety shows, producers are commonly reassigned to other sections within the same network or transferred to the network's branch offices located overseas or the countryside. These practices serve to ensure a degree of flexibility in the rigid system of lifetime employment—another key characteristic of the Japanese corporate structure in the postwar period that television networks managed to preserve even in the wake of the economic recession. Reassigning employees among sections or branch offices is a strategy both to reward talented employees by allowing them to move up in the corporate hierarchy and to demote employees who fail to live up to the expectations of their senior colleagues. As a result of these corporate practices, many producers think of themselves as something in between salaried men (*sarariman*) and artists (*geijutsuka*). Nevertheless, many admit that *authorship* and *creativity* would be equivocal terms to describe their work for three reasons: first, policies of reassigning employees among sections and branch offices circumvent the development of artistic consciousness; second, freshmen employees cannot choose which department they will be assigned to; and third, drama production involves teamwork with a subtle division of labor.

Most producers do not wear neckties—which distinguishes them from salaried men—and experience it as a shock when they are expected to don them (should they be transferred to the programming department, for example). While some consider themselves artists and others businessmen, they are closer to athletic coaches, in my opinion, whose primary aim is to set new records (namely, to win the race for the highest audience ratings both within their own networks and compared to others). When talking to producers I found it curious how often they used sports metaphors— primarily from golf and baseball—to explain their profession.

Unlike freelance scriptwriters, producers are paid monthly salaries and two yearly bonuses from their affiliated television networks. When their dramas achieve high ratings, they get additional bonuses. However, the financial incentive is by no means the only one encouraging them to achieve high audience ratings. In the headquarters of TBS, for instance, daily ratings charts are posted in front of the elevators. A producer told me that when his ratings were low he was ashamed to get into the elevator and would take the stairs instead. Another example of the same mentality further illustrates this point. I was told that within the drama section (*dorama seisakubu*) producers did not offer opinions about their colleagues' dramas before the ratings became available. The reason for this was that if their opinions were not in alignment with the ratings they might be accused of not being able to assess what is interesting to the audiences, which is considered to be an essential skill in their profession. That is to say, pressure from colleagues is just as relevant a motivation for producers to achieve high ratings as are financial rewards.

To be a producer is highly demanding both mentally and physically. Stories of mental breakdowns and suicides are not rare in the business. In the 1990s, star producers such as Ōta Tōru (Fuji) or Ueda Hiroki (TBS) were mocked as the "ghosts" of the network for they ate, slept, and lived there.[14] Ueda's career is demonstrative of the intensity of working in the drama section of a commercial television network. The first drama he was in charge of as the producer-in-chief was a detective drama (*keiji mono*), *Keizoku* (Beautiful Dreamer, 1999). The drama turned out to be a hit, and Ueda was suddenly celebrated as the young star producer at TBS. As a result he was assigned to TBS's top investment dramas *Beautiful Life* and *Good Luck*, both featuring the most sought-after tarento, Kimura Takuya. Star writers Kitagawa Eriko (*Beautiful Life*) and Inoue Yumiko (*Good Luck*) were contracted to write the scripts, and the viewing rates set records: the series finales achieved 41.3 and 37.6 percent, respectively. However, Ueda's career in drama production was only four years long. In 2001, at the age of thirty-five, he was transferred to the programming department due to failing health.

In parallel with the fragmentation of the consumer markets and the concomitantly growing commercialization of television, the work of producers has become incomparably more stressful. They are the ones who have to coordinate the division of labor within the production team and negotiate with the sponsors, the programming department, and the *tarento*[15] (celebrity) agencies. The producer works out the character set and the drama plot together with the scriptwriter and contracts the *tarento* cast in the lead roles. Because they must protect the integrity of their media personae, the *tarento* must agree to lend their names to a particular story before the programming departments can approve a drama plan. In parallel with the development of the trendy drama, *tarento* have gained unprecedented power in drama production. They are booked two years in advance, and, as replacing them is close to impossible, producers and writers have to craft roles the *tarento* find agreeable. Next the producer, assistant producer, director, assistant director, and scriptwriter will discuss the drama plan. It is generally held that if one person on the team does not like the script there will be a 20 percent loss in the target audience. Yet it is the producer whose opinion matters most, and ultimately the scriptwriter will be required to rewrite the plan as many times as necessary. When such negotiations between the producers and scriptwriters end, the scriptwriter can start writing the script itself, although the producer closely supervises the writing process.

The pressure to come up with a good story for a drama can be inferred from the ways scriptwriters complain about producers. When the star scriptwriter Kitagawa Eriko was asked if she had experienced sexual harassment while working with the male production staff, she answered that she thought of the consultations (*uchiawase*) with the producers as something very close to sexual harassment. A significant majority of the production staff is male, and they rip her scripts apart and nonchalantly say such things as "this is not interesting at all" (*zenzen omoshirokunai*) (Kitagawa 2000).[16] By relating a corresponding observation to me, scriptwriter Nakatani Mayumi has confirmed my understanding that these tensions are generated by the growing difficulties producers are facing as they try to deliver the desired high ratings to their sponsors in the era of market fragmentation:

> Often producers ask me to change the whole plot after they have approved it. Two types of producers do this. The first type cannot envision the drama from a proposal, while the other type simply changes his mind far too often. In these cases, I end up investing an unreasonable amount of time in something that is doomed to be *boring*.[17]

The adjective "boring," of course, suggests that the tedium of repeated rewriting is terribly unsatisfying for the scriptwriter. However, as I will illustrate later, such conflicts often result in scripts that are ultimately not interesting to the audiences either. If such is the case, the audience ratings will naturally be low, and for this the whole production team has to take responsibility. Sometimes drama workers mention that it is one of the most important dimensions of teamwork that team members share both success and failure. Yet scriptwriters remain the most vulnerable members of the team; because they are freelancers, they will not be rehired if their programs get low ratings. Producers whose programs get low ratings are deprived of additional bonuses and may have to take the stairs instead of the elevator, but their monthly paychecks are unaffected.

Keeping producers and directors on the corporate payroll means that Japanese television networks have yet to outsource production, in contrast to Hollywood studios, which do not employ production personnel. In Hollywood, each time a new movie or television program is made the production staff is assembled from scratch. (Both TBS and Fuji established branch production companies in the late 1990s—Fuji's Kyōdō Terebi and TBS's Dreamax—which means that the process of vertical disintegration has begun.) This means, in turn, that in Japanese drama production flexibility is demanded exclusively of the scriptwriters, who are the only freely disposable and replaceable components in the production process.

While scriptwriters speak vehemently of producers, producers constantly and bitterly complain about scriptwriters as well. Producers often wax nostalgic about older generations of scriptwriters, emphasizing that until the 1980s scriptwriters worked more autonomously and there was no need for producers' surveillance to get them to craft high quality scripts in a timely manner. As one TBS producer put it:

> These days very few scriptwriters can write high-quality scripts. Writing cool dialogue or having a fresh eye for the current fashion trends does not make a drama good. Talent and fitness are not enough for this job. One has to practice writing and composing plots as well. Among young scriptwriters, many have a good sense of what is trendy with youth, but the scripts they write are poorly composed. They should study much, much more. These days there are very few really good scriptwriters, and this is why we have no choice but to use them in a disposable (*tsukaisute*) manner. When veteran writer Hashida Sugako[18] [who was born in 1925] was young, she worked for a film company for more than ten years, where she learned the basics of filmmaking. That makes a huge difference.[19]

In other words, in the producer's opinion scriptwriters lack experience, cannot keep up with the rapid pace of drama production, and do not create scripts of sufficiently high quality.

It is curious how both producers and scriptwriters translate structural problems into a lack of professionalism on the other's part, and neither talks about the fact that the demand for trendy dramas rose sharply after they turned out to be popular with the new target audience. In terms of audience ratings, dramas took over the leading role from variety shows by the mid-1990s. Accordingly, many variety show program slots were reallocated to dramas and the demand for scriptwriters increased rapidly.[20] It is true, indeed, that scriptwriters did not have enough time to master the profession, for it takes years of writing and experimenting to develop one's own style. The sociologist Tessa Morris-Suzuki's analysis of the transformation in employment patterns in response to a shift from a Fordist system of production to flexible accumulation is pertinent. She has highlighted that flexible production tends to "reduce the useful lifespan of work-related knowledge to a length shorter than the normal working life of a human being."[21] That is, the trendy drama called for workers with new expert knowledge, and it was not only young female writers who were inexperienced in drama production, as producers were also navigating uncharted territory. Programming departments tended to assign their youngest producers and directors to these dramas as they did not want to trust the astronomical budgets that drama production required to middle-aged producers whose proficiency in youth culture was not believed to be sufficient.[22] In the late 1990s, producers who reached their forties were no longer assigned to produce trendy dramas despite the fact that this was the only genre in which they had any expertise. In other words, in drama production the shift to niche targeting decreased the productive lifespan of producers and writers; in their early forties, producers are transferred to other departments while writers are simply released.

"I WANT TO CRAFT TOUGH AND SELFISH HEROINES": THE SCRIPTWRITERS' STORY

Although scenario writing was the first task to be outsourced in Japanese television production, the turnover rate of scriptwriters was much less rapid before the mid-1980s.[23] Until then, the average productive lifespan of a television writer was more than twenty-five years, while these days only the luckiest ones remain in the business for more than eight or ten years. Currently, after young writers reach their mid-forties they are no longer contracted to write serial dramas, the source of the most prestige and money. What is left for them is to write books, articles, or scripts for feature films (*tanpatsu dorama*). These jobs pay much less generously, as feature films are produced by smaller production companies, which run on much smaller budgets than those of commercial television networks.

Scriptwriter Kitagawa Eriko has poignantly summarized the difference between older generations of professional scriptwriters and young female newcomers to the drama business. She writes, "I'm a type of person that is common among office ladies, but very rare among scriptwriters. For a while, I had an inferiority complex for being different from most scriptwriters, who were in their late fifties and thought of themselves as artists. Yet it seemed that I was in the closest position to the viewers and currently [in 1995] that has become a great advantage [*ima wa sore ga buki da to omoimasu*]."[24] In the same interview, Fuji producer Kameyama Chihiro—with whom Kitagawa made hit dramas such as *Asunaro Hakusho* (Asunaro White Paper, 1993, Fuji), *Kimi to Ita Natsu* (The Summer I Spent With You, 1994, Fuji) and *Long Vacation* (1996, Fuji)—affirmed this view, saying that Kitagawa writes only what she thinks. But Kameyama does not view this as selfish individualism (*sakkasei wo oshitsukenai*). Rather, Kitagawa is writing scripts that are the easiest for the viewers to identify with."[25]

The demand for young writers occurred suddenly and increased rapidly. In response to this, "scenario schools" were established to train new cadres of writers to meet demand. These writing schools were booming in the 1990s.[26] Enrolling in a writing school became the most common way for young women to try their luck in the television business. Attending lectures was useful not only for learning the basics of scenario writing but also for making connections in the business, as the lecturers were established scriptwriters and producers active in drama production. These connections provided some of the students with small jobs such as serving as stand-in writers (*sabu-raitā*) who write an episode when the main writer misses a deadline, or who fill plot writing jobs (*purotto-raitā*), writing rough storylines for feature dramas (while the actual dialogues are written by a more established scenario writer).

The majority of people attending writing schools are housewives or "dropouts" from the corporate world, usually former office ladies. In addition to their social proximity to the target audience, another reason for the greater number of women in these schools (and in this profession) is that this work does not provide a stable income. And, it is often said, women have the option of marrying men with stable incomes. These schools advertise their courses by emphasizing the fun side and lucrative nature of the profession and claiming that the basics can be mastered in a matter of months. To understand why housewives enroll in scenario schools in such great numbers, we have to look at prevalent gendered patterns of employment. In Japanese companies female employees (office ladies) are commonly expected to quit upon marriage (*kotobuki taisha*) and become homemakers (*sengyō shufu*). This is a reasonable system for companies; as women retire after age twenty-five, companies replace them with younger female employees, which makes it less conspicuous that women's salaries increase much more slowly (if they increase at all) than those of their male colleagues.[27] Because these women do not have any expert knowledge, they can re-enter the workforce only as part-timers employed in low-paying jobs. Mary Brinton explains this trend arguing that in Japan, in the absence of immigrant labor and any sizable ethnic minority, women serve as a readily available reservoir of unskilled labor that can be maintained or shut down as business cycles fluctuate.[28]

That is to say, housewives enroll in scenario schools hoping that they will find reemployment in a more creative and versatile business than the parcel delivery or convenience store work that is most commonly available to them. However, these housewives almost never make it into the television business. It is the other category of students, the dropout office ladies, who are the main supply of labor for television networks. For many women, marriage and child rearing are not the best career choices. These women started postponing marriage and extending their tenure despite the unwelcoming atmosphere of their workplaces. Many struggle in the corporate world until they recognize that it is a dead end for them and drop out. Among the well-known and currently working scriptwriters are such women as Nakazono Miho, who worked for an advertising company for two years, and Inoue Yumiko and Takahashi Rumi, who both worked as office ladies for small film production companies.[29] Inoue's goal to become a director was not achieved, while Takahashi felt increasingly uneasy with long commuting hours and ineffective work patterns in the company. She recounted:

> I didn't know what I wanted to do, but I was sure that the office lady job did not suit me. I thought that I could easily finish the week's five days of work within one day, and I did not understand why I had to go to my workplace five days a week. . . . I preferred to work at my own pace, and my colleagues began accusing me of being deviant. Now that I think about it, it's nice if someone is paid for her work on a monthly basis, but as time passed I started feeling uneasy about receiving my salary [whether I did my best or not]. I increasingly felt that I wanted to be paid for what I had actually completed,"[30]

Takahashi, along with the two scriptwriters mentioned above, are examples of office ladies who could not make a career in the mass media as full-time employees. These office ladies enter the scenario schools hoping that connections they make at these institutions will launch their careers as freelancers in the television business.

Another route to becoming a professional scriptwriter is to win a scenario-writing competition. Institutions such as the Shinario Sakka Kyōkai (Association of Scenario Writers), Nihon Hōsō Sakka Kyōkai (Japanese Television Writers' Association), and Fuji Television Network started organizing annual scenario-writing contests around the same time as the development of the trendy drama. On average, for example, the Fuji Network receives twenty-five hundred scripts per year for its competition named Yangu Shinario Taishō (Young Scriptwriter Award). While the prize-winning script automatically becomes a drama serial, the nine other finalists are offered the chance to work in the industry, commonly debuting as subwriters.[31]

Scriptwriting is an extremely competitive profession, and its cutthroat nature does not diminish even after a young writer manages to debut in the business. In addition to the financial instability, the job is physically and mentally grueling and involves excessively tight production schedules. From the first consultation (*uchiawase*) with the producer until finishing production of the last episode it takes approximately six months to complete a drama serial. The producer designates the theme of the drama, and it then takes two months for the scriptwriter and producer to do the research, create the plot, and develop the characters. The scriptwriter starts writing the script two months before the scheduled airing and completes it in parallel with the broadcasting of the drama. There are various reasons for this tight schedule. As the scriptwriter Nobumoto Keiko (*Hakusen Nagashi* [Those Were the Days], 1996) explains it:

> It is said that to write a good script for a three-month-long serial drama takes six months. However, it often happens that the drama plan or the casting changes, and the script for a three-month-long drama serial has to be completed in three or four months. This is a huge burden for the scriptwriter. These days, it is the casting that determines the drama, and the proposal is prepared in alignment with the profile [that is, earlier television performances and media appearances] of *tarento* cast in the lead roles.[32]

Another reason why the scriptwriter does not start writing earlier is that the sooner she starts the more grueling the rewriting process will be. Members of the drama production staff are always running late and oftentimes end up shooting the last episode the same day it is scheduled to be aired; thus, the less time left for writing the script the less difficult the subsequent rewriting and consulting will be.

Although there were male scriptwriters in the 1990s, they were, by far, outnumbered by women.[33] The scriptwriter Nakazono Miho has commented on the gender imbalance in the profession:

> Scenario writing fits women better. The script has to be rewritten countless times, depending on the sponsors' wishes or actors' capriciousness. Rewriting is much more grueling psychologically for men. They think too much about authorship (*sakkasei*) and their own politics (*jibun no porishii*). Women vehemently curse male producers, but they hang on until the end. From the male producers' point of view, what is important is that they have to spend half a year with a scriptwriter, and during these six months they see her more often that they see their wives. They are better off with female writers, whom they might even find pleasant, than with argumentative male writers with too much pride.[34]

Correspondingly, many male producers use the metaphor of marriage to describe the relationship between producers and scriptwriters. Fuji producer Ōta Tōru writes, "The relationship between a producer and scriptwriter is like a relationship between a husband and wife. As they are working on the same project, they have to support each other. It is natural that they argue with each other from time to time. These fights are exactly as if they were between a husband and wife."[35]

STRUGGLES BETWEEN AUTHORSHIP AND CAPITAL

Ōta casually likens the relationship between scriptwriters and producers to a litigious but comfortable marriage. This section, however, will show that female writers often find it more difficult to envision an easy, familial relationship with producers. I will offer two examples to illustrate how producers exert their power over scriptwriters and how it affects the drama plots and the ways young women are portrayed in them. The first is from my interview with Takahashi Rumi, the writer of the megahit *Shomuni* series (General Affairs Section 2, 1998, 2000, 2002, Fuji). Takahashi told me of her experiences writing *Hikon Kazoku* (Unmarried Family, 2001, Fuji), which was produced for the Thursday 10:00 P.M. slot and targeted at women between twenty-six and thirty-four. She had bitter memories of writing the drama, which was based on the work of the famous graphic novel (*manga*) artist Saimon Fumi.[36] (Most commonly, it is the plot and/or the main characters that are derived from the original graphic novel.) Beginning with *Tokyo Love Story*, which has become a cult drama throughout East Asia and an all-time hit in Japan, Saimon's graphic novels have been adopted for a number of dramas. As television networks have earned huge profits from her dramatized graphic novels, she is a highly respected author. Accordingly, one imagines that it must have been a nightmare for scriptwriters to work with her comics, as issues of authorship were likely to spark conflicts. In *Hikon Kazoku*, Takahashi was not allowed to rework Saimon's original text. The producer, Koiwai Hiroyoshi, instructed her to keep the original text, as it was written, down to the last punctuation mark. Strict adherence to the original text was difficult enough for Takahashi; in addition, she could not relate to the story.

Hikon Kazoku centers on a triangle relationship between a laid-off salaried man and his first and second wives. In the first episode the main character, Matoba Yōsuke, loses his job and his second wife, Hikaru, leaves him in search of meaning in her life. One day he runs into his first wife, Chikako, who has become a successful editor at a women's magazine. Having no income, Matoba has no choice but to accept the first wife's offer to move into her apartment with his son. Later Hikaru joins them. While the viewers are channeled toward the expectation that Matoba will reunite with his first wife, in the end she chooses to marry a young colleague. Takahashi had trouble identifying with this story; she has never been married or divorced and felt uneasy writing the script without changing the original.

The limitations on Takahashi's authorship and her inability to identity with the drama's plot did not comprise the full extent of her dissatisfaction while working on *Hikon Kazoku*. Top *tarento* such as Sanada Hiroyuki (Matoba Yōsuke), Suzuki Kyoka (Chikako), and Yonekura Ryōko (Hikaru) were cast in the main roles. Takahashi told me that it was not only the producer Koiwai but also Sanada who made her work difficult. Sanada Hiroyuki acted like a second producer and continually vetoed the dialogue Takahashi had faithfully copied from the original comics, following producer Koiwai's instructions. She soon found herself between two "enemies." She was supposed to mediate between the producer, who was worried about the comic artist Saimon Fumi, and the actor, who was worried about his media image. In the end, the drama was a flop (the ratings for the last episode were 11.4 percent, which meant a deficit in revenue for the network), and both parties blamed the scriptwriter for the failure. Among the 113 serialized dramas that Fuji produced between 1988 and 2003, *Hikon Kazoku* was ranked 101.

The second example of a conflict between capital (the network producer) and authorship (the scriptwriter) comes from my interview with scriptwriter Nakazono Miho.[37] This anecdote also shows that while the expertise of young female writers in women's culture is crucial to the success of these dramas, the final word is never theirs in determining what will appear on the television screen. Among Nakazono's scripts, the drama *Yamato*

Nadeshiko (Ideal Wife, 2000), which aired on Mondays at 9:00 P.M. on the Fuji network, achieved the highest ratings, 34.2 percent. As such, in 2003, this series was ranked as the sixth most popular drama on Fuji's all-time trendy drama hit list. Its main character, Jinnō Sakurako, is a young woman who wants to marry a wealthy man of high social status as compensation of sorts for a childhood spent in poverty. Sakurako becomes a flight attendant and moves to Tokyo, where she rents a tiny, dilapidated apartment so that she can spend most of her income on high-end designer outfits. Her "philosophy" is that a woman can never wear the same dress twice because she never knows when she might meet the same man while wearing the same outfit. At a friend's wedding she meets Nakahara Ōsuke, who she believes to be rich, and falls in love with him. She then learns that the young man is a dropout graduate student who studied mathematics at the Massachusetts Institute of Technology in Cambridge but currently is running his mother's small fish shop.[38] Sakurako soon recovers from her disappointment, breaks up with Nakahara, and sets out to find her prince on a white horse. She meets a much less handsome doctor who is soon to inherit his father's hospital. Sakurako is determined to marry him.

At the end of the drama, however, the former Japanese adviser of the math student arranges a job for him at a prestigious university in New York City on the condition that he completes his dissertation. Nakahara is deeply conflicted about whether to accept the position as his memories of his graduate studies in the United States are shadowed by the loss of his fiancée. She died in a car accident, and Nakahara feels responsible for her death. However, he overcomes his contradictory feelings, finishes his dissertation, and starts his teaching job in New York. Sakurako flees her wedding ceremony with the rich doctor and joins Nakahara in New York, where they get married. The drama ends with Sakurako dragging her husband from one designer boutique to another. The husband, loaded with Christian Dior shopping bags, is following Sakurako with a defeated and bitter smile on his face.

The scriptwriter Nakazono—a very competitive career woman and single mother—explained to me that the main theme of the drama was to criticize Japanese young women's fascination with the Cinderella myth. The drama was replete with sarcasm and irony, and it explicitly made fun of young women's fixation with brand names and status marriages (*tamanokoshi ni noru ganbō*). The Cindarellaesqe ending and the closing shopping scene are puzzling, however, because they appear to endorse precisely what they had previously criticized. I asked the scriptwriter about the contradiction between the drama's argument and its ending. Nakazono agreed that the last scenes contradict the overall message she intended to convey in the drama.

She explained that it was the season finale and it is over the end of the drama that scriptwriters have the least control. As the last episode tends to draw the highest ratings, producers are extremely fastidious in crafting it. In this case, the producer, Iwata Yūji, determined the episode's "happy" ending by appropriating the role of chief writer himself. He acted as a representative of his company, whose main task was to please the sponsors with high ratings. The last scenes of shopping for high-end designer goods—on Nakahara's assistant professor salary in New York City—were not in Nakazono's script. The producer was convinced that happiness for office ladies, the viewers of the drama, equates with moving up in class and financial status and being able to hop from one designer boutique to another. Nakazono told me that she felt defeated as she did not interpret the Cinderella theme as a happy story for women. But it is always the producers (or occasionally the directors) who determine the ending for dramas according to how they imagine happiness is, or should be, constructed for young female viewers.

CONCLUSION

Previous television studies have commonly centered on analyzing the ways viewers have decoded the meanings producers encoded in programs.[39] This chapter has aimed to illustrate that in conditions in which networks are juggling the conflicting interests of sponsors and viewers, the primary site of negotiation has become televisual production itself. A strategy to craft dramas that satisfy young female viewers is to engage them in the production of the dramas via young female writers, who are close in age and value orientation to the target audiences, and thus capable of mediating between the still dominantly male drama producers and female audiences. Yet this is not an unproblematic process of translation. On the contrary, it has become a crucial terrain where meanings of identity are struggled over.

The growing need for mediation between production and reception sheds light on a new trend, namely the increasing interdependence between these realms.[40] In both media studies and cultural anthropology televisual production and reception have previously been separated from each other and studied as distinct analytical spheres of cultural production.[41] For instance, anthropologists have studied television's role in the ideological construction of the nation in postcolonial and post-socialist contexts.[42] These studies considered television program production and consumption in terms of the dichotomy of (homogeneous) state power and individual agency (i.e., resistance or negotiation). In the last decade, however, audience fragmentation and the concomitant commercialization of the televisual medium have led to the transformation of national television industries. While serving the interests of both state power and commercial advertising are by no means mutually exclusive functions of television production, I wish to highlight that the newly emerging cultures of televisual production and reception require new analytical frameworks. An approach that blends ethnographic research with political economy, I would like to suggest, best equips us to analyze the ways in which the television industry was affected by and simultaneously capitalized on socioeconomic changes such as the erosion of mass middle-class society and the fragmentation of the consumer market.

In the context of the Japanese television industry, the strategy of engaging young women in drama production turned many of these programs into mega-hits. The effects of these dramas spread like ripples in a pond, as they revived the prestige of this medium for viewers and marketers. As translators between producers and viewers, young writers came to play a crucial role in the promotion of dramas. Due to their permanent presence in women's magazines and on television screens, many of them became well known to the audiences. Scriptwriters were not on corporate payroll, however, and thus lacked an institutional safety and support net. They were in desperate need of media publicity. The interviews with them in magazines and television programs served as means for self-promotion. At the same time, in the process of promoting drama serials, scriptwriters endowed these programs with a human face; their personal narratives on why they raised certain issues in their dramas or their thoughts on love, work, and friendship sutured over the increasingly elaborate and intricate mechanisms of engineering trendy dramas and concealed the growing profit-motivations of the culture industries.

The young female scriptwriter boom epitomized a new trend in that in parallel with the development of trendy drama, authorship started assuming an increasingly important role in popular discourse about television dramas. The new visibility drama producers and directors were given in the media was a calculated promotional strategy on the part of television networks. In the 1990s, producers such as Ōta Tōru or Kameyama Chihiro became household names. As popular magazines and newspapers began to talk about them alongside their dramas, these drama professionals helped their networks cut through the clutter by branding them. Equally pertinent, the new preoccupation with authorship was also a response to marketing discourses that emphasized the importance of custom-tailored quality products for young women. In the 1990s, marketing discourses commonly portrayed young women as *consumer connoisseurs* who—compared to the general population—marketers believed to be more concerned about quality than price or convenience. Authorship in drama production played an essential role in fuelling audience distinction by treating young women as special customers who deserve "quality entertainment" with high production values and top-notch celebrities. In other words, authorship served to suggest that television was no longer an anonymous mass medium that was unable to deliver high quality tailor-made entertainment to its customers.[43]

NOTES

1. This article is a slightly modified version of a chapter that appears in my book, *Scripted Affects, Branded Selves: Television, Subjectivity, and Capitalism in 1990s Japan*, forthcoming from Duke University Press.

2. Satake Taishin, *Shinarioraitā ni narō: Ninki sakka ga kataru hitto dorama sōsakuhō* (Let's Become Scenario Writers: Popular Writers Tell How to Make Drama Hits) (Tokyo: Dōbun Shoin, 1997); Satake Taishin, *Kanojotachi no dorama: Shinarioraitā ni natta joseitachi* (Dramas for Women: Women Who Become Scenario Writers) (Tokyo: Kinema Junpōsha, Kinejun Mukku, 2000); Komatsu Katsuhiko and Matsumoto Yaeko, *Shinarioraitā ni naru 10 no hōhō* (Ten Ways to Become a Scenario Writer) (Tokyo: Yōsensha, 2000).

3. In Japan, the hours between 7:00 P.M. and 10:00 P.M. are called *gōruden taimu* (coined from the English words "golden" and "time"). This is the Japanese equivalent of the U.S. term "super-primetime." *Puraimu taimu* (prime-time) refers to the period between 7:00 P.M. and 11:00 P.M. To avoid confusion, in this essay the term "prime-time" refers to the broadcasting hours between 7:00 P.M. and 11:00 P.M.

4. In drama production, ratings of 15 percent for the last episode aired is considered passable, over 20 percent is a hit, and over 25 percent is a megahit (15 percent equals fifteen million viewers).

5. Arthur De Vany, *Hollywood Economics* (London: Routledge, 2004).

6. Indeed, these male employees are the corporate elite, for the drama departments are the most prestigious sections within television networks.

7. Post-Fordist (flexible) accumulation was a response to a crisis in Fordist production (1945–1973) that was predicated on long-term and large-scale capital investments in systems of mass production and mass consumption. Post-Fordist production refers to the strategy that instead of mass-producing a single product, manufacturers target different groups of consumers with diversified product lines. See David Harvey, *The Condition of Postmodernity* (Oxford: Blackwell, 1991). In Japan, the television industry shifted to post-Fordist production much later than other domestic industries.

8. Stuart Hall, "Encoding/Decoding," in Centre for Contemporary Cultural Studies, ed., *Culture, Media, Language: Working Papers in Cultural Studies, 1972–79*, 128–38 (London: Hutchinson, [1973] 1980).

9. Satake Taishin, *Shinarioraitā ni narō,* 189–90, emphasis added.

10. Ōta, known as the "hit man" (*hittoman*), is one of Fuji's most successful producers. In 2003, his dramas occupied five of the top twelve positions on Fuji's trendy drama ranking. (The list consisted of 113 dramas in 2003.) Ōta's hit dramas include *Hyakuikkaime no Propōzu* (The Hundred and First Marriage Proposal) at 36.7 percent, *Hitotsu Yane no Shita* (Under the Same Roof) at 35.9 percent, *Hitotsu Yane no Shita II* at 35.9 percent, *Ai to Iu Na no Moto ni* (In the Name of Love) at 32.6 percent, and *Tokyo Love Story* at 32.3 percent.

11. Ōta Tōru, *Hittoman: Terebi de Yume wo Uru Otoko* (Hit Man: The Man Who Is Selling Dreams on Television) (Tokyo: Kadokawa Shoten, 1996), 22.

12. Some early trendy dramas include *Anaunsā Puttsun Monogatari* (The Edgy Newscaster), 1987, Fuji; *Otoko ga Nakanai Yoru wa Nai* (Men Cry at Night), 1987, Fuji; *Rajio Binbin Monogatari* (Radio Go Go), 1987, Fuji; *Gyōkai Kimi ga Iku* (Go Go Television Man), 1987, Fuji; *Arano no Terebiman* (The Deadly Television Men), 1987, Fuji; *Papa wa Nyūsukyasutā* (Dad Is a Newscaster), 1987, TBS; *Seisaku Ni Bu, Seishun Dorama Han* (Drama Department 2, Teenage Drama Section), 1987, Asahi TV; and *Koi wa Haihō* (Love Hurrah), 1987–88, Nihon TV.

13. See Tessa Morris-Suzuki, *Beyond Computopia: Information, Automation and Democracy in Japan* (London: Kegan Paul International, 1988); and Thomas P. Rohlen, *For Harmony and Strength: Japanese White-Collar Organization in Anthropological Perspective* (Berkeley: University of California Press, 1979).

14. Ōta, Tōru. *Hittoman;* Kitagawa Eriko, Ueda Hiroki, Doi Nobuhiro, and Takai Ichirō, *Bokura ga Dorama wo Tsukuru Riyū* (Why Are We Making Dramas?) (Tokyo: Kadokawa Bunko, 2001).

15. Unlike American celebrities, the tarento simultaneously perform in various media genres. It is a particular feature of Japanese televisual culture that *tarento* serve as hosts, guests, and contestants in game shows, they participate in variety shows, perform in television dramas, release CDs, and endorse commodities in commercials.

16. "Interview with Kitagawa Eriko," *Shūkan Asahi,* 17 March 2000, 40–44.

17. Nakatani Mayumi, interview with the author, 23 June 2003, Tokyo, emphasis added.

18. Hashida Sugako is famous for never consulting (*uchiawase*) with producers or directors. Her NHK morning drama *Oshin* (1983) achieved ratings as high as 62.9 percent in the early 1980s, and since then "whatever she touches turns gold" and no producer has been in a position to argue with her. In the 1990s, she wrote a drama for TBS, *Wataru Seken wa Oni Bakari* (Living Among People Is Nothing But Trouble/ Making It Through), the only prime-time serial targeted at elderly consumers, which was so popular that it ran for six seasons (1990, 1993, 1996, 1998, 2000, and 2002). Rumor has it that TBS directors and producers carefully avoid conflicts with her for they are worried she might "transfer" to another television network.

19. Interview in the drama department of TBS on October 12, 2002. Tokyo, Japan. (The informant asked me not to reveal his name.)

20. Besides Fuji's Monday 9:00 to 10:00 P.M. and TBS's Friday 10:00 to 11:00 P.M. slots, other drama slots were introduced or made available for trendy dramas as of the year 2000: Asahi, Monday 8:00 to 9:00 P.M. from 1993 to 2000; Fuji, Tuesday 9:00 to 10:00 P.M. from 1996; Fuji, Tuesday 10:00 to 11:00 P.M. from 1996; Nihon TV, Wednesday 10:00 to 11:00 P.M. from 1987; TBS, Friday 9:00 to 10:00 P.M. from 1988; TBS, Thursday 9:00 to 10:00 P.M. from 1957; and NTV, Saturday 9:00 to 10:00 P.M. from 1988.

21. Tessa Morris-Suzuki, *Beyond Computopia*, 144.

22. Ōta Tōru, already alluded to as one of the most successful producers of trendy drama at Fuji, was in his late twenties when he produced his first drama hit (*Tokyo Love Story*, 1991).

23. The phrase "I want to craft tough and selfish heroines" is from scriptwriter Nakazono Miho, interview with the author, 1 July 2003, Tokyo.

24. Shimazaki Kyōko, "Kitagawa Eriko: Shichōritsu tte isogiyoi kara suki" (I Like Ratings for They Are Powerful), *Aera*, 27 November 1995, 57.

25. Ibid.

26. These schools, including the Shinario Sakka Kyōkai (Association of Scenario Writers), Shinario Sentā (Scenario Center), Nihon Kyakuhonka Renmei (Japanese Scriptwriters' Guild), Nikkatsu Geijutsu Gakuin (Nikkatsu Fine Art School), and Shōchiku Shinario Kenkyūjo (Shōchiku Scenario Research Institute), offer courses ranging from two to six months, and the tuition is more than affordable. Advertised tuition fees ranged from 21,000 to 84,000 yen ($180.00 to $700.00) (Satake Taishin, *Kanojotachi no dorama*).

27. Yuko Ogasawara, *Office Ladies and Salaried Men: Power, Gender, and Work in Japanese Companies* (Berkeley: University of California Press, 1998).

28. Mary C. Brinton, *Women and the Economic Miracle: Gender and Work in Postwar Japan* (Berkeley: University of California Press, 1993). Similarly, Tessa Morris-Suzuki has explained Japanese women's role in supplying flexible, part-time labor. She writes, "The most desirable situation, therefore, is to have access to a flexible workforce: one which lacks a clear career structure, an expectation of steadily rising wages or a right to lifetime employment and the welfare and fringe benefits which that entails. Part-time workers fit the bill admirably." (Tessa Morris-Suzuki, *Beyond Computopia*, 143.)

29. Further examples are Komatsu Eriko, Nobumoto Keiko, Egashira Michiru, Yoshida Noriko, and Noroi Miyuki.

30. Satake Taishin, *Shinarioraitā ni narō*, 131–32.

31. Ibid., 190–92.

32. Komatsu Katsuhiko and Matsumoto Yaeko, *Shinarioraitā ni naru 10 no hōhō* (Ten Ways to Become a Scenario Writer) (Tokyo: Yōsensha. 2000), 162.

33. Examples include Nojima Shinji, Nozawa Hisashi, Okada Yoshikazu, Kimizuka Ryōichi, and Todayama Hisashi.

34. Satake Taishin, *Kanojotachi no dorama*, 198.

35. Ōta Tōru, *Hittoman*, 132.

36. Takahashi Rumi, interview with the author, 27 April 2003, Tokyo.

37. Nakazono Miho, interview with the author, 1 and 9 July 2003. Tokyo.

38. The main dilemma for Sakurako is: "Who, do you think, will make a woman happy? A handsome man who can't see a way out of his debts or a rich man who looks like a pig (*Shakkin mamire no hansamu otoko to, yūfukuna buta otoko, docchi ga kekkon shite onna wo shiawase ni shitekureru to omoimasu ka*)?"

39. Hall, "Encoding/Decoding."

40. Joel Stocker's study of comedy (*manzai*) production in Japan comes to a similar conclusion. See Joel F. Stocker, "Yoshimoto Kōgyō and *Manzai* in Japan's Media Culture," in Brian Moeran, ed., *Asian Media Productions*, 247–68 (Honolulu: University of Hawai`i Press, 2001).

41. On media studies, see Ien Ang, *Watching Dallas: Soap Opera and Melodramatic Imagination* (London: Routledge, 1985); David Morley, *Television Audiences and Cultural Studies* (London: Routledge, [1980] 1992); and Henry Jenkins, *Textual Poachers: Television, Fans, and Participatory Culture* (London: Routledge, 1992). On cultural anthropology, see Lila Abu-Lughod, *Dramas of Nationhood: The Politics of Television in Egypt* (Chicago: University of Chicago Press, 2005); Purnima Mankekar, *Screening Culture, Viewing Politics: An Ethnography of Television, Womanhood, and Nation in Postcolonial India* (Durham: Duke University Press, 1999); and Purnima Mankekar, "Dangerous Desires: Television and Erotics in Late Twentieth Century India. *The Journal of Asian Studies*, 63 no. 2 (2004): 403–431.

42. Lila Abu-Lughod, *Dramas of Nationhood*; Purnima Mankekar, *Screening Culture, Viewing Politics*.

43. Here, my argument is inspired by the television scholar John Caldwell's analysis of a new preoccupation with authorial intent and manufactured notoriety in the context of 1980s American network cable television as a strategy to reposition television from a purveyor of low culture to a producer of quality entertainment. John Caldwell, *Televisuality: Style, Crisis, and Authority in American Television* (New Jersey: Rutgers University Press, 1995).

Can't Live without Happiness: Reflexivity and Japanese TV Drama

Kelly Hu

Established in the early 1990s, a form of Japanese TV drama known as "trendy drama" has been prevalent for more than a decade not only in Japan but throughout Southeast Asia. Japanese trendy drama appeals to young audiences by portraying the trendiness of contemporary, metropolitan reality in Japan, a context quite different from more traditional forms of Japanese televised drama such as samurai or family drama, which make use of historical and often rural settings.[1] It is not surprising that TV drama is seen globally as a site featuring late modernity. The Latin American telenovella, for example, has been studied "in terms of its relationship with modernity: the economic, cultural, and psychic reorganization of society around the demands of consumer capitalism."[2] This paper will reveal reflexive approaches to narrating questions of modernity in Japanese society through TV drama. It will capture the ways in which the anxieties, ambivalences, and transformation of self-awareness embodied in reflexive modernity play important roles in the structure of Japanese TV drama. As shown through three case studies, Japanese TV drama develops a formula encapsulating textual reflexivity, which is especially concerned with complicated and sensitive psychological mappings of the inner self, the interaction of the self with the other, and the self coping with dilemmas in social settings.

It is beyond the scope of this study to use quantitative methodology to prove that most Japanese TV drama fits the category of reflexive scripting, but proposing that it is formulated with reflexivity is not exceptional. In her study of Japanese TV drama scriptwriters, Eva Tasi indicates that Nojima

Shinji, one of the best-known celebrity writers, is not so much engaged in the role of telling a story than in mirroring and creating "an occasion for reflexivity" that is related to "the discourse of modernity and values".[3]

The influence of this narrative strategy on audiences' reception has also been documented. Leung Lisa Yuk-ming's study of Hong Kong audiences' viewing of the famous Japanese TV dramas *Rongu bakēshon* (*Long Vacation*, 1996) and *Bīchi Bōizu* (*Beach Boys*, 1997) indicates the way in which audiences are attracted to identify with reflexive life attitudes presented in these two dramas.[4] Both dramas manifest the philosophy of "dropping out" and relaxation, a backlash against the highly competitive and stratified capitalist Japanese society. Hardworking Asians living in a highly competitive society may feel liberated by associating themselves with protagonists who rediscover and revitalize themselves through a jobless "long vacation" and happy summer days spent on the beach. Failure and depression do not mean the end of the world; instead they may lead to another, even happier stage of life. In a previous study I investigated the ways in which some online Chinese fans reflexively receive Japanese TV drama and even achieve implicit self-healing, as they are inspired by the rich amount of reflexive lines and thoughts therein.[5]

Why is the reflexivity of modernity important? According to the British sociologist Anthony Giddens's study on "high" or "late" modernity and self-identity, "the self becomes a 'reflexive project' through which self-identity is constantly redefined and reconstructed."[6] He describes "the emergence of new mechanisms of self-identity that is shaped by—yet also shapes—the institutions of modernity."[7] The project of the self parallels the development of modern institutions as both are propelled toward reflexivity by the desire for self-control and self-management. Like modern institutions, the modern individual is driven to be self-reflexive. Individuals will ask themselves questions about everything from lifestyles and relationships to body image and self-therapy.[8] Japanese TV dramas present a multitude of similar questions with choices acted out for the viewers. Such basic reflexive questions as "What should I do with my life?" "What kind of job suits me?" "Where do I stand with regard to my various relationships?" and "What makes me happy or causes me pain, and for what reasons?" make up the central themes of most trendy dramas.

If reflexive modernity is an inevitable part of global modernization and is therefore not a Western privilege, we can expect the Japanese TV industry, as a modern institution in Japanese society, to demonstrate an investment in the practices of textual reflexivity. In her remarkable study of Dutch audiences for the American TV serial *Dallas* written more than two decades ago, Ien Ang describes the characteristics of the soap opera.

> The dialogues in Dallas—dialogue is the narrative instrument of soap opera—never contain any critical and conscious (self) reflection. The characters never ponder on their position in the world, they never philosophize from a detached point of view on themselves and their relations to others. The conversations the characters have with one another, on the other hand, always express the living through or digesting of a conflict, in the here and now. There is never question of an intellectual exposition and exchange of ideas.[9]

Contrary to what Ang observed in *Dallas*, Japanese TV dramas are usually constructed with an abundance of philosophical and critical reflexivity. The protagonists in Japanese TV drama are certainly more than manipulated puppets; instead, they are endowed with the ability to reflect on their situations and confront themselves and others. Such reflexivity is embodied most clearly in the narrative style of many dramas with its constant foregrounding of "philosophies of life."

One of the major strengths of the Japanese TV drama industry since the 1990s has been that it recruits a pool of talented scriptwriters who are equipped with "mobility and reputation" that put them in "a more powerful category".[10] Established scriptwriters are not only highly esteemed and well compensated, but they also play significant roles in drama productions. They are masters at evoking pathos and a populist consciousness along with traces of rebellion and reflexivity within the framework of social norms. The best scriptwriters delve deeply into the human psyche and express a range of reflexive issues through the various twists and turns of their plots.

The reflexive TV drama scripts maintain an intricate, emotional subtlety and an attention to fragmentary, seemingly trivial moments and verbal expressions. Aside from dialogue and other conversations, there are frequent applications of voice-overs and monologues, the most direct form of self-exploration in dramas. Reflexive thoughts, in the form of concise phrases and sentences, are routinely adapted to the Japanese TV drama format. In addition to this specialized use of language, the short duration of Japanese TV dramas also fits perfectly into a reflexive narrative strategy. It should be noted that Japanese TV dramas usually contain ten to twelve one-hour episodes and are broadcast on a weekly basis. Therefore, the four annual drama seasons (of three to four months each) correspond to the poetic rhythm of the four calendar seasons, and the dramas, which are rarely rebroadcast, are packaged to be consumed accordingly. As a result, the story must be told in a precise way. Unlike long-lasting Western serials with their endless plot convolutions and indeterminate lifespans, Japanese TV dramas, with their ephemeral broadcast life and compact structure, are made to be consumed briefly.

Even the transnational cultural consumption of Japanese TV dramas can testify to the charms of brief reflexive language. Chunghua Telecommunication Company, a Taiwanese firm, attempted to advertise the new functions of its mobile phones by incorporating "classical mottos of Japanese TV dramas" into its messaging service.[11] First of all, this reveals that the brief reflexive language used in Japanese TV dramas is indeed powerful enough to be used in intimate exchanges of messages outside Japan. Second, it signifies the lively transcultural translations; the miniaturization of sentences and words produced in Japan can be recycled in Taiwan as they are compatible with miniaturized consumer products.

THE PURSUIT OF HAPPINESS

In the this section, I propose that, in terms of locating self-identity, the main theme of pursuing happiness in Japanese trendy TV dramas can be regarded as equivalent to the modern reflexive imperative. Based on requests for happiness in the three dramas I will discuss, *Hikon kazoku* (*Unmarried Family*, 2001), *Shūmatsu kon* (*The Weekend Marriage*, 1999), and *Shuiyōbi no jōji* (*Wednesday Love Affair*, 2001), this section establishes that the urge for reflexivity is mediated in the search for happiness.[12]

Happiness (*shiawase*) is a ubiquitous subject in Japanese mass culture. It has, for example, become cliché for a man to propose to a woman in Japanese TV dramas by stating, "I will bring you *shiawase*. Please marry me." In its more conventional sense, happiness can also be described as meaning hope or a blessing, but it indicates more than a state of mind or intention. It can be materialized in a social system to signify such things as success in one's studies, work, economy, marriage, and family. Besides, happiness can be experienced through seemingly petty actions in daily life such as taking a bite of delicious food or breathing fresh air on a sunny morning. Happiness can exist in the here and now or be accumulated little by little. However, in a deeper and extended sense, happiness is, after all, a lifelong goal. As some of the characters in these dramas put it:

> As long as happiness can be gained eventually, all decisions made in the past are the right decisions. (Yōsuke in *Unmarried Family*)

> I decided to move ahead with a smile, even if I am suffering. The goodness of happiness only moves ahead. Thus, only those who move ahead can grab happiness. (Tsukiko in *The Weekend Marriage*)

The biggest misfortune is that you used to have days of happiness. (Shōko in *Wednesday Love Affair*)

According to these quotations, happiness is not content to be preserved in a perfect past and present but is more or less future oriented. In addition, happiness is not guaranteed to last forever. That is why happiness matters and becomes a debatable issue in TV dramas and reality. The road to happiness requires an investment, which usually compels one to undergo pain and trauma. To obtain true happiness does not mean to achieve a stable and peaceful condition; rather it is a dynamic process that involves many dramatic tensions and requires philosophical thought.

Questions of happiness in representations of Japanese TV drama echo questions of modernity; modern individuals strive to gain happiness through the reflexive means of locating the self in a modern society. The development of modernity and globalization accompanied by increasing uncertainty and risk has profoundly transformed the psychology of personal activities in relation to the world. During transitional periods in a modern individual's life, he or she has to learn how to reorganize physic mechanisms with each new start. The self becomes a manageable and revisable project, which corresponds to the "overriding tendencies" of modern institutions toward "colonizing the future".[13] In Japanese TV drama, the search for happiness may undergo the reflexive process, which is the consequence of individuals' choices and mentalities after they have gone through life-altering experiences. The pursuit of happiness as a highlight in these dramas not only is intensified by the TV industry but also mirrors the dilemma of modernity.

Next I will analyze three Japanese TV dramas and expose the ways in which they offer rich reflexive arguments on gaining happiness through various life trajectories, transformations, and negotiations in the form of family and marriage. As a result, they reinforce the significance of self-mastery over one's fate exercised through reflexivity. The three dramas analyzed here sharply interrogate our self-identity in a modern society. How do people locate and dislocate themselves in the family and marriage through the complexity of heterosexual love, sexuality, emotional fulfillment, regulation, social functioning, and gender role playing?

UNMARRIED FAMILY:
THE RESTRUCTURING AND REDEFINITION OF FAMILY

Unmarried Family, adapted from the famous female comics writer Simon Fumi's work, tells the story of the collapse of a family and the alternative life directions and new awareness the breakdown offers to its protagonists. Forty-year-old Yōsuke, a typical middle-aged Japanese husband, has dedicated himself to a single company since his early twenties. He has doubts about neither his social position as a hardworking office employee nor as a husband and father in a traditional nuclear family until he encounters difficulties with his job and realizes that his wife, Hikaru, twenty-eight years old and married to him for eight years, wants to leave him.

She deserts the family for her dream of becoming a tango dancer. Tango dancing, which usually requires a male dance partner, is not the type of leisure activity, such as cookery or flower arranging, in which Japanese housewives usually engage. Yōsuke cannot understand why Hikaru has dumped him and their son and begs her to come back.[14]

> YŌSUKE: How can you survive without my economic support? . . . You are a mother, Shōta's mother . . . you should be responsible. Isn't the husband-wife and family relationship a matter of tolerance? Everybody survives by means of tolerance. Life is not so simple. It is impossible to live in your own way.
>
> HIKARU: Our family is built on my tolerance. . . . I have graduated from family.

Yōsuke occasionally meets his ex-wife, Chikako, who is the successful chief editor of a fashion magazine. Chikako is in love with a married man. Feeling tortured, she wants to end the affair, and so she invites Yōsuke and his six-year-old son Shōta to come and live with her, thereby creating an "unmarried family" relationship.

In David Morley's theorization of the relationships between media and home territories, he discusses the role of the family and refers to Nancy Fraser's work, stating that families are "sites of egocentric, strategic and instrumental calculation as well as sites of usually exploitative exchange of services, labor, cash and sex."[15] Tolerance can be romanticized to disguise the power structures within families. The happiness of a family is established by patriarchy and at the cost of tolerance. Such tolerance especially applies to the gendered hierarchy, in which the husband is expected to channel his energies toward the external society, while the housewife's energies are expended on home-based labor. Family and marriage in Japan are basically codependent relationships.[16] Unmarried children depend on their parents. Housewives depend on their husbands economically. Husbands depend on their wives for household management, child rearing, and housework.

The Japanese housewife is a female worker lacking economic ability. Japanese women are expected to rely on their parents before they get married and their husbands afterward. To be sure, the husband also suffers in his role as a moneymaking machine with constant worries. "Marriage for a Japanese woman is a rebirth while for a Japanese man it is a ritual."[17] Such male-centered views of marriage indicate that Japanese women have been either debased or celebrated as persons who are happily free of any economic responsibility.

This kind of gender and family relationship is often seen as providing support for Japan's postwar "miracle economy." Yet, even in the postbubble 1990s, a survey indicates that, although the numbers of career women has increased, the ambitions of Japanese women are still predominantly domestic. The problem is that the whole Japanese capitalist system marginalizes females as transitional laborers who seldom attain high positions or good salaries.[18] Most female college and university graduates anticipate becoming "office ladies" (OLs) and enduring a transitional career performing routine administrative tasks such as photocopying and serving tea or coffee. Thus, the social and economic structure is gender biased, which in turn drives Japanese females to retreat into marriage.

Marriage for Japanese women who cannot have satisfactory jobs perhaps offers a practical escape. In some dramas, such as *Love Story* (2001) and *The Power of Love* (2002), thirty-something OLs experience the double tragedy of unemployment and failed romantic relationships.[19] The solution society offers is marriage, as it is a shortcut to survival in uncertain economic conditions. However, Hikaru in *Unmarried Family* rebels against social conventions and escapes her housewifely "destiny." She discovers her own individuality by liberating herself from the imprisonment of family that Japanese society demands.

Chikako, Yōsuke's ex-wife, is a woman without a family. Her professional ambitions and her involvement with a married man highlight her position as an outcast from traditional ideas of family. While she owns a luxurious apartment, she feels emotionally empty and admits that she eats and sleeps alone most of the time. The loneliness and social isolation of a single woman in her thirties is reinforced by an ideology that privileges heterosexual marriage and family. The family has "the power to exclude others, a defensive measure to allow access to the resources of the home to a select and privileged few."[20] Living with Yōsuke and Shōta, Chikako gradually experiences the happiness of having a "family," even though its members do not all share matrimonial or blood bonds.

The failures in his marriage and career stimulate Yōsuke to grow out of his self-centered chauvinism. His interactions with Chikako subtly play with gendered role exchange. Chikako is a diligent working woman; Yōsuke becomes a househusband who performs all sorts of domestic work—cooking, cleaning, ironing, washing, and even giving Chikako massages after work—and he gradually comes to understand the loneliness of the average housewife. Yōsuke's experience at home, along with the job training he undertakes to become a nurse for the elderly, transforms his outlook. He becomes sensitive to the restrictions imposed by typical gendered practices in society and becomes more open-minded and flexible.

In an unscheduled trip to a resort city, Yōsuke, Chikako, and Shōta renew their relationships as a family. As a rich single woman, Chikako expects to stay in a modern deluxe hotel. Yōsuke makes a reservation at a traditional, Japanese-style hotel with tatami rooms designed for families. The communal baths and open spaces of the hotel encourage contact between families, and the scene evokes the nostalgia of Yasujiro Ozu's classic family movies of the 1950s. The script brilliantly contrasts symbols of the Japanese family-style hotel its Western-style counterpart. Chikako admits that deep in her heart she longs for a family:

> Here everything exudes unbearable and unpleasant scents of family. . . . Japanese feel relieved as long as they have their own families. . . . Maybe I am the one who cares about having a family most.

Although Chikako, Yōsuke, and Hikaru are situated in a repressed social milieu, eventually they find their own paths. What does *family* mean? This is the key concept that *Unmarried Family* attempts to explore. The drama deconstructs the myth of family as a modern institution that is legitimated by state and society. That is, the Japanese family is too functional in its operation and has more or less suppressed individual needs. The social and gender mechanisms of marriage and family stratify the husband-wife relationship. Yōsuke's monologue expresses his reflections on marriage and family.

> The final purpose of man and woman is not marriage. Marriage is perhaps the fatal killer of the man-and-woman relationship. This dysfunctional family has made me aware how strong family bonds are.

Finally Chikako develops another relationship with Ōkubo, a young man who is twelve years younger than she, and becomes pregnant with his child. She decides to give birth but is not prepared to commit to Ōkubo, who soon will be working overseas. Yōsuke divorces Hikaru and keeps Chikako company by living with her. The strong affective ties between Yōsuke and Chikako transcend the formal relationships of husbands and wives, lovers and friends. One year later, at a party celebrating the birth of Chikako's child in the final episode, the densely layered relationships among Chikako, Yōsuke, and Ōkubo seem at once completely oblique and unexpectedly natural.

The ambiguous ending of the story is open to interpretation. The question of whether Chikako is "married" to Ōkubo, Yōsuke, both, or neither is undermined by *Unmarried Family's* devaluation of marriage as a social form. What matters is whether the people involved are considerate enough to support each other, grounding the meaning of *family* in real relationships without the burden of social roles or kinship. The utopian approach of *Unmarried Family* envisions a future in which a family need not be established through legal procedures; instead it can be constructed through the will of people who are interested in commitment. This story implies that all the main characters involved form a kind of family attachment with each other.

The unmarried family is an ideal alternative to the inflexibility and suppression of a modern family. This drama also signals the fragility of marriage and family. It warns that happiness is not an inherent part of marriage and family, especially among those who treat these institutions as naturally legitimate. *Unmarried Family* implies that happiness may in time come to those who are keen and sensitive enough to resist the pretentious "happiness" institutionalized in the traditional marriage and family.

SET ME FREE OR TIE ME UP?
THE DILEMMA OF *THE WEEKEND MARRIAGE*

> The feelings of "never being satisfied" within the relationship . . . reflect the difficulties inherent in creating or sustaining a relation in which there is balance and reciprocity, satisfactory to both partners, between what each brings and each derives from the tie.[21]

Anthony Giddens precisely grasps the ambivalent psyche of modern people in relationships. Corresponding to the intricacy of relationships themselves, ambivalence becomes part of the essence of happiness. Happiness is generally understood to derive from living with a family in a marriage, a situation well suited to fulfilling the impulse for long-lasting intimacy. Aside from love and gender asymmetries, the most difficult hurdle to overcome in a relationship is that our desire for emotionality and independence contradicts and is negated by marriage and family as social institutions. Modern individuals desire the bricks and walls of marriage and family to ground their emotional security, while paradoxically such stability is hazardous to a lively relationship, which requires space for mobility and volatility.

Makiko Tsuchidate, the female scriptwriter of *The Weekend Marriage*, adapted it from the comic book of the same name, which she also wrote. Makiko Tsuchidate not only specializes in depicting the complexity of extramarital affairs, but also in the dark side of psychological competition and tension between sisters and mothers and daughters. *The Weekend Marriage* attempts to identify a variety of marriage styles that might be tenable in a modern society. Apart from intricate love-and-hate relationships among several men and women, the most significant theme in this drama is the exploration of emotional conflict, incongruity, and loneliness in middle-class marriage. The two main characters are sisters who are rivals and very resentful of each other. They compete with each other in the fear that one of them will be happier than the other. Interestingly, the standard of happiness itself varies throughout the dynamic changes in the relationships of the two sisters.

Yōko, the elder sister, marries a promising man who works in a DNA medical research center. Having a respectable, loving, and faithful husband, Yōko should be happy. Yet she is not fully accepted by her in-laws, and even though she has chosen to be a housewife she previously led a more independent and exciting life as a student in Spain. She is unhappy as a nameless housewife and jealous of her younger sister, Tsukiko, who is a career woman. The situation reveals the contradictions of a modern wife who wants to have control of her family life but also hopes to be recognized as a woman with outstanding abilities outside the home.

It is said that "the Japanese woman manages and controls the home as her own space, enjoys unlimited autonomy there, and frequently prevails over her husband[22] in decision making about the home and family life in general."[23] Yōko is represented as one of those women who have real power at home. As a full-time housewife, Yōko's smothering love and care compels her husband to seek a haven by renting a room outside the home. In that room, the husband meditates, relaxes, and watches porn videos on his own, things that are not so easy to do at home. The constrained marriage that Yōko's husband experiences prompts him to put forward the idea of a "weekend marriage," that is, husband and wife should live alone on weekdays and be together on weekends. The closeness of husband and wife may wear out their romantic love when they are overwhelmed by daily trivialities and boredom. The weekend marriage can help maintain a sense of freshness and keep a proper distance for both individuals. He talks with Tsukiko about it, and Tsukiko decides to try out this marriage style with her husband, Kōichi, who is also her boss at an architecture and design company. Kōichi relates the concept of the weekend marriage to the philosophy of architecture, while Tsukiko responds with different metaphors.[24]

> KŌICHI: The weekend marriage is like rooms connected by a glass door. . . . The normal marriage is like rooms connected by an iron door, which sometimes is suffocating and compels people to run away. Even with the glass door in between, the two rooms are still connected with a sense of safety and bonding.
>
> TSUKIKO: The glass door is less insecure and unstable than the iron door; however, it creates a kind of nervous atmosphere, which will keep a married couple's relationship as passionate as a single couple's relationship.

For Kōichi, the glass-door weekend marriage provides more breathing space, yet the couple is still attached. Tsukiko suggests that the weekend marriage is less controllable. With its subtle power plays, uncertainty, and freedom, the weekend marriage allows for more open romantic challenges and excitement.

The sweetness of their weekend marriage at its inception is gradually eaten up by Tsukiko's jealousy and loneliness. In contrast, Kōichi enjoys it as he can truly immerse himself in his work without feeling burdened by the family all the time. Tsukiko does not know how to manage her weekday evenings after work, as she is less busy than Kōichi is. The more time they spend apart, the less Tsukiko feels that she understands her hardworking husband. In addition, she is forced to reflect on the detachment of the weekend marriage after witnessing a conflicting and yet passionate scene between Yōko and her husband. She thinks that the married couple, which really only lives together on weekends, would begin to show their best side instead of being frank and revealing their fears and humiliations.[25]

> TSUKIKO: The glass door is most torturous. It is a kind of suspense. It's neither two people nor one person. Sometimes I wonder: is this person my husband? . . . Should not husband and wife develop affective family ties and desperately overcome difficulties together?
>
> KŌICHI: I still think weekend marriage deserves a try. We should try to cultivate the strength to live on one's own. Two people with the power to live on their

own would be strong enough to support each other in a marriage.

Finally, Tsukiko decides to train herself to become career oriented, tough, and independent, and, as Kōichi expected, she succeeds. On the one hand, it can be seen as a sign of progress and growth for a female to regain her independence. It makes sense for an individual to understand the significance of living on one's own without simply clinging to marriage and family relationships. Individuality and independence become highlighted as alternatives to loneliness; people in a marriage and family situation may come to regard intimate togetherness as a privilege while at the same time losing the ability to live on their own.

On the other hand, the reshaping of Tsukiko as a career woman is, in a sense, quite convenient for Kōichi, who undergoes no internal change as a result of the weekend marriage. That is, Kōichi's achieves his masculine life goal at the cost of Tsukiko's repression of her thirst for more time and energy invested in intimacy. Here the plot exposes a woman's dilemma in a capitalist world that emphasizes efficiency. A modern career woman like Tsukiko must be autonomous and not too emotional, and yet she has to be ready to engage in feminine tenderness. In some of the weekend scenes in this drama, Kōichi becomes a childlike boy who craves Tsukiko's mothering. It seems that the "independence" of the modern woman does not necessarily mean that she is rescued from patriarchy; rather she becomes a useful subject who responds to a competitive capitalist system and a new mode of marriage by taking on multiple roles.

In this drama another couple—Tsukiko's ex-boyfriend and his ambitious girlfriend—have a wedding in a different space. After planning the wedding, the bride gets an urgent call to travel to Paris on important business. She is not willing to miss the opportunity while the groom does not want to change the wedding schedule. Kōichi suggests that they exchange their marriage vows over cell phones in Tokyo and Paris. In this context, the portability of cell phones, which enables long-distance weddings, also suggests that modern marriage, too, can be mobile and flexible under the imperatives of global flows of people and capital. Kōichi says:

> This is perhaps the true spirit of the weekend marriage: you are experiencing "individuality" instead of "loneliness."

The weekend marriage project is an alternative to the old model of married life. What is the purpose of marriage? How does a couple cope with loneliness in marriage? What are the advantages and disadvantages of a normal marriage versus a weekend marriage? Can the weekend marriage foster one's freedom and self-sufficiency as an alternative to a traditional, all-encompassing marriage? In all marriages, how can a couple maintain mutual affection? A successful weekend marriage can be achieved, perhaps, if it is conceived as a rational goal set by a rational couple with self-control, confidence, and trust. On the other hand, a weekend marriage can be difficult if either partner has insecurities or doubts. Tsukiko's internal struggles with loneliness are the dilemma in her weekend marriage.

WEDNESDAY LOVE AFFAIR:
SEEKING LOVE IN MARRIAGE AND AFFAIRS

Wednesday Love Affair is the story of a triangular relationship involving a marriage and a serious friendship, a story of two women and a man. The famous TV scriptwriter Hisashi Nozawa, who unfortunately committed suicide in 2004, plays with sensational dramatic elements. Like most of Nozawa's work, *Wednesday Love Affair* is an exploration of complex, often puzzlelike relationships. Nozawa's philosophy in dramas reflects a tendency toward dystopia.[26] That is, his stories often start with the collapses of marriages, families, and relationships and end with the deconstruction or reconstruction of new relationships that are not guaranteed to be any more satisfactory than the original. Nozawa is interested in complicated husband-wife relationships, especially the reshuffling of couples.[27]

Nozawa feels that he should stop concentrating on the "husband-wife" relationship.[28] However, he cannot take his eyes off this small but inexplicable world. *Wednesday Love Affair* is a TV drama that again focuses on unstable husband-wife and man-woman relationships and the untrustworthy institution of marriage. Eiichiro and Ai are the ideal, thirty-something, middle-class couple without children and deeply in love. Eiichiro works as a vigorous editor in a publishing company, while Ai is an interior designer. Nothing goes wrong in their happy marriage of over three years until one day when they are invited to attend the funeral of the husband of Ai's high school classmate, Misao. During the funeral, Misao, a gloomy but charming widow in black, catches Eiichiro's eye. Eiichiro, a man who by all appearances is a good husband and would never betray his wife, crosses the line. A series of love games between Eiichiro and Misao implies that romantic love arouses a kind of excitement and danger that can be absent from a stable marriage.

Nozawa constructs several climaxes in the encounters between the three protagonists, including Eiichiro's choice between celebrating his wedding anniversary or his lover's birthday. However, the cruelest encounter, the discovery of the secret affair, ironically follows immediately after the celebration of Ai's brother's wedding. Where there is the establishment of happiness, there is also the destruction of happiness. Ai and Misao have a fight and disclose their past history of love and hatred. They used to be best friends, but they split up because they fell in love with the same boy. In addition to their romantic rivalry, undercurrents and implications of vague lesbian positionalities between Ai and Misao surface. If love can be symbolized as a battlefield, the competition between two women may stimulate passions and possessiveness over the love of the same man.

Ai confesses that she has detected Eiichiro's fascination with Misao. On the one hand, she wants to test Eiichiro's love for her. On the other, she deliberately pushes Eiichiro toward Misao as compensation for stealing Misao's high school boyfriend. In this ambivalent situation, Ai suffers deeply. Ai and Eiichiro break up at the party, and Eiichiro moves in with Misao. A marriage/family has been destroyed, and a house must be rebuilt. Ai, an interior designer, begins to remodel her house to suit a woman who lives on her own, which brings a kind of loneliness and heartache.

In this drama, Nozawa not only portrays the sparkle of an affair but also the special love between a husband and wife. Knowing that he has lost his marriage, Eiichiro feels painfully in love with Ai. He recalls the sweet moments that he has shared with her. Abandoning his pursuit of Misao, now he turns to Ai. Misao's overwhelming love for Eiichiro makes him feel withered. He describes himself as "a castrated male cat" living a tasteless, henpecked life. Misao is also aware of the boredom in their love life and the loss of the freshness they once experienced. Misao even suggests that Eiichiro get involved in playful relationships with young girls in order to revitalize himself. Once evening, at a bar after work, Misao tells Eiichiro:

> Physical attraction between lovers is inevitable. However, when it comes to the husband and wife relationship, there must be something absolute there which goes beyond physical attraction, such as absolute love, since the body will gradually wither away. . . . What is most important is to believe in the pursuit of absolute love.

Misao regards formal marriage contracts, as well as alluring bodies, as unreliable sources of passion. Only the search for absolute love is everlasting. Nozawa says, "Husband and wife are partners who have gone through the stage of being lovers and then develop other kinds of attachments to deal with everyday trivialities."[29] Husband and wife must generate a new love that transcends lovers' love if they hope to sustain a marriage that can last for over fifty years.

Eiichiro continues to feel that he is falling in love with Ai again, and he begs for a reunion. However, Misao thwarts Eiichiro and Ai's secret dating. Misao gets hurt and suggests that she and Eiichiro get married, a departure from her original plan. Eiichiro agrees, and Misao asks Ai to play the role of surrogate father at the wedding. The skillful use of clothing—Ai, with a tall figure, wears a black ensemble and Misao is in a white wedding gown—highlights the opposition and rivalry between the two women. Speaking as Eiichiro's ex-wife, Ai interrupts the ceremony.

> Before they take their vows, I want to make a vow myself. God, are you here? . . . This guy over there [Eiichiro] is going to make a vow to Misao. . . . Today he will vow to be faithful to this marriage with a true heart; however, it is hard to predict whether things will be the same tomorrow. . . . I have made up my mind that I will get my happiness—to have a good lover, to have children and live with him until we are old. I must find warm happiness. Both of you, too.

Ai's declaration that she will look for new happiness condemns the wedding vows in that they impose an eternal bond on the husband-wife relationship. The climax occurs after Ai walks away from the church. At the moment when she is to take her vows, with a calm and pretty smile and tears in her eyes, Misao says:

> I think that I cannot surpass the strong love that Ai has for you. I also want to have happiness, the warm kind. . . . If Ai can find happiness with another man, I can also live without you. . . . Eiichiro, can we dump you?

With a tone of determination and self-declaration, Misao, like Ai, leaves Eiichiro and swears to seek happiness. Love triangles such as these are predestined to be fraught with distrust, jealousy, and heartache. What remains is the strong will of two women who throw away past baggage and act on their own to search for happiness. In this case, romantic love is not so much empowered as it does not guarantee to lead to *shiawase*. Therefore, why not dismantle the triangle and start a new life with someone else? On the other hand, both Ai and Misao are still looking for love encapsulated with happiness. Romantic love in this triangular relationship is perhaps too bitter to bear; it is not the warm kind of happiness they want. The failure of the wedding once again confirms Nozawa's style of pessimism and suspicion of marriage. Romantic love, perhaps, is still one of the highest principles of life, but it is not placed above everything if the quality of love has gone sour. Ai and Misao's determination indicates that the self is more important than romantic love.

The story, however, does not end there. Several years after their breakup, the three of them meet for a picnic. Eiichiro remains single, while both Ai and Misao are married with children. After the pleasant talk and food, Eiichiro, Ai, and Misao leave in different directions. Meanwhile, Eiichiro, in a voice-over, says, "I have a feeling I was brought up by two women." Women not only nurture kids but also the adult." Eiichiro becomes aware of his growth with the help of the two beloved women, and both take on a mother-lover image. In the final scene, Eiichiro receives a cell phone call from one of the women. The audience is not told if it is Ai or Misao who is calling, but apparently "she" invites Eiichiro to a private meeting somewhere in Ginza. In the last shot, Eiichiro's face wears a mysterious smile as he looks at the camera and says, "Man and woman still have fifty years time."

It suggests that the encounters and struggles between heterosexual man and woman are never ending. It is a surprising and brilliant ending. Nozawa keeps reminding us of the central emphasis of this drama, the capricious nature of man-woman relationships. If marriage can be emptied of its original meaning, Ai and Misao, whoever they meet or marry, will not necessarily find stability or happiness. Marriage, family, love, and happiness in the course of life are relentlessly demolished and rebuilt through various reflexive trajectories of options and chances.

RATIONAL REFLEXIVITY AND THE AMBIVALENT SELF

> The "new sense of identity" . . . as required . . . is an acute version of a process of "finding oneself" which the social conditions of modernity enforce on all of us. This process is one of active intervention and transformation.[30]

The three Japanese TV dramas presented here reveal the processes and struggles of locating self-identity in institutional marriage and family. This essay has tried to grasp the ways in which reflexive problems are suggested; dramatic situations are plotted for philosophical debates; social, cultural, and gender elements are juxtaposed; and the inner self is articulated. It has also shown that the emphasis on reflexivity in association with the search for self-identity in Japanese TV dramas is assured by its specific narrative rhetoric of reflexive expression.

"Melodrama was less about an emergent liberal populism than about the anxieties of a society experiencing unprecedented moral, cultural, and socioeconomic disarray."[31] In Ben Singer's study on American melodramatic films in the early twentieth century, he relates the anxious aspects of modernity to a variety of representations in melodrama. Like American melodramatic films, many Japanese TV dramas are stories set in modern environments that map the disturbances of modern human psychology. These dramas have cultivated reflexive content that is mostly concerned with modern symptoms of individuals struggling between internal emotions and external social realities.

> It is not an excess of rationality, but a shocking lack of rationality, the prevailing irrationality, which explains the ailment of industrial modernity. It can be cured, if at all, not by a retreat but only by a radicalization of rationality, which will absorb the repressed uncertainty.[32]

Ulrich Beck's logic suggests that modern reflexivity may function as a mechanism to overcome irrationality. I find that Japanese TV dramas strangely mix up emotional subtlety and reflexive rationality. The characters in dramas are dragged into inevitable conflicts and confusions, which are not so different from melodramas worldwide. However, what makes them specific is that the characters are empowered to be self-reflexive, and even self-healing, no matter what dramatic pitfalls are imposed on them. Scenarios in which protagonists experience pain, sentiment and fragility without too much emotional excess, allowing for moments of reflexive rationality, are a common rhetorical formula in Japanese TV drama. As evidenced in *Wednesday Love Affair*, even at the most heartbreaking moment female protagonists can generate positive power through reflexive self-narration. In my view, it is emotional intensity incorporated with reflexive rationality that makes Japanese TV drama powerful, fascinating, and contradictory. It exposes a particular kind of philosophy and aesthetics, one in which emotional sentiment works through the form of rational reflexivity and vice versa.

Reflexive rationality liberates us not only from emotional intensity but also with self-assured calmness. To unleash emotion is necessary but is incomplete without consequent reflexive rationality, regardless of whether the substance of the reflexivity is mature or immature, true or false, all positions that are a matter of taste. It is the dramatized reflexive act itself that is important. Reflexivity should not be mistaken for a static state of being; rather it is an active, continuing "self-confrontation" in Beck's use of the term.[33] Reflexive rationality can come in the form of self-control, and yet it is not a totalizing power since it emerges from doubt and uncertainty. The reflexive content changes depending on time, space, and the scenario, resulting in various reflexive demonstrations in different TV dramas, but in all cases reflexivity is the site of struggle.

The reflexivity in Japanese TV dramas does not necessarily indicate that it is radical enough to direct social revolution or even that it can avoid being implicated with particular power structures or conveying certain types of ideologies. To some extent, reflexivity itself may be manipulative and authoritative, for example, by simply communicating the author's idiosyncratic reflexive declarations. Eriko Kitagawa, one of the most famous female TV drama scriptwriters, is, incredibly, worshipped as "the goddess of love." That is, reflexivity in questions of love can be mainstreamed in the marketing of "love ideologies."[34] Nevertheless, such reflexive impulses may still reinforce a sense of self-awareness and self-exploration, create alternative possibilities for resistance, or suggest ways being outside existing social norms. The reflexive approaches in the three Japanese TV dramas discussed in this essay correspond to Ulrich Beck's viewpoints on the characteristics of late modernity. Following Beck, what is discovered in the three surveyed dramas is that there are so many models for love relationships, marriage, and family that they "break apart the togetherness and multiply the questions," which in turn forces "every man and woman to operate and persist as individual agent and designer of his or her own biography."[35] The more life choices there are, the more risky it is for one to make life decisions.

> Once "democratization" was replaced by economic development as the overriding objective, most Japanese had little choice but to become socialized to corporate and national goals. As time passed, such regimentation was sweetened by the material rewards of prosperity and hardened by nationalistic appeals. The emergence of a mass consumer society created an ethos of "middle-class" homogeneity and contributed immeasurably to depoliticization (or preoccupation with personal and local matters).[36]

It is often observed that since the end of World War II, and especially since the 1960s, Japan has turned its attention away from nationalistic patriotism and toward an engagement with consumerist materialism and personal concerns. What makes Japan appear to be a homogenous "middle-class" nation is confirmed through the representations of reflexive narratives and highly developed consumerist lifestyle in Japanese TV dramas. In his case study of consuming cuteness in Japan, Brian J. McVeigh argued there are two coexisting tensions in Japanese society: "groupism" versus "individuality" and "social role" versus "self-expression."[37] Reflexive Japanese TV dramas may be related to this wider context, one in which Japanese society as a whole has been drawn into developing the consciousness or unconsciousness of focusing on the inner self and the local as a counterpoint to the imposed collective social/work/official hierarchy. Is this a consequence of the postwar national "depoliticalization" project? Perhaps. In any event, the merger of the "politics of the personal" emphasizing the subtlety of social-psychological exploration, with capitalism and consumerism has become a prevalent theme throughout the popular culture industry. Whether reflexive statements in Japanese TV dramas are made explicit through the use of "I" or implicit by proffering philosophical mottos with a hidden "I," the Japanese TV drama industry has been sophisticated in capitalizing on the business of self-reflexivity.

Minami, the main female character in the Japanese TV drama *Long Vacation* says, "If a person cannot be self-sufficient with happiness, they will not obtain happiness in marriage either." The tone taken here is a very assertive one, and the quotation highlights the significance of the self, which in turn resonates with my earlier discussion of the issue of obtaining happiness. Minami, a thirty-year-old woman who lost her job and was left at the altar by her fiancé, reflects on her single status as she experiences tremendous social pressure to get married. She confirms her right to find happiness herself rather than depending on marriage. In a modern society, happiness can never be contained in a single shape or form. Thus, the path to happiness certainly has to be found in the continuous process of exploring the interaction between the self and social institutions and the need to feel in control despite living in an age of late modernity rife with uncertainty, loneliness, powerlessness, vulnerability, jealousy, and obsession. The search for happiness inscribed in Japanese TV dramas parallels the way in which modern subjects tenaciously look for the existential meanings, which are excavated again and again in other TV dramas and by audiences in everyday life. In this world, happiness can never be promised or stable, and the search for it is not only a lifelong paradox but also a permanent theme for capitalist appropriation.

> Consuming and gazing Japan, the final object perhaps is not Japan, but the ambivalent self.[38]

The reflexive comment comes from a Hong Kong scholar, Kwai-Cheung Lo, in the preface of a book on Japanese popular culture by Hong Kong writer/cultural critic Ching-Siu Tong, an ardent fan of Japanese TV dramas. Yes, it is exactly "the ambivalent self" which compels modern individuals to be constantly reflexive. Indeed, the ambivalent self is always unsettling and contradictory, yet it provides the reflexive power for self-therapy and re-birth. "The final object perhaps is not Japan"—it is true and yet we may have to ask why it is Japan but not anything else, which is empowered to be a significant object mediating reflexivity for Asian fan audiences. Issues of transnational consumption are beyond the scope of this article, but what I have attempted to do here is capture the way in which reflexive narratives in Japanese TV dramas enrich and complicate our views and imaginations of ways to cope with the ambivalence of the self.

NOTES

1. Mimi White, *Perfectly Japanese: Making Families in an Era of Upheaval* (Berkeley: University of California Press, 2002), 190.

2. Robert C. Allen, *To Be Continued . . . : Soap Operas around the World* (New York: Routledge, 1995), 11.

3. Eva Tsai, "Nozawa Dorama: Televisual Authorship in the Currents of Suspense and Desires," *Japan Forum* 19, no.1 (2007): 33.

4. Lisa Yuk-Ming Leung, "*Ganbaru* and Its Transcultural Audience: Imaginary and Reality of Japanese TV Dramas in Hong Kong," in *Feeling Asian Modernities: Transnational Consumption of Japanese TV Drama*, ed. Koichi Iwabuchi (Hong Kong: Hong Kong University Press, 2004), 79–81. *Long Vacation* was produced by Fuji TV and scripted by Eriko Kitagawa. *Beach Boys* was produced by Fuji TV and scripted by Yoshikazu Okada.

5. Kelly Hu, "Discovering Japanese TV Drama through Online Chinese Fans: Narrative Reflexivity, Implicit Therapy, and the Question of the Social Imaginary," in *Media Consumption and Everyday Life in Asia*, ed. Youna Kim (London: Routledge, 2008), 114–26.

6. Anothy Giddens, *Modernity and Self-Identity: Self and Society in the Late Modern Age* (Stanford: Stanford University Press, 1991), 32.

7. Ibid., 2.

8. Ibid., 70–108.

9. Ien Ang, *Watching Dallas: Soap Opera and the Melodramatic Imagination* (London: Methuen, 1985), 73.

10. Eva Tsai, "Empowering Love: the Intertexual Author of Ren'ai Dorama," in *Feeling Asian Modernities: Transnational Consumption of Japanese TV Drama*, ed. Koichi Iwabuchi (Hong Kong: Hong Kong University Press, 2004), 47.

11. Chunghua Telecommuncation, "*Tiankon Shucheg*" (Skybookstore), http://www.skybookstore.com/home.htm, accessed June 2, 2002.

12. *Unmarried Family* was produced by Fuji TV and scripted by Simon Fumi, *The Weekend Marriage* was produced by TBS and scripted by Makiko Tsuchidate, and *Wednesday Love Affair* was produced by Fuji TV and scripted by Hisashi Nozawa.

13. Giddens, *Modernity and Self-Identity: Self and Society in the Late Modern Age,* back cover.

14. Page: 10
Dialogue extract follows.

15. David Morley, *Home Territories: Media, Mobility and Identity* (London: Routledge, 2000), 86, quoted in Nancy Fraser, *Unruly Practices: Power, Discourse, and Gender in Contemporary Social Theory* (Minnesota: University of Minnesota Press, 1989), 120.

16. Masahiro Yamada, *Danhsen Gishshenzu (Parasite Singles),* trans. Shenlin Li, Taipei: Hsin-Hsinwen, 2001), 70. The citation originally in Chinese is translated in English.

17. Yamada, *Danhsen Gishshenzu,* 17.

18. Yamada, *Danhsen Gishshenzu,* 67.

19. *Love Story* was produced by Fuji TV and scripted by Eriko Kitagawa. *The Power of Love* was produced by Fuji TV and scripted by Tomoko Aizawa.

20. Graham Allan, "Introduction," in *Home and Family: Creating the Domestic Sphere,* ed. Graham Allan and Graham Grow (London: Macmillan, 1989), 4.

21. Giddens, *Modernity and Self-Identity: Modernity and Self-Identity: Self and Society in the Late Modern Age,* 91.

22. Dialogue extracts follows.

23. Yuko Ogasawara, *Office Ladies and Salaried Men: Power, Gender, and Work in Japanese Companies* (Berkeley: University of California Press, 1998), 3.

24. Dialogue extracts follows.

25. Dialogue extracts follows.

26. Ching-Siu Tong, *Rijyu Yoliyun (The Playground of Japanese TV Drama)* (Hong Kong: Man Lam, 1999), 25–27.

27. For example, *Koibito yo!* (Dear Lover, 1995) is a story about two married couples who change partners. *Nemurenu Yoru wo Daite (Thinking of Your True Love,* 2002) describes the intricate involvements of three married couples in the past and present.

28. Naoki, "Rjyubiji Sheiiaur de Qiegsh" (A note on Wednesday Love Affair), http://over-time.idv.tw/esc-1459.html, accessed July 8, 2002.

29. See note 28.

30. Giddens, *Modernity and Self-Identity: Self and Society in the Late Modern Age,* 12.

31. Ben Singer, *Melodrama and Modernity: Early Sensational Cinema and Its Contexts* (New York: Columbia University Press, 2001), 132–33.

32. Ulrich Beck, "The Reinvention of Politics: Towards a Theory of Reflexive Modernization," in *Reflexive Modernization: Politics, Tradition, and Aesthetics in the Modern Social Order*, ed. Ulrich Beck, Anthony Giddens, and Scott Lash (Oxford: Polity, 1994), 33.

33. Ulrich Beck, 5.

34. Ching-Siu Tong, *Luanbudoeniag* (*Walking into Eastern West: An Anthology of Japanese Culture*) (Hong Kong: Compass Publisher, 2001), 95.

35. Beck, "The Reinvention of Politics," 15.

36. John W. Dower, "Peace and Democracy in Two Systems: External Policy and Internal Conflict," in *Postwar Japan as History*, ed. Andrew Gordon (Berkeley: University of California Press. 1993), 31.

37. Brian J. McVeigh, *Wearing Ideology: State, Schooling, and Self-Presentation in Japan* (New York: Berg, 2000), 162.

38. Kwai-Cheung Lo, "Preface," in *Luanbudoeniag* (*Walking into Eastern West: An Anthology of Japanese Culture*), Ching-Siu Tong (Hong Kong: Compress, 2001), 7–9.

Becoming Prodigal Japanese: Portraits of Japanese Americans on Japanese Television*

Christine R. Yano

On 1 April 2002, Nihon Hōsō Kyokai (the Japan Public Broadcasting Corporation or NHK) began broadcasting its latest *asadora* (morning serialized drama) entitled *Sakura* (Cherry Blossom; notably, a symbol of Japan) with the headline "Sakura, a Heroine Who Links Two Countries, Will Meet Up with the Heart (*kokoro*) of Japan."[1] The accompanying cover photo of NHK's publicity magazine showed a fresh-faced, pixie-haired, broadly smiling ingenue clutching a branch of fuchsia-colored bougainvillea against a backdrop of spring green. This announcement and other publicity sources introduced the Japanese public to the title character and newly minted NHK *asadora*. Like many *asadora*, this drama focused on a young woman facing the challenges of her surroundings, but this one had a new twist in that its heroine was not Japanese but Japanese American.[2]

The plot of the series concerns a twenty-three-year-old fourth-generation Nikkeijin (a person or persons of Japanese descent, here abbreviated to Nikkei and used as a shorthand term for Japanese American), a woman from Hawai`i, significantly named Elizabeth Sakura Matsushita who spends one year in Japan teaching English at a private middle school in rural Hida-Takayama.[3] Over the course of the year, she becomes "more Japanese than most Japanese," championing Japanese values, expressing fondness for things Japanese, and exhibiting that central feature of Japaneseness, *kokoro* (heart, mind, spirit). This essay examines the television drama *Sakura* as a media text that defines Japanese Americans not so much as Americans as prodigal Japanese separated from their homeland by a mere ocean.

217

The NHK network is not alone in creating representations of Japanese Americans. American media, too, have portrayed Asian Americans (including those of Japanese descent) in ways that beg the realities of their daily lives and subjectivities. Much of the critique of American media representations focuses on ways in which Asian Americans are exoticized, orientalized, feminized, and inevitably racialized. The processes of their representation create a sense of otherness by highlighting their difference from white America. As the historian Darrell Hamamoto points out, even though Japanese Americans have been part of American society for four and even five generations, their media depiction in the United States remains frozen in time. They are commonly portrayed as newly arrived foreigners, producing a "symbolic containment [that] implies that Japanese Americans still occupy 'probationary' status within the larger society."[4] Nikkei in these American media depictions are forever fresh off the boat and thus always foreign and exotic.

In NHK's *Sakura*, the shoe is placed on the other foot with Nikkei depicted on Japanese television. This is a process not so much of making others as of extending selves by incorporating Nikkei within the fold of Japan. In a sense, the Japanese media depiction of Nikkei agrees with that of American media, tying them more to Japan than to the place of their American births and lives. Both, in the words of James Clifford, position Nikkei as "not here to stay" in America.[5] These representations make Nikkei always and only diasporic. As Ien Ang writes, "When the question of 'where you're from' [the place of one's ancestral origins] threatens to overwhelm the reality of 'where you're at' [the place where one lives], the idea of diaspora becomes a disempowering rather than an empowering one."[6] The process, however, is more complex than this in the hands of Japanese media. Nikkei become selves with a twist, resting on an underlying racialism that creates a blood tie to all those of Japanese ancestry even while pointing up the differences wrought by the circumstances of their upbringing in America.

These contrasting media gazes from both sides of the Pacific place Nikkei in a liminal state.[7] They squirm as the gazed-upon, even as those gazes contradict each other, as well as share in the processes of representation. Edward Said addresses the power of these gazes when he writes, "The job facing the cultural intellectual is . . . not to accept the politics of identity as given, but to show how all representations are constructed, for what purpose, by whom, and with what components."[8]

This essay takes up Said's call by examining the ways in which *Sakura* is a site of narrative practices and readings on Nikkei. I analyze portrayals of Nikkei within *Sakura* as forms of ideology set forth by a statist institution, NHK. I ask what work these portraits intend. How do Nikkei, as prodigal

Japanese, become exemplars of what Japan has lost? Furthermore, how does this media image of white-collar, female, (Hawaiian) American Nikkei temporarily residing in Japan stand in direct contrast to the everyday reality of blue-collar, primarily male, South American Nikkei now resident there? And, more politically charged, how does this portrait of Nikkei position them not as Japanese Americans as much as Japanese residing in America at the ready to display and enact their loyalties to and affinity for Japan? The latter part of my essay compares these telegenic portraits of Nikkei—positive, attractive, even exemplary—with some on-the-ground responses by viewers. Through interviews conducted with Nikkei in the United States, I position the drama as but one voice among many whose constructions leave the people themselves out of their representations.

This essay adopts the strategy of tracing a media text from its producers to consumers, in the words of Faye Ginsburg, Lila Abu-Lughod, and Brian Larkin, addressing "not only how media are embedded in people's quotidian lives but also how consumers and producers are themselves imbricated in discursive universes, political situations, economic circumstances, national settings, historical moments, and transnational flows."[9] This goes beyond Stuart Hall's mechanical encoding/decoding model, which does not sufficiently account for the complexities and dynamisms that shape each side of the equation.[10] Louis Althusser's concept of interpolation—in ideal form built on a tight hierarchical relationship between producer and consumer with producers wielding the power to interpolate consumers into a certain set of assumptions, practices, and subjectivities—may be extended here.[11] In this overseas context, at least one group of consumers reads a media text at a distance from its producers. The varied reaction to the text by Nikkei ranges from one that sidesteps powers of interpolation with indifference to one whose interpolated subjectivity expresses itself through an adamant rejection of the media portrayal. In this transnational shift away from a primary audience (Japanese) to a scattered, secondary one (Japanese American) interpolation is an uneven, ambiguous, yet persistent project.

SAKURA: EYE ON NIKKEI

In Japan, *Sakura* garnered an audience viewership averaging approximately 23 percent, considered a success by NHK standards. The *asadora* genre of which it is a part is particular to NHK and distinctively frames the way Japanese viewers interpret what they see. (This is a frame not necessarily shared by Nikkei, who, for the most part, are not as familiar with the vicissitudes of NHK or the *asadora* genre.) Each *asadora* is a fixed-length serial drama, typically broadcast six mornings a week for fifteen minutes over a period of approximately six months.[12] Because it is a daytime television broadcast, in this case from 8:15 to 8:30 A.M., it is known as television geared toward women and retirees.[13] As such, its programming is widely acknowledged in Japan as conservative family drama, which may tackle social issues but with little in the way of sexuality or hard-hitting controversy. This is not reality as much as an NHK fiction that gives viewers a prescriptive dose of programming for what is considered to be the personal and national good. According to Paul Harvey, *asadora* characteristics include a focus on young women and family, a generally light-hearted, comedic tone, and, as is NHK's mandate, an educational component with regard to Japan and Japanese culture.[14] The network uses each *asadora*'s historical context and/or regional setting as an opportunity to dispense information and boost related tourism. The heroines of these *asadora* undergo some kind of personal hardship, resulting in growth and change.[15] The themes of *Sakura*—a young female put to the test in a new environment, growth and development through hardship, and reinforcement of traditional values—are themes common to the *asadora* genre and therefore part of a Japanese viewer's set of expectations.

The character Sakura is a *yonsei* (a fourth-generation Japanese American) who goes to Japan on a personal quest to discover her roots and teach English for one year.[16] She goes not as a complete stranger but as one brought up in a family enclave of things Japanese in Hawai`i. Japanese is the language of the home in Sakura's family; not only do all family members speak it, but, amazingly enough, so does her Caucasian fiancé Robert, who spent part of his childhood in Japan. Within this heavily Japan-centered family context, Sakura is singled out as a member with particularly close emotional and intellectual ties to Japan. Her interest in Japan comes through her *nisei* paternal grandfather, of whom she was a favorite.[17] He long ago imposed on the family rules to encourage speaking Japanese, eating Japanese foods, and following Japanese customs. He thus acts as the family arbiter of things Japanese.

The entire serial drama is told from this *nisei* grandfather's point of view as the voice-over narrator of events, thoughts, and reactions, as well as Sakura's guiding spirit. He even makes an occasional phantasmic appearance on the program, seen only by his granddaughter Sakura. In these ways, Sakura acts as the repository of her grandfather's spirit, including his values and practices. She combines the waning ties of each succeeding generation of the male patriline, of which she is inevitably a part, with direct ties to things Japanese through the in-marrying *issei* women in each generation of her family.

This relationship between Sakura and her grandfather and their ties to Japan and the past in many ways parallels that between Nikkei and their ties to Japan's past. Just as Sakura is a repository of her grandfather's spirit, so, too, are Nikkei—and particularly Nikkei in Hawai`i—said to be a cultural repository for Japan's rural past, carrying on the ways of Japan as distilled from the regions and time periods of their original immigration (1885–1924). Aspects of Nikkei immigrant culture in Hawai`i are considered by many in Japan to be examples of marginal survival in which the marginal members of a diasporic population tend to preserve particular elements of the home country while adopting and adapting others. Nikkei represent nostalgic exemplars of who "we Japanese" once were.

Kohki Nishitani, a Japanese national resident of Hawai`i and head of the company that assisted NHK in its on-site production there through his company, Magic Island Productions, Inc., explains:

> Japan is very Westernized, but the Nikkeijin, they still keep [Japanese] tradition. Meanwhile Japan [is] losing tradition. So Sakura is *yonsei*, but she carry—I think a lot of Japanese *sansei, yonsei* still carry—from the old people, old-style Japan. . . . They [Nikkei] still carry over. Even you go *bon* dance [Japanese folk dance] on Kauai [island]—I'm so surprised. Country *no* [Japanese rural] *bon* dance style. Japan, *ima mo nai, ne* [no longer has the old type of *bon* dance]. Doesn't have. But still they [Nikkei on Kauai] keeping [older Japanese traditions]. So we [his company] try to show Japan [NHK], hey, look, it's [Hawai`i] different. You know this is like Japan before.[18]

Nishitani, like many Japanese, links spatial and temporal dichotomies: Japan versus "the West" and past versus present. Within this configuration, Nikkei occupy a liminal space by carrying Japanese blood, Western culture (though historically excluded from certain sociopolitical dimensions), and Japan's past (rural, typically southwestern). They are thus Japan's past—or at least one imagined, regional configuration of it—residing in the West. Sakura brings this liminality to a Japanese rural village whose own connection to tradition is threatened. Nishitani's "this is like Japan before" characterization of Nikkei in Hawai`i encapsulates NHK's guiding assumption.

In the series, Sakura's family explains that retaining the Japanese language is a deliberate choice. However, it is easy for viewers in Japan to naturalize Japanese as the default language (and therefore harbor a set of linguistic expectations) for anyone with Japanese blood. As Harumi Befu points out, the ties among land, race, culture, and language are reinscribed repeatedly in *nihonjinron* (theories about being Japanese) and other nationalistic forms of discourse in modern Japan.[19] In order to dramatize the difference between Japanese and Japanese Americans, however, Sakura and other

Nikkei in the drama occasionally stumble over words and ask for help in learning new vocabulary, creating a linguistic deficiency that calls on native speakers for help. In many instances, these linguistic lapses sound at odds with the rest of their speech, which is unaccented, native-level Japanese. By contrast, non-Nikkei *gaijin* (foreign) actors in the drama speak in accented Japanese but never stumble over their words. Laura Miller's work on *gaijin tarento* (foreign media celebrities) is useful here. According to her, ethno-linguistic boundaries retain a stubborn hold on popular belief in the unique-ness of Japanese culture in Japan.[20] Therefore, media commentators focus on the mispronunciations and grammatical errors in *gaijin tarento* speech, rendering foreigners cute, endearing, and ultimately nonthreatening.[21] Part of the irony of *Sakura* lies in the juxtaposition of a Japanese actress feigning linguistic neediness while actual foreigners' linguistic flaws go unnoticed.

According to the promotional literature that accompanied the drama, Sakura is one "whose outward appearance is Japanese but whose think-ing is American."[22] The network's depiction of Sakura's Americanness goes beyond thinking to bodily matters. She runs around with arms and legs flailing and gapes, mugs, and grimaces with exaggerated facial ex-pressions.[23] Hers is a body out of control like that of a child before it has been trained in Japanese ways of sitting, standing, and bowing. For ex-ample, when she and a fellow teacher, Mr. Katsuragi, are conducting their first family visit to homes of their students, Sakura's foot falls asleep and she cannot stand up.[24]

KATSURAGI:	Can't you even sit properly?
SAKURA:	What?
KATSURAGI:	It was just for twenty minutes.
SAKURA:	But I'm an American.
KATSURAGI:	Don't say that with a Japanese face. (episode 16)

Later, when her family comes to visit her in Japan, the same thing happens to her father, who ends up falling over when he tries to rise from the dinner table (episode 55).[25] Untrained bodies mark the foreignness of these Japanese Americans.

Part of what redeems Sakura is that which is often a source of conster-nation and rebuke: her body. She is shorter than many of her junior high students and appears to weigh less. With her pixie haircut and thin, boyish figure, she looks more like a *shōjo* (young, unmarried girl between the ages of approximately eight and sixteen) than the university graduate student in her twenties that she is in the story. Her clothes, too, tend to downplay adult sexuality; she typically dresses in long pants and shirts that cover most of her torso and limbs. With her conservative, childlike appearance, she presents little threat to Japanese viewers. Hers is a body and character in contradistinction to that of the stereotypical Westerner: tall, overbearing, and aggressive.

People assume certain things about her because she is American, and at times she disproves them. For example, on her first morning her homestay mother serves her two fried eggs and toast while everyone else in the family eats rice and miso soup. She is dismayed and says that she prefers rice, explaining that in her family her grandfather's policy was to have rice for breakfast. Amid this, the homestay family's teenage daughter reacts with excitement at being able to eat Sakura's toast.

GRANDFATHER:	Bread won't sustain you throughout the day.
SAKURA:	I agree. Rice gives you power.
GRANDFATHER:	I agree.
FATHER:	It looks like Sakura and Dad think alike. (episode 19)

Several things are going on in this scene. For one, like many other aspects of contemporary Japan, food becomes dichotomized as Japanese (rice) or Western (bread). What you eat for breakfast is interpreted as an indicator of who you are, including your relationship with things Japanese.[26] Second, the teenage daughter's enthusiastic reaction to being able to eat Sakura's toast pantomimes what is considered to be Japanese youth's appetite for things Western and, to some extent, urban. The teenager's life in this rural village is a period of biding one's time until one can leave for the city, where one may eat bread with abandon. Third, rice is imbued with both physical and symbolic power.[27] Bread (that is, "Western ways") is a flash in the pan, a quick fix; Japanese people need rice (that is, "Japanese ways") to sustain themselves throughout the day. Fourth, Sakura is placed in the position of teaching Japan's youth (and adults) the ways of their own forefathers. She is a cultural repository that links her more closely to grandfathers on both sides of the Pacific than to those her own age. In these ways, Sakura creates multiple bridges: between Japan and its past, Japan and America, older and younger generations in Japan and urban and rural in Japan.

In fact, Sakura becomes a catalyst for Japanese around her to consider their relationship to Japan. In one scene, Sakura expresses great interest in her homestay family's long-standing business of candle making. The family business is in danger of demise for want of a successor, and Sakura takes it on herself to learn about this regional tradition. She watches the grandfather painstakingly craft each candle, taking copious notes, and we watch as the family, including the young son Daisuke, watches her watching.

FUDEKO (mother):	Ms. Sakura is certainly earnest about this.
KEN'ICHI (father):	She's been like that since morning.
GRANDMOTHER:	I wish the family would take a lesson from her. (episode 27)

Sakura the American is the exemplary student who promises to save a family enterprise, a regional tradition, and a link to Japan's past.[28]

In another scene Sakura and other non-Nikkei foreigners gather to learn calligraphy from a Japanese master. Later, inspired by Sakura's enthusiasm for the beauty of the art, her host family gathers around the dining table and practices calligraphy themselves. Each writes some abstract word or expression that is relevant to their lives or personalities.

GRANDFATHER:	It's nice to sit down and use a brush and ink once in a while, isn't it?
SAKURA:	Calligraphy is a wonderful tradition of Japan. Each Chinese character has a deep meaning.
GRANDMOTHER:	Sakura, since you came here, you've made us think about a lot of things.
FATHER:	It's strange to have an American teach us about Japanese culture and tradition. (episode 43)

In both of these scenes, the grandfather leads off as the practitioner of a traditional art form. Others may or may not join in, following Sakura's example. But careful attention is paid to Daisuke, the thirteen-year-old grandson of the family, out of concern for the patrilineal flow of past ways and practices. In her respect for tradition, Sakura becomes both the taught and the teacher, the observer and the observed, in a kind of embedded triangulated relationship between younger Japanese, older Japanese—particularly males—and Nikkei, here female.

Gender plays an important role in this triangle. In many ways, Sakura could not have been a man. Adopted into this host family, she can become another daughter who, within the patriarchal family system, must be brought up, protected, made marriageable, and then let go. Daughters, in other words, have mobility by way of marriage as daughters-in-law. They function as mediators between persons, families, and communities. Their in-betweenness makes them sojourners in transit, accommodating themselves to those around them and therefore necessarily attentive to the subtlest conditions and requirements. Mothers-in-law and daughters-in-law within this system have a stereotypically tense relationship as trainers and trainees in the ways of the household. Women in Japan are the caretakers of family traditions, especially as practiced within the household. (This stands in contrast to the homestay grandfather, who upholds his family's public tradition of candle making. This also stands in contrast to Sakura's paternal grandfather in Hawai`i, who took it upon himself to impose Japanese traditions on his family.) As Harvey writes, "Men may often carry out traditions, but it is women [in *asadora*] who retain the knowledge."[29] Women also have a particular relationship with tradition as people who move from their natal household to their conjugal one. Unlike men, they undergo the processes of being an outsider, a trainee, and ultimately a keeper. Sakura fits into this family system not only as a daughter but also as a daughter-in-law, an outsider trainee and eventual caretaker of the ways of Japan.

More than a woman, however, Sakura is a *shōjo*. She is *kawaii* (cute) physically and socially. These elements bundle together the traits of being vulnerable, dependent, hapless, childlike, and endearing. Her dependence—to some extent linguistic, as she makes some implausible blunders despite her otherwise native facility with Japanese—calls on those around her to help, thus sealing their relationship with her. She is the one that the community of Japanese must raise. If Sakura were a boy, she would also be raised, but placing a male in Sakura's position would emasculate him. Sakura's dependency only feminizes her.

I argue that in this drama Nikkei become *shōjo*, bound to dependency through her hybridity. Nikkei retain this liminal state of (pre)pubescence, not fully adult, not fully Japanese, but always with the potential to learn and become. The tightrope for Nikkei as depicted by NHK is their very hybridity, with one foot in each country, both child and adult. Being Japanese for Sakura becomes something that must be taught and learned on a racial foundation that justifies these lessons. Japaneseness incorporates both the racial and cultural, both nature and nurture, a balancing act between something that must be taught but only to students who can claim the birthright of race. This is part of the lesson of Nikkei in the NHK drama: they can learn to become Japanese because their blood gives them the ability, as well as the right, to do so. In the process, Sakura herself becomes a lesson to Japanese viewers on being Japanese, on the beauty and value of their own culture. In one scene, the homestay grandfather and Sakura have a heart-to-heart talk late at night while drinking sake.

GRANDFATHER: Sakura, you're such a caring person (*yasashii ko*). People [in Japan] these days are sensitive to what's been done to them, but when it comes to doing something to others they're totally insensitive. They always blame someone else. Why do you think I let you stay with us here?

SAKURA: I don't know.

GRANDFATHER: It's because I felt that you'd understand the heart of the Japanese (*Anta ni wa nihonjin no kokoro o wakaru to omotta kara*).

SAKURA: The heart of the Japanese?

GRANDFATHER: The heart that even the Japanese today have forgotten. The humility it takes to give in to others. . . . A strong determination to take on something without blaming others. I felt that you had those qualities.

SAKURA: No, I don't.

GRANDFATHER: [sips *sake*] You could say that it's the heart of Japan.

SAKURA: The heart of Japan?

GRANDFATHER: The first time you came to this shop. . . . When I saw the look in your eyes as you watched me making my candle, I thought that you'd understand. The heart of Japan.

SAKURA: I'd be so happy if that were true.

GRANDFATHER: Don't ever forget that heart.

SAKURA: I won't. (episode 101)

In the span of this three-minute scene, the word *kokoro* (heart) is invoked no less than seven times. This becomes NHK's mantra of Japaneseness.

What about others who are not racially Japanese? In this NHK drama, there are various characters who are *gaijin* residents of Japan. One of them is even married to a Japanese woman and operates a tofu restaurant whose customers are primarily other *gaijin*. The restaurant serves Japanese food exclusively and has a "speak Japanese only" policy, not unlike that imposed by Sakura's grandfather on his Nikkei family. It is, in other words, a place where *gaijin* can practice or play at being Japanese, eating Japanese food, speaking Japanese, or learning calligraphy from a wizened old master. These *gaijin* study Japanese language, food, and culture as a pursuit of *benkyō* (study). There are limits, however, to this space for becoming Japanese. For one thing, it is a bounded space, owned and operated by *gaijin*. It is not a Japanese space but one set aside for those who want to study and practice the language and customs. As such, it is always set apart and performed as *gaijin* doing Japanese things such as eating Japanese food (cooked by *gaijin*) and speaking Japanese (primarily with other *gaijin*). The patrons are young, unmarried, multiracial, and transient *gaijin* from Europe and America. In fact, the extent to which these *gaijin* can become Japanese (or as Japanese as Sakura is allowed) is limited. They are always quarantined by their phenotypic difference, hitting a glass ceiling of acceptance because they do not have the racial authority to fully adopt these cultural ways. Unlike Sakura and other Nikkei, who always have the potential to become Japanese, these non-Nikkei *gaijin* can only practice and perform; they can never become.

In contrast to Sakura is her younger teenage sister, Stephanie "Momo" (Peach) Matsushita, who visits from Hawai`i. Momo is taller and darker complexioned than Sakura, with long hair dyed brown and a broad, open smile. Her size is cause for attention and wonder, especially by the teenage boys at the school, who describe her as *"iroppoi"* (sexy). Seated at a lunch table with her, they ask questions such as "How tall are you?" and "What are your measurements?" which she blithely ignores. Instead, she eats hungrily and even finishes the leftovers from the lunch of one of the students. The boys look at each other in amazement, commenting, "No wonder she's so big!" (episode 58). Unlike Sakura, Momo has a *gaijin* body and sexuality. She greets people with a smacking kiss on the cheek, leaving traces of lipstick in a trail of boisterous interactions.

The presence of Momo heterogenizes NHK's portrait of younger Nikkei, but her effect is limited, especially given her minor role. For one thing, she speaks Japanese as well as Sakura. She ultimately shares the same values even though they come bundled in a rougher, less palatable form. And, like all children, Momo simply needs to learn. There is nothing fundamentally "wrong" with her. What is right is that she is racially Japanese. Her shortcomings may be overlooked as similar to those of others—including many children and young adults in Japan—who also only need to learn how to become culturally Japanese.

The drama paints this version of Nikkei unproblematically. Sakura is young, attractive, fluent (except for occasional gaps), highly educated, and in love with Japan. She is not confronted with such negative stereotypes of Nikkei as "dumb Japanese" who lack the cultural knowledge that should course through their veins or as Japanese who could not succeed in their own country and were forced to migrate. Instead, she is welcomed, in part because of her Japanese face, her disarming, childlike ways, and her admiration for Japan. She retains her distinctiveness from Japanese by her candor, impulsiveness, expressiveness, and high energy, yet, these elements of difference never fundamentally challenge the status quo. If anything, they hark nostalgically back to the kind of people the Japanese supposedly once were. Nikkei exemplify retro-Japanese, showing Japanese as tied to tradition, appreciative of their rural lives, and treating each other with compassion. Furthermore, these catalysts for change come within the packaging of *shōjo*—young, female, and desirable—tied to Japanese culture through grandfathers, both biological and adoptive.

The drama also paints a historical picture of Nikkei as Japanese brethren who have undergone great hardship. When Sakura's natal family visits her in Japan, her father is asked to speak to the students and teachers at the Japanese school (episode 59). His speech highlights the pain and suffering that Japanese immigrants endured in their struggle to make a living in Hawai`i and elsewhere. He describes their backbreaking labor and the debt he owes them. He turns *hole-hole bushi* (song of canefield workers), a work song and lament sung by Japanese immigrant women as they toiled in Hawai`i's fields, into a Nikkei anthem iconic of that labor. His speech, as well as a moving performance of *hole-hole bushi* by Sakura's grandmother, elicits tears from his audience, including Sakura and the rest of her family.[30] This provides an emotional climax to the drama and an opportunity for a phantasmic appearance by Sakura's paternal grandfather. In this immigrant story, Nikkei—in particular Nikkei women—emerge as heroic in their suffering.

What is significant here is to consider Nikkei who go unacknowledged in NHK's drama. These include Nikkei who might pose a threat to patriarchal, heterosexist stability: political activists, labor union organizers, criminals, or female leaders.[31] It also includes Nikkei who disrupt the category of Nikkei such as persons of partial Japanese descent, now common among *yonsei*, as well as Okinawan immigrants and their descendants, who often faced discrimination from other Nikkei.[32] This also includes Nikkei who increasingly populate Japan's workforce, primarily men from South America (Peru, Brazil) engaged in blue-collar jobs.[33] Although the Japanese government has made accommodations for this influx, such as creating Japanese-language learning opportunities in the public schools for immigrant children, the general public tends to regard these Nikkei with suspicion and unease.

By contrast, the Nikkei who inhabit *Sakura* are mirror images of the unproblematized Japanese upheld as models of family life: a middle-class urban family living in a three-generation household led by a male bread-winner. They engage in the practices of Japan: eating Japanese foods, speaking Japanese, and espousing the values of a past era. These Nikkei are nothing less than Japanese who happen to live overseas, forever diasporic in their close ties to Japan. They are the prodigal daughters of Japan.

READING NIKKEI IN *SAKURA*: NIKKEI VIEWERS

Sakura was broadcast not only in Japan but also overseas. It was shown in various parts of the world, in some cases with only a few weeks' delay (primarily for subtitling purposes).[34] In Hawai`i it was broadcast from May through November 2002 on the pay-per-view cable network NGN.[35] In parts of California it was broadcast in 2003.

When considering Nikkei's reaction to *Sakura*, we have to consider who they are and what they have invested in their identity as Nikkei. In Hawai`i, *Sakura*'s viewers have self-selected for their interest in things Japanese through their monthly investment in an NGN subscription.[36] They are also those with enough disposable income to make that investment. Some may have an interest in particular features of NGN's programming such as live sumo tournaments (NHK broadcasts dubbed in English) or daily news (NHK broadcasts in Japanese, no subtitles). Others have lived in Japan and want to maintain their ties to the country through this media connection. In fact, they are a relatively small minority in Hawai`i.[37]

Although many viewers interviewed for this essay readily accept and enjoy NHK's version of Nikkei as entertainment, some express disgruntlement at their own portrayal. This disgruntlement rests not only on the many errors in the portrait but also in the muting of their voices in the process. The most glaring mistake in the portrait is that of language. Sakura and her family are far too fluent in Japanese to be credible to anyone who has spent even the briefest amount of time with Nikkei, especially those of the *sansei* and *yonsei* generations. One *sansei* female journalist from Hawai`i now living in Japan writes:

> My gripe with this drama is that it is not realistic at all. No fourth-generation Japanese-American girl can speak Japanese as fluently as Sakura can. . . . I am very disappointed . . . that NHK did not

229

> get more advice from some "real" fourth-generation kids because
> it is giving the Japanese audience the wrong impression of what
> the situation would really be like.[38]

An *issei* woman in her sixties recounts from her own family experience: "I have two children, and even if I have taken them to Japan and they have studied Japanese, they soon forget the language. *Sakura* is not the reality. *Sansei* and *yonsei* in Hawai`i can't speak Japanese" (personal communication 5/15/03).

Glen Fukushima, a longtime Nikkei resident of Japan and president of the American Chamber of Commerce there in 1998–99, notes the following discrepancies between NHK's Nikkei and those in real life.

> 1) the main character . . . is a Yonsei born and raised in Hawaii
> who has never been to Japan but she speaks flawless Japanese;
> 2) her English is not Hawaiian [inflected]. . . ; 3) she and her fam-
> ily members all speak Japanese in their home in Honolulu; 4) her
> Caucasian boyfriend . . . communicates with her in fluent Japa-
> nese; and 5) she is so thoroughly familiar with Japanese customs
> that she knows how to pray formally in front of her ancestors'
> altar when she visits her maternal grandparents in Tokyo for the
> first time.[39]

Fukushima's points about language and customs are well taken, especially when contrasting Sakura with real *yonsei*, many of mixed blood, and few of whom speak Japanese.[40]

Fukushima points out that the series emphasizes the hardships of the plantation days for Nikkei in Hawai`i, including racial discrimination: "While there is no need to deny this history, a rather one-sided view of the United States is conveyed when the drama fails to mention the prominent role Nikkei have come to play in Hawaiian society—whether in politics, government, business, law, media, academia, etc."[41] He criticizes NHK for both the inaccuracies and the partial picture of Nikkei.

Fukushima is not alone. In October 2002, the *Mainichi Daily News* writer Ryann Connell compiled a litany of complaints about *Sakura* by Nikkei in Hawai`i, as well as others in Japan, with an article entitled "Soap Stinker Gets Up Nose of Japanese-Americans." Besides language, other complaints arose over the depiction of a typical family home in Hawai`i: "Some scenes had Sakura with her family in Hawaii. The living room was too cramped. It was like Tokyo." Another complained about the dress styles: "Sakura's mother and grandmother were dressed too plainly. In Hawai`i, even old women get around in T-shirts, shorts or aloha shirts."[42]

One Nikkei noted the lack of physical expressiveness in NHK's version of Nikkei romance: "She [Sakura] treated him [her fiancé] as though he was a stranger. . . . When an American meets their fiancé, at the very least they'd kiss. It was really weird that they didn't kiss or hug."[43] In fact, the physical relationship between Sakura and her Caucasian fiancé is, by American standards (and perhaps even Japanese standards, revealing much about NHK and its depiction of romance vis-à-vis other Japanese media), extremely restrained and distanced. They physically interact more like siblings than lovers.

Language, customs, housing, dress, and sexual prudishness, however, are not all there is. One seventy-seven-year-old *nisei* man I spoke with complained: "Sakura was too outspoken. Hawai`i people are more reserved. I guess movies are always like that, but I didn't like it. Not the way they portrayed that girl."[44] What this man reacted to was NHK's depiction of a Nikkei who would act impulsively, without reserve, walking into a situation as a newcomer, and set about changing things to suit her own values and beliefs. In this, NHK took a stereotype of Americans—as geared toward action rather than reflection—and foisted it on Nikkei. They also generalized Nikkei themselves, not necessarily distinguishing Hawaiian residents (who tend to be less aggressive and more reserved) from those living elsewhere in the United States (who some would say have more closely assimilated to mainstream American values and actions).[45]

One *yonsei* Japanese American woman I spoke with recalled that Sakura and her family were so unrealistic that after a while she forgot that they were supposed to be Nikkei at all and took them as simply characters in a Japanese drama.[46] Indeed, it is the unqualified Japanese sense that unnerves some Nikkei watching the show. Although the drama revolves around Nikkei, it is strictly a Japanese story told by Japanese to Japanese. While few would argue that media are meant to truly capture life, it is the sense of appropriation, especially amid much-touted on-location research and attention to detail, that makes these violations an affront for many Nikkei viewers.

CONCLUDING THOUGHTS

In conclusion, let us return to the questions posed by Said with which I began this essay: how are these representations of Nikkei—like all representations—constructed, for what purpose, by whom, and with what components? These questions take this analysis beyond an image study concerned with the accuracy of the portrait and toward a more productive examination of the sociopolitical contexts of media production.

In the United States, Nikkei have been stereotyped as a model minority, quietly assimilating and adopting the American dream even as media depict them as "forever foreigners." In Japan, Nikkei are stereotyped as a different kind of model minority, one with a dream of Japan as the homeland to which one returns. They, too, are fresh off the boat, but it is a boat that assumes a return trip. The fact that NHK ties this homeland to fourth-generation Nikkei suggests that the dream of "home" continues in those who are well past any direct connection to Japan. According to this, Japan is a "natural," blood-based homeland.

What does it mean to say that Sakura is "more Japanese than most Japanese," that her sense of cultural identity—of being and doing Japanese—surpasses that of Japanese? At the most fundamental level, it suggests that identity is external to oneself; that there are different degrees of being Japanese; that cultural identity is a process, an act, and an achievement; and that one may lose one's identity while another person may gain one. Yet identity within the racialized ideology of NHK remains tied to biology. Sakura is, after all, of Japanese blood and therefore carries within her what is understood as a certain birthright. Therefore, she stands in contrast to the many *gaijin* in Japan who might attempt to likewise achieve linguistic fluency, adopt many of the customs, and enthusiastically pursue a life in Japan, even in some cases marrying Japanese. They may "do Japanese," but they can never "be Japanese" like Sakura.

How does Sakura surpass Japanese? She does so through a Nikkei time warp that distills the values and some of the practices of a previous era in Japan and maintains them in diasporic outposts. In this, Nikkei are depicted as nostalgic exemplars of what Japan has lost. Moreover, Sakura becomes "more Japanese than the Japanese" by means of her enthusiasm and passion in direct contrast to the apathy of Japanese who take the identities, traditions, and practices labeled "Japanese" for granted. This critique, in particular, is leveled by older, more conservative Japanese toward youths who are considered to have strayed too far from their identity as Japanese. *Sakura* and the Nikkei within the drama are a media primer on becoming Japanese taught by one whose blood makes her an insider even while her citizenship makes her an outsider.

The question arises, why now? Why does Japan look to Nikkei at this point in time? I suggest several elements that contribute to this. For one, ever since the economic downturn of the 1990s and 2000s Japan's tightly knit system based on postwar growth and prosperity has been called into question. Media and government point fingers in various directions to address what are perceived as not only economic but also political and social ills. They target the very foundation of institutions such as the family, educational system, and workplace. Japan, say media and government pundits, is in a state of crisis. Calls for reform often take a nostalgic, even nationalistic turn, suggesting that the way to move forward is to look back. According to this, Japan has lost its way through the haze of Western-based modernity and must return to its fundamental roots of spirituality and values. One place to find living examples of these roots is overseas in communities of Nikkei. I am deliberately pointing up the irony of Japanese looking to Nikkei as a repository of their roots even as Sakura travels to Japan to find her roots.

Nikkei, however, are more than past Japanese. They are past Japanese who can frequent cosmopolitan circles because of their linguistic and cultural ties to Euro-America. Although Euro-America may not always accept them fully as citizens, they stand with one foot in the door more easily, perhaps, than Japanese. Here language plays a crucial role. In fact, many Japanese may be the truer cosmopolitans because of their international travel and epicurean knowledge of foreign (particularly European) ways, foods, and products.

Sakura is supposed to be "a heroine who links two countries." She embodies the very link between the two countries in terms of her biology (Japanese) and culture (American or an admixture of Japanese and American). Therein lies a second reason why a statist institution such as NHK might pay particularly close attention to Nikkei. I argue that Nikkei are seen as a potential bank of unpaid primordial ambassadors of Japan residing within the United States. The network assumes a continuing tie between Nikkei and Japan as a "home country" even for those who have never set foot on the country's soil; do not understand, speak, read, or write Japanese; and/ or have no abiding interest in or affinity with Japan. It is believed that even the non-Sakuras among Nikkei can become part of a biological bridge intended to foster pro-Japanese sentiment in the United States if given the proper encouragement, support, and instruction.[47] Ironically, this attitude toward Nikkei by the Japanese government and related institutions such as NHK exactly parallels the assumptions made by the U.S. government during World War II that led to the internment of Nikkei.

Nikkei are not alone as targets of this kind of ambassadorship. The Japanese government has engaged in the practice of creating its informal global ambassadors through expensive policies and practices such as the Japan Exchange and Teaching (JET) program. Since its inception in 1987, JET has annually hosted approximately six thousand foreigners for a one- to three-year stay in Japan. Although teaching foreign languages such as English and interacting with Japanese are important parts of the program, an equally—if not more—important element is returning the grantees to their respective home countries with positive attitudes toward Japan.[48] Under this strategy, the JET program creates thousands of informal ambassadors for Japan yearly.

Sakura depicts Nikkei as both conduits of Japanese tradition in Japan and racialized ambassadors for Japan living in the United States. They are not Japanese American as much as Japanese in America. It is exactly as a Japanese in America now returned to Japan that Sakura does the greatest damage to her credibility for many Nikkei viewers. By negating decades of political struggle and assimilation in favor of the simplistic blinders of race, NHK and its *asadora Sakura* created its own version of Nikkei forever tied to blood.

The racialization of Nikkei by the media occurs on both sides of the Pacific, where they are depicted as inextricably tied to Japan and diasporic in their identity. A television show such as *Sakura* erases the gap between (Japanese) face and (American or Japanese American) thought, suggesting that thought is far more malleable than face and thus nurture may be overcome by nature. At the same time, these Nikkei become exemplars for contemporary Japan as themselves forever Japanese through language, food, bodies, practices, and values even while those in Japan are said to face constant threats to their national-cultural identity. The notion that Nikkei can become "more Japanese than the Japanese" suggests that in this NHK world identity may boil down to a simple daily fare of rice rather than bread and tea rather than coffee as long as one starts from the common ground of race. The lessons of NHK's Nikkei gazing become lessons for all Japanese on the seeming simplicity of *nihon suru* ("doing Japan" so to speak) in order to "be Japan." Japan thus becomes a predicate in search of a subject the whereabouts of which may be found in Honolulu as easily—perhaps more easily—than in Tokyo.

NOTES

*This article is based on but is a substantial revision of my "Gaze Upon Sakura: Imaging Japanese Americans on Japanese TV," in *Gender and Globalization in Asia and the Pacific: Method, Practice, Theory*, edited by Kathy E. Ferguson and Monique Mironesco (Honolulu: University of Hawai`i Press, 2008), pp. 101–20.

1. NHK, *Sakura* (Cherry Blossom) (Tokyo: NHK Publications, 2002). The *asadora* was broadcast April through September 2002 on NHK Monday through Saturday from 8:15 to 8:30 A.M. with a rebroadcast from 12:45 to 1:00 P.M. It was also broadcast

on NHK Satellite 2 Monday through Saturday from 7:30 to 7:45 A.M. The cumulative week's installments were rebroadcast on Saturdays at 9:30 A.M.

2. This was not the first time NHK created a drama series about Nikkei. In 1983–84, *Sanga Moyu,* broadcast on Sunday nights during prime time, depicted the divided loyalties of a Japanese American in Los Angeles during the 1930s and 1940s. Based on a novel by Yamazaki Toyoko entitled *Futatsu no Sokoku* (Two Homelands), the television series (and book) generated controversy among Nikkei because it gave the misleading impression that many Japanese Americans during World War II shared these divided loyalties. Glen Fukushima, "Japanese Americans in the Japanese Media," *Hawaii Pacific Press,* 30 June 2002.

3. According to Emiko Ohnuki-Tierney, cherry blossoms have been symbolic of Japan since the Edo period (1685–1867) when the capital, Edo (now Tokyo), was deliberately planted with cherry trees in various locations for their beauty. Emiko Ohnuki-Tierney, *Rice as Self: Japanese Identities through Time* (Princeton: Princeton University Press, 1993), 55. She discusses the cherry blossom as symbolic of the life force in Japan, specifically in terms of agrarian productivity and gendered female reproductivity (27–33).

A Japanese middle name is common among second- and third-generation Nikkei, but less common in the fourth generation. The fact that in the drama most people, including her family members, call the heroine by her Japanese middle name is not typical.

4. Hamamoto, *Monitored Peril,* 11.

5. James Clifford, *Routes: Travel and Translation in the Late Twentieth Century* (Cambridge: Harvard University Press, 1997), 255.

6. Ien Ang, *On Not Speaking Chinese: Living between Asia and the West* (London: Routledge, 2001), 34.

7. I do not deal here with Japanese American depictions of themselves in the media, although more on this and other related Asian American media representations are discussed in Jun Xing's *Asian America through the Lens: History, Representations, and Identity* (Walnut Creek: Altamira, 1998). Counterprogramming is discussed in Darrell Hamamoto, *Monitored Peril: Asian Americans and the Politics of TV Representation* (Minneapolis: University of Minnesota Press, 1994), 206–37.

8. Edward Said, *Culture and Imperialism* (New York: Knopf, 1993), 314.

9. Faye D. Ginsburg, Lila Abu-Lughod, and Brian Larkin, "Introduction," in Faye D. Ginsburg, Lila Abu-Lughod, and Brian Larkin, eds., *Media Worlds: Anthropology on New Terrain,* 1–38 (Berkeley: University of California Press, 2002), 2.

10. Stuart Hall, "Encoding/Decoding," in Stuart Hall, Dorothy Hobson, Andrew Lower, and Paul Willis, eds., *Culture, Media, Language,* 128–38 (London: Hutchinson. [1980] 1973).

11. Louis Althusser, *Lenin and Philosophy and Other Essays* (London: New Left, 1971).

12. The *asadora* was first screened in 1961. It is patterned after British radio soap operas in its brief, daily format. See Paul S. Harvey, "Nonchan's Dream: NHK Morning Serialized Television Novels," in D. P. Martinez, ed., *The Worlds of Japanese Popular Culture*, 133–51 (Cambridge: Cambridge University Press. 1998), 135.

13. School-age and younger children also constitute part of the audience since the show is broadcast on satellite television (NHK-2) at 7:30 A.M., typically when children are eating breakfast. According to Harvey, *asadora* have been watched by most adults under the age of forty at some point during their childhood as "part of the fabric of Japanese life" (ibid., 141–42). This gives the genre further significance as a socializing agent within the context of the home.

14. Ibid., 136–39.

15. The NHK 2001 *asadora* that preceded *Sakura* was *Churasan*, about a young woman from Okinawa who moves to Tokyo to become a nurse and in the process becomes exemplary of Japaneseness. Many parallel themes in *Sakura* can be found in *Churasan* as well. The network's 2003 *asadora* was *Kokoro* ("Heart, Mind, Soul," a theme repeatedly invoked in *Sakura*), about a young woman who quits her job as a flight attendant to eventually take over her mother's restaurant business.

According to Aoki Shinya, the assistant producer of *Sakura*, the actress chosen to play the main character of an *asadora* is typically an unknown or a newcomer to show business. Watching the actress make her first appearance in a title role is part of the show's appeal (personal communication, 2 June 2002). Indeed, the publicity for *Sakura* repeatedly mentions that Takano Shiho was chosen for the leading role from among nearly twenty-five hundred aspiring actresses. An *asadora*'s production process becomes part of the Japanese audience's viewership. Both NHK and the Japanese audience may be said to "discover" this new talent and participate in her public upbringing.

16. Although the television show identifies Sakura as a *yonsei*, NHK's reckoning seems to be based on age rather than generation. Her mother is from Japan, making her *nisei*, or second generation, on her maternal side. Even on her paternal side, her grandfather may have been born in Hawai`i, justifying Sakura's *yonsei* status, but he lived in Japan from the age of six through twelve, making him far closer to an *issei* (first-generation Japanese American) culturally. Furthermore, her grandmother was born in Japan, making Sakura *sansei* or third generation. By my count, she is of generation 3.25. This sounds like a lot of mathematical splitting of hairs, but it impacts the individual in terms of his or her ethnic-cultural identity.

17. In fact, Sakura's grandfather is *kibei nisei*, a Japanese American who is born in America, is raised in Japan, and subsequently returns to America. *Kibei nisei* typically speak Japanese as a mother tongue and are culturally far closer to Japan than to the land of their birth.

18. Nishitani Kohki, personal communication, 27 August 2003.

19. Harumi Befu, "Nationalism and *Nihonjinron*," in Harumi Befu, ed., *Cultural Nationalism in East Asia: Representation and Identity*, 107–35 (Berkeley: Institute of East Asian Studies, University of California, 1993), 115.

20. Laura Miller, "Crossing Ethnolinguistic Boundaries: A Preliminary Look at the *Gaijin Tarento* in Japan," in John Lent, ed., *Asian Popular Culture*, 189–201 (Boulder: Westview, 1995), 190–91.

21. Ibid., 198.

22. NHK, *Sakura*, 7.

23. Gaping and mugging as a style of acting are admittedly a part of the genre, whose actors sometimes perform in comic book, light comedic fashion. However, the actress playing Sakura is made to gape and mug more than usual.

24. The English translations of the dialogue come from subtitles provided in later broadcasts by the Nippon Golden Network (NGN).

25. Note, however, that it is not only Americans and other foreigners who become the butt of jokes about the pain and discomfort of sitting on one's knees. The 1987 film *O-sōshiki* (The Funeral), by Itami Jūzo, mocks Japanese people's discomfort when sitting on the floor, showing them squirming, rubbing their feet together, and even falling over when they try to rise from a seated position, just as Sakura's father did.

26. Christine R. Yano, *Tears of Longing: Nostalgia and the Nation in Japanese Popular Song* (Cambridge: Asia Center, Harvard University, 2002), 206, n. 3.

27. Ohnuki-Tierney, *Rice as Self.*

28. This process of an outsider taking an interest in Japanese arts and crafts and stimulating Japanese to do the same finds a historical parallel in the life and career of Ernest Fenollosa (1853–1908), who went to Japan initially to teach philosophy at the University of Tokyo and ended up championing traditional Japanese art. Fenollosa played key roles in the founding of what has become Japan's premier institution of higher learning in the arts, Tokyo Geijutsu Daigaku (Tokyo University of Fine Arts and Music), and the creation of the renowned Asian collection at the Boston Museum of Fine Arts. The point to be made here is that in the historical case of Fenollosa, as well as in this media representation of Sakura, Japanese took far more interest in their own arts and traditions after an outsider expressed enthusiasm for them.

29. Harvey, "Nonchan's Dream," 140.

30. In this episode, the *hole-hole bushi* is sung by Sakura's grandmother, an in-married urban *issei* who never worked a day in the sugarcane fields. The program thus treats all older Nikkei women as having endured the hardships of plantation life.

31. In retelling Japanese American history, *Sakura* fails to mention the role of the Japanese American labor activists who led major plantation strikes in 1909 and 1920, organized labor unions in 1946, and continue to stand at the forefront of labor unrest, especially in white-collar unions where their numbers are greatest.

32. Lane Hirabayashi, Akemi Kikumura-Yano, and James Hirabayashi assert the importance of discussing Nikkei identities in the plural to acknowledge differences based on prefectural background, the immigrants' destination (urban or rural), the

dynamics of community formation, and gender. See Lane Ryo Hirabayashi, Akemi Kikumura-Yano, and James A. Hirabayashi, "The Impact of Contemporary Global-ization on Nikkei Identities," in Lane Ryo Hirabayashi, Akemi Kikumura-Yano, and James A. Hirabayashi, eds., *New Worlds, New Lives*, 19–28 (Stanford: Stanford Univer-sity Press, 2002), 20.

33. In 1990, Japan revised its immigration laws to permit overseas ethnic Japanese to enter the country as long-term residents in hopes of building a supply of ethni-cally acceptable unskilled workers. As of 1996, there were 233,478 South American Nikkei registered as residents in Japan, making them the third-largest minority group in the country. Joshua Hotaka Roth, *Brokered Homeland; Japanese Brazilian Mi-grants in Japan* (Ithaca: Cornell University Press, 2002).

34. *Sakura* was broadcast in forty-one countries as part of NHK's "world premium" programming, which includes news, dramas, sports, arts, and culture.

35. The Nippon Golden Network has been broadcasting Japanese-language pro-gramming to cable subscribers since 1982. As of August 2003, it was broadcasting to approximately seventeen thousand households, sixteen thousand of them in the state of Hawai`i and the rest in Southern California (mostly in the Gardena, Torrance, and South Bay areas, which have relatively large Nikkei populations). *Sakura* was broad-cast in Hawai`i six days a week from 7:00 to 7:15 P.M. and rebroadcast from 8:15 to 8:30 A.M. the following morning. California subscribers received *Sakura* broadcasts sev-eral weeks after the episodes were shown in Hawai`i. In 2003, two California cable networks also began broadcasting *Sakura*: United Television Broadcasting, based in Los Angeles; and Fuji Telecast, based in San Francisco.

36. The monthly cost of an NGN hookup is $15.95, as of the date of the series' broadcast. Although this does not sound prohibitively expensive, several people with whom I spoke, especially retirees, gave price as the reason why they did not subscribe.

37. The methods I used to solicit Nikkei opinions on *Sakura* included appearing on the Japanese-language radio station KZOO in Honolulu for a half hour to dis-cuss this research and ask for phone-in opinions (I only received two phone calls) and posting a query on a Nikkei listserve, the Nikkei-network (I received four re-plies from the continental United States). I also interviewed six viewers of *Sakura* in Hawai`i introduced to me by acquaintances.

38. Sandy Ito, "Spotlight," *Eye-Ai* 26, no. 303 (2002): 17.

39. Fukushima, "Japanese Americans in the Japanese Media."

40. For this poem, see Carrie Takahata, "Being Yonsei," in Jonathan Okamura, ed., *The Japanese American Contemporary Experience in Hawai`i*, special issue of *Social Pro-cess in Hawaii* 41 (2002): 73–74.

41. Fukushima, "Japanese Americans in the Japanese Media."

42. Ryann Connell, "Soap Stinker Gets Up Nose of Japanese-Americans," *Mainichi Daily News*, 2 October 2002.

43. Ibid.

44. Personal communication, 18 May 2003.

45. In fact, Nikkei from Hawai`i make this distinction very clear, even going so far as to give Nikkei from the continental United States a derogatory label, *kotonk*, which refers to the sound of something hitting one's head.

46. Personal communication, 15 July 2003.

47. In 2002, I attended a luncheon meeting hosted by the new consul general of Japan in Hawai`i with two other leaders of Nikkei organizations. My initial thoughts were that he wanted to understand the state of Nikkei in Hawai`i and provide support for their organizations. This turned out to be true, but his rationale was not quite as benign as I had assumed. He explained that the Japanese government was interested in helping Nikkei with the understanding that Nikkei, in turn, would help Japan in times of need, supporting its positions vis-à-vis the United States. Nikkei, in other words, were expected to become Japan's private ambassadors. This link between the Japanese government and Nikkei through organizations, sponsorship, and activities helped frame NHK's *Sakura* within a covert political agenda.

48. David L. McConnell, *Importing Diversity: Inside Japan's Jet Program* (Berkeley: University of California Press, 2000).

Global and Local Materialities
of Anime

Mitsuyo Wada-Marciano

The emergence of anime as an area of study offers us a rich opportunity to explore various issues of popular culture and globalization. Anime is most prominently characterized by its range of media formats, termed the "media mix" (comics, film, original video animation [OVA], television, computer games, DVDs, video releases, and their accompanying merchandise) and its transnational ability, which represents a particularly current example of global transformation in popular culture.

At the same time, the transformative quality of anime makes it elusive in terms of its discursive development as an academic discipline since it requires an ever-expanding knowledge of technology and culture in flux. In the U.S. academy, anime is emerging as a course subject in East Asian studies, communication studies, and film studies, but there has been little discussion among scholars about productive approaches to teaching and research, and, moreover, there is little consensus about what anime actually is.

This essay offers a critical reappraisal of the emerging discourses in anime studies and some proposals for alternate areas of inquiry. Before elaborating on those aspects, the current state of anime studies, how it is approached in media studies, cinema studies, and Japanese studies needs to be examined. Put simply, what has been done and what has not been touched on in anime studies? Subsequently, what might be the possibilities for teaching and researching anime in the connection between anime and cultural globalization or the connection between anime and local cultural specificities? In many ways, the global force of anime has been treated much too unproblematically. I will offer a view of anime as a contested site of global and local forces by focusing on anime's formative roots in Japanese television to address the neglect of the local experience in anime studies.

ANIME STUDIES:
PRIVILEGING TEXT OVER VERNACULAR EXPERIENCE

Anime has been viewed as a perfect example of global culture. When early anime TV series such as *Astro Boy* (1963) were released in the United States, most viewers did not even realize that they were from Japan. It was mainly due to the creator Tezuka Osamu's intention to make it a worldwide product and anime's transformative nature combined with relatively easy dubbing and reediting that anime could be accepted without cultural resistance. Moreover, setting the diegetic space in the future formed the prototype of a denationalized image and established the pattern of the dominant *mecha* genre (aka robot genre) in anime. Anime has continuously demonstrated its adaptive qualities, assimilating itself within kids' cultures in various areas of the world for the last four decades and becoming a shared cultural memory. In doing so, it has attained a level of ubiquity by masking its origins to a certain degree.

However, once anime emerged as an object of study it came to stand for nothing but a Japanese cultural artifact. Many of the discourses in both journalism and the academy have described it as the extension of Japanese "pictocentric culture," connecting it with *ukiyo-e, manga,* and pictographic script.[1] Furthermore, some try to explore the contemporary Japanese cultural reflection of anime in terms of the "changing position of women in Japanese society."[2] In this way, some studies hypothesize anime, oddly, as a "mirror" image or challenge to the society while ignoring its place within a range of social, cultural, and textual practices. In order to distinguish anime from animation in general, the association between it and Japan or Japanese culture is seemingly inevitable, yet there is a persistent gap between the transnational image of anime and the discourse of it as the signifier of a fixed Japanese identity. This gap has been either suppressed or not adequately problematized in anime studies. At this global/local juncture of anime, what aspects have been devalued, or even erased in anime studies?

Anime started with mid-1970s TV programs in Japan, yet the current international boom occurred with the animation film *Akira* (1988), which established a filmic experience as the standard reference of anime abroad.[3]

Indeed, the global success of anime largely rests on minimizing the local spectatorial experience of TV anime. Current anime studies largely misappropriate the term *media mix*, using it as a buzzword to signify anime's morphing capacity without addressing the specificity of media, the ways in which different modes of production and distribution affect spectatorship, and anime's content. It is crucial to contextualize the cross-marketing of anime in multiple formats historically and in particular media registers. The transformation of sponsorship and marketing dynamics, for example, from the top-down toy company sponsorship of robot TV anime in the early 1980s to the present close collaboration among various producers, such as software, music, and publishing companies, at all levels of anime planning and production, represents different versions of economic models with consequently radical differences in anime form as well. Anime studies tend to homogenize these different modes, for instance, relegating TV anime, as having less aesthetic and discursive value, within the larger category of anime. Little work has been done on Japanese TV anime since that would force a reassessment of the paradigm of anime as global culture. If we pursue anime studies, we should not replicate this pattern, erasing the vernacular core of anime as a popular cultural experience. Without grasping this experience, we cannot hope to understand the attractions and continued innovations of Japanese animation.

ANIME AND ITS HISTORICITY

It may seem a minor point that we use the same term *anime* as it is used in Japan instead of *animation*. This shared English origin of the term makes anime more familiar to us, and it furthers the illusion of the ubiquitous status of anime historically and geographically.[4] *Anime* is an abbreviation of the Japanese word *animēshon*, a word borrowed from English. However, in Japanese, *anime* is not necessarily equivalent to the generic meaning of *animation*, and it historically appeared as "a phenomenon of popular culture" during the so-called first anime boom in the mid-1970s.[5] The TV series *Star Blazer* (1974), *Galaxy Express 999* (1978), *Gundam* (1979), and *Macross* (1982) formed a group of animation texts and constructed their child audiences as consuming subjects by tying the programs to toy makers such as Bandai. With the growing popularity of anime as a cultural phenomenon, the term *anime* became synonymous with every permutation of it.

The term *anime* itself needs to be examined in the historical and local specificity of the 1970s. Prior to the 1970s boom, other terms were used to describe animation such as *dōga* (moving image), *manga eiga* (cartoon film), and *terebi manga* (TV cartoon program).[6] Amid the current discourse of anime studies, the term *anime* is often used to describe the entire historical range of Japanese animation.[7] It bears stating that many early Japanese animations, such as *Panda and the Magic Serpent* (1958) and *The Great Adventure of Hols, Prince of the Sun* (1968), were not called anime, nor did they represent the same industrial paradigm of multiple product tie-ins or cross-media formats that 1970s anime initiated.[8]

Set within this specific temporal and spatial context, the assumption that "anime is Japanese animation" is misleading. Most problematically, equating anime with Japanese animation reifies it as a uniquely Japanese cultural product tied to an imagined pictorial tradition rather than the industrial and economic contexts of late 1970s TV. Indeed, many of the discourses surrounding anime tend to conflate historical contexts, collapsing broad cultural moments to reveal the Japanese national traits underpinning anime texts. Thus, for example, the *mecha* genre of the 1970s is often freely interpreted as a reflection of the World War II experience and postwar Japanese pacifism rather than part of the 1970s animation industry revitalization, that is, the expansion of TV, film, publishing, and toy markets. After all, *anime* is a commercial term invented and promoted with multiple marketing, targeting, and formatting strategies in Japan and subsequently adapted to a global cultural level.

Interestingly, whether one is analyzing the 1979 TV series *Gundam* or the 1993 film *Patlabor II*, the reference has often been to the same monumental, national events, such as World War II, as if Japan was caught in the never-ending cycle of victimhood and traumatic recovery.[9] Never mind the fact that *Gundam,* with its merchandise tie-ins, is a kind of extended commercial while *Patlabor II* is not.[10] What needs elaboration is the intertextuality among TV programs, the ways in which a program such as *Gundam* invokes the earlier "jumbo latex suit genre" *Ultraman* TV series (1966–2008) or the even earlier *Godzilla* film series (1954–2004). And, while the *Godzilla* series has certainly been interpreted as "monstrous bodies [that] became replacements for tangible markers of loss [from World War II]," there is a significant lightening of political weight in the comforting repetition of sequels and TV series.[11] This sets apart such anime as *Gundam* from the original traumatic narrative. As Yoshikuni Igarashi writes, "The [*Godzilla*] sequels did not inherit the original's critical perspective on the foundational narrative [of loss]."[12] Without locating these anime programs in the flux of Japanese popular culture, the intertextual references and signs of TV's industrial cultural formulas, the connection to such nation-forming events as the war seems at best overdetermined.

ANIME AS UPROOTED TEXT

The majority of anime discourses have dealt with characters, themes, genres, and authors for purposes of categorization and discussion. This preference for textual analysis continues to be the dominant approach in anime studies. In the process of constructing a body of knowledge in anime studies, anime has been dislocated from specific patterns of reception whether culturally, temporally, or technologically configured. The facts of how anime is tied to local specificity and needs, for instance, in the form of TV series, have often been neglected or erased.

This is partially due to the vicissitudes of viewing technology concurrent with the beginning of anime's current popularity in the late 1980s in the United States. In this period, Video Home System (VHS) hardware became widely affordable to anyone. Although we acknowledge anime's range of media formats—film, TV, OVA, and Internet image sharing—in reality we usually do not distinguish these format differences in anime studies. The over ten-year gap between the beginning of the anime boom in Japan and the boom in the United States determined the different cognitions of anime and indeed its reception from the distinctly separate precedents of TV and VHS. Except for the limited amount of kids' anime on morning TV, most of the American adult or teenage audience's experience of anime has been constructed through videotapes and DVDs, a private spectatorial mode that cannot retrieve the public function of TV anime, which enhances the ideological bond of viewers to a cultural moment.[13]

The emphasis on textual analysis in journalistic and academic discourse has also pushed anime studies to follow what are, on occasion, essentializing tendencies in the academy, paradigms that have often been criticized for creating a canon and the hierarchy surrounding it. The allegorical reading of national cinema or literature, for instance, also parallels the aforementioned overdetermined association between the *mecha* anime genre and the Japanese war experience. Thus, anime studies in the United States, intentionally or not, is being organized around canons, which serve to legitimize the academic discipline. With anime studies as a forming discipline, discussions often center on the visually more complex anime "films," but not on the domestic and mass-produced anime TV series.[14] Big budget anime films such as *Metropolis* (2001), *Princess Mononoke* (1997), *Ghost in the Shell* (1995), and *Akira* are frequently discussed, along with their contemporary critical themes of technological alienation, environmental issues, cyborg feminism, and postmodernity, while the vast majority of TV anime series have been neglected, since an analysis would require an examination of anime's connections with local audiences and the complex popular culture of Japan.

This application of already established canonization practices has created a curiously "official" version of anime, separated from its intrinsic value as commodity and reconstructed as national identity. In my subsequent discussion of the film *Metropolis*, I reveal how such tendencies cyclically influence the content of anime films as Japanese producers attempt to efface anime's history, "rewriting" it as high art for an international audience.

The pervasive term *otaku* (enthusiastic fans) has also been conveniently used in anime studies to compensate for the lack of a thorough reception study and to create an imagined resemblance between Japanese and international fandom. Matt Hills indicates that "fan identity is prioritised over national identity," and "[t]his identification can be read as an attempt to 'naturalise' fan identity by implying that fandom is an essentially transnational/transcultural experience."[15] In such a broadly ahistorical and denationalized context, the question arises, what is *otaku*, anyway? Antonia Levi writes that it is "a word that *completely defies translation*. Technically, it is a formal usage of the Japanese word meaning 'your.'"[16] This "untranslatable" quality of the word functions as a substitute discourse for the actual anime audience, and it gives the nuance of insidership to the critic through the word's evocation of the mysterious atmosphere of Japan. This untranslatable word was, arguably, first nominalized by the Japanese writer Nakamori Akio, who adopted it from *manga*, anime, and science fiction fans, who used it as a colloquial expression, addressing each other as *otaku* (you) instead of by name. The term has a feeling of closeness, and yet it also includes the awkwardness of the ritualized clique codes of adolescents. One can come up with various definitions for the term and seek slightly different "origins"; however, the problematic side of these *otaku* discourses is not only the fan identity's substitution over national identity but also the construction of a pseudo-national identity itself. If *otaku* means "enthusiastic anime fans," which anime are these *otaku* following? Do they all like the same anime or are there no factions in the *otaku* culture? The term *otaku* has been used in Japanese anime studies as a mechanism for uniting anime as a monolithic group of texts consumed by this pseudo-national identity. In these *otaku* discourses, variations in audiences—from general TV viewers watching the long-running *Sazae-san* (1969–present) at the family dinner hour to viewers who record every single episode of after-midnight anime programs such as *Serial Experiments Lain* (1998)—are completely suppressed. I must hasten to add that this misuse of the term *otaku* occurs in Japan as well; the self-appointed *otaking* (*otaku* king) Okada Toshio points out its similar domestic usage: "'What is *otaku*?' this question has been unfairly discussed based on preconceived images, and *otaku* have been discriminated against and the term has never been fully examined. That's the misfortune of *otaku*."[17]

GRASPING THE VERNACULAR ANIME EXPERIENCE

After his film *Spirited Away* (2001) received the Grand Prix at the Berlin International Film Festival 2002, Miyazaki Hayao made the following statement: "If I may reveal my real feeling about anime now, I think Japanese anime has been facing its bottom."[18] His utterance seems to contradict the film's success and that of his previous film, *Princess Mononoke,* as well as the fact that the Japanese animation industry had been increasing both anime film productions and anime TV programs in the anime boom of the 1990s. He continues:

> The director An'no Hideaki, who is about twenty years younger than me, said that his generation is the first copy generation, and his later generation is even the copy of the copy. Now we have the generation of the copy of the copy of the copy. You can imagine how distorted and watered down the result is. They [the younger animators] are not drawing what they have actually seen. I feel the same way as An'no when I am working with these younger animators. How to overcome this situation is not for my generation to solve, but is an assignment for them.[19]

While Miyazaki's comments are directed at anime generally, in his focus on the issue of originality he seems to be criticizing the self-referential tendency of limited TV animation. Yet it is precisely this aspect of TV anime that accounts for its attraction to fans. The success of An'no's TV series *Evangelion* (1995–96), for instance, is due to the fact that it references textual elements from the *mecha* genre such as the reluctant boy hero inside the giant robot in *Gundam.* The spectator's pleasure is based on the shared "experience" between the animators and themselves; in the recognition of twists on older patterns, the experience resembles an "interactive" communication among participants. Originality in TV anime does not exist in Miyazaki's sense, but it emerges in the wide range of entry points for the anime audience to participate in creating their own textual experiences, expanding even the parameters of "textuality." Such activity, in John Fiske's terms, signals the text's "potentiality rather than its concrete existence."[20]

In what follows, I argue that TV anime, through its multitude of interactive sites, often subverts the aesthetic hierarchy of textual meaning, creating its own criteria within the vernacular anime experience. TV anime programs such as *Serial Experiments Lain, Cowboy Bebop* (1998–99), and *Boogie Pop Phantom* (2000) represent a radical expansion of anime's ongoing commodification of variegated media platforms. Such TV anime programs displace the central position of the anime text, as Miyazaki sees it, by merging it within a spectrum of media sites. As such, they present a profound challenge to what constitutes a traditional visual narrative structure since their "texts" need never end but may continue in venues such as Internet fan sites, computer games, and fanzines. This is why I also argue that much of the established film and literature-based approaches to anime, which emphasize thematic or symbolic readings of narrative and image within a text, do not adequately address the processes of media consumption—the complex interplay of commodity, consumer, and technology—and their reflection onto the anime text as well. In order to better explain how this confluence of media formats operates within the aesthetic constraints of TV-limited animation, I will here briefly elaborate the industrial, economic context that shaped 1990s TV anime.

As I mentioned, the anime boom started in the late 1970s, and the second boom occurred in the 1990s. Despite the fact that Japan's economic situation has been in steady decline since the early 1990s, the Japanese anime industry continued to expand. In 1990, there were about 250 anime programs on TV, and by 1998 the number had increased to about 300.[21] By embracing so-called Big Friends (ōkina otomodachi, a resurgent otaku fan base) who could appreciate the referential codes of various anime, the second anime boom expanded the variation and time slots of TV anime programs. With their "potential for high referentiality," as defined by Okada, the Big Friends have enlarged anime's multiple textualities in several ways.[22] Many are in their twenties and thirties and have more disposable income than the majority of younger anime audiences. Thus, they can participate in the expanded range of anime texts by buying related games and hardware.

Also, in terms of cultural economy, they enrich the viewing process with their knowledge of referentiality even beyond the category of anime. Okada notes, "In general, people call one who knows a field well otaku, but what I mean by high referentiality is not being trapped in one field but rather having crossover cultural knowledge."[23] The participation of the Big Friends enriched the fandom discourse, creating home pages, for instance, that used critical terms and theories to discuss anime and related phenomena. Okada himself, in fact, is an example of the Big Friends, as he moves between production, writing, and teaching about anime. The Big Friends have transformed anime viewers' social position from that of passive consumers to active participants, often providing critical feedback that changes the direction of a production. At the end of the Evangelion series, for example, the director An'no visually inserted negative comments from his fans in its last episode as his response; this can be read as another example of the "interactive" anime experience.

The referential fluency of the Big Friends also extended across the boundaries of anime and computer games. In 1990s, the *bishōjo* game (cute girls game) became one of the dominant game softwares in Japan. One of its subgenres, the *noberu* game (novel game), in which a player "reads" the given multistories, such as taking a walk with interchangeable cute girls, has become especially influential for game users of the Big Friends' generation.[24] This relatively less active game—a player only reads the written text and chooses movements scene by scene—changed the speed and visual standards for viewers of both computer games and anime. Viewers became increasingly sophisticated as they moved among different technological visual platforms, and they developed an appreciation for the slower pace and the psychologically interior possibilities of limited animation. For anime, the influence of computer games caused a significant shift in visual norms away from the frenetic, "realistic" movement of full animation, toward a hybrid of limited animation and an increasing number of still images with an emphasis on highly defined backgrounds and atmosphere. In effect, the shift in anime has decentered the long-standing dichotomy of Disney-style full animation versus Japanese and/or TV limited animation as well as displacing the hierarchical notion of their respective high and low aesthetic values.

THE ATTRACTIONS OF TV ANIME: *SERIAL EXPERIMENTS LAIN*

There is mutual reciprocity between the Japanese broadcast system and the sophistication of its viewers so that both nurtured or influenced the media-mix culture in 1990s TV anime. In 1997, Tokyo TV, which had heavily promoted TV anime for decades, started opening its after-midnight slots to anime programs; other networks, such as Nippon TV, Asahi TV, and Fuji TV, followed close behind. In 1998, some satellite TV stations became available to the public, and cable TV was introduced in urban areas. Cable and satellite technologies brought a dramatic increase in the amount of programming and a wider audience in the 1990s, and the Digital Terrestrial Television system has further increased demand since 2003.[25]

These transformations gave momentum to anime's expansion after the mid-1990s. In particular, the shift from the golden-time TV slot, with its high ad prices and stiff competition for ratings, to the after-midnight slots changed the dynamics of profit and content by making anime programs less dependent on advertising revenues. Advertising during the after-midnight TV slots, when programs such as *Serial Experiments Lain* (1:15 to 1:45 A.M.) and *Initial D* (1998, 3:20 to 3:50 A.M.) are aired, is much less expensive than during other hours, and the late slots also allow anime productions to operate with fewer regulations over program content. Instead of aiming for high TV ratings, these past-midnight anime productions began to play a different role in the new format of media mix, acting as promotional spots for repackaged DVDs or to encourage follow-up sales of computer games deploying the same characters and settings. CDs were also sold featuring various programs' theme songs. These changes in broadcasting have determined anime's increasing relations with other media commodities as well.

The explosive success of *Evangelion* from 1995 to 1997 established the now prevalent marketing strategy of media mix, in this case tying the anime to related productions by King Records, Kadokawa Publishing, and the Sega game and video software company. This production system influences not only the promotional role of TV anime programs but also the program's format. To boost sales, the software makers kept the price of videos and DVDs affordable; in consequence, anime series gradually became shorter and typically adopted a standard of 13 episodes (although *Evangelion* retained a long run of 26), which is noticeably different from such long-running anime programs as *Sazae-san* (1,820-plus shows from 1969 to the present) and *Pokémon* (200-plus episodes from 1997 to the present). One could argue that the 13-episode structure is inherently weak in establishing characters and narrative development, but many of these after-midnight anime programs have devised innovative ways to convey more "atmosphere" without causality, to promote feeling over logic, and to employ visual strategies that require a high degree of hermeneutic sophistication from viewers.

In *Serial Experiments Lain* there is little resolution of plot elements or defined beginnings and endings. The episodes' abstract titles, such as "layer 03: PSYCHE," "layer 05: DISTORTION," and "layer 12: LANDSCAPE," indicate the lack of an episodic structure and point to the series' creation of atmosphere through the piling on of images, which are often repeated across episodes. Repetition of an exact library of images, such as Lain, the fourteen-year-old protagonist, commuting to and from school or accessing her computer, conveys a sense of temporal stasis. The program embeds the surreal sequences of the wired world in these repetitions of mundane everyday life, thus creating a vaguely structured narrative around scenes that have no discernible pattern of cause and effect. It should be noted that a same-title book has been published with detailed episode summaries in the United States to help remedy audience uncertainty regarding plot.[26] The uncertain narrative does not necessarily work against the popularity of the program since the loose structure approximates many game formats in which the individual interprets the story case by case and sequence by sequence.

The assimilation between Lain and the audience creates a pseudo-interactive tie between the TV program and its consumers. The narrative reproduces the interaction between two increasingly entwined worlds by using the character Lain's double identities: one belongs to the real world and the other to the wired world.[27] The program intertextualizes the culture of the Internet albeit in a hyper form by dramatizing the contrast between the user's solitary physical existence and her detached immersion in the multifaceted commotion of the Web. In this way, the program co-opts the audience's experience and interest in the Web's "unlimitedness" and its possibilities for the reinvention of the self. The TV program locates its narrative in the urban junior high school student's everyday life, which is a further simulation of its targeted audiences' experience.

In place of narrative, *Serial Experiments Lain* highlights psychological impressions in its visual images so that the momentary still images have fundamentally different structural meanings than those in earlier TV anime programs, which relied on limited animation techniques only for the sake of saving cels and production time. Here limited animation and still images become virtues rather than constraints to creating a character that is neither talkative nor active. In *Lain*, for instance, the program uses her silence and static images to create interior depth. The opening title sequence shows Lain walking across a pedestrian bridge; the wind blows her hat away, and then the scene freezes with the hat in midair as Lain continues walking. This use of a still image within limited animation provokes a psychological dialogue between the viewer and anime, creating an effect of viewer alienation from the usual protocols of reproduced screen "reality." This leads to a moment of engagement in which the viewer can wonder what it all means, which is a fundamental attraction of watching anime. *Evangelion*, as a forerunner of such techniques, boldly used sequences of sustained still images, as in a scene in which the characters Asuka and Rei stand in an elevator, motionless and wordless yet in a psychological struggle, which continues for an unheard of fifty seconds.

A further attraction of the figure Lain lies in the gap in the complex psychological character presented in the prepubescent girl's body. Lain's figure shares *Ghost in the Shell*'s image of the final cyborg body with the protagonist, Motoko, a similarly prepubescent girl made immortal and omniscient by merging with the "Net," which is also appropriated in Lain's wired intelligence. Lain's image samples the attractive qualities of previous anime figures known as *moe-kyara* (from *moeru kyarakutā*, "attractive characters"), typically girl figures with some individualized, fetishized aspect. Inside the anime diegesis, Lain is viewed as a childlike figure even by her classmates and parents; visually she is often shown wearing a bear pajama outfit at home or a cowl with a bear emblem when she is outside. The bear ears of her pajama hood make reference to a standard *moeru* trope, that of the young girl with animal or mythical features such as Ram-chan in *Ranma 1/2* (1989). The attraction of *moe-kyara* rests in the precise balance between fetishized and sexualized aspects in the childlike character; its attraction makes the figure an ideal vehicle for the promotion of media-mix and related products.

Near the end of the series, when Lain's character completely merges with the Wired realm, the opening montage features animated images of Lain being watched by fans on TV, and later episodes have a grainy screen image of Lain saying, "I promise you I'll always be right here. I'll always be right next to you, forever." Lain's image is marked by this ubiquity in the anime culture even in the publicity narrative surrounding the image's creation. The director reportedly chose the Lain figure while surfing the Internet, selecting a drawing from the home page of an art school graduate.[28] This story blurs the line between fandom and animators, amateur and professional, especially in the way the student artist, Abe Yoshitoshi, was discovered and later became an anime illustrator. This narrative also furthers the myth of fans creating their own anime while consuming such images. This particular pattern of cultural production and consumption strongly influences fandom's way of receiving anime itself, as fans create their own fanzines, anime festivals, and reconstruct versions of anime using characters, satire—even changing existing endings. As Henry Jenkins notes about TV fandom, "For the fan, watching the series is the beginning, not the end, of the process of media consumption."[29]

It should be clear at this point that determining the attraction of anime involves locating it and its textuality within the local consuming culture. The mistake that is often made in American anime studies is to apply a few cases, such as *Sailor Moon* (1992–95) and *Pokémon*, to the rest of Japanese animation and neglect the sources of attraction in the local consumer culture of the domestic Japanese audience. Many contemporary TV anime subvert the standard criteria of animation, which rests on the primacy of Disney-style full animation. The dichotomy, still prevalent in anime discourses, between Japanese "limited" animation (animation with as few cel frames per second as possible) and Disney's "full" animation (animation typically with twelve cel frames per second) is essentially false and outdated when applied to anime. While scholarly works make frequent reference to this comparison, they seldom discuss the technical aspects of limited animation and the way it constructs meanings, values, and attractions in a specific popular culture. Especially in the case of contemporary TV anime programs, Disney-style marketing is of little concern to anime producers; what they most consider to increase their sales is how to constantly fit their product to domestic consumers' needs and tastes. In other words, what they compete against are the formats of computer games, with which they share most of their target audience. As I outlined earlier, the postmidnight TV anime, in targeting Big Friends and the new computer-game and Internet generation, naturally started to merge with the cultural formation of media-mix and interactive technologies. However, the ultimate difference between the two media (computer games and TV anime) is in the computer game's interactive structure versus anime's noninteractive viewing formation. In consequence, anime's assimilation of the interactive mode of games and computers has been the overriding force reshaping its narrative modes, aesthetic forms, and reception patterns.

CENTERS AND MARGINS

The release of the animation film, *Metropolis,* to near unanimous critical praise and equally unanimous box office failure signals a rift in anime's position in global and local popular cultures. It points to the ongoing pattern of globalization as configured in the hegemonic structure of center and periphery, that is, the center created through the dominance of Western modernity. The Japanese animators' desire to be acknowledged by that center within the classical dictates of film art signifies an acceptance of the full animation paradigm with its connoted values of Disney-style auteurship, "full" in the sense of a large amount of artistic labor or "full" signifying the completion of an aesthetic vision. The producers of the film themselves would seem to have internalized the dichotomy of limited versus full animation as a referendum on the historical legacy of Japanese animation. The film's combination of limited animation and computer graphic effects directly mimics the full animation style of old Disney cel animation in which the effects of gravity are exaggerated in characters' movements. The film's frenetic style is an attempt to relocate Japanese animation within the ideological classicism of Disney. Thus, it can be seen as a calculated bid for "anime classicism" within the politics of global aesthetics.

In his review of *Metropolis*, the critic Mark Vallen positions the film in the global discourse of animation.

> James Cameron (*Aliens, Terminator, Titanic*) saw Rintaro's film and had this to say about it: "*Metropolis* is the new milestone in anime. It has beauty, power, and above all . . . heart. Images from this film

> will stay with you forever." While it's hard to rebuff the opinion of someone like Mr. Cameron . . . I would disagree with him on one point. *Metropolis* does not just set a "new milestone in anime". . . it sets a milestone for ALL animation. Rintaro's production could well change the face of animation. Henceforth, this film will be the yardstick by which all animated features are measured against.[30]

Here praise is given as a measure of the film's global reach, its power to re-shape the whole animation field. Such a view reifies the category of animation as a universal yardstick (in contrast to the locality of anime) and, all the praise notwithstanding, merely reiterates the value of animation within the paradigm of Disney's centrality. Indeed, the film seemingly fulfills Tezuka Osamu's ambition (the film is based on his original comic published in 1949) to have his animation work included in the canonical tradition of Disney-style full animation. The film's director, Rintaro, seems to have inherited Tezuka's desire for international recognition, a long-standing obsession among many Japanese filmmakers. In contrast, through their heteropathic connections to popular culture—literature, comics, games, music, and so on—TV anime series have been targeting the domestic audience but they have been problematically viewed as a "stigma" on anime generally by the majority of anime artists such as Rintaro and Miyazaki in their bid for anime's admittance to the historical tradition.

There is a strong bias among the auteur animators against the lack of originality, which they see in TV anime. Read further, this speaks of their discomfort with the secondary role of anime in a chain of commercial practices. Needless to say, as auteurs they have tried to distance themselves from the past associations of cheap, offshore, factory labor and toy merchandising, which were formative practices in the postwar years of Japanese animation. For such an exercise in national self-esteem, the reinvention of the anime tradition requires rewriting history itself, that is, erasing the local cultural experience of TV anime.

In *Metropolis*, nostalgia serves as a brutal, excising force regarding anime's actual past. The film's nostalgic aesthetic—its retro-futurism, film noirism, jazz score, and narrative of labor union struggle—is both reverential and referential to classical cinema rather than anime per se or other contemporary forms in popular culture. In this sense, although Tezuka insisted that Fritz Lang's 1927 film *Metropolis* had no influence on his comic, that influence is present in the anime film, particularly in its ambivalence toward technology and its treatment of class struggle. In thematic and iconographic terms, *Metropolis* presents a denationalized urban dystopia, literally configuring the city space as a vertical hierarchy of working class and ruling class, robot and human (members of the ruling class lead upscale lives in the urban space while the working class toils below). In this regard, the film makes visual and thematic reference to 1920s social progressive film drama such as Sergey Eisenstein's *The Battleship Potemkin* (1925), King Vidor's *The Crowd* (1928), and Fritz Lang's *Metropolis* (1927). The resultant "canned feeling" from the 1920s makes the film both retro and nostalgic, reflecting a desire for the period in the cinema when capitalism was still questioned. The film's assimilation of classical cinema and its proscriptive stance toward anime culture perhaps best explain its inability to effectively target its audience. Its nostalgia, which is further enforced by the director's and screenplay writer's act of making the film a tribute to Tezuka, reflects the desire for an imaginary classical anime that actually never existed in Tezuka's oeuvre. Tezuka's TV anime series were mostly done in limited animation, so the film's imagined past has more to do with early Disney than Japanese animation. In this sense, the film tries to erase the history of anime and the dominance of limited animation TV series and reduce its commercial ties to cheap commodification. In doing so, the film also reinforces the notion that full animation is of higher aesthetic value.

It is revealing to see the parallel here between Japanese anime auteurism and current discourses in U.S. anime studies; in both cases, the tendency is to locate anime's place within the cognitive pattern of the West as the center and Japan as the periphery, a pattern that has been constructed under the conditions of modernity. In anime studies the central problem lies in the discursive constructs of anime as a global culture, which we share on more or less equal terms, and anime as the other's culture, sufficiently different from ours and therefore worth learning about. Yet the separation of anime into global and local polar opposites tells us little about the ways in which these spheres are mutually constitutive in the permeability of local culture to global influences and in new cultural productions marked by local specificity. Both levels of interaction can be seen, for instance, in Japanese anime's hybrid full-animation tradition and TV's limited animation. As the world is neither completely whole nor completely fractured, I see the "gap" in anime (global and at the same time local) as the most attractive aspect of this cultural phenomenon. For anime studies, a paradigm shift is needed, one that makes room for "the complex process of global integration."[31]

NOTES

1. David Kehr, "Anime, Japanese Cinema's Second Golden Age," *New York Times*, 20 January 2002, B1.

2. Kyu Hyun Kim, "Girl (and Boy) Troubles in Animeland: Exploring Representations of Gender in Japanese Animation Films," *Education about Asia* 7, no. 1 (spring 2002): 38.

3. The titles of Susan J. Napier's books, *Anime from Akira to Princess Mononoke* or *Anime from Akira to Howl's Moving Castle*, overtly reveal the tendency toward emphasizing film texts. Susan J. Napier, *Anime from Akira to Princess Mononoke: Experiencing Contemporary Japanese Animation* (New York: Palgrave, 2000); *Anime from Akira to Howl's Moving Castle: Experiencing Contemporary Japanese Animation* (New York: Palgrave Macmillan, 2005).

4. The term's origin is debatable. In contrast, Antonia Levi writes, "The Japanese took the word from the French to describe all animated films." Antonia Levi, *Samurai from Outer Space: Understanding Japanese Animation* (Chicago: Open Court, 1996), 1.

5. Napier, *Anime from Akira to Princess Mononoke*, 3.

6. The major animation production company's name, Tōei Dōga (Tōei Moving Image Company), and its film festival, Tōei manga matsuri (Tōei Cartoon Film Festival), are some examples, although the latter's name was changed to the Tōei Anime Festival in the 1990s.

7. The reference book on Japanese animation, *The Anime Encyclopedia: A Guide to Japanese Animation since 1917*, also uses the term *anime* as follows: "The period up to 1945 is covered in two generic sections, EARLY ANIME and WARTIME ANIME." Jonathan Clements and Helen McCarthy, *The Anime Encyclopedia: A Guide to Japanese Animation since 1917* (Berkeley: Stone Bridge Press, 2001), x. As its title indicates, another useful guidebook, *Anime: A Guide to Japanese Animation (1958–1988)*, also uses *anime* interchangeably with *Japanese animation*: "'Anime' is the expression used by the Japanese to designate animated features, an art which has, in less than a century, attained an unimaginable popularity in the Occident." Andrea Baricordi, Massimiliano De Giovanni, Andrea Pietroni, Barbara Rossi, and Sabrina Tunesi, *Anime: A Guide to Japanese Animation (1958–1988)*, trans. Adeline D'Ooera, ed. Claude J. Pelletier (Montreal: Protoculture, 2000), 8.

8. This film was produced by Tōei Dōga and distributed through the Tōei Film Company. Takahata Isao directed it, and Miyazaki Hayao worked as a background designer. Released in July 1968, it targeted child audiences through the Tōei manga matsuri. The media-mix business strategy was not yet employed in its promotion.

9. Articles that typically employ this pattern of association include David Vernal, "War and Peace in Japanese Science Fiction Animation: An Examination of *Mobile Suit Gundam* and *The Mobile Police Patlabor*," *Animation Journal* IV, no.1 (fall 1995): 56–84; and Michael Fisch, "Nation, War, and Japan's Future in the Science Fiction Anime Film *Patlabor II*," *Science Fiction Studies* 27, no.1 (March 2000): 49–68.

10. *Patlabor* was originally "made on video because sponsorship was initially unavailable to make it for TV. . . . [T]he show was soon heading for broadcast and movie success." Clements and McCarthy, *The Anime Encyclopedia*, 294.

11. Yoshikuni Igarashi, *Bodies of Memory: Narratives of War in Postwar Japanese Culture, 1945–1970* (Princeton: Princeton University Press, 2000), 114.

12. Ibid., 118.

13. Azuma Hiroki, a cultural critic, reads the same tendency in a more positive light since he interprets it as evidence of respect toward anime as a "textual" subject in the United States in contrast to the purported informational emphasis in Japanese anime discourses. Azuma Hiroki, "An'no Hideaki ha ikanishite 80 nendai Nihon anime o owarasetaka: Shinsei evangerion ni tsuite [How An'no Hideaki Terminated the Japanese Anime of the 1980s: About *Evangelion*]," *Eureka* 28, no. 9 (August 1996): 112–23.

14. Some exemplary anime TV programs, widely discussed in both journalism and academia, are *Sailor Moon, Evangelion,* and *Pokémon.*

15. Matt Hills, "Transcultural *Otaku*: Japanese Representations of Fandom and Representations of Japan in Anime/*Manga* Fan Culture," paper presented at the conference, Media in Transition 2: Globalization and Convergence, Massachusetts Institute of Technology, 10–12 May 2002.

16. Levi, *Samurai from Outer Space*, 2.

17. Okada Toshio, *Otaku-gaku nyūmon* [Introduction to *Otaku* Studies] (Tokyo: Ōta Shuppan, 1996), 8.

18. Miyazaki Hayao, interview with anonymous journalists, *Animage* 25, no.4 (April 2002): 5–15.

19. Ibid.

20. John Fiske, "Moments of Television: Neither the Text nor the Audience," in Paul Marris and Sue Thornham, eds., *Media Studies: A Reader,* 337–45 (Edinburgh: Edinburgh University Press, 1996), 337.

21. Ogawa Bi'i, "Gekizoshita *anime* taitorusū [The Marked Increase of Anime Production Numbers]," *Animage* 25, no.4 (February 2002): 68.

22. Okada Toshio, *Otakugaku nyūmon*, 28.

23. Ibid.

24. Azuma Hiroki, *Dōbutsukasuru posutomodan* [Animalizing Postmodernity] (Tokyo: Kōdansha Gendai Shinsho, 2001), 108–25. English translation is also available. *Otaku: Japan's Database Animals*, trans. Jonathan E. Abel and Shion Kono (Minneapolis: University of Minnesota Press, 2009).

25. "Gekizōsuru TV anime no butaiura [The Background of the Growth in TV Anime]," *Animage* 21, no.5 (May 1998): 100–105.

26. Bruce Baugh and Lucien Soulban, Serial Experiments Lain *Ultimate Fan Guide* (Guelph, Ontario: Guardians of Order, 2002).

27. Clements and McCarthy summarize the narrative adequately, "[The] 14-year-old Rein Iwakura meets a school friend on the Wired, a super-Internet that allows almost total immersion in cyberspace—but Chisa died by her own hand days ago.

Now she says God is in the Wired. Understandably shaken, Rein is further baffled by a strange encounter in a club, where a junkie is so scared by her sudden, chilling response to his pestering that he kills himself. Rein learns more about the Wired, drawing her further into another existence, one where Lain, her second self, lives an independent life in the electronic impulses. . . . Lain starts putting in appearances in the real world, causing her double to wonder which of them is real. Uncertain of her true origins or existence, or of reality itself, Rein/Lain crosses paths with the god-like entity Deus (creator of the Wired, now dwelling inside it) in a surreal struggle." Clements and McCarthy, *The Anime Encyclopedia*, 350.

28. Konaka Chiaki, "Rein o hagukumi rein na sutaffutachi [The Staff Members Fostering Rein Are 'Rein' Themselves]," *Animage* 21, no.10 (October 1998): 58.

29. Henry Jenkins, *Textual Poachers: Television Fans and Participatory Culture* (New York: Routledge, 1992), 278.

30. Mark Vallen, "Review of *Metropolis*, dir. Rintaro," *Black Moon*, September 2001, http://www.theblackmoon.com/Deadmoon/metro.htm, accessed 7 May 2002.

31. Ien Ang, *Living Room Wars: Rethinking Media Audiences for a Postmodern World* (London: Routledge, 1996), 153.

Becoming Kikaida: Japanese Television and Generational Identity in Hawai`i

Hirofumi Katsuno

Long before the appearance of *Pokémon*, *Sailor Moon*, *Dragon Ball Z*, and *Power Rangers*, another Japanese superhero won over the hearts of children in 1970s Hawai`i. During 1974 and 1975, the Japanese-language television station KIKU-TV aired a *tokusatsu*—a live-action television program depicting superheroes and monsters—entitled *Jinzō Ningen Kikaida* (Mechanical Man Kikaida, known simply as *Kikaida* in Hawai`i).[1] *Kikaida* started a craze among young fans, especially boys, and garnered higher ratings than any action program produced in the continental United States. The tremendous success of the show was amplified by a merchandising bonanza of related goods including dolls, T-shirts, books, and soundtrack records from Japan.[2]

Twenty-six years later, in November 2001, KIKU began rebroadcasting the series and issuing collectibles at the request of die-hard adult fans, generating a second *Kikaida* boom. Twenty-first century *Kikaida* fans, dubbed by KIKU "Generation Kikaida," cover a large demographic base, including children and original fans (now in their thirties and forties) from widely varying ethnic backgrounds. Governor Benjamin Cayetano officially declared 11 April 2002 Kikaida Day in Hawai`i, which featured guest appearances by the Japanese stars and wildly popular public events, further cementing the place of Kikaida within local culture.

This study treats the *Kikaida* revival in Hawai`i among adult devotees as a confluence of nostalgia, media fandom, and locality, and examines how fans from a particular age cohort become part of Generation Kikaida. To a large extent these fans construct identities upon their interactions with the television show and the memorabilia it spawned. I am primarily concerned with the ways in which generational identity is shaped not only by media text or fan interactions but also by the dialectical relationship between marketers and fans embedded within a larger sociocultural and geopolitical context.

The formation of generational identity is closely related to collective memory. Both phenomena occur as a result of the collective actions of individuals responding to the notion of a shared past. As Ron Eyerman points out, shared experiences only suggest a potential for the formation of a generational identity. Such an identity will not come about without "significant collective action, which both articulates this consciousness and also puts it into practice."[3] Collective memory and representations of a shared past must be reformulated to construct a view for the present and future that enables a generation to form a subjective awareness as a social and historical agent. Generational identity is therefore produced through a symbolic process involving, according to Mike Hepworth, "variable interaction between memories of participation in events of collective generational significance and contemporary circumstances."[4]

In the case of Generation Kikaida, generational consciousness emerges through a kind of media fandom in which fans construct memories through consumer practices. Marketers also take part in the creation of generational identity through what Marita Sturken calls "technologies of memory," which include the rebroadcasting of the television show, newly released products, various *Kikaida* events, and an official website (www.generationkikaida .com).[5] These commemorative mechanisms structure the shared experiences of Kikaida fans.

These marketing and consumer processes are closely related to Hawaii`s locality, in terms of both its sociocultural specificity and its geopolitical position in the global economy vis-à-vis the continental United States and Japan. Kikaida, a Japanese superhero, provides an alternative to popular American superheroes like Superman, Batman, and Spiderman. Kikaida also supports KIKU's corporate identity as part of a local culture industry, linked to Japan but operating on the periphery of the United States. Tangled relationships among text, marketer, and viewer are embedded within a larger historical specificity, prompting questions as to how the text is being marketed and consumed during this particular period, and why a Japanese television program has once again become popular in contemporary Hawai`i.

The first part of this essay explores how promoters recontextualize *Kikaida* to further their own commercial interests by marketing memory and nostalgia. I argue that the representation of *Kikaida* as a local icon in KIKU-TV's revival campaign operates strategically against the hegemony of national or global cable networks to secure a corporate identity as a local television station with ties to Japan. The second part of the essay focuses on how the cultural expressions of fans collectively form a generational identity. Kikaida mediates between fans and their past within the contemporary context.

METHODOLOGY

This study is based on fieldwork conducted in Honolulu between April 2002 and May 2003. My methodology included participating in fan events, monitoring fan-based websites, and conducting one or more hour-long interviews with a total of fifteen fans and KIKU-TV marketers of *Kikaida*. In this essay, I focus primarily on six individuals with whom I conducted particularly rich interviews. Some of them had forgotten about *Kikaida* until its resurgence, while others had been continual fans for more than ten years. Their identities as *Kikaida* fans cannot be separated from their specific backgrounds, subjectivities, and agencies. The generational identity they share is articulated through interactions between fans, where the text-audience encounter is reinterpreted and renegotiated.

My study examines narratives at fan events, on websites, and in interviews. It is important to remember that, as Lawrence Grossberg points out, fans' relations to popular texts often involve a particular sensibility sometimes described as a "feeling of life."[6] This affect signifies what matters most to fans in their relations to media texts.[7] In an attempt to understand the impact of this affect on the creation of generational identity, I concentrated on fan interactions with *Kikaida* products in most of my interviews. At certain times during the interviews fan collections and products became productive sites of narrative, while at other times the material objects became texts in and of themselves, representing what could not be verbalized by the interviewees.

THE SOCIAL HISTORY OF KIKAIDA

Kikaida was originally produced by the Japanese television and film production studio Toei in 1972. It was in the heyday of *tokusatsu* superhero programming lasting from the late 1960s to the early 1980s. The scripts for the program were written by the well-known *manga* (comic book) artist Ishinomori Shotaro, who collaborated with Toei in the creation of numerous superheroes.[8] One of his masterpieces, *Kamen Raidā* (Masked Rider), established the concept of *henshin* (metamorphosis) as a central component of Japanese *tokusatsu*. Metamorphosis would become a central theme in the *Kikaida* series as well.

The *Kikaida* plot circumscribes an epic battle between the eponymous hero and the nefarious "Dark," an organization attempting to conquer the world through the use of androids. At the beginning of the series, Dark captures Dr. Komyoji, an authority on robotics, and his daughter/assistant Mitsuko, and tries to exploit their expertise for the creation of androids. While imprisoned by the organization, Dr. Komyoji secretly creates a conscience circuit and installs it in a mechanical human. The result is Jiro, a motorcycle-riding, guitar-playing, denim-clad humanoid figure who metamorphoses into Kikaida, a red and blue, evil-fighting android. Professor Gill, the head of Dark, discovers Dr. Komyoji's plan prior to the completion and installation of a conscience circuit. Kikaida rescues Mitsuko and together with her escapes from Dark, but Dr. Komyoji ends up with amnesia, wandering from place to place. The forty-three episodes of *Kikaida* follow Jiro/Kikaida's journey with Mitsuko and her younger brother Masaru in search of Dr. Komyoji.

Fans in Hawai`i emphasize that *Kikaida* and other Japanese *tokusatsu* programs were revolutionary in introducing new types of superheroes to the television screen in the 1970s. They argue for the distinctiveness of *Kikaida* on the basis of the following: (1) a relatively complex and continuous story line within a set number of episodes; (2) exotic characters, both heroes and villains, and the visual elaborateness of their costumes; (3) the emphasis on metamorphosis; (4) physical combat techniques based on martial arts; and (5) catchy theme songs.

As with most of Ishinomori's works, the plot of *Kikaida* is pervaded by existentialist themes. The consequence of Jiro's imperfect conscience circuit is an ongoing internal struggle between good and evil, human and android. Hakaida, a bad android created to kill Kikaida, also suffers from an identity crisis. After Kikaida's defeat by another evil android in episode 42, Hakaida loses control, saying, "What am I? What purpose was I created for. . . . What is left for me to live for?! What is my purpose? How will I live from now on? . . . I despise Professor Gill for creating me!" Some fans feel that this interior complexity of the androids is one of the show's biggest appeals. For instance, Saburo, a 38-year-old Philippines-born Chinese male, local comic distributor, and huge Hakaida fan, explains:[9]

> Hakaida is not like . . . bad guys [who] are just straight-on bad guys. Then nobody will sympathize with that. But if you make

him complicated, if you give a motivation, give a reason, people then like the character.[10]

Kikaida debuted in Hawai`i on KIKU-TV in February 1974, achieving overnight popularity. Its success precipitated the broadcast of many other *tokusatsu* programs from Japan, including *Kamen-Rider V3*, *Go Ranger*, *Robocon*, *Diamond Eye*, and *Inazuman*. These programs aired on KIKU until the early 1980s. *Time* magazine reported that *Kikaida* and other superhero programs featuring martial arts were amongst the top children's programs in Hawai`i in 1975, even surpassing *Sesame Street* in the Nielsen ratings.[11] The rising popularity of these shows produced a marketing bonanza. In January 1975, the local Japanese department store Shirokiya reported Christmas holiday sales of over six thousand Japanese superhero dolls. The store also sold 48,000 Kikaida T-shirts in about six months. The Japanese-owned Honolulu supermarket Daiei sold more than four thousand *Kikaida* soundtrack albums in a single month in 1974.[12]

In August 1974, a seven-actor *Kikaida* stage troupe in full costume was invited to perform at the fiftieth annual state fair, attended by about ten thousand local Hawaiian children and their parents, as well as then governor George Ariyoshi. The success of this first performance led to two more live shows featuring the Japanese actors from the actual *Kikaida* program. The State of Hawai`i later bestowed the title of "honorary citizen" on actors Ban Daisuke (who plays Jiro in *Kikaida*) and Ikeda Shunsuke (Ichiro in *Kikaida 01*), as well as the Toei producers.

The increasing circulation of *Kikaida* products in Japan, dating from the mid-1990s, and the resurgence of the *Kikaida* boom in Hawai`i are more than coincidental. Although *Kikaida* has not experienced a huge revival in Japan, its popularity has risen amongst a small fan group in response to an overall revival of 1970s and 1980s *tokusatsu* television programs. Several toy companies released faithful reproductions of *Kikaida* characters. Multiple tribute books and a sound-track CD followed. In addition, Ishinomori Productions produced a 2000 animated version of *Jinzō Ningen Kikaida* in Japan. All of these products were targeted at Japanese fans in their thirties and forties who enjoyed the series in the 1970s, but many ended up as exports to Hawai`i, with the help of the Internet.

An unforeseen consequence of the revival in Hawai`i was a rebounded fandom of Japanese *Kikaida* fans visiting Hawai`i for the events. One major Japanese travel agency, Kinki Nihon Tourist, created a tour in which fans could participate in a *Kikaida* dinner show in Hawai`i in April 2002. *Kikaida* fans from Hong Kong also visited an anime/*tokusatsu* exposition in Honolulu in the summer of 2001. Although the creation of Generation

Kikaida in Hawai`i is still tied to Japanese market trends, the larger mediascape of *Kikaida* extended far beyond the marketers' original scope. Fandom in Japan and Hawai`i, therefore, is synergistic.

MARKETING COLLECTIVE MEMORY

The resurgence of *Kikaida* was brought about by a confluence of conditions. As I have mentioned, it began shortly after the 25th anniversary of *Kikaida* in Japan in 1997, when fans in Hawai`i started purchasing *Kikaida* tribute products such as books, action figures, and CDs over the Internet. According to Joanne Ninomiya, president of JN-Productions (JNP), a company closely affiliated with KIKU, unofficial *Kikaida* fan clubs based in Hawai`i began appearing on the Internet in 1998.[13] Collectors' events were held, and fans pressured KIKU via email and telephone calls to re-air the show. In May 2001, Ninomiya decided to reacquire the broadcasting and merchandising rights. A DVD series that included new English translations and other commercial goods such as T-shirts and posters was produced locally by JNP under the brand name Generation Kikaida.

Chance Gusukuma, a thirty-three-year-old Okinawan-American employee of JNP, observes that the boundary between producer and fan is extremely blurred in the *Kikaida* revival.[14] Fans not only successfully convinced KIKU to re-air the show, but continue to influence the revival campaign as well. Most events are supported by fans—some volunteers and some employed for the purpose—who take care of incidental tasks such as regulating lines and cleaning up venues, but who also perform more instrumental duties, including creating costumes, arranging and performing music, and acting as extras onstage.

As Henry Jenkins suggests, fan culture usually includes not only the consumption but also the production of texts such as fanzines, songs, costumes, and poems.[15] However, it is unusual for such secondary products to become integrated into media marketing strategies, as has happened in Hawai`i. Gusukuma explains this phenomenon by noting that five out of the six members on the *Kikaida* project team are themselves *Kikaida* fans. As a small local television station, KIKU may have also found it necessary to integrate this bottom-up labor force into the production process in order to manage the campaign at the current scale.

It is important to remember that *Kikaida* is not produced by KIKU and JNP, but by Toei; the relationship is thus not merely producer-consumer but is triangular, involving Toei, KIKU/JNP, and fans in Hawai`i. Both marketers (KIKU/JNP) and fans appropriate *Kikaida* for their own intents and purposes. While fans actively produce "past" memories through their consumption, as well as production, marketers try to localize Kikaida by marketing collective memory as part of the official history of contemporary Hawai`i. Both of these seemingly different projects of history and memory are produced thorough a narrativization process that blurs the boundary between media and fans.

The metamorphosis of Kikaida from Japanese superhero to local icon has been facilitated by KIKU/JNP through various fan events accompanying the continuous rebroadcasting of the show.[16] Some of these functions have taken a commemorative form, including an exhibition of fan collections of *Kikaida* goods at the Japanese Cultural Center of Hawai`i in March and April 2002, and various autograph sessions by the performers of the original series.

The incorporation of *Kikaida* into official events sponsored by the state government of Hawai`i has helped legitimize the superhero as a local icon. As mentioned above, the state government declared 11 April 2002 Generation Kikaida Day in Hawai`i. Kikaida was part of the halftime show during the homecoming football game at the University of Hawai`i in October 2002. Kikaida also appeared at various Children and Youth Month events in June 2002 and onstage at the State Farm Festival in July 2002. In addition, the release of the DVD series by JNP further contributed to the history-making project. Each DVD contains promotional spots for KIKU as a special feature and comes with a brochure on the history of the show. The catchphrase of the campaign, "Generation Kikaida," evokes a sense of lineage and tradition.

The *Kikaida* revival campaign has much to do with KIKU's corporate identity as a relatively small, ethnic TV station. In the 1970s, there were only five channels including KIKU in Hawai`i, of which three were major national network affiliates. Today KIKU has lost some of its audience in proportion to the decreasing number of Japanese speakers in Hawai`i. In addition, American national cable television networks have dominated television in Hawai`i since the 1980s. Now KIKU competes with more than sixty channels from the continental United States. By promoting *Kikaida* as a local icon, KIKU hopes to capture a particular segment of the mediascape; that is, it is attempting to secure a position and identity as part of the "local" culture industry. Its marketing strategy is therefore embedded within global media politics.

FORMATION OF A GENERATIONAL IDENTITY THROUGH FANDOM

Fans relate to popular texts through both affect and ideology. Affect may appear elusive, formless, or chaotic, but in reality "operates within and, at the same time, produces maps which direct our investments in and into the world. . . . Affect is what gives 'color,' 'tone,' and 'texture' to our experiences."[17] Raymond Williams addresses a similar phenomenon when he speaks of the "structure of feeling," meaning "those elusive, impalpable forms of social consciousness which are at once as evanescent as 'feeling' suggests, but nevertheless display a significant configuration captured in the term 'structure.'"[18] However, as Grossberg emphasizes, determining why a popular text produces an affect requires an understanding of its ideological justification. Fan practices, identities, pleasures, meanings, desires, and fantasies are articulated through specific ideologies that distinguish one form of fandom from another. Authenticity and difference are claimed in relation to genres (rock versus pop) and at the level of specific texts (*Star Trek* versus *Star Wars*). In other words, the seemingly oppositional elements of feeling, and ideology (the former supposedly inchoate and chaotic, the latter rigid and explicit) form a complementary dialectic in fandom.

The affective and ideological elements of receptivity to popular texts are seen in the consuming practices of fans in which the specificity of text, viewers, medium, period, and locality all play a part. In the following subsections, I explore the particular sensibility underlying *Kikaida* fandom and its relationship to the construction of a generational identity. I focus on community formation, consuming practices, and fan narrativization of texts in fandom.

Consumption and Production by Fans

Consumption of *Kikaida* includes not only watching the television series but also purchasing related products such as action figures, cards, posters, and T-shirts. Consumption goes beyond the purchase itself, however. Fans use, clean, decorate, modify, repair, and photograph these products, incorporating bodily practices that Grant McCracken calls "possession rituals."[19] Possession rituals allow mass-produced products to be appropriated as extensions of self. The products are personalized as part of a world of goods reflecting the fan's experiences and concept of self and the world.[20] In the case of *Kikaida* fans, watching the television series and possessing related products are two forms of consumption in a dialectical relationship. Possessions reflect how fans watch the television show and vice versa.

Collecting is one of the most popular consuming practices among *Kikaida* fans. Russell Belk defines *collecting* as "the process of activity, selectivity, and passionately acquiring and possessing things removed from ordinary use and perceived as part of a set of non-identical objects or experiences."[21] Collection as a source of self-completion happens through the "principle of organization."[22] The construction of a "seriation" makes a collection.[23] Indeed, each collector has his or her own system of classification. Each collector's world of goods is closely related to their system of values. For instance, some individuals collect only goods related to a particular character from the television show while others collect only vintage paraphernalia from the 1970s.

Of the fans I interviewed, one of the biggest collectors is Anthony, a 39-year-old Portuguese, Spanish, Hawaiian, and Puerto Rican American who first saw *Kikaida* during his middle school years. He later became a world-class triathlete. He began collecting *Kikaida* products in early 2000. He explains his motivation as follows.

> [In my childhood] I had a lot of other *tokusatsu* figures, but among them Kikaida was the best. He was the pioneer of superheros in Hawai`i. . . . I started this [collection] because I grew up with it, and it just came back recently. . . . And, because I grew up with it and loved it so much, I wanted to get back into [it] again. *Kikaida* is part of my childhood, a happy time of my life.[24]

Although the show includes other popular characters such as Kikaida 01, Hakaida, and Bijinda, he only collects products related to the central protagonist, Kikaida. He also limits his collection to objects such as posters, T-shirts, and large toys that are big enough to autograph easily; he seeks autographs on his collected items whenever Ban Daisuke visits Hawai`i for fan events. During our interview, Anthony talked mostly about his meetings with Ban Daisuke, recalling interactions from the 1970s as well as from the present revival period. He talked at length about personal attributes such as the actor's voice, appearance, height, and attitude.

According to Susan Stewart, a souvenir "represents not the lived experience of its maker but the 'secondhand' experience of its possessor/owner. . . . [It] displaces the point of authenticity as it itself becomes the point of origin for narrative."[25] This conception of souvenirs might be applied to the role autographs play for Anthony. They are proof of his contact with Ban and mnemonic traces of Ban/Jiro's authenticity. Moreover, these autographs become authentic in and of themselves as Anthony constructs narratives around his interactions with a childhood superhero.

Fandom leads other collectors to create original products. Pomai is a Portuguese American born in 1968 and raised near Honolulu. He works as a graphic designer in the advertising section of a large carpentry store. When he was younger, Pomai sometimes accompanied his father on business trips to Japan. He always looked forward to buying Japanese toys on these trips. Like many children raised in mid-1970s Hawai`i, he was deeply absorbed by *Kikaida* as a child but stopped following it as he grew older. He became involved in the *Kikaida* as a result of a brief conversation with a coworker, who simply asked, "Remember *Kikaida*?" Soon after this exchange, Pomai researched *Kikaida* on the Internet and found a Hawai`i fan-created website. He downloaded several pictures and decided to make some masks. Since 1998, he has created several life-sized Kikaida figures and other *tokusatsu* superhero masks and costumes. These products have been exhibited at various fan events and in the gallery of the Japanese Cultural Center in Hawai`i. Pomai enthusiastically explains the aesthetic process of making a Kikaida mask in conjunction with a *Kikaida* festival and exhibit:

> The way I created this mask, you know, I basically took a bowl and cut it out. It's not a design that you can just pull off casually. You cannot just put it together and say okay. . . . People have seen some other Kikaida costumes and said okay, that's okay, but I think people really have to go the extra step to create the character. . . . It's a challenging design to replicate because you cannot just create the asymmetrical design just by having a simple head and painting it red and blue. You need to have that ridge. And no other superhero has that. I think for all of the Hawai`i kids who drew it, you know in the artwork, they always remember drawing that ridge. It's so unique. The asymmetrical design was so unique. . . . The design was dynamic and so perfect. Still is. His design is so timeless.[26]

What matters most in Pomai's relation to *Kikaida* is the visual aspect of his work. The reproduction of the design becomes a mnemonic device encapsulating certain childhood experiences, such as drawing Kikaida in art class. Apart from *Kikaida* DVDs and videotapes, he does not collect products released by JNP or Japanese toy companies. He made a solitary exception for a Kikaida model kit made of polyurethane casting resin. According to Pomai, this kit represents the most realistic reproduction of the original character. He told me that it is not easy to build the figure, but it is the challenge that attracts him as fan-cum-designer.

He goes on to describe the response he received when he wore the Kikaida costume he made for the first time:

When I created the costume in 1998, I did it in two months' time after work, always after I came home. And I had a whole suit and boots, everything. When I wore it on Halloween night, all the local Hawai`i people there just went nuts. The public reaction was so refreshing, to finally see Kikaida again. There were people just on their hands and knees, just worshipping the character. Everybody was saying, like, "Kikaida! Kikaida! Remember Kikaida!" They were so happy to see Kikaida. . . . There were people forty years old, forty-five, my age, thirties, just like they became a child again. I guess [I got such an enthusiastic reaction] because my costume came out so good and because they weren't exposed to Kikaida for so long.[27]

The public display of Pomai's mask and costume embodies what Walter Benjamin calls "aura," the irreducible specificity or uniqueness of an object in an age of mechanical reproduction.[28] It distinguishes him as a craftsman from general consumers as well as other fans. These practices involve *Kikaida* closely in the realm of Pomai's lived experiences.

Still another expression of *Kikaida* fandom is through music. Ronnie is a 38-year-old Spanish and Portuguese American, also born and raised in Hawai`i. He works at a music store and is a musician and music producer. He reconnected with *Kikaida* earlier than most other Hawaii fans, however, by playing for Japanese tourists.

In the nineties, I started music full-time, here and on the mainland. What I used to do was, ah, we had Japanese visitors, and we thought they would know the *Kikaida* song. We sang the whole song. You don't know if they knew it or not, but that's what we always did. I started it. I created a *Kikaida* song, and the whole band played it, too.[29]

In 2000, Ronnie caught on to the *Kikaida* revival during its nascent stage. He began interacting with other fans online and decided to make a remix of *Kikaida* songs.

What I did was my tribute, my musical tribute. Like Sean [another fan] makes costumes, his way of tributalizing his memories. In the Yahoo groups, some people have their collectible toys. So I decided that I wanted to do my tribute by music. I did. I have five [songs] now.[30]

JNP now broadcasts these songs at fan events. They are also distributed among fans.

Most of the fans I talked with emphasized the appeal of *Kikaida*'s visual and musical aspects. The *Kikaida* theme song has become their anthem. They confess that when they watched the series again for the first time they had forgotten the story lines, but they immediately remarked the visual and auditory aspects of the series. This may be because as children they not only watched the show but also played with action figures and heard and sang along with the theme song repeatedly on television, the radio, and record albums. Nostalgic consumption and production in the present conjures embodied memories through the senses of touch, sight, and sound. Although they can never regain the sensory experiences of their childhood, their bodily practices in the present "tributalize" their memories. By employing the power and skills belonging to adulthood to produce and purchase, they actively create and appropriate nostalgia for their childhood and its superheroes.

Forming a Fan Community and Narrativizing Kikaida

Gender marks *Kikaida* fandom in important ways. Firstly, there are far more male than female fans. In the words of many fans, *Kikaida* was and is a "boy thing." Little boys grew up learning elements of masculinity through the superhero Kikaida. Secondly, gender differentiates fan relationships with the characters in the television program. Both male and female fans identify themselves reflexively with androids of their own gender: Kikaida, Hakaida, and Kikaida 01 for men, and Bijinda (a female android character) for women. Interest in human alter egos, however, always gravitates to the opposite sex; that is, the gaze of the male fan is usually directed toward Mari (the human alter ego of Bijinda), while female fans yearn for Jiro.

Thirdly, fan practices differ by gender. Although many women attend fan events, particularly autograph sessions with Ban Daisuke, they are rarely involved in the more extreme fan production activities. Most of the figure doll collectors are male. As Joanne Ninomiya points out, a number of male fans volunteer to participate in public *Kikaida* events largely out of a desire to wear costumes from the series on stage.

Nila is one of the few ardent female *Kikaida* fans. A Filipino American, she was born and raised in Hawai`i. Now 35-years-old, she was seven when *Kikaida* first aired. In her childhood, she also enjoyed watching other Japanese children's programs broadcast by KIKU, such as the anime show *Candy Candy*, which featured nurses and, according to her, influenced her decision to become a nurse. Her practices in the revival boom are primarily continuous rereadings of the text and participation in the local and web-based fan community. Nila was one of the first members of several Internet fan clubs and remains active in them.

Nila rediscovered *Kikaida* in 2000 after many years of not giving the show much thought. She was just learning to use the Internet when she stumbled across a *tokusatsu* fan's website that included information on *Kikaida*. She then attempted to find a *Kikaida* fan club on the Internet but was unsuccessful. She contacted Stuart, the designer of the *tokusatsu* website, and proposed organizing a fan club. Stuart did so, and Nila became its first member. More fans soon joined, and the club became very active after KIKU began rebroadcasting *Kikaida* a year later. Nila looks back on the formation of the fan community:

> I realized this [maintaining the fan club] is a great way to get fans together. Then I got involved in the whole, you know, the fire just caught on, just, ah, sparked. The whole passion for *Kikaida* overwhelmed. I guess *Kikaida* was always in our hearts. But this revival sort of opened our hearts. And I guess it helped . . . reconcile childhood dreams to the present, make it kind of come together for us.[31]

Nila emphasizes the feelings of passion and enthusiasm that keep her involved in *Kikaida* fandom today. Her excitement about reconnecting with the past is made possible only through interactions with other fans from the same generation in the present:

> It's sort of like you lock away your precious toys and memories. And then something triggers it. You meet the right people who have the same interest and excitement toward it. . . . And then you realize you are not alone. It kind of unifies our generation in that sense, who have the same enthusiasm, who have the same passion for the sense of past, the childhood memories. . . . I was thinking, why *Kikaida* is so popular now and why we are getting back into it [is] because it lets you feel like a child again. It gives you the same spirit, energy, enthusiasm, innocence, and, ah, so many memories, wonderful memories.[32]

As Mike Featherstone points out, "There is nothing so powerful as the image of an integrated organic community in the childhood one has left behind. . . . Successive generations always have recourse to the myth of 'the good old days,' or the existence of a harmonious community."[33] Nila describes the ideological reality of a nostalgia that fosters a sense of belonging, warmth, and togetherness amongst fans by drawing on the mythical security of a childhood long past.

In their discussion of the revival of Batman in the United States, Lynn Spiegel and Henry Jenkins note that "Childhood memories evoked a pleasure in liminality as people moved fluidly between imagining themselves as children and recognizing their current status."[34] Pleasure in the liminal experience also defines the relationship between *Kikaida* and adult fans in Hawai`i. These fans are not Goffmanesque performers, constantly in negotiation and conflict, but players whose interactions shape an ambiguous identity between childhood and adulthood.

This pleasure in liminality is also recognizable in Jason, a teacher at an English-language school in Honolulu. Jason is 75 percent Filipino and 25 percent Portuguese. Born in 1970, he watched *Kikaida* from age four to six. After the revival campaign began, Jason started to learn martial arts, seeking a new sense of masculinity in the physical strength of Kikaida's technological body. As a child, he also enjoyed watching other *tokusatsu* TV series aired by KIKU. When he saw *Star Wars* in 1977, he became so absorbed in the film series that he eventually attended film school at the University of Southern California in Los Angeles. Once in California, however, he reconnected with *Kikaida* as a way of asserting his Hawaiian identity:

> My sister gave me a car, and I needed to get a California license plate. I was feeling a little bit homesick for Hawai`i. And I was thinking if I get a license plate, that gives an idea of my identity. . . . So I decided to get it [inscribed with "Kikaida"]. Because, of course, in L.A., so few people knew about it, I had a feeling that no one else would have that license plate. I was happy to get it. . . . I think the bigger influence on me going to film school is *Star Wars*. But I went back to *Kikaida* as my source after I graduated because I was getting nostalgic.[35]

Jason left California to teach English in Japan. He arrived just as the 1970s *tokusatsu* superheroes were enjoying a revival in popularity. He started collecting the action figures related to the television programs and taping shows aired on a cable channel devoted to *tokusatsu*. He even sent fan letters to Ban Daisuke and eventually met the actor. He was disappointed that he could not share this experience with others, however:

> I wished I had more friends who like *Kikaida* as much as I do, but there weren't any. . . . Besides my sister and cousin . . . I didn't talk [to anyone] about *Kikaida*. I didn't know there were *Kikaida* fans around me. . . . Of course, no way in California.[36]

Jason then discovered the Internet fan club that Nila and Stuart had created. He regularly posts opinions on the website and meets other members at fan events.

> Now it's nice because I make all these new friends. We have something in common because all the friends I have now are *tokusatsu* fans, *Kikaida* fans. . . . I met them within the last couple years. They are all in my generation. We still relate to that. We all watched it together in different homes. . . . I guess because *Kikaida* was so much Hawai`i then, it's one way for people my age to identify with each other, to relate to each other, to talk or joke around.[37]

While fans' practices are highly individuated, it is the sense of participation in a community that sustains fandom. Consuming *Kikaida* as a member of a community enables a circulation of meanings and the construction of collective memory.

Although a presumed collective memory is the basis for the construction of Generation Kikaida, this does not mean that all members of this generational group share the same memories. Each fan produces his or her own personal memories through different consuming practices. At the same time, though, fans often speak for others, as well as themselves, through their interactions. They forget or purposely delete omit details, alter the chronological order of a series of events, consciously or unconsciously, or even interweave other people's stories with their own. These dynamic communicative processes allow fans to represent a collective memory of their own personal images and stories, and this idea of a collective memory partly explains the frequent use of the pronoun *we* in fan narratives of childhood memories.

Another common characteristic of these narratives is the frequent mention of "Japan" and the "Japanese" in discussions of *Kikaida* experiences. Fans explain a current interest in Japan as having originated in the imaginary space of Japanese-based media culture in 1970s Hawai`i. Although my identity as a Japanese researcher may have influenced fans to talk about Japan, it also seems true that *Kikaida* fans construct mythical connections to Japan. For fans, this legitimizes the internal structure of the generational group and establishes a further claim to a collectively shared past.[38]

Jason, for example, portrays *Kikaida* as mediating both his childhood memories of learning to read and his later interest in Japan and the Japanese language:

> *Kikaida* gave me a lot of influence. When I saw the *Kikaida* show, I was hearing Japanese but reading English [subtitles]. This is how I started to try learning to read. . . . It was also the first time for me

to pay attention to a foreign language. . . . [Many years later] I applied to the JET [Japan Exchange and Teaching] program because
I always wanted to visit Japan, because of that show.[39]

Ronnie similarly traces his general interest in Japanese culture to childhood memories of *Kikaida* and other programs on KIKU. His use of *we* suggests that he ideologically shares these memories and interests with others:

> I think the series did interest me in Japanese general culture, be-
> yond the hero things. . . . Because we watched KIKU, we also saw
> everything they showed, including the commercials. That's why
> we got interested in Japanese culture. Oh, not only that, even the
> music. J-pop. Back then, Saijo Hideki and Go Hiromi. I kind of got
> into that, too. We know all that too.[40]

For Ronnie, who grew up in Hawai`i, the symbolic image of Japan is largely
contextualized within the local, multiethnic community of Hawai`i. When
Ronnie uses the term *Japanese culture*, he is primarily referring to elements
that have become local to Hawai`i, particularly food.

> I remember that [in the TV program] Mitsuko and Masaru are
> eating *musubi* [rice balls]. I'd never tried it, and I don't think I even
> liked it, too. But when I saw them eating it, you know, like, "Oh, I
> wanna copy them" and ate it. That's kind of silly, but that's what I
> thought. . . . Since then, I like Japanese food.[41]

Images of Japan also help to explain fan infatuation with the heroine,
Mitsuko. Almost all fans claim that their enthusiasm for *Kikaida* owes, at
least in part, to the romantic relationship between Jiro and Mitsuko. Some
male fans even call Mitsuko their "first love." Fans emphasize Mitsuko's
devotion to Jiro despite knowing that her love will never come to fruition.
Anthony says that the image of Mitsuko strongly influenced his concept of
the ideal woman:

> I liked Mitsuko. I liked her. She influenced my ideals of what real
> women should be like. . . . Honestly, I have no attraction to white
> women. I am serious. When I look at them, they look boring. I
> have problems with Haole [Caucasian] women. You know, they
> think you are bunk. Local girls [non-Caucasians, born and raised
> in Hawaii] they are lazy and no work. . . . When I look at Japa-
> nese women, they look exciting, enjoyable, lovable, and attrac-
> tive.[42] But looking at other types, they don't attract me at all. I'm
> not prejudiced or anything, but I'm telling the truth. . . . Japanese

women make the best mothers, too. Most of them are loyal to their men. They don't cheat on their men. They don't look at the other men.[43]

Anthony finds in *Kikaida* an old-fashioned, heterosexual, romantic ideal of femininity in relation to the stereotypical image of Japanese women circulating in his community.

Thus, adult fans use the *Kikaida* text to reshape childhood memories and constitute adult identities. No matter how nostalgically fans talk about *Kikaida*, their fanship is grounded in current perspectives. Their images of Japan are also a response to their personal backgrounds and the various social discourses on Japan surrounding them in the local community of Hawai`i.

CONCLUSION

In this essay, I have tried to trace the birth of a cohort that took place not in the 1970s, when children watched a wildly popular Japanese television show, but among the contemporary adult fans that these children became, who derive meaning in their lives as members of Generation Kikaida. The success of the revival lies partly in the specific locality of Hawai`i. Local ethnic discourses here, as well as the accessibility of *Kikaida* goods through local Japanese department stores and the Internet, enable Japanese media texts to appear meaningful in fans' everyday lives. The material element of this fandom is extremely important since it interacts directly with the text. In the mediascape of *Kikaida*, where textual and material products leap transnationally beyond marketers dreams, fans narrate themselves as both individuals and members of Generation Kikaida, bound to an alternative space inhabited by transformative superheroes from Japan.

Ien Ang writes that media consumption is "an integral part of popular cultural practices, articulating both 'subjective' and 'objective', both 'micro' and 'macro' processes. . . . It is in this very living out of their everyday lives that people are inscribed into large-scale structural and historical relations of force which are not of their own making."[44] Although fan relations to *Kikaida* operate within a particular sensibility connected to a pleasure induced by nostalgia, the contexts in which their actions take place are embedded within a complex macrodynamic of sociocultural, economic, and geopolitical forces. The intertwining of personal and collective fantasies transforms the media text into consumer identities for a particular generation. Generation Kikaida may not have existed prior to KIKU/JNP's enterprising efforts, but through the agency of this label longtime fans from all walks of life have seized the opportunity to reinvent themselves as media stars in their own right.

NOTES

1. In this essay, I consider the sequel series *Kikaida 01*, which aired in 1973–74 in Japan and 1975–76 in Hawai`I, to be part and parcel of *Kikaida*.

2. Throughout this essay, "Kikaida" is italicized whenever the reference is to the television show rather than the protagonist.

3. Ron Eyerman, "Intellectuals and the Construction of African American Identity: Outline of a Generational Approach" in June Edmunds and Bryan S. Turner, eds., *Generational Consciousness, Narrative, and Politics*, 51–74 (Lanham, Md.: Rowman and Littlefield, 2002), 52.

4. Mike Hepworth, "Generational Consciousness and Age Identity: Three Fictional Examples," in June Edmunds and Bryan S. Turner, eds., *Generational Consciousness, Narrative, and Politics*, 131–44 (Lanham, Md.: Rowman and Littlefield, 2002), 135.

5. Marita Sturken, *Tangled Memories: The Vietnam War, the AIDS Epidemic, and the Politics of Remembering* (Berkeley: University of California Press, 1997).

6. Lawrence Grossberg, "Is There a Fan in the House? The Affective Sensibility of Fandom," in Lisa A. Lewis, ed., *The Adoring Audience: Fan Culture and Popular Media*, 50–65 (London: Routledge, 1992), 56.

7. Ibid., 56, 60.

8. Kikaida simultaneously appeared in the weekly comic magazine *Shōnen Sandē* as an integral part of a marketing strategy pervasive in the Japanese culture industry known as media mix, which consists of the selling of a text or "character" simultaneously through various media such as television, comics, music, video games, and toys. Ishinomori is known as a pioneer of media-mix entertainment. See Otsuka Eiji and Sasakibara Go, *KyōYō to shite no manga/anime* (Manga/Anime as an Education) (Tokyo: Kōdansha, 2001).

9. This and other names are combinations of pseudonyms, nicknames, and real names, as per interviewee requests.

10. Personal communication, 10 January 2003.

11. "Clockwork Sushi," *Time*, 5 May 1975, 61–62.

12. "Heroes and Villains," *Honolulu*, November 2000, 134–36.

13. Personal communication, 17 January 2003.

14. Personal communication, 5 March 2003.

15. Henry Jenkins, *Textual Poachers: Television Fans and Participatory Culture* (New York: Routledge, 1992)

16. *Kikaida* and *Kikaida 01* were aired four times each between November 2001 and August 2003.

17. Grossberg, "Is There a Fan in the House?" 57.

18. Terry Eagleton, *Ideology: An Introduction* (London: Verso, 1991), 48; Raymond Williams, *Marxism and Literature* (Oxford: Oxford University Press, 1978).

19. Grant David McCracken, *Culture and Consumption: New Approaches to the Symbolic Character of Consumer Goods and Activities* (Bloomington: Indiana University Press, 1988), 85.

20. Ibid., 86.

21. Quoted in Tim Dant, Material Culture in the Social World (Buckingham: Open University Press, 1999), 148.

22. Susan Stewart, *On Longing: Narratives of the Miniature, the Gigantic, the Souvenir, the Collection* (Baltimore: John Hopkins University Press, 1984), 155.

23. Dant, *Material Culture in the Social World*, 149.

24. Personal communication, 15 April 2002.

25. Stewart, *On Longing*, 135–36.

26. Personal communication, 17 January 2003.

27. Ibid.

28. Walter Benjamin. *Illuminations*. Hannah Arendt, ed. (New York: Shocken, 1969).

29. Personal communication, 25 January 2003.

30. Ibid.

31. Ibid.

32. Ibid.

33. Mike Featherstone, "Localism, Globalism, and Cultural Identity," in Rob Wilson and Wimal Dissanayake, eds., *Global/Local: Cultural Production and the Transnational Imaginary*, 46–77 (Durham: Duke University Press, 1996), 51.

34. Lynn Spiegel, and Henry Jenkins, "Same Bat Channel, Different Bat Times: Mass Culture and Popular Memory," in Roberta E. Pearson and William Uricchio, eds., *The Many Lives of the Batman: Critical Approaches to a Superhero and His Media*, 117–48 (New York: Routledge, 1991), 138.

35. Personal communication, 5 May 2002.

36. Ibid.

37. Ibid.

38. In order to legitimate the distinctiveness of this generational fandom, fans sometimes label other generations—particularly younger ones—with names such as the high-tech or MTV (Music Television) generations. For instance, one interviewee, Florencio, told me that "people between twelve and twenty, who are MTV Generation, do not like watching *Kikaida*. They are exposed to other media

entertainment like video games, computers, and cables." Personal communication, 5 January 2003.

39. Ibid.

40. Personal communication, 25 January 2003.

41. Ibid.

42. Here the speaker refers to Japanese nationals rather than Japanese American women.

43. Personal communication, 15 April 2002.

44. Ien Ang, *Living Room Wars: Rethinking Media Audiences for a Postmodern World* (London: Routledge, 1996), 137.

Contributors

Noriko Aso is Assistant Professor of History at the University of California, Santa Cruz. Her publications include "Sumptuous Re-past: the 1964 Tokyo Olympics Arts Festival" in *positions: east asia cultures critique*, vol. 10, no. 1, and "Shiteki na kōkyō: maboroshi no Shibusawa Seien-o Kinen Jitsugyō Hakubutsukan" in *Rekishi to minzoku* 23 (February 2007). She is currently completing a book manuscript on museums in Imperial Japan.

JungBong Choi is Assistant Professor in Department of Cinema Studies at New York University. He is the author of *Digitalizing Television in Japan: Economy, State, and Discourse* (Verg, 2007) and is currently working on a book manuscript titled *Transnational Vector of National Cinema*.

Stephanie DeBoer is an Assistant Professor of Film and Media Studies in the Department of Communication and Culture at Indiana University, Bloomington. Her research and teaching interests include transnational Japanese and Chinese language, film, and media, inter-Asia cultural studies, and digital media in the context of globalization. Her article, "Co-Producing Cross-border Action: Technologies of Contact, Masculinity and the Asia-Pacific Border," is forthcoming in an anthology on trans-Asian screens from Hong Kong University Press. She is currently writing a book manuscript on Asia Pacific film, television, and media co-productions from the second half of the twentieth century.

Aaron Gerow is Associate Professor in Japanese Cinema at Yale University. His books include *Kitano Takeshi*, *A Page of Madness*, and *Research Guide to Japanese Film Studies* (co-authored with Abé Mark Nornes). His book on 1910s Japanese film culture, *Visions of Japanese Modernity*, will be published by the University of California Press in 2010.

Shuhei Hosokawa is Professor at the International Research Center for Japanese Studies. His principle areas of study include popular music and Japanese-Brazilian culture. He co-edited the book, *Karaoke around the World: Global Technology, Local Singing* (Routledge, 1998), and has published articles in such journals as *Cultural Studies* and the *British Journal of Ethnomusicology*. Currently he is writing about the music history of modern Japan and the literature of the Japanese-Brazilian community.

Kelly Hu is currently Associate Professor at the Graduate Institute of Mass Communication, National Taiwan Normal University, Taipei, Taiwan. Her publications in recent years include a book chapter "Discovering Japanese TV Drama through Online Chinese Fans: Narrative Reflexivity, Implicit Therapy, and the Question of the Social Imaginary" (*Media Consumption and Everyday Life in Asia*, 2005), and a journal paper "Made in China: the Cultural Logic of OEMs and the Manufacture of Low-cost Technology," (*Inter-Asia Cultural Studies*, vol. 9, no. 1 [2008]). The other journal paper "Chinese Subtitle Groups and the Neoliberal Work Ethic," written in Chinese, will be published soon in the *Journal of Mass Communication Research*, vol. 100 (2009). Her email is kellyhu87@gmail.com.

Koichi Iwabuchi is Professor of Media and Cultural Studies at the School of International Liberal Studies, Waseda University. He has been working on cultural globalization and transnationalism, East Asian media cultural connections, multicultural questions and cultural citizenship, and cultural policy issues. He is co-editor with Chris Berry of the book series, TransAsia: Screen Cultures (Hong Kong University Press). His publications include *Recentering Globalization: Popular Culture and Japanese Transnationalism* (Duke University Press, 2002) and *East Asian Pop Culture: Analyzing the Korean Wave*, co-edited with Chua Beng Huat (Hong Kong University Press, 2008). His new book, *Undoing Cool Japan: Culture and Dialogue in the Age of Brand Nationalism* (tentative title), is forthcoming from Paradigm Publishers in 2010.

Hirofumi Katsuno is a Ph.D. candidate in anthropology at the University of Hawai`i, Manoa, currently completing his dissertation on the development of robot culture in Japan. He has published some articles on Japanese media culture.

Gabriella Lukacs is Assistant Professor of Anthropology at the University of Pittsburgh. Her book *Scripted Affects, Branded Selves: Television, Subjectivity, and Capitalism in 1990s Japan* is forthcoming from Duke University Press.

Eva Tsai, a Ph.D. from the University of Iowa, is Associate Professor of Mass Communication at National Taiwan Normal University. Her publications on Japanese TV culture, stardom in Asia, and academic labor can be found in the journals, *Inter-Asia Cultural Studies*, *Japan Forum*, and *Modern Chinese Literature and Culture*, and in the following two anthologies: *Feeling "Asian" Modernities: Transnational Consumption of Japanese TV Dramas* and *East Asian Pop Culture: Analysing the Korean Wave*. She is working on a manuscript about Japanese TV drama writers and investigating girl culture through stationery arts and industries.

Mitsuyo Wada-Marciano is Associate Professor in Film Studies, School for Studies in Art and Culture, at Carleton University, Canada. Her research interests are Japanese cinema, especially its relationship to Japanese modernity in the 1920s and 1930s, the impact of new media on Japanese cinema, and East Asian cinemas in global culture. She is the author of *Nippon Modern: Japanese Cinema of the 1920s and 1930s* (University of Hawai`i Press, 2008); the Japanese translation was published by Nagoya University Press in 2009. She is also the co-editor of *Horror to the Extreme: Changing Boundaries in Asian Cinema* (Hong Kong University Press, 2009). Her articles and reviews are published in *Film Quarterly, Camera Obscura, Canadian Journal of Film Studies, Post Script, The Journal of Asian Studies, Asian Cinema, Social Science Japan Journal,* and *Intelligence*. She is currently completing a book on digital technology's impact on Japanese cinema in the 1990s and 2000s.

Christine Yano is Professor of Anthropology at the University of Hawai`i. Her previous books are *Tears of Longing: Nostalgia and the Nation in Japanese Popular Song* (Harvard University Press, 2002), *Crowning the Nice Girl* (University of Hawai`i Press, 2006), and *Airborne Dreams: Race, Gender, and Cosmopolitanism in Postwar America* (forthcoming, Duke University Press). Her current research interests include "pink globalization" (cute culture), Obama-mania in Japan, and Pan American World Airways in postwar Japan.

Mitsuhiro Yoshimoto is Associate Professor in Department of East Asian Studies at New York University. He is the author of *Kurosawa: Film Studies and Japanese Cinema* (Duke University Press, 2000) and *Empire of Images and the End of Cinema* (Ibunsha, 2007). He also co-authored *Site of Resistance* with Masao Miyoshi (Rakuhoku Shuppan, 2007). His new book on conspiracy and image is forthcoming in fall 2010.

Index